THE HISTORY OF

AMERICAN PAINTING

THE MACMILLAN COMPANY
NEW YORK · BOSTON · CHICAGO · DALLAS
ATLANTA · SAN FRANCISCO

MACMILLAN & CO., Limited
LONDON · BOMBAY · CALCUTTA
MELBOURNE

THE MACMILLAN COMPANY
OF CANADA, Limited
TORONTO

STUART, GIBBS–CHANNING : WASHINGTON, OWNED BY S. P. AVERY, JR.

THE HISTORY OF
AMERICAN PAINTING

BY

SAMUEL ISHAM

ASSOCIATE OF THE NATIONAL ACADEMY OF DESIGN, MEMBER OF
THE SOCIETY OF AMERICAN ARTISTS

*WITH TWELVE FULL-PAGE PHOTOGRAVURES AND ONE HUNDRED
AND FORTY-ONE ILLUSTRATIONS IN THE TEXT*

NEW EDITION

WITH SUPPLEMENTAL CHAPTERS BY

ROYAL CORTISSOZ

MEMBER OF THE AMERICAN ACADEMY OF ARTS AND LETTERS

New York

THE MACMILLAN COMPANY

1936

COPYRIGHT, 1905 AND 1927,

BY THE MACMILLAN COMPANY.

———

COPYRIGHT, 1933,

BY JULIA ISHAM TAYLOR

———

Set up and electrotyped.   Published November, 1905.
New edition with supplemental chapters by Royal Cortissoz, October, 1927.
Reissued October, 1936.

Norwood Press
J. S. Cushing Co. — Berwick & Smith Co.
Norwood, Mass., U.S.A.

PREFACE

THIS volume was first published in 1905, in a series projected under the editorship of John C. Van Dyke to assemble the materials for a history of American art in all its phases. Its success was immediate and lasting. Since the book went out of print the demand for it has steadily continued, finally causing the preparation of the present edition. The source of this popularity undoubtedly lies in the author's peculiar fitness for his task. In order that the series might be authoritative in opinion each volume was placed in the hands of a practitioner of the craft surveyed in it. The late Samuel Isham was abundantly qualified by experience to write of American painting.

He was born in New York in 1855 and was graduated from Yale just twenty years later. Professor Niemeyer, in the Art School there, grounded him in draughtsmanship and in the succeeding three years he studied under Jacquesson de la Chevreuse, in Paris. Returning then to this country he abandoned the subject and entered the legal profession, following it for full five years; but the passion for art was revived in him and in the early eighties he definitively adopted the career of a painter. In Paris once more he frequented the Academie Julien, to be trained by Boulanger and Le Fevbre. His progress was rapid, developing him into a figure and landscape painter of marked ability, well disciplined in technique, an artist giving gracefully decorative expression to such ideas as are suggested by the titles of some of his pictures, "Psyche," "The Apple of Discord," "The Lilac Kimono," "Seated Lady in White," "Girl with Branch," and "Music."

From the first his work was well received. In France his pictures were accepted at the Salon and at home he met with the same cordial appreciation. He was elected a member of the Society of American Artists, then, in 1891, enjoying all its prestige as the most advanced of organizations here. In 1900 he was made an Associate of the National Academy of Design and he became an Academician in 1906, when the

v

Society was merged back into the older body.   Isham belonged to the
New York Water Color Club and to the Architectural League.   His
work figured in exhibitions throughout the country and he often served
on their juries.   He was thus in the thick of the artistic events of his
time, down to the day of his death at Easthampton, in 1914, and his
book is consistently a study of American painting from the painter's
point of view.

It has been in sympathy with that point of view that the chapters
continuing his narrative have been written.   They have been planned
to indicate the fruition of careers still in progress when the book was
originally published, and to carry the record down to our own day.
Certain significant movements and types have been discussed but, as
Isham himself states in his introduction, "the ungrateful and impossible
task of recording the names and works of every meritorious painter
has not been attempted."

ROYAL CORTISSOZ

CONTENTS

vii

CONTENTS

ILLUSTRATIONS IN TEXT

PLATES

INTRODUCTION

As the United States of America is the youngest of the great nations of the world, but recently come to full rank among them, so the development of the arts within it has been short and has not yet reached completeness. The whole course of American painting from its beginnings down to the present extends over no great space of time, and a few long artist-lives span it in a surprising manner. One does not have to be beyond middle age to remember Professor S. F. B. Morse, yet Morse was a student under West, the almost legendary founder of the craft, who got his first colors from the painted savages of the forest; and West, moreover, was still living when Daniel Huntington, even now painting among us, was born. Yet the course of our art though short has not been unbroken. It has not the interest of organic growth, of logical development, but has continually deserted one set of models to follow another, retaining at each change hardly any tradition of its former ideals. In general, however, it divides itself with sufficient distinctness into three periods, which may be characterized as the Colonial, the Provincial, and the Cosmopolitan.

At first such art as the struggling colonies possessed came from visiting English craftsmen usually of the most unskilful type. Soon, however, they had disciples and rivals among the native-born, of whom some of the most promising and enterprising went to England to perfect themselves. Two or three of these were men of quite unexpected ability. A recent critic has said that the best were but second-rate English painters; but they were second-rate only if Reynolds and Gainsborough be placed in a class by themselves as alone first-rate. With the best of the others Copley and Stuart are substantially on an equality, and West, though now antiquated, was an important influence in the art of his time. That they were *English* painters, however, cannot be well denied. Copley and West remained to the end British subjects, and the long line of American students who passed through the studio of West returned home with English methods and English ideals.

The intellectual dependence on the mother country naturally lasted long after the political ties were broken; but separation, the social changes resulting from the change of government and the ruder, more isolated life incident to the development of the interior of the country, weakened the influence of English art until it slowly disappeared. In its place came all manner of strivings of native talent to satisfy the æsthetic cravings of native taste, crude at first but gradually improving under the influence of Düsseldorf, Rome, and later of Paris. One interesting result of the movement was the development of a native landscape school, and it finally culminated in a few men whose original talent, strengthened by adverse surroundings, has not been surpassed since.

With the conclusion of the Civil War came another change. The succeeding generation of artists departed for Europe almost in a body. They studied in the best *ateliers* of the Old World, side by side with the men who are now the leaders of European art; they contended with them for the school prizes and later showed pictures alongside of theirs in the exhibitions; they accepted European standards of workmanship and also to a great extent European tastes and interests. They no longer reflected the culture, the likes and dislikes of their compatriots as, in spite of foreign travel or training, the elder generation had done. They appeared almost as aliens. Even after their return, when they had begun half unconsciously to reflect native ideas in their work, they still tested it by comparison with what was being done elsewhere. In fact, American painting had become an integral part of the painting of the world. The methods, the ideals, the achievements of Europe were all open to the American artist who, according to his temperament and ability, chose or rejected what he would. The old period of isolation was passed.

It is along these latter lines that our painting is developing, adapting itself to native needs and to a new-found native taste with a rapidity that precludes any adequate record. The amount of space devoted to men like West or Chester Harding in the present volume may seem entirely disproportionate when compared with that given to living men of equal or greater abilities; but even if the earlier men who are comparatively few in number were completely omitted, the space gained would suffice no better for individual criticism of the men of to-day. Moreover, a history of American painting should have its importance not through its description of isolated men or their works, but as a record of the growth of the country in intelligence and culture; as a part, in fact, of that *History of Taste* which still awaits its author. The lives of the early painters have consequently been given in some detail so that it may be seen not only what manner of men they were but also how they were formed by their surroundings and the sort of public to which they catered.

For the same reason an attempt has been made to note the rise and growth of the different art organizations and their social and intellectual character, and also to give some record of the foreign influences that have been brought to bear upon them. The artists have changed their ideals but not accidentally or arbitrarily. Even when some of them seemed to be opposing the taste of their countrymen, they were in fact but aiding it in a necessary and inevitable advance. It is this development of painting and of the appreciation of painting which it has been the aim of this book to trace, and mention of the lives and works of individual painters has been made as they seemed to illustrate such development. The ungrateful and impossible task of recording the names and works of every meritorious painter has not been attempted.

HISTORY OF AMERICAN PAINTING

CHAPTER I

THE PRIMITIVES

American Painting entirely derived from Europe. — Artists among the Early Explorers. — Le Moyne. — Joannes With. — Culture of the French Superior in the Beginning to that of the English. — Conditions of Early Colonial Life. — Some Pictures brought over. — Early Painters. — Smybert. — Greenwood. — Theus. — Feke. — Kilburn. — Blackburn

THE fundamental and mastering fact about American painting is that it is in no way native to America, but is European painting imported, or rather transplanted, to America, and there cultivated and developed; and even that not independently, but with constant reference to the older countries, first one nation or school having a preponderating influence, then another. There is no local tradition or influence; no ancient archaic style to be vaguely felt even in the latest and most varied achievements. The Indians of the Atlantic seaboard were skilled in war and hunting, some of them were wise in council, sound reasoners, and with a striking and picturesque eloquence, but in all that touched art, even of the rudimentary savage type, they were far behind their brethren of Mexico and Peru. Even had they been equally advanced, it is doubtful if their carvings and paintings would have left perceptible traces. The immigrants who permanently occupied the country were not in a frame of mind to learn from the savages, nor were they, in most of the English colonies, greatly interested in anything pertaining to sculpture or painting.

With the French colonists it was different; they were far more advanced in all that touched the refinements of life, and their leaders often were at home in the highly cultivated French court, where all the arts were encouraged to the utmost. The French colonies were sent out more or less under court patronage and for the glory of the French name. Their promoters desired, as a rule, to enrich themselves, but also to gain renown, to enlighten the world, to found states which should reflect the glories of France. They were interested in the beauties of the country, in its people, and in its fauna. The large intellectual interests of the pioneers of Canada are in strong contrast to the narrow, incurious Puritan mind. Thoreau describes Governor Winthrop's surmises about the great lake and the hideous swamps about it where the Connecticut and the Potomac took their rise, and his recording among the memorable events the expedition of Darbey Field (an Irishman, which accounts for his enterprise), who went to the top of the White Hill, from whence he saw eastward "what he judged to be the great lake which the Canada River comes out of;" and Thoreau compares these wild conjectures with the adventures and discoveries of Champlain, of which "we have a minute and faithful account, giving facts and dates as well as charts and soundings, all scientific and Frenchmanlike, with scarcely one fable or traveller's story."

One French expedition, and that of the earliest, was even supplied with an official artist, whose adventure merits some notice, as he was the first professional painter of the New World. In 1565 that picturesque moral character, Sir John Hawkins, had for the second time captured a cargo of negroes on the African coast and transported and sold them into slavery in the Spanish West Indies, all to his great profit, though to the scandal of the more conservative of his countrymen. Scandal, not because the sacking of negro villages was considered in any way reprehensible, but Spain claimed and was generally allowed a monopoly of commerce with the Western continent, and Sir John had been infringing on her preserves to the extent of attacking the towns and forcing them to permit him to trade. On his way home, after disposing of his live stock, he put in at the mouth of the St. John's River in Florida for water, and found there a French colony in great distress. It was the far-sighted Admiral Coligny who, at the beginning of the Huguenot troubles in France, had furthered the idea of planting a Protestant state in the New World. One futile attempt had been made in Brazil. The Florida one was undertaken a few years later, under the leadership of Jean Ribaut, who had returned to France, leaving his lieutenant, Laudonnière, in command; and his party, who were most unfitted for the rôle of colonists, being mostly soldiers, young

Huguenot nobles, adventurers, and everything except farmers, had come, through improvidence, discontent, rebellion, and gold-seeking, to a point where famine stared them in the face.

Hawkins treated them with kindness, furnished them with provision, and left them a ship for their return to France, taking Laudonnière's bill for payment. He had hardly left and they were still waiting for a favorable wind to embark when Ribaut came with relief, and the settlement was in the way of becoming permanent; but within a week from Ribaut's arrival another fleet appeared. They had been betrayed to Spain by the court party at home and the Spanish admiral, Pedro Menendez de Avilés, had been sent out against them. He slaughtered the whole colony without quarter, cruelly and, the French claim, treacherously. A handful alone escaped, among them Jacques le Moyne de Morgues, the artist of the expedition. Le Moyne had been left with the sick and disabled, and on the Spanish attack fled to the woods, from whence he saw a comrade (who, in desperation, had given himself up to the Spaniards) hewn to pieces before his eyes. He finally succeeded in reaching the coast, and was picked up by one of the small vessels which had escaped and was brought to England. It is interesting to add that two years afterward a simple gentleman of Mont-de-Marsan, Dominique de Gourgues, neither powerful nor rich, but fired with wrath at the cruelty of the Spaniards and the apathy of the court, raised at his own costs three small vessels and a handful of men, sailed for Florida, enlisted the Indians (who were friendly to the French), and after succeeding in his desperate venture and completely exterminating the Spanish colony, returned home, leaving the ruins of the settlement to the aborigines.

In the second of the *Voyages*, published by De Bry, in 1591, may be found the *Brevis Narratio* of Le Moyne's experiences, illustrated with copper plates by De Bry after his drawings. The engraving is of good commercial quality, but there is not much art in the compositions nor (though figures of turkeys and alligators give some local color) is there much to distinguish the country and its inhabitants from Thracia or Cathay as shown in similar publications of the time. Even the portrait from life of the great King Saturiona, except for his scanty attire and plentiful painting or tattooing, shows

no racial characteristics; and the same criticism may be made on the
illustrations to the first of De Bry's *Voyages*, which, although published earlier, had reference to a later expedition, Raleigh's Virginia
venture of 1585.   The artist, Joannes With, presumably from Germany or the Netherlands, was sent out with the parties by the publisher as a special artist (*eius rei gratia in illam provinciam annis*

FIG. 1. — ILLUSTRATION FROM DE BRY'S *Voyages*.

1585–1588 misso), but though all was "dilligently observed and
expressed to the life," yet the series of men and women of the Indian
tribes has an addition of half a dozen or so of plates of ancient Brit-
ons, which the painter asserts are much the same thing, and which
certainly seem the same in his illustrations.   These works were followed in the succeeding century by many others calculated to gratify the interest excited in the strange New World, containing many
illustrations of the cities, peoples, animals, and plants of America,

often done by men who had been on the spot ; but, apart from the fact that the English settlements got far less attention than the West Indies and Brazil, the interest was mainly scientific, and the artists had no more real connection with the art of the countries they visited than the explorers who to-day illustrate the Congo basin or Man- churia. Few of the draughtsmen were English, and if we wish traces of a taste for art, we must turn to the French rather than to the English settlers. Even before De Bry's publications in Ramusio's *Voyages* of 1556, there was a recognizable view of Hochelaga (later Montreal), and in 1558 there appeared at Antwerp, Thevet's *Les Singularitez de la France Antartique*, which contained a cut of a buffalo, probably from a drawing by Thevet himself, and fairly well done. Later there appeared another artist who, though also an amateur, was far better known than even Le Moyne. Samuel de Champlain, that gallant, steadfast gentleman, adorned his journal with colored pictures of harbors, rivers, animals, blockhouses, skir- mishes with Indians (who shoot their unfortunate victims full of arrows until they look like porcupines), and other occurrences of interest, as may be seen in the manuscript preserved in Dieppe to this day. Parkman says they are " in a style which a child of ten might emulate," but they elucidate the text, and no English pioneer had advanced even as far as that.

There was continually among the French explorers of Canada an effort toward a life adorned with the graces and refinements which they had left behind. Champlain himself, on his return from an exploring expedition, was welcomed at Port Royale by a *fête* where Neptune and his tritons, issuing from beneath an arch blazoned with scutcheons and the arms of France, declaimed a greeting in good French verse. And later yet the fiery Frontenac, who in his early days in France had lavished money and boasted of the perfection of his *cuisine* and establishment generally, cared for the intellectual pleasures of cultivated life and got himself into difficulties with the clergy through his masquerades and plays.

But these incursions into art left no permanent results ; no more did the portraits of saints and the lurid representations of the suffer- ings of the damned which the Jesuit priests carried through the wilds to turn the hearts of the bloodthirsty Hurons to grace, nor the other religious paintings of the same type with which Spain endowed the churches of Mexico and Brazil.

It is interesting to conjecture what might have been the result had France won in the duel for the possession of the continent.

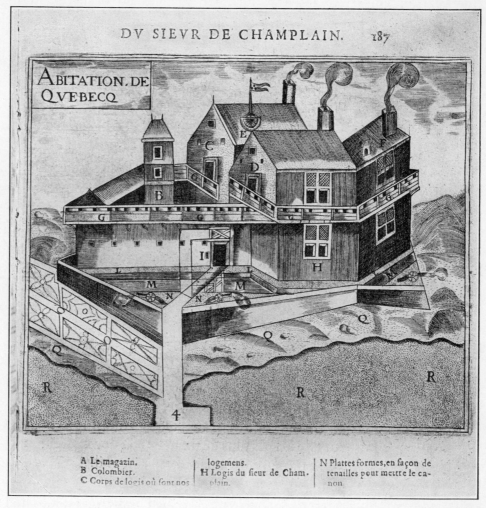

DV SIEVR DE CHAMPLAIN.   187

ABITATION. DE QVEBECQ

A Le magazin.
B Colombier.
C Corps de logis où font nos

logemens.
H Logis du sieur de Cham-
plain.

N Plattes formes, en façon de
tenailles pour mettre le canon

FIG. 2. — ILLUSTRATION FROM CHAMPLAIN'S *Voyages*.

It is doubtful if it would have been as advantageous artistically as is generally supposed, for the fact is that the permanent development of American art was through the English-speaking race, and its difficult beginnings were not among the cavaliers of the South nor the Dutch of New York, who might be expected to retain some sympathy with the decorative side of life, but among the Puritans of

Boston and the Quakers of Philadelphia. In general the early colonists brought no paintings in their baggage and little thought of them in their minds. Whatever their aspirations, whether for freedom of conscience or for gold mines, the settlers passed their first years in misery and squalor. They lived in hovels dug in the sides of the hills, and the rude log hut was a luxury. A greater degree of comfort soon came in, but even the towns were long unpaved and poor, although the accounts vary greatly according to the reporter. Thus, in the middle of the seventeenth century, Johnson describes Boston as "a city-like Towne crowded on the Sea, banked and wharfed out with great industry and cost, the buildings beautifull and large; some fancily set forth with Brick, Tile, Stone and Slate, and orderly placed with comeley Streets." The less partial eyes of the Old World Royal Commissioners saw it a few years later. "The houses generally wooden, their streets crooked, with little decency and no uniformity." There was a steady improvement with time. Brick came into general use after the beginning of the eighteenth century, and "what is now known as colonial architecture gradually developed, some of its best examples dating from about 1720."

This was written particularly of Boston, but it applies equally well to the other cities of the colonies. Both in New England and Pennsylvania religious prejudice was opposed to most forms of art, and New York kept to its traditions as a trading post rather than an intellectual centre. Some of the patroons on the Hudson may have brought with them an ampler culture, at least it was so of the De Peysters, and there still remain portraits of Colonel Abraham and his wife which must have been painted in Europe about 1700. Mrs. Brown of Laggan, who was at the homestead about 1760, reports it well supplied with canvases. "The best bedroom was hung with family portraits, some of which were admirably executed; and in the eating room which, by the bye, was rarely used for that purpose, were some fine scriptural paintings; that which made the greatest impression on my imagination and seemed to be universally admired, was one of Esau coming to demand the anticipated blessing; the noble manly figure, and the anguish expressed on his comely though strong featured countenance, I shall never forget." Even the lesser people

among the Dutch immigrants cultivated the arts to some extent, as
the inventory of Jonas Bronck, the shadowy eponymous hero of the
Borough of the Bronx, Manhattan, bears witness. He was a sub-
stantial burgher but no patroon, yet he left eleven pictures, as well
as a number of books and a Japanese cutlass.

FIG. 3. — ELIZABETH PADDY WENSLEY (EXAMPLE OF EARLY WORK), PILGRIM HALL, PLYMOUTH.

While such cases may have been rare, especially in the English
colonies, yet constant intercourse with the mother country was
maintained, and the governors and other officials sent out from England brought with them the refinements of life and maintained a
certain state. There was a natural demand for likenesses of prominent persons, legislators, or divines. Portraits, more or less authentic,

FIG. 4.—SMYBERT: FAMILY OF BISHOP BERKELEY, YALE UNIVERSITY.

of the early governors and worthies, the Winthrops, Winslows, Calverts, Mathers, and the like, are still extant, many painted in England, but some produced in the colonies. Cotton Mather relates in his *Magnalia* how "Mr. Edward Rawson, the honored Secretary of the Massachusetts Colony, could not, with all his entreaties persuade John Wilson to have his picture drawn; 'What! such a poor vile creature as I am! Shall my picture be drawn! I say no; it never shall,'" and it was not, though "The limner was introduced with all things ready." Wilson died in 1667, a very early date to find an artist in Massachusetts; and the probabilities are that he was a very bad one, though his experience will gain the sympathy of portrait painters. Other worthies, however, were less modest or showed it in a different way, and the early art of the colonies was mostly confined to portraiture or to the painting of signs and coaches, both much more elaborate then than now. There were more practitioners during the eighteenth century than is usually supposed, though they were but indifferent workmen, and it is well-nigh impossible to place any names on the canvases that survive from the period before 1750. Records of them appear here and there. As early as 1715, John Watson, a Scotchman, came to this country and set up his easel at Perth Amboy. After his first visit he returned to Europe and brought back to his adopted country many pictures, which with his own compositions formed no inconsiderable collection in point of number. He painted portraits and ideal heads of kings and heroes, and his painting house, with the shutters divided into squares and decorated with personages in antique costume, still remained to awaken the childish wonder of Dunlap. He died at an advanced age, and left a reputation for lending money to his sitters and being a usurer and miser.

The earliest artist whose works are known and of sufficient merit to warrant serious consideration was John Smybert (or Smibert, for he spelled his name both ways), who came to America in 1728 with Bishop Berkeley when that worthy divine attempted to start his college in Bermuda, and who remained after the return of his friend the bishop and settled in Boston, where "he married a woman of considerable fortune" and resided there until his death.

Smybert was really a fair painter according to the English stand ards of his day, which were not high, since he lived just before the brilliant flowering of English art at the end of the eighteenth century. He was Scotch by birth, born in Edinburgh, in 1684, and in his youth was apprenticed to a house painter and plasterer; but a taste for drawing made him leave the more mechanical branch of his profession and come to London, where he supported life by coach-painting and copying old pictures. He increased his skill by studying in the Academy of Sir James Thornhill, who was then the leading native artist in England and almost the first to receive any public recognition. Sir James was a man of good birth, which undoubtedly helped him to success, and he decorated, at so much a square yard, staircases, galleries, and ceilings, including the dome of St. Paul's, in the style of Verrio and the foreigners that he succeeded. He was wealthy and maintained his Academy at his own expense. Smybert had there, for a fellow-student, Hogarth, with whom the series of great English portrait painters begins, and who clandestinely married Thornhill's daughter.

After his coach-painting days, Smybert went, in 1717, to Italy and on his return set up as portrait painter with success and was particularly patronized by the "Virtuosi" of London, a society of amateurs of the fine arts, containing men of some celebrity like John Wooten, Thomas Gibson, and George Vertue. And he was also well known to Horace Walpole, from whose anecdotes of painting we get most of our knowledge of Smybert before he sailed for America, and who regarded his departure for an uncivilized country, just when fortune began to smile on him, with the amused superiority of a man of the world and a dilettante. "Smybert," he says, "was a silent and modest man who abhorred *finesse* in his profession and was enchanted with a plan which he thought promised tranquillity and an honest subsistence in a healthy and elysian climate, and in spite of remonstrances engaged with the Dean."

His most important work and his best is the picture of Bishop Berkeley and his family, now in the Dining Hall, Yale University, a group containing eight figures suggesting the one described in the *Vicar of Wakefield* whose dimensions rendered it impossible to enter the house and relegated it to the yard. It is well if somewhat stiffly arranged, the painting is dry and hard, and the

FIG. 5.—BLACKBURN: PORTRAIT OF JOSHUA WARNER, BOSTON MUSEUM.

shadows black and without transparency, but the drawing is good, and the character of the different persons well given, with a certain liveliness and animation in their expression. This, which is one of the earliest of his works in America (he is said to have begun it, or at least the studies for it, during the voyage), seems to have met with general approbation, for he had many orders and painted a long line of divines, magistrates, and justices with their wives and children, of unequal merit, and (although his reputation has probably suffered from the reckless attribution to him of the work of inferior men) mostly stiff in pose and labored in treatment. Yet his portraits were by far the best executed in the country up to the time of his death, and we owe him a debt of gratitude for the sincerity with which he has preserved for us the likenesses of our early worthies, men like Jonathan Edwards or John Endicott of Massachusetts, and the others who out of their unskilfully drawn eyes stare at us stiffly from his canvases. Much of his work is preserved, and Perkins gives a list of thirty-six pictures by him which he considers authentic.

Smybert died in 1751, and from that time the number of painters in America multiplied, though their merit did not increase. Smybert's son Nathaniel followed his father's profession and showed promise, but died young, in 1756.

John Greenwood was also a contemporary, and all over the colonies there were artists like Theus, whose name Dunlap has preserved and who painted portraits in South Carolina "certainly as early as 1750," and Robert Feke, of an old New England family, who worked about the same time. All of these did work that, without being of great merit, still was not grotesque, and even had some dignity and beauty. In the New York *Gazette* of July, 1754, there was published a notice to the effect that

"LAWRENCE KILBURN, Limner

"Just arrived from London with Capt. Miller, hereby acquaints all Gentlemen and Ladies inclined to favor him in having their pictures drawn, that he don't doubt of pleasing them in taking a true Likeness, and finishing the Drapery in a proper manner, as also in the Choice of Attitudes suitable to each Person's Age and Sex, and giving agreeable satisfaction as he has heretofore done to Gentlemen and Ladies in London."

His notices continued to appear until 1772, when he seems to have abandoned the practice of art and opened a paint store, selling among other items, "yellow oker, prusian blue, and verdigrease," and finally, in 1775, comes a notice for the payment of debts due him to Judith Kilburn, his executrix. Similar notices of other painters were published subsequently, and other names appear in the old records, some of them connected with the beginnings of West and Copley; but oblivion has swallowed up the works of most of them.

The neglect is not unmerited. The work is poor and without artistic interest, though the portraits are often the only likenesses we have of men important in their day, and the costumes are amusing. Bad as they are, the *technique* usually suggests Continental work rather than English, which is natural, for English painting was hardly begun, and the wandering craftsmen in America got what ideals they had from men like Kneller and Lely. Most of them probably learned their trade before coming to America, and renewed their artistic inspiration from such prints and portraits as they could get a sight of. The general result was about what one might expect an unskilful sign painter to produce when attempting to copy Sir Godfrey Kneller from memory.

Of one man we know something more. Jonathan B. Blackburn came to Boston about 1750 and remained some fifteen years. Mr. Perkins has been unable to trace his early life, but says that "there was a travelling artist of the same name about a generation before him, and he may have been his son, but there is no proof of it." He gives a list of some fifty pictures by him which are still preserved, including a number of full lengths and two family groups, and surmises that he remained in Boston until his pupil or imitator, Copley, had begun to paint better than himself. Blackburn, however he may have got his training, was a respectable painter and might fairly rival Smybert or the youthful Copley. His portraits are rigid and the modelling dry, like those of his contemporaries, but they are serious work, and he sometimes shows a feeling for color in delicate grays and quiet tones which is entirely his own, and he was, moreover, capable of composing a group fairly well.

COPLEY: PORTRAIT OF MRS. FORD, HARTFORD ATHENÆUM.

CHAPTER II

COPLEY AND HIS WORK

AMERICAN ART FIRST BECOMES OF SERIOUS IMPORTANCE WITH COPLEY AND WEST. —
COPLEY'S FAMILY. — HIS STEPFATHER, PETER PELHAM. — COPLEY'S EARLY
TRAINING. — HIS MARRIAGE AND LIFE IN BOSTON. — EXHIBITS IN LONDON. —
FINALLY GOES ABROAD AND IS FOLLOWED BY HIS FAMILY. — SETTLES IN LONDON. —
WORKS PAINTED THERE. — HIS DEATH. — HIS PERSONAL CHARACTER. — HIS
PAINTING. — SINCERITY OF HIS WORK DONE IN AMERICA. — IMPROVEMENT OF HIS
WORKMANSHIP IN ENGLAND

In spite of the modest merits of their predecessors, it was with
Copley and West that American painters first took a recognized
position in the world of art. Neither of the men were geniuses, but
they had respectable talents; and both for what they did and for
what they were, each occupies securely a little niche in the temple of
Fame which shields him against oblivion.

With no similarity of character or of work, there is still a curious
parallelism in their lives — each born in different provinces of a new
country where art was still in its infancy, and each coming to
London to gain wealth, honor, fame, and finally to die there at an
advanced age, just as their vogue was beginning seriously to decline.
They were almost exactly contemporaries, having been born and
dying within a year or so of each other.

Copley was the elder, which of itself should give him precedence;
but it is also convenient to consider him first because his beginnings
are interwoven with the earlier men, and his work shows their style,
which he carried on and perfected, being brought up and working at
Boston, which was, as much as any place could be, the centre of the intellectual life of the colonies. He did not go to England until he was
nearly forty, and led there a rather retired and quiet life, in pointed
contrast to West, who had scarcely any professional instruction in
America, and was hardly of age when he left, but who advised,
taught, and assisted two generations of younger men in their beginnings.

John Singleton Copley was born in Boston, July 3, 1737. His father was of a Yorkshire family long settled in County Limerick, Ireland, where he married and with his wife came to Boston in 1736. He died in the West Indies about the time of his son's birth. His widow went into the tobacco trade and sold, as one of her notices sets forth, "the best Virginia Tobacco, Cut, Pigtail, Spun, by Wholesale and Retail, at the cheapest rates," and was long a popular and well-known dealer in Boston. Nine or ten years after her first husband's death she married Peter Pelham, an event of the greatest advantage and importance to the boy.

Pelham was a mezzotint engraver of serious merit. John Chaloner Smith's "Catalogue of British Engravers" shows that he executed some thirty-six plates, more than half of them in England. His American work consists largely of heads of divines from unskilful originals, and of necessity without beauty, but occasionally, as in the portrait of Sir William Pepperell after Smybert, he got a fairly attractive subject, and produced a good plate. He came to America about 1726 but found little call for his skill there, so that he took advantage of his education, which seems to have been unusually good, by opening a school where he taught "Reading, Writing, Needlework, Dancing, and the art of Painting upon Glass." He continued his school after his marriage, and also practised his art when he found opportunity. He seems to have claimed and been allowed a good social standing, writing "gentleman" after his signature in a surety bond, the other witness being but a perukemaker. When he died he is described as "schoolmaster."

He engraved a number of portraits of divines, some of them from his own paintings, and was a man well known and esteemed. It is certain that Smybert was intimate with him and reasonably certain that under the circumstances then prevailing at Boston he knew the other painters and engravers there. He died in 1751, when his stepson was but fourteen; but the boy was precocious and had already made some progress in drawing. His first known work is said to be a portrait of his stepfather, and a couple of years after he painted a portrait of his stepbrother, Charles Pelham, and the next year, when he was sixteen, published an engraving of the Rev. William Welsteed from a painting by himself. He continued

Cottonus Matherus

FIG. 6. — PELHAM: ENGRAVING OF. COTTON MATHER.

to paint portraits, and in 1754 produced an allegorical picture thirty inches long by twenty-five wide, of Mars, Venus, and Vulcan, and the next year a miniature of Washington, who came to Boston in the first flush of his reputation as an Indian fighter.

Copley was then a boy of seventeen, and it only needs this account of his boyhood to show how inexact and misleading is the often-quoted statement from a letter by his son, Lord Lyndhurst, to the effect that his achievements were remarkable, "considering that he was entirely self-taught, and never saw a decent picture with the exception of his own until he was nearly thirty." While Perkins's suggestion that he may have been the pupil of Blackburn seems to rest on nothing but its inherent probability, he had exceptional facilities for his early training under his stepfather, and there were a good many pictures more than "decent" in Boston and its vicinity at that time, and Copley was in the way of seeing most of them. Besides the Smyberts and Blackburns there were portraits by foreign artists, some Knellers, and alleged Van Dycks, one of Governor Belcher by Liotard, a likeness of Richard Saltonstall said to have been painted in Holland in 1644 by Rembrandt, and particularly a copy by Smybert after Van Dyck of a cardinal's head which now hangs in the Harvard Memorial Hall, and which was studied in turn by Copley, Trumbull, and Allston.

There seems never to have been any doubt about Copley's vocation; at seventeen he was recognized as a painter and had continual opportunity to exercise his skill. He is said to have been quiet and reserved as a boy, and his career is undiversified either by struggles against poverty or Bohemian outbreaks. He accepted the rather rigorous life of Boston, and he maintained and insisted upon his social standing as one of the upper class. His life was uneventful, but prosperous and dignified. In 1769 he married a daughter of Richard Clarke, a wealthy merchant of the town and agent of the East India Company, a marriage in every way fortunate. The strongest affection united them throughout their lives, and Mrs. Copley, who possessed much personal beauty, was introduced by her husband a number of times into his pictures. He lived in a solitary house on Beacon Hill, surrounded by his farm, as he called it, of eleven acres, in which he took great pride and pleasure.

It was there in 1768 that Charles Wilson Peale, his junior by four years, came to him for instruction, and there Trumbull, then a boy of sixteen, visited him, finding him about to receive a party of friends at dinner, and remembered to the end of his life his costume and appearance. "An elegant-looking man, dressed in a fine maroon cloth with gilt buttons," and probably the impression was influential in determining him later to become a painter himself. It is worth while to add that the visit was not made "at the time of his (Copley's) marriage" (he had been married two years), nor did he wear "a suit of crimson velvet with gold buttons," both of which statements are carelessly made by Dunlap, and being more picturesque than Trumbull's own accounts have been generally copied by biographers.

Thus Copley passed his early manhood with such an honorable position and so assured an income that he hesitated to leave it for the larger but more hazardous opportunities of London. He himself wrote in 1767: "I am now in as good business as the poverty of this place will admit. I make as much money as if I were a Raphael or a Correggio, and three hundred guineas a year, my present income, is equal to nine hundred a year in London." These reflections were probably prompted by the reception at the London Society of Artists of his portrait of his half-brother, Henry Pelham, known as the "Boy with the Squirrel," which he had sent to West with a letter requesting that it might be shown in the exhibition. The letter was delayed, and the rules of the society, then a comparatively new institution, forbade the admission of anonymous work; but West, from the pine of which the stretcher was made and from the flying squirrel, recognized the painting as the work of an American, and with his customary kindliness urged that it should be hung, praising the "delicious color, worthy of Titian himself." The picture was shown in the exhibition of 1766, and much admired. His name appeared in the catalogue as Mr. William Copely of Boston, New England. The next year, when he sent a full length of a lady with a bird and dog, he is Mr. Copley, and in 1768 his name is given in full and correctly. He sent that year a half-length portrait of a gentleman and another of a lady, the latter in crayon. In 1771 and 1772 he appears again as Mr. Copely with, in the latter year, the

letters F.S.A. after his name, showing that he had been elected a
Fellow of the Society of Artists. This was probably done through
West's influence, who was in correspondence with Copley and had
invited him to come to London and make his house his home. In
consequence of this, he sailed for England in June of 1774, leaving
his family in Boston, and apparently in the expectation of returning
there. West received him on his arrival, took him to see the pictures in the Queen's Palace, introduced him to persons likely to be
helpful to him, and furthered his interests in every way in his power.
He stayed in London during the summer, painting a number of portraits, including those of Lord and Lady North and heads of the
King and Queen, and in the autumn left for Italy, passing the winter in Rome, where he spent his time studying the antiquities, copying both from the statues and paintings, and finishing a group of
Ralph Izard of South Carolina and his wife, the only portraits which
he did there.

The growing political disturbances in America, as well as the
favor with which his painting was received, caused Copley to send for
his family, and in July of the next year, while he was at Parma copying the "St. Jerome" of Correggio, for which he had a commission, he
learned of their arrival in London, and after a trip down the Rhine
and through the Netherlands joined them before the end of the
year. Mrs. Copley left behind her in America Mrs. Pelham, the
artist's mother, and in her care an infant only a few weeks old, which
she was afraid to expose to the trials of an ocean voyage, and which
died soon after. She took with her three children, and was soon
afterward joined by her father, Mr. Clarke, and her brothers, who
had previously moved to Canada. Mr. Clarke was a strong Tory.
It was to him that the tea was consigned which was dumped into
the harbor at the " Boston tea party," and in other ways he suffered
so heavily for his views that he subsequently received a pension
from the British government up to his death.

Copley, on the contrary, favored the American party, but without
strong feeling. He writes to his wife on her arrival in England,
when war was imminent: " You know, years ago, I was right in my
opinion that this would be the result of the attempt to tax the colony;
it is now my settled conviction that all the power of Great Britain

will not reduce them to obedience," but he adds a postscript instructing his half-brother " on no account whatever to take part in the present dispute."   He, more than West, seems to have kept his sympathies to himself during the war, and to have regarded it as something in which he had no personal concern, and to have cared more for his family relations and for his advancement in his art than for public questions.   He nevertheless was grieved at the suffering caused by the war, and rejoiced at its close.   He was working at the time on a portrait of Elkanah Watson, in the background of which he had introduced a ship.   On Dec. 5, 1782, they listened together to the King's speech recognizing America's independence, and on their return to his house Copley at once painted on the ship's mast the first American flag displayed in England.

When they first settled in England, Copley lived in Leicester Square, but shortly after he purchased the house 25 George Street, Hanover Square, which was to be his permanent home, and after his death, that of his son the Lord Chancellor.   It was a handsome mansion, and in it Copley led the dignified, stately life which was dear to him.   His house was known to all Americans visiting London, and its hospitality was offered to all those of sufficient social standing.   His talents brought him ample patronage from the first. His life was quiet, devoted to his family, and uneventful except for the pictures which his steady industry produced — not only portraits but also a series of figure pieces, many of large size, one of the first being " A Youth rescued from a Shark," a replica of which now hangs in the Boston Museum.   The " Youth " was Brooke Watson, who had been a companion of Copley's on his voyage to England, and who had related his adventure so frequently and vividly that the painter succeeded in giving an appearance of reality to a very exceptional scene.   Brooke Watson himself was not an altogether admirable character.   His youth was devoted to the slave trade ; he served under Wolfe at Louisburg, and later was Commissary General to the army under Lord Dorchester.   When the Revolution broke out, he assumed sympathy with the national cause and used his position to act as a spy for the British.   In spite of his later elevation as Lord Mayor of London and Baronet of the United Kingdom, there are those whose sympathy is with the shark.

FIG. 7.—COPLEY: PORTRAIT OF JOHN HANCOCK, BOSTON MUSEUM.

About the same time Copley painted the " Family Picture " of his own household, including himself. " The Death of Lord Chatham " was finished before 1780 and followed by the " Death of Major Pierson," the " Siege of Gibraltar," 1790, the " Surrender of Admiral de Windt to Lord Camperdown," and " Charles I demanding the Five Impeached Members."   Later he turned more to religious subjects, painting a " Red Cross Knight " about 1789, and half-a-dozen years later, " Abraham's Sacrifice," " Hagar and Ishmael," " Saul reproved by Samuel," " The Nativity," the " Tribute Money " (his diploma picture), " Samuel and Eli," also large portrait groups such as the " Three Princesses," children of George III, the " Fitch Picture," the " Western Family," and the " Knatchbull Family."

This latter picture painted for Sir Edward Knatchbull had been plentifully adorned with legends illustrating the laborious deliberation of the painter's work.   Begun in 1800, the baronet fondly thought that it might be finished in a month, but it was not finally put in place until 1807, and in the meanwhile the wife first represented had died and her effigy had been effaced and replaced by that of a second one; two children had also gone the way of all flesh (though their portraits remained), and four more had arrived.   It is even said that Sir Edward desired his first wife introduced floating as a guardian angel over the group, but that his second objected so decidedly and strenuously that her likeness was painted out for the second time.

Toward the end of Copley's life his vogue as a painter began to decline, many of his large compositions remained unsold, including an equestrian portrait of the Prince of Wales and " The Offer of the Crown to Lady Jane Grey," a canvas with the figures half life-size, a scale which was unusual with him.   Then, too, Sharpe, the engraver, caused him much trouble by his dilatoriness in finishing the plate of the " Siege of Gibraltar," which dragged along through several years after the prints had been promised and subscriptions received.   All this with his large establishment and his expensive manner of life involved him in financial difficulties, and to insure his son's advance in the study and practice of the law he was forced frequently to borrow money from his son-in-law, Gardiner Greene

of Boston, who had married his eldest daughter and returned with
her to America in 1800.   He died in 1815, too soon to enjoy the
great success of his son, and was buried in the parish church of
Croydon.

Copley's strongest personal trait seems to have been his family
affection.   It was not demonstrative.   With his birth and training in
colonial Boston that was not to have been expected, but he was
a good son and a good husband, and he aided his half-brothers to
the best of his ability.   The radical difference of political views
caused no dissensions between him and his father-in-law, who lived
with him until his death, and his wife and children loved and
honored him.   Apart from his family life he was a rather reserved
man, wrapped up in his work, not genial, and with a disposition
to brood over his griefs.   The breaking of a box of casts which he
had sent from Italy was a disappointment, which, in the words of
his son, " he never ceased to regret during the whole course of his
life," and the sale of his Beacon Hill " farm " embittered his existence.   He felt that he had been wronged, defrauded of a fortune,
though apparently he only made the mistake, personally or through
his agent, of selling the property just before its great rise in value,
and even the future Lord Chancellor, when he made a trip to America for that purpose, could find no legal flaw in the transaction.

Copley's painting separates itself into two pretty sharply marked
divisions, according to whether it was done before or after he left
Boston.   The latter half is far more skilled and complete technically;
but it is the earlier work, the long series of portraits of our colonial
dignitaries, divines, judges, and merchants with their womankind
which is most interesting and characteristic, and which gives him
his peculiar importance.   They are the only pre-revolutionary relics
on which we can depend to put before our eyes the very age and
body of the time.   The lack of facile skill makes their veracity
more convincing than that 'of the canvases of Gainsborough or Reynolds, where temperament or training idealized or Italianized the
sitters into something rather different from what their contemporaries saw in daily intercourse.   Gainsborough was a poet, Reynolds
an eclectic, wise in all the traditions of the craft, who could at will
see with the eye and work with the hand of Van Dyck or Titian —

FIG. 8.—COPLEY: MRS. SCOTT, OWNED BY GEORGE SCOTT WINDSOR, BOSTON.

or come pretty near to it. Copley had no such temperament or training. The sitters themselves in the cold, clear light of New England were what he tried to put on the canvases, unmodified by any golden mist of Venice or facile brush work of the Netherlands.

This is not to make him the equal, much less the superior, of the men just named. His surroundings forced upon him a greater sincerity, which seems also to have corresponded with his temperament. He began under the influence of his stepfather Pelham, and though the latter died when he was a boy of fourteen, yet his influence shows through much of his early work. The engraving, in mezzotint, of Welsteed, made when he was sixteen, much resembles the average work of Pelham and is more like the production of a mediocre craftsman than the early effort of a boy of exceptional talent. Copley very soon gave up engraving and seems never to have returned to it in any form, but his early works show its influence in a blackness of shadow and a hardness of style. They were in addition stiff and ungraceful, and in the faces was a sincerity of plainness which must have been trying to the sitters. Even Smybert, whose work resembles that of Copley at this period, and whose colonial dames are rigid and unbending enough, yet manages to put into their faces a comeliness and charm unknown to the youthful Copley, still struggling uncompromisingly with the difficulties of drawing. His improvement was steady, but it took him long to master certain details, like the rendering of eyes, which Smybert never became entirely sure of. At first they were little better than dark slits, and in his best colonial work the lids are often unnaturally prominent. He learned nothing by heart, acquired no ready formulas for execution. He had to see every detail in front of him and put it down exactly as it was. He worked laboriously, mixing each tint with his palette knife, holding it up and matching it to his sitter's face before he placed it on the canvas. This made him a slow executant, and there are many stories of the tedium of sitting to him; sixteen sittings of a whole day each were not considered too much for a head alone, and when at a much later period he painted the children of George III, the whole party, — the princesses, their attendants, even the spaniels and the parrots — broke into open revolt, which was only quelled through West's intervention with the old king.

D

The pictures thus produced were without beauty of tone or richness of color. Something must be allowed for the fading of the flesh tones, probably put in with carmine, but the effect must always have been crude and harsh. The high lights are chalky white, the shadows black or brickish brown; a cold raw blue (like Prussian blue) is often painfully prominent, and there is no attempt to soften the opposing tints nor to blend them. The paint is laid on heavily and worked smooth until there are no brush marks visible. There is no attempt to keep the shadows transparent nor much glazing or working over. It follows the style of his predecessors, founded on German or French models, and shows no trace of the richer, ampler work already beginning in England, where the traditions of Van Dyck were being revived. Nevertheless, in spite of these faults, or possibly on account of them, his portraits have remarkable qualities. The figures are well placed on the canvas, in good if rather rigid poses, the backgrounds, especially in the full-length portraits, are sufficiently furnished with curtains, tables, and Turkey rugs, but over and above all else is the thorough, unwearied sincerity of the work. Copley knew his sitters, knew their position in the community, their dignity, their character, their wealth. He was in sympathy with them and judged by their own standard those airs and graces which to a European might seem provincial and uncouth. Holmes has well called his portraits the titles of nobility of the Bostonians of his day. He painted them as they were, — serious, self-reliant, capable, sometimes rather pompous in their heavy velvet coats, but men to be depended on in an emergency.

The women were fit mates for the men, their faces stamped with that character which left its impress on every child of the ample families of the time. The least successful are the younger women, and at times there is a difficulty in reconciling his portraits with the reputation of the sitters for grace and beauty handed down in the old diaries and letters; but in time his sincerity triumphed even here, and while the portrait remains crude, hard, and without charm, yet we recognize that it is the portrait of a charming woman. This lack of charm tells terribly against them when hung in a gallery with other pictures; but when seen in the places for which they were destined, the halls or rooms of old colonial houses of Boston or

FIG. 9.—COPLEY : FAMILY GROUP.

[From a Copley Print. Copyright 1898 by Curtis & Cameron, Publishers, Boston.]

other of the New England cities, or brought together in official groups as in the Harvard Memorial Hall, their inherent strength makes itself felt. They take their places as the true *genii loci* as nothing else could do. Even their faults strengthen the impression. If a bit of drawing, a hand for example, has been too difficult, it remains always the sitter's hand, badly drawn perhaps, but not replaced by anything more facile but less true, and the same faithfulness pervades all the details and accessories.

The velvet coats and embroidered waistcoats of the men, the satin robes and laces of the women, are of undoubted genuineness. Even if the satin looks like tin, we know that it is satin; and if a colonial worthy goes to the expense of silk stockings, not even the most casual observer could mistake them for wool. In time this unremitting labor began to have its result. During the last ten years or so of his Boston life, Copley was master of his trade and could produce what he tried to. That his portraits still remained dry and hard, without atmosphere, was because he had not seen enough good work to recognize what he lacked. His color, too, is mostly displeasing, or at least not pleasing, and there are but few of his canvases that merit the praise West bestowed on "the delicious color" of his "Boy with a Squirrel." But he was now in a position to benefit at once from increased knowledge. He was no sooner abroad than his style gained in ease and simplicity. His portrait of Ralph Izard and his wife, painted when he was in Rome, shows still something of the old stiffness of attitude, the over-filling with detail; but the work is smoother, more graceful, though still minutely finished in all its parts in a way more characteristic of the Continental work of the time than the English, where the example of Reynolds had produced a broader, more effective handling.

With his London life Copley's work took on more and more of the English manner. His "Family Picture" of himself, his wife, his father-in-law, and his four young children, painted a few years after his arrival, shows this alteration, but retains also the finer qualities of his colonial period and is one of his very best works. The composition is not in perfect unity, and the tone is cold, with much of a sort of claret color and his old unpleasant blue, but they are softened and harmonized with skill, and the shadows and blacks are soft, rich, and

deep.   The painting of the heads is superb, drawn impeccably, full
of character, and with only a touch of the old rigidity, the children
especially most happy in attitude and expression.   This was his first
family group in England, and Mrs. Amory says he had done nothing
at all of the kind in America, with the exception of his boyish allegory of " Mars and Venus."   His groups were certainly rare, which
seems rather strange, considering the example of Smybert and Blackburn and the large dimensions of some of his portrait canvases.   It
is surprising also that with so little experience he should have succeeded from the beginning with complicated compositions.   The
" Family Picture " was preceded by the " Youth rescued from a
Shark," and followed by the series of his historical pictures, inspired
doubtless by West's, who, as will appear in his life, was the founder
of the school; but surpassing their prototypes, they remain to-day
masterpieces of the kind.   It is not too much to say that no other
artist of the time could have produced the " Death of Chatham."
To the sincerity of the emotion, without false sentiment or bombast,
the skill of the arrangement of grouping and light, the clear characterization of the heads, is added a peculiarly interesting arrangement
of the scarlet and white of the peers' robes, which forces the scene
upon the mind.   It is not poetry, the gods did not make Copley
poetical; but it is splendid prose, and its immediate successors were
of the same quality.

These compositions, however, were but incidents in his work.
Portrait painting was the business of his life from beginning to end,
but his latter work has less importance in a history of American
painting.   Probably it should be called better than his earlier.   It
certainly had fewer glaring faults, but it also had less personality.
His earlier work is unmistakable anywhere, his latter often approaches
so closely to that of the brilliant circle of contemporary portrait
painters in England that it is practically indistinguishable from it.
A little extra firmness and solidity of drawing persists to the end;
but the poses, the dark backgrounds, the rich color, the glazings, are
all of the school.   Like Reynolds, he sought for "the Venetian," the
marvellous medium supposed to have been used by Titian, which
like the philosopher's stone would by its own virtue transform the
leaden tones of mediocre painters into gold.   He even thought a

few years before his death that he had found it, but he was then only one of many who could paint glowing canvases. Patronage fell off; almost his last important work, the equestrian portrait of the Prince Regent, from which he hoped great things, remained unsold; his health declined, and his life did not long outlast his popularity.

CHAPTER III

CAREER OF BENJAMIN WEST

BENJAMIN WEST. — HIS BIOGRAPHER, JOHN GALT. — ANCESTRY AND CHILDHOOD. — EARLY
PATRONS AND INSTRUCTION. — LEAVES PHILADELPHIA FOR NEW YORK AND SAILS
THENCE FOR ITALY. — STUDY AND WORK IN ITALY. — ARRIVAL IN LONDON AND
SUCCESS THERE. — HIS MARRIAGE. — INTRODUCTION TO THE KING AND RISE IN
ROYAL FAVOR. — "DEATH OF GENERAL WOLFE." — FOUNDING OF THE ROYAL
ACADEMY. — LOSS OF ROYAL PATRONAGE ON THE FAILURE OF THE KING'S MIND. —
"CHRIST HEALING THE SICK," AND OTHER LATE WORKS. — HIS DEATH. — WEST'S
CAREER. — FORTUNATE THROUGHOUT HIS LIFE. — HIS TRAINING. — HIS PUBLIC. —
QUALITY OF HIS WORK. — HIS PERSONAL CHARACTER

THE life of Copley was long, honorable, and successful, but it
was not picturesque. It was his surroundings when a boy that
turned him to art, and he followed painting, without enthusiasm, as
the most obvious means of earning a livelihood. With his industry
and intelligence, his success would have been equally assured if
chance had directed his talents into law or trade. With West it
was different. His career has long been used as a triumphant demonstration of the theory of God-given genius, which, like lightning,
strikes where it will, and develops in spite of the most uncongenial
surroundings. The story of his childish attempts at drawing has
been worked into a sort of tradition, and is known to thousands who
never saw one of his pictures, nor ever heard the name of Copley.
The story is a remarkable one, but it has been aided greatly in
popularity by the telling. John Galt was, as one may say, the official biographer. He was a writer of ability, who tried his hand at
everything, — poems, plays, essays, novels, — a precursor of the "Kail
Yard" school, whose Scotch dialect stories have had sufficient vitality
to warrant their reprinting within the last few years. But between
his romances and his plays, he was a man who, as he himself
says of Plutarch, "had no taste for the blemishes of mankind. His
mind delighted in the contemplation of moral vigor; and he seems
justly to have thought that it was nearly allied to virtue; hence
many of those characters whose portraiture in his works furnish the

FIG. 10.—STUART: PORTRAIT OF BENJAMIN WEST, NATIONAL PORTRAIT
GALLERY, LONDON.

youthful mind with inspiring examples of true greatness, more authentic historians represent in a light far different."

" More authentic historians "— Dunlap, for instance — do not diminish the " true greatness" of West ; but they explode some of the embellishments with which Galt, in the interest of morality, saw fit to adorn it. And yet the life of West is best told by including copious extracts from Galt, who received many of the details from him and whose style is in harmony with his subject.

Benjamin West was born in 1738, at Springfield, a little Pennsylvania settlement, and his childhood knew all the rigor and simplicity of frontier life ; but his family were people of position in England and of good descent. The first to embrace the Quaker faith was Colonel James West, the companion of John Hampden, and West's maternal grandfather was a confidential friend of William Penn. When the West family came to America, in 1699, John, the father of Benjamin, was left to complete his education at the great school of the Quakers at Uxbridge, and did not join his relatives until 1714. Shortly after his arrival he married, and as a part of his wife's marriage portion received a negro slave ; but during a voyage to the West Indies, in the course of trade, he was so shocked by the cruelties of slavery that on his return he released his slave and continued to debate the subject of slavery with his neighbors at their meetings, until a resolution was passed " that it was the duty of Christians to give freedom to their slaves." The discussion spread until, in 1753, it was ultimately established as one of the tenets of the Quakers that no person could remain a member of their community who held a human creature in slavery. An echo of this faith appeared long afterward, when the son offered his ample galleries in London for the meetings of the Committee of the Society for the Abolition of the Slave Trade ; and what other details have been handed down about John West show him, though but a storekeeper in a small village, yet a man of character, and respected.

Benjamin was the youngest child of a large family. On Sept 28, 1820, Edmund Peckover, a celebrated preacher of the Quakers, preached in a meeting-house erected by the father of Mrs. West, who was present and so affected by the fiery and minatory discourse that she gave birth to her infant immediately after ; and

such was the agitation into which she was thrown that the consequences nearly proved fatal to herself and her child.   Mr. West
was much impressed by the occurrence, and his feelings were shared
by Peckover, who " took him by the hand, and with emphatic solem-
nity said that a child sent into the world under such remarkable
circumstances would prove no ordinary man ; and he charged him
to watch over the boy's character with the utmost degree of paternal
solicitude."

Such are the omens and prodigies with which Galt surrounds the
birth of his hero.   They sound rather absurd to the taste of the
present day, and their bathos is not diminished by the fact that
West was really born on Oct. 10, 1738, and Dunlap's comment that
Peckover did not come to America until five years after that date.

It was when he was six that the well-known incident occurred of
his attempting to draw with red and black ink the portrait of his
sister's baby which he had been set to watch.   The next year he
went to school, but still continued his drawing, until one day a party
of friendly Indians, amused at the sketches of birds and flowers which
he showed them, taught him to prepare the red and yellow colors
with which they painted their ornaments.   His mother furnished
indigo, the cat's fur was clipped to make brushes, and with these
primitive materials he produced some paintings which were seen
by a Mr. Pennington, a Philadelphia merchant related to the Wests.
They seemed to him remarkable productions for a child of eight, and
he promised to send him a box of paints which, on his return home,
he did.   The boy's delight at the gift was unbounded.   He kept it
by his bed at night and deserted school in order to give himself up
to art.   Besides paints and canvas, the box contained six engravings
by " Greveling," Galt says.   Presumably Gravelot's, whose volumi-
nous works, besides the charming illustrations with which his name
is naturally connected, contain many copies after the followers of
Raphael and the Fontainebleau school.   When his mother, learning
that he was not at school, finally discovered him in the garret hard
at work, he had combined two of these engravings on a single canvas
with so much skill that she refused to let him finish it lest he should
spoil it, and it was preserved to be exhibited sixty-six years after
with the " Christ healing the Sick," the painter declaring to Galt

that "there were inventive touches in his first and juvenile essay which with all his subsequent knowledge and experience he had not been able to surpass."

A few days after Mr. Pennington made another visit to the Wests, and took the boy with him to Philadelphia, where he composed a picture of a river, with vessels on the water and cattle on the banks, and where he met with a professional painter, one Williams, who had painted a picture for one of Mr. Pennington's acquaintance who asked the artist to show it to young West. The interest and enthusiasm of the boy impressed Williams, who asked if he had read any books on the lives of great men, and finding his reading limited to the Bible, he lent him the works of Fresnoy and Richardson on Painting. Their perusal gave to him the idea of an artist's career, and soon after his skill brought him his first pecuniary profit.

A cabinet-maker had given him some clean poplar boards, and he made drawings on them in ink, chalk, and charcoal. Mr. Wayne, a gentleman of the neighborhood, noticed them, and asked for two or three of them afterward, complimenting the young painter and giving him a dollar apiece for them, and Dr. Johnston Morris, another neighbor, soon after gave him a present of a few dollars to buy materials to paint with. These were the first public patrons of the artist, and it was at his own request that Galt set down their names and deeds. A year after the visit to Philadelphia he was invited to spend a few weeks at the house of a Mr. Flower, who had sent to England for a governess for his daughter; she was interested in West, and finding him unacquainted with other books than the Bible and Fresnoy and Richardson, she read to him from Mr. Flower's library "The most striking and picturesque passages from translations of the ancient historians and poetry," and it was thus that he heard for the first time of the Greeks and Romans.

The wife of a Mr. Rogers (a friend of Mr. Flower's) was greatly admired for her beauty, as were also her children. On Mr. Flower's suggestion and with his father's consent the boy went to Lancaster to paint their portraits in which he was so successful that he had all the orders that he could conveniently fill. Among others he painted the portrait of a gunsmith, William Henry, who had acquired a handsome fortune in that profession and was a man of intelligence. He admired the painting, but said "that if he could paint as well he would not waste his time on portraits but would devote himself to historical subjects; and he mentioned the Death of Socrates as one of the best topics for illustrating the moral effect of painting." Upon the confession of the painter that he knew nothing of Socrates, Mr. Henry took from his library a volume of the English translation of Plutarch and read the story. West's imagination was aroused, and he executed a painting of the subject which when finished attracted much attention and was of peculiar advantage to him, for at that time Dr. Smith, Provost of the College at Philadelphia, happened to be at Lancaster. After seeing the picture and talking with the artist "he offered to undertake to make him to a certain degree acquainted with classical literature; while at the same time he would give him such a sketch of the taste and character of the spirit of antiquity as would have all the effect of the regular education requisite to a painter."

Benjamin accordingly went to the capital and resided at the house of Mr. Clarkson, his brother-in-law, a gentleman who had been educated at Leyden and was much respected for the intelligence of his conversation and the propriety of his manners. Provost Smith gave to his pupil a peculiar training. "He regarded him as destined to be a painter and on this account did not impose on him those grammatical exercises of language which are usually required of young students of the classics, but directed his attention to those incidents which were likely to interest his fancy, and to furnish him at some future time with subjects for his easel. He carried him immediately to those passages of ancient history which make the most lasting impression on the imagination of the regular bred scholar and described the picturesque circumstances of the transactions with a minuteness of detail which would have been superfluous to the general student." It was at this time when confined in bed during an illness that he discovered for himself the principle of the camera obscura.

At the end of his Philadelphia studies the question of settling him in some profession for life came up, and Galt gives a description of a solemn scene with discourses, prayers, and a final dedication of the youth to art with the kisses of the women and the laying on of hands by the men — a performance which Dunlap points out would be entirely contrary to Quaker custom, and which could never have occurred as described, although it is probable that it was at this time, the boy having attained his sixteenth year, that it was decided that he was to make painting his profession. He consequently returned to Philadelphia, where he lived for the next few years with his brother-in-law, continuing his studies with Provost Smith in the evenings, but devoting the day to portrait painting. He also found time to paint a composition of " The Trial of Susannah," "drawing the principal figures from life," says Galt, but Dunlap who had seen it says that the composition was largely from a print.

He was living at this time most frugally to save enough money for a visit to Europe, and it was this consideration which caused him to pass a year in New York. The city was distasteful to him, and he found there less intellectual and refined life than in Philadelphia; but he could charge £10 for a half-length portrait and £5 for a head, double his previous rates. His economies were finally sufficient for a short trip in Italy, which he was enabled to make under exceptionally favorable conditions. A ship laden with wheat and flour was being sent to Messrs. Rutherford and Jackson in Leghorn, a well-known firm, and Mr. Allen their Philadelphia agent, wishing his son to see something of the world, decided to send him abroad by her, which Provost Smith hearing of at once begged that West might accompany him. This was granted and in addition a Mr. Kelly, whose portrait he was painting at the time, presented him with an order for £50 on his agents.

He reached Rome in July of 1760, where the picturesqueness of his position as the member of a strange and fantastic religious sect come from the distant wilds of America (still a half-fabulous country) to study the fine arts was in every way calculated to arouse the interest and curiosity of the society of cosmopolitan dilettanti settled there. His courier spread his fame and the day of his arrival, before he had had time to dress, he was called on by Mr. Robinson, afterward Lord Grantham, who took him that evening to a party where he met some of the best people in Rome, including the old Cardinal Albani, whose blindness had not diminished his reputation as a connoisseur, and who was much amazed to meet an American who was not a savage. He asked if he were white, "as white as I am," which amused West, who was very fair, while the old cardinal was as dark as an Indian.

Every one was interested to see the effect which the sight of Rome would have on the open mind of the newcomer, and a party was arranged to accompany him the next day. It was then that he made his well-known remark about the "Apollo Belvidere," "It is a Mohawk warrior"; but the works of Raphael and Michael Angelo

FIG. II. — WEST: DEATH OF WOLFE.

did not immediately impress him, and he was honest enough to say so. He soon began work, painting a portrait of Mr. Robinson, which he showed to Raphael Mengs, the most prominent of the painters then in Rome, who praised it generously and gave West excellent advice as to his study in Italy. The story of his portrait reached Mr. Allen, and he and Mr. Hamilton united in giving West unlimited credit at their agents'. This enabled him to remain three years in Italy, spending his time in travel, copying the old masters. and in painting a "Cymon and Iphigenia," also an "Angelica and Medoro."

His career there, with the exception of an illness at the beginning, was most successful. He gained many friends, some reputation, and was made a member of the Academies in Florence, Bologna, and Parma. When he finally reached England in the autumn of 1763 he found there his good friends, Mr. Allen, Governor Hamilton, and Dr. Smith who were in a position to introduce him advantageously. His romantic history, his personal manners, and the friends and reputation he had won during his Italian sojourn were all factors in his favor. He finished the " Angelica and Medoro," begun in Italy, and exhibited it with the " Cymon and Iphigenia " and a portrait of General Monckton at the Spring Gardens Exhibition in 1764. His success was immediate. He had many commissions, and Lord Rockingham offered him a permanent engagement at £700 a year to embellish with historical paintings his mansion in Yorkshire, which he declined.

With the growth of his prosperity he abandoned the idea of returning to America. At his desire his father came to England, bringing with him the lady his son had chosen for a bride, and in September of 1765 they were married and settled permanently in London. Galt gives no details of the marriage, nor does Dunlap ; but in fact the family of Miss Shewell, the bride, were much opposed to the match, and when West wrote to the lady saying that his father would sail for London by a certain brig, and if she with her maid would accompany him, they could be married on arrival, her brother discovered the letter and promptly locked up his sister until the ship should have sailed. Three good friends of West, however, concluded that this was not to be endured. A rope ladder was smuggled in under the maid's petticoat, the ship set sail as if to depart, but anchored again lower down the river; at night the mistress and maid descended from their prison, were received by the three conspirators, all got into a coach, lost their way, and finally after driving about all night reached the brig in the morning, when the lady safely embarked. Her assistants in this romantic adventure were Francis Hopkinson, William White, who was afterward the first Bishop of the American Episcopal Church, and Benjamin Franklin. The future bishop was then but a lad of seventeen, but to the end of his life he prided himself on his youthful exploit.

Archbishop Drummond, at that time particularly well received

E

at court, became one of West's patrons, commissioned him to paint "Agrippina landing with the Ashes of Germanicus," and strove with energy to raise a fund of £3000 for the artist to rid him of the drudgery of portrait painting and enable him to devote himself to nobler flights.　It was with deep chagrin that the good archbishop saw the subscription stop at half the amount sought and the scheme abandoned, but he was of far greater service to West in another way, for it was he who presented him to the King.　The royal patronage was almost a necessity to the artist if he were to continue in his chosen line.　The large size of the canvases needed for the paintings calculated to ennoble human nature rendered them unsuitable for any ordinary dwelling and difficult to dispose of.　An offer to paint an altarpiece for St. Paul's was refused with energy by the bishop who " would not suffer the doors to be opened to intro-duce popery," though several lesser churches received religious pic-tures by him without objection.　His " Orestes and Pylades " and the " Continence of Scipio " brought him nothing but fame.　His house was thronged by admiring crowds, his servants received a small fortune in tips for showing his pictures, but no one even asked their price.

It was a decisive moment in West's career when Archbishop Drummond induced the King to send for him and his picture of " Agrippina landing with the Ashes of Germanicus."　An officious messenger who forestalled the archbishop in announcing his good fortune to West described the King to him.　" His Majesty is a young man of great simplicity and candour; sedate in his affections, scrupulous in forming private friendships, good from principle, and pure from a sense of the beauty of virtue," and so the painter found him.　He received West with all the simple bonhomie which made George III such an excellent family man and so poor a monarch. He presented him to the Queen, admired his picture, and suggested to him a new subject, saying, " The archbishop made one of his sons read Tacitus to Mr. West but I will read Livy to him myself — that part where he describes the departure of Regulus."　The artist declaring the scene admirable for a picture, the King gave him a commission on the spot, and from that time began the long friend-ship between them which ended only with death.　The " Regulus " was successful in pleasing the royal taste and was followed by a series of other works produced with amazing rapidity for the same patron, culminating in a command to decorate the royal chapel at Windsor.

This was not undertaken by the King without grave deliberation. The question whether pictures in such a place leaned toward popery, and what was and what was not permissible was too congenial to him to be hastily dismissed. There was much taking counsel with bishops and deans as to the propriety of the act, and finally there was a list drawn up of subjects, which, as Bishop Hurd the spokesman said, " Even a Quaker might contemplate with edification." The latent sarcasm was not lost on George, who rebuked it, saying: " The Quakers are a body of Christians for whom I have a high respect. I love their peaceful tenets and their benevolence to one another, and but for the obligation of birth I would be a Quaker."

It was at this time that West made an innovation for which, if for nothing else, his name would deserve to be honored in the annals of art. He began a picture of the death of General Wolfe after the capture of Quebec, and it was reported that he proposed to represent his characters in the costumes which they actually wore. Such a degrading of lofty emotions by vulgar and commonplace details was unheard of. Archbishop Drummond, seriously alarmed, called on Reynolds and laid the case before him and together they visited West and tried to dissuade him. The King himself heard of the discussion and questioned West, who answered with admirable good sense that the event to be commemorated happened in the year 1758 in a region of the world unknown to the Greeks and Romans, and at a period of time when no warriors who wore such costumes existed. " The subject I have to represent is a great battle fought and won and the same truth which gives law to the historian should rule the painter. If instead of the facts of the action I introduce fictions, how shall I be understood by posterity? The classic dress is certainly picturesque, but by using it I shall lose in sentiment what I gain in external grace. I want to mark the time, the place, and the people, and to do this I must abide by truth."

After the picture was completed, Reynolds after studying it long and carefully declared: " West has conquered; he has treated his

subject as it ought to be treated; I retract my objections.   I foresee
that this picture will not only become one of the most popular but
will occasion a revolution in art."   It was about the same time that
West performed his other great permanent service to art in being
mainly instrumental in founding the Royal Academy.   Picture
exhibitions were a comparative novelty in England and had had
a curious origin.   When the Foundling Hospital was finished,
Hogarth presented to it his portrait of Captain Coram.   Five years
later the building was enlarged and other artists gave or promised
works.   These proved a great attraction.   The room where they
were hung became a favorite resort of the public, and the artists
gained reputation.   This suggested the first public exhibition of
paintings in 1760 at the Great Room of the Society of Arts, Manufactures, and Commerce.   The next year the artists divided, some
remaining at the Society's room in the Strand and some exhibiting
at the Great Room, Spring Gardens.   These later became the
" Incorporated Artists," and continued to hold exhibitions with
increasing success until their very prosperity caused their downfall.
The money received from admission fees accumulated until it
became a large sum, and the projects for the disposition of this gave
rise to such unseemly bickerings that a number of the artists,
including West, who was a director, and Reynolds, withdrew from
the association.

There was difficulty about forming another society.   Reynolds
was but lukewarm and hesitated about committing himself.   When
the dissenting artists met for organization, neither West nor
Reynolds were present, and after a long wait they were on the point
of adjourning when both appeared.   West having through his position at court secured the favor of the King had gone to Reynolds's
house and decided him to attend the meeting, which immediately
proceeded to organize the Royal Academy and elect Reynolds
president.   The first exhibition was held in 1768.

West was now in the full tide of success.   He had early set up
an extensive establishment with long galleries and a lofty suite of
painting rooms, filled with sketches and pictures by himself and
some works of the old masters.   Here he worked with unremitting
industry, and here he received with unfailing kindness all who came

SIR BENJAMIN WEST : PORTRAIT OF QUEEN CHARLOTTE AND THE PRINCESS ROYAL.

to ask his aid or advice. His pictures were mostly commanded by the King, who gave to him a yearly salary of a thousand pounds in addition to payment for specific work. When the royal chapel was approaching completion, he was engaged to cover the walls of the hall of Windsor Castle with scenes from the life of Edward III.

In 1792, upon the death of Reynolds, West was unanimously elected president of the Royal Academy. His first reverse came when the King's mind began to fail and Wyatt, the royal architect, without preliminary warning, announced to him that the pictures being painted for the chapel at Windsor must be suspended. He appealed and, on the King's regaining his senses, was most kindly received and told to go on with his work, but this was their last interview. The old King's madness became incurable and on his superannuation all of West's commissions were countermanded and his yearly salary stopped, and now "he submitted in silence — he neither remonstrated nor complained."

While suffering these rebuffs he was also deposed from the presidency of the Academy (in 1801). He had taken advantage of the Peace of Amiens in that year to go to Paris and see the collections of art plundered from the whole of Europe and brought together in the Louvre. He was received with much honor by the French artists and statesmen, and he was filled with admiration for Napoleon and his schemes for the regeneration of Europe. He had two interviews with the Emperor, and the accuracy with which he judged his character may be gathered from his recommending confidently to him the example of Washington. This visit was supposed to have offended the King and so West was replaced in the presidency by Wyatt. But the reverse was only temporary. The King's favor in his lucid intervals remained unchanged, and Wyatt was so manifestly unable to fill the place that West was reëlected president the next year with but one dissenting vote which Fuseli admitted that he cast for Mrs. Moser, saying "one old woman is as good as another." West retained the office until his death.

In spite also of loss of royal patronage and advancing years, his greatest popular successes were yet to come. He was applied to for a subscription toward the building of the Philadelphia Hospital, and replied that his means would not permit him to offer

money, but that he would give a picture, and for the purpose painted
an enormous composition of " Christ healing the Sick," which when
exhibited in London created a sensation. The British Institution
offered three thousand guineas for it, which could not well be
refused; but a replica (with some changes) was painted and sent
to America, where its exhibition was a permanent source of
revenue for the Hospital, earning $4000 from admission fees
in the first year. This was followed by a series of huge religious
paintings, the " Descent of the Holy Spirit at the Jordan," a " Cruci-

FIG. 12. — WEST: DEATH ON THE PALE HORSE, PENNSYLVANIA ACADEMY.

fixion," sixteen by twenty-eight feet, an " Ascension," the " Inspiration of Peter," " Christ Rejected," seventeen by twenty-two feet,
and finally " Death on the Pale Horse," fifteen by twenty-six feet.
This latter was painted from a smaller picture which he had taken
with him to Paris, and which his admirers there had declared to equal
the old masters. All of these were admired both by the critics and
the greater public. The " Death on the Pale Horse," in particular,
was successful in exciting emotions which their possessors believed
to be noble and profitable.

But the admirers of these works seldom bought, and the pictures
were disposed of with difficulty. West, in spite of his splendid con-

stitution and regular life, was getting old. In 1817 his wife, to whom he had been married over fifty years, died, and it was a hard blow to him. He painted up to the last, but in 1820, in his eighty-second year, he too succumbed, and was buried in St. Paul's near Reynolds and Wren, with splendid ceremonies.

The career of West is calculated to confute the pessimists who find no good in human nature. It is not so much that he was a good man himself; good men there have ever been, but as a rule their good deeds shone in a naughty world. West was not only good himself, but the cause of goodness in others. Surely no man was ever so generously and so efficiently aided throughout his whole career. From the painted savages of the forest to the King on his throne, all delighted in being of use to him, and he never failed to accept the proffered help, never failed to utilize it to the fullest extent, and never forgot to be grateful. At the end of his life he remembered his first patrons who had given him a few dollars for his works, and it was at his request that Galt recorded their names.

It is not enough, however, that friends should be willing to aid: they must aid wisely, and here West's good fortune shines. He was lucky, lucky from the beginning in having parents who, contrary to all expectation from their creed and surroundings, were interested in and encouraged his childish scrawls; lucky in getting a paint-box, and lucky in coming in contact with Williams, a practising painter. The loan of the "works of Fresnoy and Richardson" were factors of the utmost importance in deciding his choice of a profession. Both works have become antiquated now, but both had a great vogue in their time. Fresnoy was Charles Alphonse Dufresnoy, a French painter of the seventeenth century, whose Latin poem *De Arte Graphica*, modelled on the Horatian plan, described the nobility and utility of art, and laid down rules for simplicity of composition, breadth of light and shade, and the like. Dryden, among his other works as a publisher's hack, turned out a translation in English prose in a week, which must have been the version West received. A later metrical rendering had notes added by Reynolds himself. The other work, *Richardson on Painting*, was an English treatise written in much the same spirit, wherein "the whole art of painting

is divided into Invention, Expression, Composition, Colour, Handling and Grace and Greatness," with chapters on each.　A second
book, the *Connoisseur*, gives rules for judging pictures with a certain
number of points for each quality by adding up which the merit of
the work is definitely ascertained, and also a description of the
works of the great masters and of the qualities peculiar to each.　It
is written in the taste of the time, but with clearness, enthusiasm,
and much good sense, and is eminently calculated to arouse a boy's
ambition.　Dr. Johnson writes: " The true genius is a mind of large
general powers accidentally determined to some particular direction.
Sir Joshua Reynolds, the greatest painter of the present age, had
the first fondness for his art excited by the perusal of Richardson's
treatise."

Both the fact and the moral reflection might be equally well
applied to West.　Leslie even, who doubts such decisive effect
of any book, yet adds, " if ever books could infuse a love of art and
an ambition to shine as a painter, into a mind hitherto insensible
to such things, Richardson's discourses would be the most likely
to do so."　That West promptly caught the " ambition to shine
as a painter " is shown by the story of his ride on a horse with
a boy who avowed his intention of becoming a tailor: a decision
he supported so firmly and with such good and prosaic reasons
that West, who had determined to be a painter, a person whom he
defined to his friend's amazement as " a companion of Kings and
Emperors," refused to ride longer on the same beast with him.
Long afterward, " when directing his friend Sully how to find
the house in which he was born, the old gentleman in describing
the road pointed out the spot where he had abandoned the intending tailor."

He was lucky again in the prescience of Provost Smith, who
resolutely filled his mind with vague enthusiasm and visions of
antiquity to the neglect of what are ordinarily considered the
principia of knowledge; for West remained an uneducated man
to the end and was as Cunningham says, " the first and last President of our Academy who found spelling a difficulty."　It was
fortunate, too, that he went first to Italy, so that he was enabled to
appear in England as an established artist instead of a beginner.

He was lucky in securing the patronage of the King, which was almost indispensable to him. But most of all he was lucky in being by character, by training, by countless little personal traits, absolutely fitted to the ideals of the time.

It was an interesting London to which he came, — the London which lives for us in the pages of Boswell. It had ceased to be feudal or renaissance, and had become mercantile and bourgeois. The glowing, unregulated inspiration of the Elizabethans had died out. The writers wrote according to classical rules, and took pleasure in their servitude; and the public delighted in the polished verse of Pope, the allegories and visions of Addison, and the moralizing of Johnson, to say nothing of those classical tragedies of whose resounding verse few to-day can read a page except as a task. The town was firmly established as a world centre and yet was not become unwieldy. Those of any intellectual prominence still knew each other personally, and private friendships and hatreds still gave flavor to work. The middle classes were rising into prominence and the authors and artists could turn to the great public and were not forced to submit to the tyranny of the patrons, though still finding them serviceable.

For artists it seems as if there never was another London like it. It was the dawn of the only great epoch of British painting. When West came there, Hogarth was still alive (he died the next year); Wilson was forty-nine, producing his best work, but ignored by the public; Reynolds was forty and in the full tide of his success as a portrait painter, with a great house in Leicester Square and making £6000 a year; Gainsborough was still at Bath, but sent his portraits regularly to the London exhibitions, and removed there himself in 1774. The town was full of " cognoscenti " and " dilettanti," delighting to discuss art, though as yet their admiration was reserved for foreign work. Hogarth's splendid craftsmanship had been treated with contemptuous neglect, though his engravings brought him in large sums. Wilson sold his fine landscapes to dealers and pawnbrokers for a few pounds, but even the most indurated prejudice had to make an exception in favor of English portraiture. There was no foreigner then living in England or elsewhere; no Holbein, no Van Dyck, not even a Lely, whose work

could an instant bear comparison with that of Gainsborough or
Reynolds; and when West painted the stories of antique heroism
or biblical virtue, whose recital had so often awakened their sensibility and painted them in the sort of late, impersonal Italian,
eclectic style, which illustrated all of the rules of art, the more
advanced of the "cognoscenti" could contain themselves no
longer; they saluted him as a great artist, and the public followed.

And yet it must be admitted that his paintings, while essential,
were not the only nor the chief causes of his success. The story
of his life was as effective in London as in Rome. The manner
in which in a wilderness inhabited by savages he was inspired even
from the cradle by unmistakable genius, caught the popular imagination, and every incident about him tended to strengthen the
effect: his youth, his reception at Rome, his success there, his
membership in the Italian academies, the charm of his manner,
the purity of his life. Even trivial things like his picturesque
comment on the " Apollo," his discovery for himself of the camera
obscura, or even his skill in skating, which his friend Lord Howe
(afterward of Revolutionary fame) induced him to display on the
" Serpentine " — all spread his name and fame. As Galt says, " It
would almost seem as if there had been some arrangement in the
order of things that would have placed Mr. West in the first class
of artists although he had himself mistaken the workings of ambition for the consciousness of talent."

Posterity seems to have decided that some such mistake was
made. West's fame has steadily declined, and his works now are
seldom mentioned except as warning examples of false taste.
More than that, the reaction against the point of view that he
represented in art has now reached its farthest point, so that he
is not infrequently held up to scorn and contempt. This is unjust,
for West had talent as well as industry, but it is unlikely that any
revulsion of artistic standards will ever restore him to popular
favor. The very character of his work is against it. Huge compositions made without feeling for the decorative necessities of the
places they are to occupy will arouse the attention and usually the
admiration of contemporaries, but whether they line the Gallerie
des Victoires of Versailles, or the hall of Windsor, they are tedious

for a later generation. And such works must be popular or they lose all excuse for their existence. A chosen few may cultivate a liking for quaint, obsolete, old-time sentiment in easel pictures, prints, or miniatures, but canvases twenty feet or more long are not for the cabinets of amateurs. " Time's great antiseptic, Style," might have saved them, but they have no "style." West had not even the sincerity which gives vitality to Copley's work. His early portraits painted before he left New York are occasionally more graceful than the Copleys of the same date, but they carry no such conviction of reality.

After he reached Italy he began to paint those " subjects the moral interest of which outweighs their mechanical execution." He gained great facility and an acquaintance with all the technical expedients of his profession; but the rapidity of his production, his admiration for the followers of Raphael, and his early saturation with a vague and windy enthusiasm from Richardson prevented him from ever gaining any mastery of beautiful workmanship. In fact, he never felt the need of it and considered his art mainly as an aid to virtue, declaring in his discourses that "the true use of painting resides in assisting the reason to arrive at certain moral influ- ences, by furnishing a probable view of the effects of motives and passions." He painted, as a rule, thinly and had a way of marking out his figures with a sharp outline, suggesting work done from an engraving. His color was poor, the costumes of his figures tinted in tones of red or pink or yellow, arranged according to the most approved rules and relieved by dark shadows and backgrounds usually of a disagreeable brownish tone produced perhaps from his admiration for the old masters of the Bolognese school. Lester (in his *Artists of America*) sums up his work in a criticism that is worth giving at length, for it shows that the judgment of 1848 still remains good to-day with the exception that at that time West was at least discussed; to-day he is ignored.

" In all his works the human form was exhibited in conformity to academic precepts — his figures were arranged with skill — the coloring was varied and harmonious — the eye rested pleased on the performance, and the artist seemed, to the ordinary spectator, to have done his task like one of the highest of the sons of genius.

But below all this splendor there was little of true vitality — there
was a monotony of human character — the groupings were unlike
the happy and careless combinations of nature, and the figures
seemed distributed over the canvas by line and measure like trees
in a plantation.   He wanted fire and imagination to be the true
restorer of that grand style which bewildered Barry and was talked
of by Reynolds.   Most of his works, cold, formal, and passionless,
may remind the spectator of the Valley of Dry Bones, when the

FIG. 13. — PRATT: AMERICAN ACADEMY, METROPOLITAN MUSEUM.

flesh and skin had come upon the skeletons and before the breath
of God had informed them with life and feeling."

Something might be saved from this general condemnation.   The
"Death of Wolfe," apart from being a courageous innovation, is finely
grouped and will hold its own against any of the numerous similar
scenes produced more or less in emulation with it; the "Battle of
La Hogue" is equally good, and all of his modern scenes have value;
but it must not be forgotten that his preëminent success was in no
way proportionate to a preëminent skill, even in suiting the peculiar

taste of the time. The works of Fuseli, Barry, or Haydon had as great elements of popularity. It was West's character and temperament which gained him wealth and honors while the others struggled and starved. More specifically it was the favor of the King, but that is only another way of saying the same thing. Besides, as far as one may judge, he would have succeeded without royal patronage, though not to an equal degree. He had the dignified, kindly, passionless temperament of the Quakers, and he kept it throughout life, though he relinquished most of the peculiar observances of the sect. Cunningham says, "The grave simplicity of the Quaker continued to the last in the looks and manners of the artist," but Dunlap, who knew him well, denies this utterly. He behaved like other people, had no desire to wear his hat in unusual places, powdered his hair, dressed well, and "his well formed limbs," as Dunlap discreetly puts it, "were covered by garments of texture and color such as were worn by other gentlemen." Leigh Hunt, whose mother was a relative of the artist, says that "the appearance of West was so gentlemanly that the moment he changed his gown for a coat he seemed to be full dressed." His Quakerism was of the spirit, not of the externals, and it served him well. His position at court rendered him an object of envy to less-favored artists. Reynolds was politic enough to conceal his feelings, but others were less reticent; toward the end of his life his success, his honors, his wealth, and probably, to be fair, a growing recognition of the defects of his painting, unchained against him a storm of vituperation.

Peter Pindar, who was then enormously popular, even brought the King into his doggerel rhymes, beginning —

> "Of modern works he makes a jest
> Except the works of Mr. West."

and later Byron himself slashed at —

> "the dotard West
> Europe's worst daub, poor England's best."

But West never answered, never attacked, nor blamed any one. This might have been policy or Quaker training, but no policy nor creed will explain his unfailing readiness to aid or encourage others. He had received many benefits, and he conferred them still more liberally, apparently with no feeling that it was particularly creditable, but rather that it was the only and inevitable course; that to miss helping any one was inconceivable.

He was a quiet, home-keeping body, staying in his own house or going to the palace, where he had free entrance at all times. His presence at Gainsborough's funeral is mentioned as exceptional in his retired life, and though he had many friends, his friendships were always on a dignified and distant footing. He had no part in Johnson's famous Club, and is not even mentioned in Boswell's *Life*. Johnson, through his friendship for Reynolds, seems even to have been opposed to him, judging by his remark, " I had rather see the portrait of a dog that I know than all the allegorical paintings they can shew me in the world; " but when the Great Chan of letters, old and suffering, refused the offer of a hundred pounds a year from Dr. Brocklesby, saying, " God bless you through Jesus Christ but I will take no money but from my sovereign," it was West who told the King of it, and that the old man needed such assistance. Fear of injury to his personal interests did not affect him. It has been told how he welcomed Copley, who was likely to become a dangerous rival, and secured him royal commissions. Haydon's works, too, were enough like West's to be preferred by many, but West went to Haydon's studio when he was painting his " Solomon " and heartily praised it; at the end of the interview, as Leslie relates it, " But," said the good old man, " get into better air; you will never recover with this eternal anxiety before you. Have you any resources ? " " They are all exhausted." " D'ye want money ? " " Indeed I do." " So do I," said he; " they have stopped my income from the King, but Fauntleroy is arranging an advance, and if I succeed, my young friend, you shall hear. Don't be cast down; such a work must not be forgotten." In the course of the same day West sent him a check for £15.

His unfailing kindness to young artists and students will appear in the lives of the younger generations of American painters. They were all his pupils, and his aid, while more essential to such strangers in London, was not limited to them. Every morning until he began to paint, at ten, his studio was open, his counsel and assistance were given freely and kindly to all comers. At his death his old servant might well say with tears in his eyes, "Ah, Mr. Leslie, whom will they go to now?" Nor was his counsel mere kindly platitude. He was a successful master, his pupils reflect credit on him, and his criticisms show not only academic knowledge but a sympathetic alertness in comprehending new work. When Constable showed him his early studies, West encouraged him and said, "You must have loved nature very much before you could have painted this," and then after touching in some lights with chalk, added, "Always remember, sir, that light and shadow *never stand still."* Constable said it was the best lecture, because a practical one, on chiaroscuro that he had ever heard, and considering West's training, and the fact that Constable remained utterly unrecognized for many years, its insight is wonderful.

The only fault which his detractors can bring against him is his self-complacency, and that was in a way essential to his integrity. He could not with clear conscience have occupied the position he did unless he had believed himself a great artist, born for great things, and he did so believe. When his work for the King was stopped, his letter of remonstrance which he wrote rings with a consciousness of merit, and his observation during his trip in France that "I was walking with Mr. Fox in the Louvre and I remarked how many people turned to look at me. This shows the respect of the French for the Fine Arts," is naïvely amusing, for the "Mr. Fox" was Charles James Fox, one of the three most powerful statesmen of England, and a less simple mind might have attributed some of the attention to him.

It is a pity that his painting had no more enduring qualities, but he was a noble figure to begin the series of American painters. He was the first to attain prominence, and he remains to this day the most successful. Tuckerman, who is not well disposed toward him, yet says truly, "His reputation has a benign, conservative charm based upon rectitude and benevolence; exemplary in life, kindly in spirit, more than one generation of American Artists had cause to bless his memory."

CHAPTER IV

EARLY PUPILS OF WEST IN LONDON

WEST'S STUDIO FROM THE BEGINNING THE RESORT OF AMERICAN STUDENTS. —
MATHEW PRATT. — ABRAHAM DELANOY. — CHARLES WILSON PEALE. — HIS VERSA-
TILITY. — HIS WORK. — LATER PUPILS. — DUNLAP AND HIS "HISTORY OF THE ARTS
OF DESIGN IN AMERICA."— HIS LIFE. — ROBERT FULTON. — RALPH EARLE.— GILBERT
STUART. — LIFE IN NEWPORT. — LIFE IN LONDON. — INTRODUCTION TO WEST

WHEN West came to England he was still a very young man,
but from the first he took the position of counsellor and helper
toward his compatriots who came there to perfect themselves in the
fine arts, and up to the time of his death the stream of American
painting may be said to have flowed through his studio. The com-
mencement of his teaching coincided with his decision to permanently settle in London, for his wife and his first pupil came to him at
the same time. When, in 1764, West's father brought to England
Miss Shewell, his future bride, Mathew Pratt, who was a relative of
the lady, accompanied them and became a member of West's household. Pratt was a Philadelphian a few years the senior of West and
was already a practising artist, having been apprenticed at the age
of fifteen to his uncle, James Claypoole, from whom he learned "all
the different branches of the painting business, particularly portrait
painting," the phrase showing the standing of art in the colonies at
that time. He followed his profession for some years in Philadelphia, diversified only by a trading venture to Jamaica, which turned
out most unfortunately, for he was captured and plundered by a
French privateer and lost a great part of his property. He received
from West (to use his own words) "the attentions of a friend and a
brother," remained in England some four years, perfecting himself in
his art which he continued to practise afterward in Philadelphia
with reasonable success. He painted portraits; he painted groups
which were favorably spoken of, but his crowning achievements seem
to have been his signs, of which he painted many, and Neagle says
they were the best he ever saw. He also assisted C. W. Peale in

FIG. 14.—C. W. PEALE: WASHINGTON, METROPOLITAN MUSEUM.

setting up his museum and lived to a good age, successful in his modest art. Tradition says of him that "he was a gentleman of pleasing manners, and a great favorite with the first citizens in point of wealth and intelligence."

In 1756 Pratt exhibited in Spring Gardens a painting now in the New York Metropolitan Museum, "The American Academy," a representation of the interior of West's studio with West himself giving instruction, and four pupils, including himself, diligently employed in copying casts. One of these was a student whom West had about this time and who pursued much the same ideals as Pratt, but with less success. This was Abraham Delanoy, Jr., who visited England about 1766. His father was Abraham Delanoy of New York, to the merit of whose pickled oysters and lobsters Fate has granted an endurance of fame denied to the art of his son. The latter made but a short stay in London, and on his return painted what portraits he could. In January of 1771 there appeared this advertisement in the New York *Gazette* and the *Weekly Mercury*: —

" To the Publick

LIKENESSES

Painted for a reasonable price by A. DELANOY JR. who has been taught by the celebrated Mr. Benjamin West in London."

Less than six months after another advertisement shows that he had old Madeira and other wines for sale and a large list of groceries, but the notice ends with, " Most kinds of PAINTING done as usual at reasonable rates." Dunlap knew him a dozen years later and pitied him. " He was consumptive, poor and his only employment sign-painting." He describes him further as " of mild manners, awkward address and unpresupposing appearance. I presume he died about 1786."

Pratt and Delanoy were fair examples of the ordinary practitioner of painting in America at the time, lineal descendants of still earlier men. They multiplied in numbers toward the end of the century, travelling from city to city and gaining a precarious livelihood by painting portraits at a few dollars a head, and when that failed turning to the more mechanical branches of their trade. Records of them crop up in old letters and diaries, and Dunlap has preserved the names of some like the three generations of Parissiens, of French extraction, — father, son, and grandson, — who painted portraits and miniatures of varying atrocity in New York; or Woolaston, in whose honor Francis Hopkinson published laudatory verses in 1758. Other men of this type besides Delanoy got together enough money to make the trip to England and there received counsel of West, and have a right to be numbered among his pupils; but their names and works have made no record.

The next artist whom we know to have worked under West was Charles Wilson Peale, a man of a higher class. Even judged by the European standard he was a passable painter, and he is also interesting as a type of the ingenious mind that could turn to anything and that, from instability or necessity, frequently deserted art for other pursuits. This inventive, mechanical genius is supposed to be the birthright of the Yankee, but it was in Chesterton, Maryland, that Peale was born in 1741. As a boy he was apprenticed to a saddler in Annapolis, and his natural versatility made him also a coach-maker, a clock-maker, a silversmith, and finally the sight of some paintings by a Mr. Frazier inspired him to add painting to his other accomplishments.

During a trip to Philadelphia he procured painting materials and a book to instruct him, *The Handmaid of the Arts*, and on his return to Annapolis an English artist, Hesselius, gave him some instruction. Soon after he had a chance to make the voyage to Boston, passage free, in a schooner belonging to his brother-in-law, and promptly availed himself of the opportunity. As has been mentioned, he saw Copley, was kindly received by him and had a picture loaned him to copy. This was in 1768–1769, and his stay in Boston was not long. He wished to go to England, and on his return to Annapolis a number of gentlemen raised a sum of money sufficient for his needs, which he promised to repay in pictures on his return. He reached London the next year with letters to West, who aided him in his kindly way, and when at the end of a year Peale's scanty funds were exhausted, received him into his own house so that he might not lose the benefits anticipated from his voyage. Peale returned from London to Annapolis in 1774, but two years later came to Philadel-

FIG. 15.—C. W. PEALE : PORTRAIT OF THE PAINTER, PENNSYLVANIA ACADEMY.

phia, and as a captain of volunteers joined Washington, and was present at the battles of Trenton and Germantown. Even in the midst of war's alarms he continued to practise his art, and his diary of the time is a curious jumble of marches, casualties, and sittings for miniatures. In 1779 he left the army and represented Philadelphia in the Pennsylvania legislature, but continued his painting until, in 1785, the finding of the bones of a mastodon caused him to conceive the idea of forming a museum. All sorts of curiosities rapidly accumulated, so that he finally removed his collection to a hall specially enlarged for the purpose and there lectured on Natural History before the most distinguished citizens. In the light of modern science he may not have discoursed very wisely about "the Mammoth, or great American Incognitum, an extinct immense carnivorous animal" (to quote from the title of a tract by his son Rembrandt), but his observations and opinions were important enough at the time to lead to a considerable correspondence with Cuvier and other prominent naturalists. In spite of these scientific excursions, however, he still painted portraits and retained his interest in the fine arts. He opened a school, attempted to have exhibitions, and after several failures was finally instrumental in founding, in 1805, the Pennsylvania Academy of the Fine Arts, which still remains a flourishing institution and the oldest of the sort in the United States.

Peale painted fairly good portraits, by far the best that were executed in the country between Copley's departure in 1774 and the return of Stuart in 1793. His earlier works show strongly the influence of Copley: not only what in Copley was the development and culmination of the characteristics of the early colonial practitioner, but also personal traits, the stiffness of pose, the rawness of tone, even the difficulty of drawing the eyes, which is still noticeable in his early portrait of Washington. He never attained to Copley's sincerity, but he mitigated somewhat his crudity of coloring. In his later work the effects of his foreign travel are manifest in a greater facility and in a greater knowledge — it improved as he grew older and lost entirely (probably owing to his study under West) its archaic colonial stiffness. A full-length portrait of himself at the age of eighty-three, drawing a curtain and displaying the marvels of his museum, is in the Philadelphia Academy. The background and details are thinly painted in West's worst manner, but the head is excellent, well drawn, well lighted, and solidly painted. It shows him as he was, a hale old man who had never known sickness and who died in 1827 not from old age but through incautiously exposing himself. He had had many children and had seen fit to impose upon them the most distinguished names, so that he could boast himself the father of Raphael, Angelica Kauffman, Rembrandt, Rubens, and Titian. In spite of their titles, however, only two were prominent in art.

Rembrandt Peale, who lived until 1860 and who wrote many reminiscences of his early days, says that his father was a fellow-student under West with Trumbull and Stuart, and even tells a story of West's remarking to Trumbull in explanation of some hammering noise that "it was only that ingenious young Mr. Peale repairing some of his bells and locks." The story fits Peale excellently, and we know that he did patch up a broken and discarded palette so that West used it to the end of his life; but chronology shows that Peale had returned to America before Trumbull or Stuart reached London. He belongs, in fact, to the first group of West's pupils, the successors of the old colonial school whose fame never spread beyond America, and not widely there. Stuart, Trumbull, and Dunlap are of a later period.

Dunlap was the youngest of these, the last to come abroad, and he never was much of a painter at best; but he deserves an honorable mention in any record of American art as its chronicler. He is our American Vasari. His *History of the Arts of Design in America*, published in 1834, is the foundation of all that we know of our earlier men. He was born in 1766, so that he was a contemporary of the beginnings of painting in the colonies; he was with West in London as a very young man, and later his erratic fortunes made him a wide traveller and gained him an extended acquaintance. He was always interested in art, and when in his old age he undertook to write his history he used not only his personal recollections, but applied to his friends and all others who were likely to know the facts. Besides this he had a feeling for accuracy rare at the time. Like Herodotus, he relates many fables, but he relates them as they were told him and gives his authority. He has been called "the acrimonious Dunlap," but the reader of to-day will not find the epithet justified. He wrote of men still living or but recently dead; he wrote not only of their works but of their lives, and he wrote something more than mere indiscriminate adulation. He had a good eye for character, and he had fixed moral standards. It is only in his pages that we seem to touch the reality of West and Stuart and Trumbull and Allston and Sully. Men were as sensitive then as to-day, and the men of whom he wrote and their friends were displeased at his frankness; but viewed at the present distance of time he seems rather kindly. He had his dislikes, but he was harder on no one than on himself. One of his charms is his old-fashioned style, as remote from that of the present day as Bacon's, a little ponderous but clear and animated. Being of his time he had to moralize some, but he does it briefly and compensates for it by introducing innumerable anecdotes, including some remarkably good ones. All of his successors have poached on his preserves, but none has paraphrased them without loss of point or character.

He sets forth frankly in his own life his intention to "show the causes that at the age of twenty-three, and after a long residence in London, left me ignorant of anatomy, perspective, drawing, and coloring, and returned me home a most incapable painter," and he succeeds in making it perfectly clear. He was born in Perth Amboy in 1766, an only child of well-to-do parents, and was brought up in a household where the servants were negro slaves with whom as a child he continually associated; and he got little discipline then or later, for the outbreak of the war obliged his family to move several times, and while it filled his boyhood with picturesque sights of soldiers and camps, prevented his receiving regular schooling. He had a taste for drawing, arising perhaps from the fact that his father had a number of well-illustrated books. He began to copy prints, and when the family removed to New York, his father tried to find an instructor for him. Ramage the miniaturist was too busy to take pupils; Delanoy who lived on Maiden Lane was unprepossessing personally, and so William Williams was engaged, and Dunlap went to his rooms "in the suburbs, now Mott Street." He got no serious instruction, but from seeing Williams's crayon portraits he began to attempt them himself. He drew all his relatives and friends, and finally strangers began to employ him at three guineas a head. He even made a drawing of Washington and Mrs. Washington, and succeeded in getting what were considered likenesses.

At this time, 1783, Joseph Wright, the son of Mrs. Patience Wright, celebrated for her profiles in wax and her patriotism, also made portraits of the same illustrious sitters. The next year Dunlap started for London. He had begun painting in oil by doing a head of Lord Hood on a sign for Delanoy, who found the likeness too difficult for him, and he had managed to paint a full-length portrait of Washington (presumably not from nature, but from his earlier drawing), represented with the battle of Princeton very much adapted from the " Death of Wolfe," in the background. When he reached London he showed this to West, who received him kindly, smiled at the transposition, and offered his casts and his counsel to the young student, but to small profit. Dunlap was now a boy of eighteen, with some money, with no habits of steady work, and with an enormous capacity for enjoyment. He does not seem to have been dissipated, much less vicious; he was simply too busy enjoying the sights, the theatres, the parks. He had, also, a shyness, a *mauvaise honte*, which prevented his asking counsel from those above him. Either West or Trumbull would have been glad to help him, but he rather avoided their advances. The reports of his idle life reached West, probably with some exaggeration, and may have made him less ready to offer his aid, especially as his son, Rafe West, showed a tendency to be led away into the same paths of idleness.

After about four years of this life, Dunlap returned to America. He tried portrait painting, but his equipment was small, and he was conscious of the superiority of Joseph Wright, who was his neighbor. After a few years he gave it up and joined his father in business. From now on, through his long life, he had a most varied career; business, literature, leasing a theatre, acting as assistant paymaster of the army, alternated with the painting of miniatures, portraits, and great religious compositions. He was unfortunate financially, always in need of money, living from hand to mouth, yet retaining the esteem of the community, and doing what he could to make the world better. An active member of the Abolition Society, at his father's death he liberated his slaves. He was instrumental in re-establishing the American Academy of Fine Arts, of which he became director and keeper, and later he joined in founding the National Academy of Design. Toward the end of his life he

FIG. 16. — DUNLAP: ARTIST SHOWING PICTURE TO HIS PARENTS, NEW YORK HISTORICAL SOCIETY.

painted some big canvases of religious subjects, and their exhibition from town to town brought him in some money.

Another pupil of West, whose fame is independent of his skill as an artist, is Robert Fulton, who, after painting portraits and land-scapes in America, went to England as soon as he was of age, entered West's studio about 1786, and gave promise of becoming a painter of merit. From there he went to Paris, where he remained seven years, worked at his art, painting easel pictures, and also the first panorama seen there, whose memory is still preserved in the name of the *Passage des Panoramas,* where it was exhibited. Even in

Paris, however, his time was mostly taken up with experiments with a submarine boat, which he perfected so that it made several successful trips. Later his development of the steamboat entirely stopped his practice of art ; but, like Morse at a later day, he became a patron of his old profession, and bought a number of West's paintings at the sale of the Boydell gallery, including the " King Lear," now in the Boston Museum of Fine Arts.

The same year that Fulton entered West's studio another pupil, Ralph Earle, left it, or, rather, left London, for he had been there twelve years and must have been independent of his master by that time. He had painted portraits before he left America "in the manner of Copley," which was simply the common manner of the time, and after his return he continued to work with success. Dunlap speaks rather slightingly of him and says that " he prevented improvement and destroyed himself by habitual intemperance." This charge it is impossible to refute, but Earle had very creditable skill as an artist. In London he had been made a member of the Royal Academy and had painted the King, and in America he painted many portraits fairly well, being especially skilful in arranging family groups, producing some in New York but more in Connecticut, where he was the best painter of his time — his work comparing favorably with that of Charles Wilson Peale.

Earle reached London a few years after Stuart, and Fulton and Dunlap later yet; but the two latter produced no important work as painters and the portraits of Earle belong by their style to the primitive period of our art. Gilbert Stuart's painting is of a higher type. He was the best of all the earlier artists, and in fact it is only within comparatively recent times that we could boast of painters in any way his equals. He was born at Middletown near Newport on Dec. 3, 1755, and baptized in April of the next year, being entered on the parish record as " Gilbert Stewart son of Gilbert Stewart the snuff-grinder." The spelling Stewart may be due to the carelessness of the clerk. He never used it himself, but the entry is also noteworthy because for a long time he signed his name Gilbert Charles Stuart, the Charles probably being inserted by his father, who was according to the family tradition a strong Jacobite who had been forced to escape from Scotland after

FIG. 17.—EARLE : MRS. BENJAMIN TALLMADGE, OWNED BY FREDERICK S. TALLMADGE.

Culloden. He was the son of a Presbyterian clergyman of Perth and was put in charge of the first snuff-mill built in the colonies by Dr. Moffatt, a fellow-refugee. In this mill, which was also a dwelling house, the painter was born. He was the last of three children; the eldest, James, died young; the second, Ann, married and was the mother of Gilbert Stuart Newton.

The snuff business was not successful and the Stuarts moved to Newport, then one of the most flourishing of New England cities and with a society both cultivated and intelligent. Here the boy got some schooling and even became something of a Latin scholar. But his spirits were too buoyant for a student. Dr. Waterhouse, who was his schoolmate, describes him as "a very capable self-willed boy, who, perhaps on that account, was indulged in everything, being an only son; handsome and forward and habituated at home to have his own way in everything, with little or no control from the easy, good-natured father." He was precocious, making at thirteen black-lead drawings good enough to discourage the attempts of Waterhouse. It was about this time that he first began to paint in oil, and some of his early portraits executed when he was fifteen or sixteen have been preserved. There was a considerable Scottish colony at Newport, and from the well-known clannishness of the nation they would be likely to feel an interest in his early attempts. One of the colony, a Mr. Cosmo Alexander, is said to have "painted for his amusement," and something slighting in his tone toward art offended Dunlap, who suggests that he did not know much about it; but he is probably the Cosmus Alexander who in 1765 exhibited a portrait in the London Society of Artists, and consequently must have been something of a painter. He opened a studio in Newport and received the patronage of the Scottish people there and through them became acquainted with young Stuart, whom he liked so well that he took him with him to South Carolina and thence to Scotland. Then Alexander unfortunately died after commending his pupil to Sir George Chambers; but when the latter also died, Stuart was left in a difficult position. He finally reached home in a collier by way of Nova Scotia. He was in rags and characteristically would never tell his experiences, for it was his way to cure disagreeable facts by ignoring them.

His foreign experience must have been useful to him in giving him an opportunity to see some good pictures and showing him his deficiencies, for he set hard to work to learn drawing, hiring in conjunction with Dr. Waterhouse a "strong muscled blacksmith" to pose in the evening. He was now about nineteen and commenced portrait painting in form, and one of his first works showed a remarkable characteristic — his power of visual memory, which he retained to the last. He painted a portrait of his grandmother, who died when he was a boy of ten or twelve, and the likeness was so striking that her son, his mother's brother, a prosperous merchant and banker of Philadelphia, gave him commissions for his own likeness and that of his wife and children. Others followed his example, among them the aristocratic Spanish Jews of whom there were many in Rhode Island; and then the painter, piqued at some affront real or imagined, refused the request of a public committee for a full-length portrait of Abraham Redwood and received all expostulations in sullen silence, a sort of twist of temper with which his friends became very familiar. This seriously diminished his popularity, and the approaching war may also have made portrait painting less remunerative; then, too, his friend Waterhouse, who understood him and to whom he could talk about art and music, left for London in March, 1775.

Soon after Stuart followed him, just how and when is stated in contradictory ways by the different authorities. Dunlap was told by him that he embarked from the port of Norfolk in Virginia. Dr. Waterhouse says, " Mr. Stuart was shut up in Boston when the first blood was spilt at Lexington and escaped from it about ten days before the Battle of Bunker Hill," that is on June 7, 1775. Mason, his latest biographer who had the assistance of his daughter in preparing his memoirs, declares that " with but one letter of introduction in his pocket, he embarked on board the last ship that escaped detention in Boston Harbor in the spring of 1775 and sailed for Great Britain." If this is so, he may have had the family of Copley for fellow-passengers, for there is a not very well authenticated story of Lord Lyndhurst, soon after he had made his famous speech denouncing the Irish as aliens, in blood, in language, and in religion, being at a public dinner and being asked by the

FIG. 18.—STUART: ELIZABETH BEALE BORDLEY, PENNSYLVANIA ACADEMY.

King across the length of the table, " And pray when did you come to the country, my Lord?" To which he retorted, " May it please your Majesty, I sailed from Boston on the last ship that left that port carrying the English colors." Probably some confusion of this story is responsible for Mason's statement.

At all events, in the late autumn of 1775 Stuart arrived in London, poorly equipped in money and acquaintances. His friend Waterhouse, upon whom he seems to have depended, was away in Edinburgh, at the time, and he suffered severely. It is to this period probably that the anecdote belongs of his entering a church where he heard the organ playing. Finding that there was a competition for the post of organist, he offered himself as a candidate and secured the place at a salary of £30 a year, for he was as fond of music as of art and had practised both with equal enthusiasm. He related this anecdote frequently in later life and illustrated his skill by playing on a small organ. How long he retained the position has not been recorded, but probably not long. When Dr. Waterhouse returned to London the next summer, he found Stuart with but one picture on his easel, and that was a family group for Mr. Alexander Grant, a Scotch gentleman to whom he brought letters, and who had paid for it in advance. " It remained long in his lodgings, and I am not sure that it was ever finished."

Of the doctor's relations to the painter we have only his own account, but there is no reason to doubt that, and it shows him a devoted and much-enduring friend. He got him lodgings, he got him sitters, " of my allowance of pocket money he always had two-thirds, and more than once the other third," twice he paid his debts and took him out of a sponging house; worse than the rest, when he got up a subscription for an engraving of Dr. Fordyce, a popular medical lecturer, and incautiously turned the proceeds over to Stuart, the latter would not even begin the portrait. As he states, " this was a source of inexpressible unhappiness and mortification, which at length brought on a fever, the only dangerous disease I ever encountered. After my recovery I had to refund the money, when I had not a farthing of my own, but what came from the thoughtful bounty of my most excellent kinsman Dr. Fothergill, who would never after see Charles Gilbert Stuart." In spite of everything, the bonds that united these two curiously assorted friends never relaxed. Stuart throughout his life was recognized as exempt from the ordinary obligations of life; he borrowed and did not pay, he promised and did not perform. He was improvident when providence was a duty, and yet with it all so gay, so brilliant, so talented, with a so ingratiating personal charm that he was loved like a child, and those who suffered most by his faults strove hardest to find some excuse for them.

Stuart was in London some three years before he saw West. This long delay is strange. West's accessibility was well known, and Waterhouse had been introduced to him on his arrival in London by the painter's father. It is only fair to conjecture that Stuart's temperament had something to do with it, for the visit must have been suggested to him. There are even two accounts of how they finally met. Waterhouse says that he " called on Mr. West and laid open to him his (Stuart's) situation, when that worthy man saw into it at once, and sent him three or four guineas, and two days afterward he sent his servant into the city to ask Mr. Stuart to come to him, when he employed him in copying." Sully, on the contrary, relates that Mr. Wharton, an old friend of West's, told him: " I was with several other Americans dining with West when a servant announced a person as wanting to speak to him; 'I am engaged,' but after a pause he added, 'Who is he?' 'He says, sir, that he is from America.' That was enough; West left the table immediately and on returning said, 'Wharton, there is a young man in the next room who says he is known in *our* city; go you and see what you can make of him.' I went out and saw a handsome youth in a fashionable green coat, and I at once told him that I was sent to see what I could make of him. 'You are known in Philadelphia?' 'Yes, sir.' 'Your name is Stuart?' 'Yes.' 'Have you no letters for Mr. West?' 'No, sir.' 'Who do you know in Philadelphia?' 'Joseph Anthony is my uncle.' 'That's enough, come in,' and I carried him in and he received a hearty welcome." These accounts may be partially reconciled by supposing that this was Stuart's first appearance after West had sent for him, but the relaters evidently are in error in some of the details.

TRUMBULL: BATTLE OF BUNKER HILL, YALE SCHOOL OF FINE ARTS.

CHAPTER V

STUART AND TRUMBULL

ORIGINALITY OF STUART'S WORK. — VISITS IRELAND. — RETURNS TO AMERICA AND PAINTS WASHINGTON. — QUALITY AND CHARACTERISTICS OF HIS PAINTING. — TRUMBULL. — YOUTH. — MILITARY EXPERIENCE. — FIRST TRIP ABROAD AND ARREST. — SECOND TRIP ABROAD. — PAINTS BATTLE OF BUNKER HILL. — THIRD TRIP ABROAD AS SECRETARY OF JOHN JAY. — FOURTH TRIP ABROAD. — COMMISSIONS FOR DECORATIONS OF THE CAPITOL

IT was late in 1778 that Stuart entered West's studio and for nearly four years he continued to work under him as student and assistant. Waterhouse left about the same time for Leyden and did not see his friend again for many years, his place as guardian providence being taken by West. That he endured the vagaries of his irresponsible pupil was perhaps to be expected, but that Stuart, with his sensitive, passionate nature, never mentioned his old master without affection speaks well for them both. How he lived during this period is not clear; some of the time he was in West's house. When Trumbull presented his letter of introduction in 1780, West, after receiving him kindly, referred him to Stuart in an adjoining room for painting materials and casts to copy. He found him "dressed in an old black coat with one half torn off the hip and pinned up, looking more like a poor beggar than a painter." Trumbull's sense of what was fitting for an artist, gained from the establishments of Copley and West, was naturally shocked; but Dunlap suggests that Stuart's torn coat was probably only used for painting. There is also a tale of Trumbull's finding him once (date not mentioned) sick abed and being told afterward that the trouble was simply hunger, he having eaten nothing for a week except a ship biscuit. But the story had passed from Stuart to Trumbull, from Trumbull to a Mr. Herring, and from him to Dunlap, and is of dubious verity; certainly while he was with West he was unlikely to want the necessaries of life.

What the artistic effect of his stay with West was it is difficult to determine.   He absolutely failed to acquire any of the characteristics which might naturally be expected.   He shows no trace of West's handling, he got no taste for composition.   In fact, it is a mystery where he gained his *technique;* it bears no resemblance to that of Gainsborough, Reynolds, or, least of all, to West.   Dunlap tells a couple of stories which he heard standing by Stuart's easel as he was painting a friend and which illustrate this as also the intercourse between master and pupil.   " Mr. West," Stuart says, " treated me very cavalierly on one occasion, but I had my revenge.   It was the custom, whenever a new Governor General was sent out to India, that he should be complimented by a present of his Majesty's portrait, and Mr. West being the King's painter was called upon on all such occasions.   So when Lord —— was about to sail for his government, the usual order was received for his Majesty's likeness.   My old master, who was busily employed upon one of his ten-acre pictures in company with prophets and apostles thought he would turn over the King to me.   He never could paint a portrait.   'Stuart,' said he, ' it is a pity to make his Majesty sit again for his picture; there is the portrait of him that you painted, let me have it for Lord ——; I will retouch it and it will do well enough.'   *'Well enough !* very pretty !' thought I, ' you might be civil when you ask a favor.'   So I *thought* but I *said* ' Very well, sir.'   So the picture was carried down to his room and at it he went.   I saw he was puzzled.   He worked at it all that day.   The next morning, 'Stuart,' said he, ' have you got your palette set ? '   ' Yes, sir.'   ' Well, you can soon set another, let me have the one you prepared for yourself; I can't satisfy myself with that head.'   I gave him my palette and he worked the greater part of that day.   In the afternoon I went into his room and he was hard at it.   I saw that he had got up to the knees in mud.   'Stuart,' says he, ' I don't know how it is, but you have a way of managing your tints unlike everybody else, — here, take the palette and finish the head.'   ' I can't, sir.'   ' You can't ? '   ' I can't indeed, sir, as it is, but let it stand until to-morrow morning and get dry, and I will go over it with all my heart.'   The picture was to go away the day after the morrow, so he made me promise to do it early next morning.   You know he never came down into the painting room, at the bottom of

FIG. 19.—STUART: GENERAL KNOX, BOSTON MUSEUM.

the gallery, until about ten o'clock. I went into his room bright and early and by half past nine I had finished the head. That done, Rafe and I began to fence; I with my maul stick and he with his father's. I had just driven Rafe up to the wall, with his back to one of his father's best pictures, when the old gentleman, as neat as a lad of wax, with his hair powdered, his white silk stockings, and yellow morocco slippers, popped into the room looking as if he had stepped out of a bandbox. We had made so much noise that we did not hear him come down the gallery or open the door. 'There, you dog,' says I to Rafe, 'there, I have you and nothing but your background relieves you.' The old gentleman could not help smiling at my technical joke, but soon looking very stern, 'Mr. Stuart,' said he, 'is this the way you use me?' 'Why, what's the matter, sir? I have neither hurt the boy nor the background.' 'Sir, when you knew I had promised that the picture of his Majesty should be finished to-day, ready to be sent away to-morrow, thus to be neglecting me and your promise! How can you answer it to me or to yourself?' 'Sir,' said I, 'do not condemn me without examining the easel. I have finished the picture. Please to look at it.' He did so; complimented me highly; and I had ample revenge for his 'It is well enough.'"

The second Stuart story, told under nearly the same circumstances, gives a view of the studio at a later time when Trumbull was there. "I used very often to provoke my good old master, though heaven knows, without intending it. You remember the color closet at the bottom of his painting room. One day Trumbull and I came into his room, and little suspecting that he was within hearing, I began to lecture on his pictures, and particularly upon one then on his easel. I was a giddy foolish fellow then. He had begun a portrait of a child, and he had a way of making curly hair by a flourish of his brush, thus, like a figure of three. 'Here, Trumbull,' said I, 'do you want to know how to paint hair? There it is, my boy! Our master figures out a head of hair like a sum in arithmetic. Let us see, — we may tell how many guineas he is to have for this head by simple addition, — three and three make six, and three are nine, and three are twelve, — ' How much the sum would have amounted to I can't say, for just then in stalked the master, with palette knife and palette, and put to flight my calculations. 'Very well, Mr. Stuart,' said he, — he always *mistered* me when he was angry, as a man's wife calls him my dear when she wishes him at the devil, — 'Very well, Mr. Stuart! very well indeed!' You may believe that I looked foolish enough, and he gave me a pretty sharp lecture without my making any reply. When the head was finished there were *no figures of three in the hair.*"

In 1782, after four years with West, encouraged by his master and others, Stuart left him, took an expensive house, and set up portrait painting on his own account. He had already exhibited at the Royal Academy, once in 1777, before he met West, and again in 1779 and 1782, the latter year having three portraits which gained him much praise. His success was rapid, his prices rose in two years from five to thirty guineas for a head, and this, with his rapidity of execution, meant a large income, which he squandered with incredible heedlessness. Herbert, in his *Irish Varieties*, relates how Stuart hired a French cook and chose forty-two persons whom he found amusing, — painters, poets, musicians, actors, and the like, — and invited them to dine with him. "After dinner he said to his friends, 'I can't have you all every day in the week, but I have contrived it so that the party shall vary without further trouble. I have put up seven cloak pins in my hall, so that the first seven who come in may hang up their cloaks and hats; the eighth man seeing them full, will go away and probably will attend earlier the next day. Then it would not be likely that any of the party of one day would come on the next, nor until the time for the forty-two be expended, and Sunday should not be excepted.' This compact was understood, without trouble of naming or inviting. I had a different company every day and no jealousies of a preference given to any one. I tasked myself to six sitters a day," said Stuart, "these done I flung down my palette and pencils, took my hat and ran about and around the park for an hour, then home, got ready for dinner, approached my drawing-room with the certainty of meeting as clever men as could be found in society; and what added to this comfort, I knew not what or who they might be until I saw them, and this produced a variety every day without any trouble. Oh, it was delightful solace after such labor! I assure you, my friend, it was the greatest of all human luxuries." "It must have been expensive." "It was more

FIG. 20. — STUART: FRANCES CADWALADER (LADY ERSKINE).

than I calculated on, but it enabled me to support my labor on six sitters." "How did Mr. West approve of it?" "He shook his head and observed that it would eat itself out. It did so; for in about six months the party was broken up, some going into the country, others out of the country — John Kemble, Irish Johnston, and others. It died a natural death, greatly to our regret."

All of Stuart's life in London was in harmony with this example. He lived in splendor, became a great beau, and enjoyed himself to the full. Even marriage had no restraining effect. He treated its obligations as lightly as others. His bride, whom he married in 1786, was a daughter of Dr. Coates and a sister of one of his intimate friends who, while admiring Stuart's genius, knew perfectly his reckless habits and did his best to prevent the match; but the painter had his way in that as in other things. Soon after his negligence and extravagance produced their result, and to escape his financial and other entanglements he moved to Dublin. The legend is that his creditors pursued him there and that he painted the nobility and gentry while in jail for debt; whether this be true or not, it is certain that he found Irish society peculiarly congenial and had ample occupation. He stayed there five years, when he sailed for America, moved as he declared by an intense desire to paint the portrait of Washington. His natural restlessness was probably quite as great an influence, and five years in Dublin were sure to have rolled up a mass of broken obligations, debts, and other embarrassments that it suited his temperament better to avoid than to meet.

He landed at New York in 1792, stayed a couple of years, then removed to Philadelphia, and there accomplished his wish of painting Washington. Stuart had mixed familiarly in the most distinguished society. He had painted portraits of three kings, to say nothing of less exalted persons. He was not embarrassed in the presence of the mighty; on the contrary, he had snubbed the great Dr. Samuel Johnson himself. When the doctor, in West's studio, remarked that the young man spoke very good English, and turning to Stuart rudely asked him where he had learned it, Stuart promptly retorted, "Sir, I can better tell you where I did not learn it — it was not from your dictionary," and

Ursa Major took the rebuff in good part.   It is a curious example
of the reverence in which Washington was held, of the *aura* which
surrounded his person, that in his presence Stuart was embarrassed,
almost awe-struck.   In his first sittings the rattle of talk with which
he was accustomed to divert his sitters failed him.   Though the
President was kindly and courteous, he was ill at ease, and the
portrait was not a success.   At least, Stuart held that it was not,
and stated that he had destroyed it.   He may have destroyed it
or he may only have said so; it is certain either it or copies of it
by him are in existence, the best being the so-called "Gibbs-Chan-
ning" picture, showing the right side of the face.   He was so
dissatisfied with the expression that the President consented to
sit again, the result being the "Athenæum" head on an unfinished
canvas, showing the left side of the face, which remains the accepted
likeness of the Father of his Country.   He also painted a full-length
for Lord Lansdowne.   These were the only portraits which he made
from life; but he produced countless replicas of them all, especially
of the "Athenæum" head.

   Gilbert Stuart still holds his place among our best painters, and
even among his great contemporaries in England.   His scope was
limited.   While they covered large canvases with full-length figures
and groups, using every aid of composition and costume to produce
their effects, and showing the result of this practice even in the
arrangement of their half-length portraits, Stuart painted heads, and
little besides heads, as far as known not a single group, a few full-
lengths, more half-lengths, a large number of what used to be called
Kit-Kats—canvases thirty by twenty-five inches, and many even
smaller than that.   The heads are placed near the centre of the canvas, often so near it that the figure, which was painted in afterward,
is cramped as it would not be if the head were higher.   There is no
effort to diversify the attitudes; and the costumes, while skilfully and
sufficiently done, are but accessories to the heads, and there is no
attempt to make them of important pictorial interest.   The heads
themselves are all painted in a cool, diffused light, seldom relieved by
heavy shadows or dark backgrounds.   There is nothing striking,
nothing forced; it is only a head — a head with its ordinary lighting
and expression.   No artifice is used to throw it into undue promi-

FIG. 21.—NEAGLE: GILBERT STUART, BOSTON MUSEUM.

nence. Within these limitations (and they are serious ones) they are unsurpassed. No one of his contemporaries had a surer feeling for the construction of a head or a surer insight into character. There are contradictory reports of his industry or indolence in studying drawing; but whether by industry or nature, he possessed it thoroughly, as far as the human features were concerned.

Where he acquired his *technique* as a painter is even more mysterious. It seems to have been original with him. He could have got little teaching from Cosmo Alexander in Newport or in his erratic life before meeting West, and yet he had exhibited a full-length portrait in the Royal Academy when he entered West's studio, and his style then was already formed, as the stories which Dunlap heard him tell will show. Exactly what the influence of his stay in West's studio was is difficult to determine; the obvious effects to be naturally looked for he seems to have completely escaped. He got no taste for imitating the old masters, nor any liking for allegory, nor any skill in composition or in the handling of large canvases. We have seen that he consciously avoided his master's handling. Dunlap recognized their " difference of opinion and style," and in connection with it mentions the following circumstance which took place about 1786, on the occasion of a visit to his old master's house and gallery in Newman Street: " Trumbull was painting on a portrait, and the writer literally *lending him a hand* by sitting for it. Stuart came in, and his opinion was asked as to the coloring, which he gave very much in these words: ' Pretty well, pretty well, but more like our master's flesh than Nature's. When Benny teaches the boys, he says " yellow and white there," and he makes a streak, " red and white there," another streak, " brown and red there for a warm shadow," another streak, " red and yellow there," another streak. But Nature does not color in streaks. Look at my hand, see how the colors are mottled and mingled, yet all is clear as silver.' "

No better description of his own style could be given. He paints with an unequalled purity and freshness of color, very delicate and sure in the half-tones, varying his color to suit the individual, but with a pearly brightness which is characteristic. The paint is put on thinly, as a rule, in short, decided touches, without heavy impasto, "mingled and mottled," as he himself says, and his execution

H

was surprisingly sure.   Two or three sittings sufficed for a head, which he painted at once in its true colors, disturbing the paint as little as possible after it was on the canvas and without resorting to the glaz-ings and varnishings so much in vogue in England.   This sureness of touch was the more remarkable because even in his youth Stuart's hand was trembling and unsteady; and in his later years, when some of his best work was done, an eye-witness says that "his hand shook so that it seemed impossible that he could paint.   The last time I saw him I think he was painting the portrait of Josiah Quincy (in 1824).   Stuart stood with his wrist upon the rest, his hand vibrating, and, when it became tolerably steady, with a sudden dash of the brush he put the color on the canvas."   The brilliancy and preservation of his works to-day attest the soundness of his practice. He painted with a restricted palette, which the curious may find in Dunlap and Mason, with his method of setting it; but let them not hope to produce the same results.   Stuart's style was his own.   He did not learn it from others, and though he gave advice freely and generously, he could not teach it to any successor.

With Stuart at West's was Trumbull, who was at his best an excellent artist, and whose works still hold their rank not only for their historical interest, but their artistic merit.   He was born at Lebanon, Connecticut, in 1756, the youngest of the six children of Jonathan Trumbull, later governor of Connecticut, whose title of Brother Jonathan, given him by Washington, has become a national personification.   John Trumbull was a sickly child, with the mind more active than the body, an infant prodigy of learning, qualified to enter college at twelve, and who actually entered Har-vard in the middle of the junior year when fifteen.   He was much younger than the other members of the class which, together with his natural reserve and the fact that he entered his class late, after friendships had been formed, caused him to make few intimate acquaintances.   He spent his spare pocket money on French lessons, and studied all the prints or books on the fine arts which he could find in the college library.   It was while at college that he made his visit to Copley and received his ideas of the dignity of a painter's life.   The same year his tutor wrote to his father: "I find he has a natural genius and disposition for limning.   As a knowledge of that

FIG. 22. — TRUMBULL: GOVERNOR CLINTON, CITY HALL, NEW YORK.

art will probably be of no use to him I submit to your consideration whether it would not be best to endeavor to give him a turn to the study of perspective, a branch of mathematics, the knowledge of which will be at least a genteel accomplishment, and may be greatly useful in future life." The governor replied, " I am sensible of his natural genius and inclination for limning: an art I have frequently told him will be of no use to him."

After his graduation, in 1773, he attempted painting with home-made material, and also taught school in Lebanon; but war being manifestly imminent, he began training the young men of the school and village, and after the battle of Lexington, when the first regiment of Connecticut troops was formed, he was made adjutant. The regiment was stationed at Roxbury, from whence the young adjutant saw the smoke of the battle of Bunker Hill. Later, when Washington arrived, Trumbull was advised by his brother to make a drawing of the British works on Boston Neck, which he partially finished and to which he attributes his appointment as second aide-de-camp to the general. Dunlap, who at the end of his life heartily disliked Trumbull, says that he always thought he was appointed because his father was governor of Connecticut. Both facts probably had their weight. Soon after, when General Gates was ordered to take command of the " Northern Department," he appointed Trumbull deputy adjutant-general, with the rank of colonel, and in that capacity he took part in the unfortunate expedition to Albany and Ticonderoga. There was little fighting, but he seems to have been active and efficient, and likely to prove a valuable officer; yet when the next February he received his commission, he returned it and resigned from the army because it was dated September instead of June. This was the turning point in Trumbull's career. Dunlap argues at length that Trumbull was in the wrong. Professor Weir, in his recently published memoir, thinks him in the right; but whether right or wrong about the proper date of his commission, there can be no justification for his retirement from the army in a huff on account of a possible error of a few weeks in the commission which made him a colonel at twenty. This irritability, this punc-tilio, this suspicion that he was being injured, this inability to ignore trifles, continued with him to the last, and embittered his life.

He retired to Boston and in 1778 served a few weeks as a volunteer in the futile attempt to recover Rhode Island.

This was his last experience as a soldier; he resumed the study of painting, and in 1780, under the influence of Sir John Temple, sailed for France on his way to London. In Paris he met Franklin and received a letter to West, who welcomed him cordially and said, "In an adjoining room I will introduce you to a young countryman who is studying with me — he will show you where to find the necessary colors, tools, and so forth, and you will make your copy in the same room." This was Stuart, who started Trumbull on his studies; but he had hardly begun when the arrest and execution of André caused Trumbull to be imprisoned. West hurried to the King and received his assurance that "in the worst possible event of the law his life should be safe." He was permitted to choose his prison and to arrange for his comfort. West sent him painting material and pictures to copy. Stuart painted his portrait; altogether the seven weeks of his imprisonment do not seem to have been unprofitable; at the end of the time he was released on bail (furnished by West and Copley) and returned to America. He became contractor for army supplies, but the signing of articles of peace put an end to that, and he had to determine anew his future occupation in life. His father urged the law, but that was revolting to him, "being rendered necessary by the vices of mankind." He "pined for the arts," and dwelt upon the honors paid to artists "in the glorious days of Greece and Rome." To this "Brother Jonathan" retorted, "You appear to forget, sir, that Connecticut is not Athens," yet yielded to the strong inclination, and in January, 1784, Trumbull was back again in London working under West.

It was in West's studio that, after a year or so of hard student work, he painted the "Battle of Bunker Hill" and the "Death of General Montgomery." They are modelled after the "Death of Wolfe," and manifestly owe much to West's influence; but the small scale demanded a *technique* quite different from West's own. The canvases are but twenty-five by thirty inches, and the execution has a miniature-like brilliancy. The coloring and grouping is excellent, especially in the Bunker Hill, which is a remarkable achievement for so young and inexperienced a painter, and he never

quite equalled it again. After the completion of these works and
on the invitation of Jefferson, at whose house he stayed, he took them
with him to Paris, and there saw David and many of the other
French artists, returning " with his head half turned by the attention
which had been paid to his paintings and by the multitude of fine
things he had seen."   Encouraged by his success, he planned
a series of illustrations of American history, and for that purpose
began a series of miniature heads from life which are invaluable
historical documents.   He painted the portraits of the French
officers for his " Surrender of Cornwallis " (finished in 1781) while
on his visit to Jefferson in Paris, where he returned again a few
years later.   On this second visit Jefferson offered him the position
of secretary, which he declined, urging the obligation of art.   He
returned to America in 1789 and continued the collection of heads
for his historical paintings, and also worked on the " Declaration
of Independence " while circulating the subscription list for the
engravings of the " Battle of Bunker Hill " and the " Death of
Montgomery."   He was successful in both of these and also painted
some portraits, including the full-length ones of Washington and
of General Clinton, now in the New York City Hall.

   In 1794 he embarked again for England, this time as secretary
to John Jay, and while there was appointed one of the commissioners " to carry into execution the seventh article of the late
treaty, relating to the damage done to the commerce of the United
States by irregular and illegal captures by British cruisers."   In
this diplomatic employment he spent seven years without deserting
the practice of the fine arts, for he finished the " Battle of Princeton " in 1795 and the " Capture of the Hessians at Trenton " soon
after.   On his return to America he tried again to take a position
as painter in New York, and executed a number of portraits, one
of the best being that of Alexander Hamilton, which was not done
from life but from the bust by Ceracchi.   His success, however,
was not sufficient to satisfy him, and after four years he returned
again to London and to West, and tried to establish himself there,
but unsuccessfully; his return was delayed by the outbreak of the
War of 1812, but as soon as peace was declared he returned to New
York with the idea of utilizing his historical material in a series of

pictures. His friends aided him and finally he received a commission
to paint four of the eight commemorative pictures in the National
Capitol.   He was eight years at the task, which he finished in 1824,
receiving $32,000 for the four paintings.   Trumbull clearly merited
the commission from his achievements as a painter, and from
the series of portraits in his possession, of which he could avail
himself; but the event did not justify expectation.   His style had
changed and was now but a feeble imitation of West's; his
strength and inspiration (always rather dependent on his surroundings) had diminished, and the resentment of Vanderlyn and others
at the award long embittered his personal relations to them.

FIG. 23.—ALLSTON: THE PROPHET JEREMIAH, YALE SCHOOL OF FINE ARTS.

CHAPTER VI

ALLSTON, MALBONE, AND VANDERLYN

DIFFERENT CHARACTER OF WEST'S LATER PUPILS. — ALLSTON. — FAMILY. — EARLY
YEARS. — COLLEGE LIFE. — SAILS FOR ENGLAND WITH MALBONE. — MALBONE AND
OTHER MINIATURE PAINTERS. — ALLSTON IN ENGLAND. — VANDERLYN. — HIS LIFE
WITH ALLSTON IN ROME. — HIS SUCCESS IN PARIS. — REMBRANDT PEALE

WEST'S later pupils began life as American citizens. Vanderlyn
(born in 1776) marks the dividing line, which corresponds here to a
real division quite apart from the accident of nationality. When
West's father wrote to him in Rome, in 1762, that from there he
should "return home," he meant that he should go to England, and
to most Americans at that time "home" had the same significance.
They were colonists in a strange land, generally with no expectation
of return, yet their hearthstones were still across the Atlantic. They
were not, save in exceptional instances, from the wealthy or aristocratic class, but still they had been in contact with cultured life in
a land rich in beautiful and stately buildings and all the adornments
of a long-established civilization. They came to the little cities or
to the forests of the New World with a perfect knowledge of what
was lacking there. The fathers of West and Stuart, the father and
stepfather of Copley, arrived in America men grown, with their education and character formed. This could not continue. The proportion of native-born increased, and of those who had a certain
native culture distinct from the standards of England or Europe.
The effect of this change increased with time, but it was already
visible in the group of men who came to West in his old age.

The standard-bearer of the group was Washington Allston.
More forgotten now than West or Trumbull, he once filled all who
knew him with confident assurance of his greatness; but he left
behind him only a few unsatisfactory, tentative efforts, which have
gradually lost interest as the charm of his personal character becomes

a fainter and fainter memory.   He was born in 1779, in the Waccamaw region in South Carolina, a long strip of land between the Waccamaw River and the ocean, from three to six miles wide, on which in Revolutionary times several patrician families lived in a sort of feudal state — one of the most distinguished among them being the Allstons, who furnished the state with a long line of governors, soldiers, and other dignitaries.   The painter's uncle was Colonel William Allston of Marion's staff, and a brother officer, General Horry, grows rapturous over the hospitality of Waccamaw lavished on the ragged troopers in the intervals of the raids of the "Swamp Fox."   The mahogany sideboards, the fish, flesh, and fowl of the fattest and finest, the pitchers of old amber-colored brandy from "demijohns that had not left the garret for many a year," and "the smiles of the great ladies" were a welcome change from the forest camps and the sweet potatoes baked in the ashes.

Allston's father married twice, the painter being the son of the second wife.   Before he was two years old his father died, and when he was seven his mother married Dr. Henry C. Flagg of Newport, who had been chief of the medical staff of Greene's army and who settled in the South after the war.   There was no objection to him except that he was a Northerner; but the faith of the slave-holding whites of the South in their own exclusive aristocracy was already formed, and Mrs. Flagg was declared to have disgraced herself and her family, and was disinherited.   As in the case of Copley, however, the marriage seems to have been advantageous to the boy, between whom and his stepfather there existed always a sincere affection, although they were but little together.   For soon after the marriage, Allston, in the interests of his health, was sent to school at Newport, Dr. Flagg's birthplace and still one of the more important of American seaports, with a pleasant social life and artistic traditions of Smybert and Stuart, and there Allston remained at the private school of Robert Rogers, one of the best in the country, until he entered Harvard.   He showed as a boy unusual taste for drawing, and found in the town friends to assist and encourage him, and particularly made the acquaintance of Malbone, two years his senior and already beginning to paint miniatures.

He entered college so well prepared that his scholastic duties sat

lightly upon him, and he could take a fair rank as a student while
having time left for more congenial things.   He did much miscellaneous reading, heard what music he could, wrote poetry, and was
cheerfully convivial at times, according to the standards of the day,
which were somewhat more liberal than at present.   His animal spirits
overflowed, he took part in college pranks and heard the chimes at
midnight, but with a loftiness of character which kept him from anything degrading.   He was, in short, the radiant young genius, slender,
graceful, handsome, with blue eyes, silky black hair, and pale, clear
complexion, liked and honored by the most dissimilar of his fellow-
students; cordial to all and yet with an aristocratic distinction that
marked him as a higher being.   Radiant with health, brilliant in
intellect, with the most delicate sensibility and the noblest moral
aspirations, to crown all he was also in love and his verses were
inspired by the lady who was afterward to become his bride.   It is
no wonder that he was elected class poet, nor that he read a poem on
Energy of Character, the lack of which kept him from success.

During his college life he still continued to work at art, drawing
after engravings, copying the best pictures he could find, and painting some original productions, — landscapes, comic scenes, groups
of banditti, the " Buck's Progress," illustrations to the *Mysteries of
Udolpho*, and all the natural contents of a young collegian's brain.
Some of these paintings were surprisingly good, and one of them, a
landscape with figures on horseback, was afterward exhibited at
the Royal Academy, London.

Upon his graduation he returned to Charleston, where he was
welcomed by his relatives, and found there also Malbone, who had
been in Boston during his college course, and whose congenial disposition and tastes increased the friendship already formed in Newport.   Charles Fraser, also, was making his first efforts in art, but
wiser than most of his fellows delayed giving himself up to it
entirely until he had by practice of the law gained enough to
insure him against want.   Bembridge, too, had had his headquarters at Charleston, but his vogue could have now given small
encouragement to the ardent youths, for he had left there from lack
of employment and moved to Philadelphia, where he married and
lived.   A contemporary of West, he had not gone to England to

perfect himself, but remained at Rome several years as a pupil of Mengs and Pompeo Battoni, and returned to his native land a fairly skilled practitioner to paint many portraits, now forgotten, and to endure the usual privations and want.

Allston painted away industriously, mostly at imaginative work, banditti, of course (they were his favorite subjects at the time), but also on a composition of "Satan rallying his Hosts," and some portraits. He did not lack patrons, but his ambition was for wider and completer knowledge and training. His family would have preferred another career, but yielded, not unwillingly, to his manifest predilection for art. The next year he embarked with Malbone for England, where he received the usual kindly welcome from West, and in return not only gave him his friendship, but sincerely admired his works. He placed him first among living artists, and this not on account of his earlier pictures, of which he had seen engravings in America, but for his later works, and especially the "Death on the Pale Horse." This love for mystery and vision is characteristic, as is also his praise of the nightmares of Fuseli, for Allston delighted in his emotions. As a child the negro-witch stories filled him with delicious terrors, and while in college he would steep himself in romantic tales of mystery and horror. Anything which could stir his feelings was sure of his admiration, even his own boyish representation of a gashed and bloody throat in one of his outlaw pictures. Malbone shared with him West's aid and praise, and also his admiration for the old painter; but not for Fuseli, who appealed less to his temperament.

The friends saw together the sights of London, especially the pictures; but Malbone, in spite of inducements to stay in England, returned to Charleston in the winter of 1801. Afterward he visited most of the larger cities, and was fully occupied with commissions for the few years he had to live. He died in 1807 of consumption, aggravated by too constant application to his work. Though toward the end of his life he painted some portraits in oil and landscapes, Malbone's reputation rests on his miniatures, which are excellent and would hold a respectable place anywhere. He had gained, with little aid from others, a sound method of work and sufficient skill in drawing, and had an innate feeling for beauty and grace. As All-

FIG. 24.—ALLSTON : SPANISH GIRL, METROPOLITAN MUSEUM.

ston said, " No woman ever lost any beauty from his hand." There is a sweetness and charming purity of expression about his works, which his sound draftsmanship and recognition of character prevent from falling into insipidity, the pitfall for most of his craft who attain facility. Miniature painting was an important branch of the profession at that time, and practised with every degree of skill. All of the portrait painters at times turned their hand to it, even men like Copley and Trumbull, and it descended through all the grades, down to profile drawing machines and black silhouettes. Charles W. Peale painted many miniatures and rather good ones; his brother, James Peale, confined himself mainly to them, as did some of the numerous Peale family of the second generation — Raphael, the son of Charles W., and Sarah M. and Anna Claypoole, daughters of James. There was also John Ramage, an Irish gentleman, who painted miniatures in Boston, moving to New York in 1777, and flourishing there until age and (Dunlap hints) dissipation diminished his skill. Some of their work is fairly good. That of Charles Fraser, the early friend of Malbone, is still better. As already stated he accumulated a modest competence at the law before devoting himself entirely to art, and lived in comparative comfort and dignity, painting countless portraits in little of the distinguished Southern families, and many landscapes and compositions. He died in 1860, at the age of seventy-eight, still regretting the years that he had sacrificed to the law. There was also Benjamin Trott, who studied under Stuart and Robert Field, of whom he is said to have been jealous, and a multitude more ; but none equals Malbone, who stands, by general consent, without American rivals until comparatively recent times.

Allston remained in London for a couple of years after Malbone left him, until in the summer of 1803 Vanderlyn came on from Paris for a few months, and the two returned there together. John Vanderlyn was then on his second trip to Europe. He was born in 1776 of Dutch stock, at Kingston on the Hudson, which town was burned the next year by the British, Vanderlyn's family being among the principal sufferers. He got a fair education at the Kingston Academy, and when sixteen entered the employ of Thomas Barton, an Englishman, who was the chief importer of engravings in

I

New York. He encouraged the boy's tendencies toward painting, and Archibald Robertson, a Scotchman, who came to the country in 1791, gave him some instruction and employed him to copy several of Stuart's portraits, including one of Aaron Burr. Vanderlyn acquitted himself so well that Burr was interested, sent for him, and took him under his protection. This is related with abundant detail by Dunlap. Tuckerman's account is that Vanderlyn was employed ir. a blacksmith's shop near Kingston, and that Burr, his horse having cast a shoe, stopped there to have it replaced. He saw some charcoal sketches on a door, found that Vanderlyn was the artist, and told him if he should decide to practise art, to " Put a clean shirt in your pocket, come to New York, and call on me." A few weeks later, as Burr was at breakfast, a brown paper parcel was handed to him, containing a coarse shirt, and he found Vanderlyn at his door and received him into his family.

This story is more picturesque than Dunlap's, and therefore more likely to be widely received, but it is almost certainly false. In any case, however, Burr aided Vanderlyn. He sent him to Philadelphia for eight or nine months to study under Stuart, and on his return employed him to paint his portrait and that of his daughter, Theodosia, and later supplied him with means for a five years' stay in Paris. In 1801 he returned with copies and studies made abroad and again painted a portrait of his patron and his daughter. He painted some other portraits and two views of Niagara, which were subsequently engraved, and sailed again for France early in 1803, crossing from there to England, where he first met Allston, and, as has been said, returned with him to Paris. There Allston stayed only long enough to see the city and the wonderful collection of pictures in the Louvre, the spoils of the French arms from all Europe, and then proceeded through Switzerland to Italy, admiring the scenery, visiting the more important cities, staying at Siena to learn the language, and finally arriving at Rome, in 1804, where Vanderlyn joined him the next year.

They could hardly have chosen a time when there was a more brilliant assemblage of foreigners in the city. It was a foreigners' city. Italian art was exhausted. The great traditions handed down through working artists had died out. Tiepolo, the last who

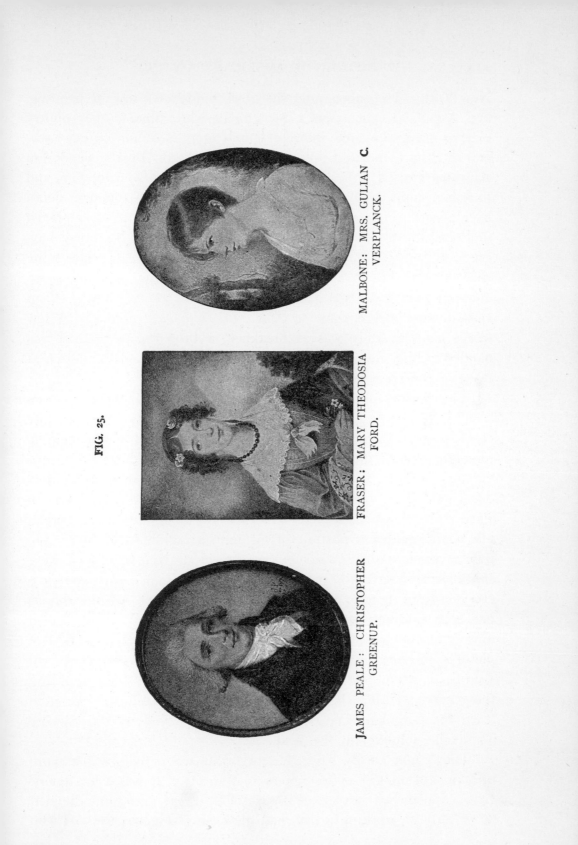

FIG. 25.

JAMES PEALE: CHRISTOPHER GREENUP.

FRASER: MARY THEODOSIA FORD.

MALBONE: MRS. GULIAN C. VERPLANCK.

had inherited a breath of the old divine afflatus, died in 1770, and even the holders of the empty training had ceased. Pompeo Battoni and the men whom West met were no more, and their place was filled with strangers — not coming like Mengs to learn of their Italian contemporaries, but enthusiasts for the old work, striving to go back and take it up again anew where some favorite master had left it in the sixteenth or seventeenth century, or inspiring themselves by the memories and visions that hung about the ancient mistress of the world. Cornelius was there and his group of ascetics, believing with true German thoroughness that they had only to put themselves into what they supposed was the fifteenth-century frame of mind to produce fifteenth-century pictures, and Thorwaldsen mingling Canova and archaic Greek sculpture with an infusion of genius. The English painter, Turner, was at this time enriching his observation by travel on the Continent; and may have been in Rome.

The surroundings were an intellectual intoxication to Allston, and when, the next year, Coleridge came to Rome, he had some one to appreciate and share his enthusiasm. He and Vanderlyn were still but students, working evenings from the model in the Academy and painting occasional pictures, but rapidly advancing. They plotted together to start some question of art or literature on Coleridge's visits, and he would for hours pour forth as wonderful talk as ever issued from the lips of man. He was then at the height of his powers, not yet a victim of opium, and even Allston could not equal him; but they were congenial spirits, and the artist added another to his intimate, enduring friendships. Coleridge declared in one of his letters that, with the exception of the Wordsworths, there was no one to whom he felt himself so strongly drawn.

Washington Irving, who came to Rome at the same time as Coleridge, and who had already met Vanderlyn in Paris the preceding year, was a younger man than Allston and fairly dazzled by his charm. He even thought seriously of deserting literature for art, for no reason save the prospect of living in community with Allston. He saw the absurdity of such a scheme, but he relinquished it with regret. Allston produced no important works in Rome, though one may suspect his influence in the " Marius " of Vanderlyn, painted in 1807: not in the handling or technical side of the painting, for Vanderlyn was older and with more practical experi-ence than he, but in the concepti of the subject.

The next year Vanderlyn took his " Marius " to Paris with him and exhibited it at the Salon, where it received a gold medal, being specially designated by the Emperor himself, whose eye was caught by the picture as he was conducted through the exhibition, and

FIG. 26. — VANDERLYN: ARIADNE, PENNSYLVANIA ACADEMY.

who abruptly ordered, " Give the medal to that." To be sure, the Emperor knew nothing about art, but his taste was the taste of the day. The picture was generally admired, and Vanderlyn remained seven years in Paris, esteemed and comparatively pros-perous. In 1812 he exhibited his " Ariadne," which increased his reputation, and three years later sailed for New York; but before this time he was enabled to repay in some measure the early kind-ness of Burr. When the latter, ruined in fortune and honor, fled to Paris, Vanderlyn received him as a friend and aided him to the extent of his powers, being in fact his only support during the first years of his disgrace.

At the time of Vanderlyn's stay in Paris, American artists had some reputation there, enough at any rate to cause David to ask why the best English painters were all Americans. This was owing to the visits of men like West and Stuart and Trumbull, and also perhaps of Rembrandt Peale, who reports the remark. The latter had been a short time in West's studio while Allston and Malbone were there, and he made two trips from America to Paris during Vanderlyn's residence in the city. He painted portraits of the distinguished men for his father's museum, and discussed with them science, philosophy, and the bones of the mastodon which his father had discovered. He was successful enough to have Denon, who was Director General of the Museums, offer him government employment, and David, who had refused to sit for any other painter, allowed him to make a portrait, and pressed him to remain, saying that, "as Gérard had commenced history and could paint no more portraits, he would give him all the Imperial portraits to paint," adding, "I prefer Gérard to you, but I prefer your portraits to any others here." Rembrandt Peale, however, was too restless to take advantage of these offers and chose rather to return home, there to emulate his father in the variety of his occupations.

CHAPTER VII

THE LAST PUPILS OF WEST

ALLSTON'S RETURN TO AMERICA AND MARRIAGE. — SAILS AGAIN FOR ENGLAND. — S. F. B. MORSE. — CHARLES ROBERT LESLIE. — ALLSTON'S WORK IN LONDON. — FINAL RETURN TO AMERICA. — LESLIE'S WORK. — GILBERT STUART NEWTON. — MATHER BROWN. — REMBRANDT PEALE'S LATER LIFE. — MORSE'S WORK IN AMERICA. — VANDERLYN'S LIFE. — ALLSTON'S LIFE IN AMERICA. — "BELSHAZZAR'S FEAST." — ALLSTON'S POSITION IN AMERICA

IN 1809, a year or so before Peale's return, Allston, who on Vanderlyn's departure from Rome had moved to Leghorn and from there to London, sailed for Boston. The determining motive for this was his engagement to Miss Channing, formed while he was still an undergraduate in Harvard and which had lasted now eleven years with more fidelity and sentiment than passion. He stayed in America a couple of years, visited his mother in South Carolina and painted her portrait, also one of Dr. Channing and some small canvases. He delivered the poem before the Phi Beta Kappa Society at Harvard in 1811, and the same year returned to London with his wife and with S. F. B. Morse, who had joined himself to them, and who looked up to Allston with the reverence and enthusiasm that he invariably inspired in young men, in spite of their utter difference of temperament and upbringing. For Morse was of the sternest Puritan stock, son of the Rev. Dr. Jedidiah Morse, an unshaken pillar of the faith, and had been reared in all the strenuousness of a Puritan household. He had a brother who found leisure to read the Bible through twice, knew long portions of it by heart, and who frequently conducted family worship before he died at the age of three years and ten months. This sounds like cruelty but it was not so to the infant of a century ago, who frequently took a fearful joy in such accomplishments. Under the rigid forms of the Morse family there was affection, intelligence, and more liberality than would be supposed.

MORSE: PORTRAIT OF MRS. DE FOREST, YALE SCHOOL OF FINE ARTS.

Samuel Finley Breese Morse, born in 1791, was the oldest of three sons, who lived beyond infancy, and he showed the usual early symptoms which proclaim the future painter. The profession naturally did not seem a desirable one to his parents, but he was permitted to practise it as well as he could even during his college course at Yale, where he painted a family group which is still preserved. Shortly before his graduation in the class of 1810 he met Allston and wrote to his family, choosing art as a profession, and saying that when Allston returned to England in the spring he "should admire to be able to go with him." His family yielded and he went to London, whither six months later came Leslie and joined him in his pursuit of art and admiration of Allston.

Charles Robert Leslie was born of American parents in London, in 1794, and so was some three years Morse's junior. When a boy of six his family moved to Philadelphia and there he was brought up; sketching everywhere, practising drawing, but especially haunting the theatre, making friends with the actors, painting scenery and portraits. Some of his water-color portraits of actors in costume are still preserved and are remarkable for a boy of sixteen. They are drawn in pencil, their firmness and accuracy of outline showing no signs of the beginner, and tinted with washes of thin color allowing the lines below to be seen. They may have been suggested by some of the colored prints of Rowlandson or his contemporaries, but they have a grace and sincerity all their own. It was with works like these that he accumulated enough for his trip abroad and for the "cheerful, innocent, scrambling student life," as he called it. Leslie's character was peculiarly sunny, modest, and pure. He soon took rooms with Morse and visited West, now growing old and out of royal favor, but still valiantly at work on huge canvases and unwearied in kindly aid to students. Copley, too, advised his young compatriots; but it was to Allston that they turned with the deepest reverence and who awakened their highest enthusiasm.

In order that there might be no mistake about his allegiance, Morse wrote home in 1813, "You must recollect when you tell friends that I am studying in England that I am a pupil of Mr. Allston and not Mr. West." This is not derogatory of West, whom both Morse and Leslie admired, but is Morse's personal tribute of adoration to Allston, who was at the time of his second visit to England at his culminating point. He was happy in his wedded life, beloved with a peculiar intensity of affection by the choicest spirits of the time, with the future bright before him, and producing works which won him much admiration and some money. He painted a great picture, eleven feet wide by thirteen high, "The Dead Man restored to Life by touching the Bones of the Prophet Elisha," now in the Pennsylvania Academy and which, exhibited in the British Institution, gained a prize of two hundred guineas. He painted "The Angel releasing Saint Peter from Prison" for Sir George Beaumont, a portrait of Coleridge now in the National Portrait Gallery in London, the "Cavern Scene from Gil Blas," "Uriel in the Sun," which brought him a gratuity of one hundred and fifty guineas from the British Institution, and a "Jacob's Dream," bought by Lord Egremont. And then after a seven years' stay, just when his position seemed to be assured and a future like that of West open before him, he returned to America and remained there the rest of his life.

It is difficult to know why he did so. There are reasons in plenty, but they do not seem sufficient. He had been seriously sick in 1813 from overwork on his "Dead Man restored to Life," so that his constitution was probably weakened, and when, two years later, his wife died, he felt her loss with all the sensitiveness of his nature; but instead of unnerving him, he found in work a refuge from his sorrow. His income, too, was less than convenient, and he had made his arrangements to return before the appearance of the Earl of Egremont as a patron; yet making allowance for all, it is not clear why he should have been disheartened, or why, if disheartened, he should have thought the future promised more in America than in England. He spoke himself in later years of "a homesickness, which (in spite of the best and kindest friends and every encouragement as an artist) brought me back to my own country," but it is probable that there was also a general feeling at the time that America offered great opportunities to an artist. The new republic had increased rapidly in wealth, population, and territory. The War of 1812 had proved that its independence from Europe was real; and the collapse of Burr's ill-fated Louisiana expedition that its government was stable. Far-sighted men already saw its enormous future power. The advance in the arts had been rapid, American painters were honored abroad, and it was natural to anticipate a great artistic movement — something like that which had just taken place in England. Why this failed, why the very force of the material growth choked the intellectual, will be related more at length in the coming chapters, but it is mentioned here to

FIG. 27. — LESLIE: SANCHO PANZA AND THE DUCHESS, NATIONAL GALLERY, LONDON.

explain the return of so many promising men and the almost complete failure of their subsequent productions.

The fault was not in the men, but in their environment. Leslie remained in England, save for one flying trip to America, lured by the offer of the position of Professor of Fine Arts at West Point, the utter impossibility of which position he had the good sense to recognize at once and to resign it and return to his accustomed work. He is consequently to be counted as of the British school rather than the American, and ranks high among his contemporaries. His paintings in the unheroic line of anecdotic *genre* — with subjects from Shakespeare's comedies or *Don Quixote* or the *Spectator* — are filled with a love of the sweet, wholesome things of life, and that delight in all the old picturesqueness, which is doubly keen after the deprivation from it in a new country, and which gives the charm to Irving's *Bracebridge Hall* and *Old Christmas*.

Even those who are not inclined to admire pictures that are only illustrations of literature are forced to make a reservation in favor of Leslie's. They are well painted, with a sure and brilliant touch, the faces are animated and characteristic, without being forced into caricature, the grouping, the costumes, the whole *mise en scène* is charming and shows how he profited by his boyish familiarity with the theatres and actors of Philadelphia. His color, too, is personal with a milky whiteness in the lights and a velvety shadow quite unlike the warm tones generally popular at the time and agreeing perfectly with the story that he once at a brilliant dinner party sat silent through the whole talk, twiddling a silver spoon and watching the reflections on it. Leslie lived long in England, successful, honored, and loved, and died there in 1859. The painter George D. Leslie is his son.

Almost equally promising was the career of Gilbert Stuart Newton, a nephew of Gilbert Stuart, whose father's royalist sympathies caused him to move to Nova Scotia, where the boy was born in 1795. He soon came to Boston, where he studied painting with his uncle until puffed up with youthful pride he cried out at him one day, "Now, old gentleman, I'll show you how to paint," which so enraged Stuart that, not happening to have the gout at the time, he kicked his nephew out of the studio. Newton did not come back, but went to London and flourished. His best works are small *genre* pieces, much in Leslie's style, but looser in handling, warmer in tone, with a sentiment less frank and simple, and more in sympathy with the public of the Books of Beauty which flourished then.

Besides these men there was Mather Brown, a Bostonian, who went early to London and remained there. He was a pupil of West's, who attained to lesser fame, but was yet appointed portrait painter to H.R.H. the Duke of York, and is represented by a number of canvases in the National Portrait Gallery, though Leslie describes his studio in later years as lined with wretched canvases two or three deep against the walls. Probably others still more completely forgotten remained to seek fame abroad, but soon after the close of the War of 1812 there was a general return to America of her painters who had won their first laurels. The older men who had returned twenty years or more before, like Peale or Stuart, without increasing their fame, had not done so badly, and now that they were growing old there seemed a chance for the younger men. A number of them preceded Allston. Rembrandt Peale returned in 1810 or 1811, Vanderlyn and Morse in 1815, Trumbull in 1816, and Allston two years later. Peale had much of his father's versatility and energy, and followed his career pretty closely. He brought back with him his picture of the "Roman Daughter," which he exhibited at the Pennsylvania Academy in 1812; then finding that his services were not in demand, he moved to Baltimore, and, after the paternal example, established a museum and gallery of paintings which he conducted for nine years. At the end of that time he produced "The Court of Death" and exhibited it throughout the country to his great profit, gaining nearly $9000 in a single year. It was a huge canvas, not badly done, with the king of terrors seated in the centre, and a line of all sorts and conditions of men approaching him from either side — an allegory very simple and intelligible and well calculated to the moral taste of the day. Its popularity was enduring, and it continued to be shown from time to time until it found a final resting place in the Detroit Art Gallery.

After this Peale took up portrait painting more vigorously, visiting New York, Boston, and Philadelphia. He produced a likeness of Washington from memory, which he succeeded in having bought by Congress. He went abroad again for short visits, he continued to paint, introduced illuminating gas into Baltimore, wrote memoirs and many reminiscences of the men with whom he had come in contact, and became in his old age a sort of dean of the profession, being for many years the only surviving artist who had painted Washington from life. He died in 1860. He was an accurate painter and (probably on account of his work in Paris) better trained in drawing than most at the time, but his color was dull, his painting lacked light and was decidedly inferior to his father's.

Much the same type of artist as Peale with the same energy, enterprise, and mechanical ingenuity was S. F. B. Morse, who reached New York some four years later. He had been obliged to return from lack of funds, and his struggle against adverse circumstances was severe, although his success as a student had been rapid and remarkable. He exhibited in the Royal Academy of 1813 a painting of a "Dying Hercules," which had already won him honors in another form. Following the example of Allston, he had modelled in plaster first the torso and then, encouraged by his success, the whole figure. West praised it and finding that there was a competition for a single figure, he sent it to the Adelphi Society of Arts and was rewarded by gaining the gold medal which was presented to him with much ceremony. Many years later this figure reappeared with dramatic effect after all copies of it had been apparently lost or destroyed. When he had finally succeeded with the problem of telegraphy, and had been commissioned to set up his instruments in the Capitol at Washington, it was necessary to place batteries and wires in the basement of the building, and there groping around in the long-disused vaults he saw a strangely familiar object and recognized with amazement a cast of his "Hercules." It was as if this witness of his early success had appeared to congratulate him in the crowning moment of his life. The presence of the statue was explained later. Of the six casts originally made, he had given one to Bullfinch the architect, who had stored it in the Capitol, and after his death it had been forgotten. But the coincidence was striking.

Morse found small demand for his painting at first and went from city to city trying to find patrons for portraits at the modest price of fifteen dollars a head. He was most successful in Charleston, where in 1818 he painted fifty-three portraits in five months, returning afterward for a number of winters. He brought many of the heads north with him in the summer and there filled in costumes and backgrounds. He painted groups and figure compositions, and in 1823 exhibited an interior of the House of Representatives filled with diminutive portraits of the members, but for some reason the picture, which had cost him two years of hard work and which he

FIG. 28.—NEWTON: YORICK AND THE GRISETTE, NATIONAL GALLERY, LONDON.

had hoped to exhibit with profit, did not succeed with the public and was rolled up and put away as a failure. He also devoted himself more and more to mechanical inventions, for which he had always had a gift, and with his brother introduced a pulsating pump from which they received some profit. These alternated with his painting according to his necessities and the promise of gain, but the turning point in his life came later, in 1832, as he was returning from a trip to England. The conversation in the cabin of the ship turned one evening on electricity. Morse knew little about it except what he had learned from a few lectures heard at Yale, though to those he had listened with particular interest. The question was asked as to the length of time necessary for the current to pass through a wire, and when it was declared that the transit was instantaneous, Morse remarked, " If the transit of electricity can be made visible in any part of the circuit, I see no reason why intelligence may not be transmitted instantaneously by electricity." The company broke up, but Morse went on deck with his mind full of the idea and jotted down in a note-book the first skeleton of the " Morse alphabet," and from that time painting ceased to be foremost in his thoughts.

It was a serious loss, for Morse, without being a genius, was yet perhaps better calculated than another to give in pictures the spirit of the difficult times from 1830 to 1860. He was a man sound in mind and body, well born, well educated, and both by birth and education in sympathy with his time. He had been abroad, had seen good work, and received sound training. His ideals were not too far ahead of his public. Working as he did under widely varying conditions, his paintings are dissimilar not only in merit but in method of execution; even his portraits vary from thin, free handling to solid impasto. Yet in the best of them there is a real painter's feeling for his material, the heads have a soundness of construction and a freshness in the carnations that recall Raeburn rather than West; the poses are graceful or interesting, the costumes are skilfully arranged, and in addition he understands perfectly the character of his sitters, the men and women of the transition period, shrewd, capable, but rather commonplace, without the ponderous dignity of Copley's subjects or the cosmopolitan graces of a later day.

K

The struggles incident to the invention and development of telegraphy turned Morse from the practice of art; but up to the end of his life he was interested in it and aggressive in any scheme for its advancement.   His influence in founding the National Academy of Design will be spoken of later, but his purchase and presentation to Yale College of the " Prophet Jeremiah dictating to the Scribe Baruch," by his friend and master, Allston, may be mentioned here as one example from many of the use made of the wealth which finally came to him.

To Allston himself, to Vanderlyn who returned in the same year as Morse, to Trumbull who came the next year (1816), fate was less kind. Between Vanderlyn and Trumbull an animosity arose almost at once, originated probably by the award of the decorations in the Rotunda of the Capitol to Trumbull, but strengthened and elaborated by many petty acts of mutual dislike.   Trumbull undoubtedly had much more political " influence" in the special sense of the word than Vanderlyn and knew how to employ it, but in all fairness the commission was due to him on his apparent merits.   His reputation was well estab-lished, he had painted historical compositions of great merit, and he had an invaluable collection of portraits painted from life of the principal actors in the struggle for independence.   Vanderlyn felt himself the better painter, and said so.   It was true enough, for he had had a sound training in France and was at the height of his powers, while Trumbull's skill was on the decline, but that could not be known at the time.   The older man triumphed, and there was much ill-feeling which Trumbull seems to have manifested indirectly in various petty ways.   Vanderlyn secured rooms in the New York city almshouse to exhibit his " Marius," " Ariadne," and other works, but during an absence from town the permission was revoked, he was ordered to remove his canvases, and Vanderlyn saw therein the spite of Trumbull.   Later he embarked on the exhibition of pano-ramas and obtained a permit to erect a building for that purpose in City Hall Park, and there showed views of Paris, Athens, Mexico, Versailles (painted by himself), Geneva, and the three battles of Lodi, Waterloo, and that at the gates of Paris.   The enterprise was not very successful; the building called the Rotunda was burdened with a debt, and finally, owing to unpaid obligations, seized by the city

FIG. 29.—MORSE: LAFAYETTE, CITY HALL, NEW YORK.

without remuneration to the artist and used for various purposes, being at one time the seat of the Court of Sessions and afterward of the Marine Court.

With the failure of these schemes Vanderlyn became discouraged, returned to Kingston, led a life of obscurity, and was frequently in need of money. Although his time was largely occupied by his exhibitions and panoramas, he had painted a number of portraits and other pictures in the years following his return, but he was a laborious and slow executant, sometimes taking sixty sittings for a portrait, so that they afforded him little profit, and during his Kingston residence he seems to have practically ceased work. Finally, in 1842, toward the end of his life, Congress urged by his friends awarded to him the commission for one of the panels in the Capitol. The subject was the "Landing of Columbus," and the price $1200; but the recognition came too late to Vanderlyn. Long inactivity had diminished his skill. He went to Paris to execute the work, and Bishop Kip, his biographer and friend, who saw the picture in 1844, reports that "it was advancing under the hand of a clever French artist whom Vanderlyn had employed. Of course the conception and design were his own, but I believe little of the actual work."

This is fully borne out by the canvas itself, which shows the ordinary facile Parisian work of the time, but no trace of Vanderlyn's own manner, which was of an earlier date, firmer, more serious, more solid. This workmanship as shown in his youthful works is his distinguishing characteristic. He was the first of our artists to study in France instead of England, and to acquire the accurate French draughtsmanship then enforced by David and his school. The "Marius" is decidedly Davidian in conception. The "Ariadne" is an admirable piece of solid modelling, an academic study from the life, rather devoid of charm, the legs and feet being especially clumsy and inelegant, but executed with a faithfulness and capacity unknown in England. Even his portraits, though the portraits of that time seem now all executed on one pattern, have a certain unidealized actuality which is felt when they are compared with his London-trained contemporaries, and also a firmer modelling and a solider, more opaque painting as compared with their transparent shadows and backgrounds. The end of Vanderlyn's life was unhappy, passed partly in Washington, where he painted an occasional portrait, and partly at Kingston.   He was convinced of his own ability and bitter against a world which would not recognize or employ it.   He was sensitive, he was poor, and he was distrusted as a sensualist from his paintings of the nude.   He died in 1852 in absolute want.

His former companion, Allston, had preceded him by nearly a dozen years, dying in 1843.   Vanderlyn was in Paris at the time, working on his panel for the Capitol, and wrote, " When I look back some five or six and thirty years since, when we were both in Rome together, and next-door neighbors on the Trinità del Monte, and in the spring of life, full of enthusiasm for our art, and fancying fair prospects awaiting us in after years, it is painful to reflect how far these hopes have been from being realized."   This is true enough in a way, for Allston failed more signally than Vanderlyn to produce works commensurate with his early promise, but his latter life is far from being so painful and bitter a story.   It is, in fact, a curious triumph of faith over works.   He was welcomed to Boston and America with enthusiasm, and for twenty-eight years held here an unchallenged supremacy as the head of American art, almost as the head of all art.   The personal charm of his youth remained undimin-ished in age and attracted to him the choicest spirits, the brightest talents, the purest enthusiasts, who worshipped at his shrine with a faith that knew no doubts; while for the great mass of the people he was a mighty unknown, who served to justify the claims that America was supreme in painting as in territory, liberty, and intelligence.

And this reputation was maintained in spite of the fact (or per-haps on account of it) that there were hardly any works produced to justify it.   He brought back with him from London the unfinished canvas of " Belshazzar's Feast," and that mysterious work might have served as the original for Balzac's *Chef-d'œuvre Inconnu.*   Its shadow hung over his whole life, taken up, put aside, recommenced, altered, arousing the highest hopes in his friends and the wildest praises from the ignorant.   It hangs to-day a battered wreck in the Boston Museum of Art, still unfinished, dingy, antiquated, showing to the casual observer no particle of true feeling or skill.   Pitiful wreck as it is, it might still awaken a sort of resentment in the friends of Allston, for after his temperament and surroundings it was the most potent influence in paralyzing all his efforts. He might perhaps have applied himself to the production of other work if his *magnum opus* were not always there as an obstacle and excuse. Immediately after his return he settled in Boston and remained there until 1830, when he married again and moved to Cambridgeport, where he had a large studio near his house. His second wife was a daughter of Chief Justice Dana, and fortunately had sufficient means to remove all danger of crushing poverty from his later years, though he often needed money, for Allston had more than a poet's ignorance and indifference in financial matters. He was not extravagant, his tastes were simple, but he would not occupy his mind with thoughts about money. When his mother's estate was settled, he accepted a sum much below the value of his share in order to have it paid at once, and then deposited in a bank, drawing what he needed until it was exhausted, with no effort to invest it so that it might earn a permanent income. There is no record that he despised or hated money or money making. It simply did not interest him. His ideas, his imaginations, his dreams, were too precious to be curtailed by the prosaic worries of real life, or rather his dreams were his real life.

During his later years he still painted. "The Prophet Jeremiah," "Saul and the Witch of Endor," "Spalatro's Vision of the Bloody Hand," and in a softer vein "Beatrice," "Rosalie," "The Spanish Girl," were done in America, yet on the whole he produced little. He himself never doubted of his industry, but there was always the "Belshazzar's Feast" to serve as an excuse for not working on other things, and when in 1836 he was offered by Congress a commission for one of the panels of the Capitol, with freedom to choose what subject he would, he wrote elaborately, giving many reasons for declining, but not the true one — that he had no longer the energy and ambition to attempt such a task.

But his life was happy. He was surrounded by friends who loved and admired him and who shielded him from any harsh contact with an uncongenial world. He went little into general society, but had his own circle to which visiting strangers who were found worthy were admitted and listened spellbound in the great studio until they left at one or two o'clock in the morning; even then their host protested that the evening had scarcely begun, for it was one of the habits of Allston's later life to sleep by day and to talk and read and work by night.

Talk leaves no permanent record, but they were not men to be easily mistaken, those admirers of Allston. From Coleridge, who said of him "that he was gifted with an artistic and poetic genius unsurpassed by any man of his age," to Lowell, who declared that he was to be classed at once " with those individuals, rarer than great captains and almost as rare as great poets, whom Nature sends into the world to fill the arduous office of Gentleman," he came in contact with the choicest minds of his time and made on them all the impression of something wonderful, of something quite beyond the dull average of humanity. It is inevitable that such rare spirits should fail to express themselves in enduring form. The materials, the carved stone or the painted canvas, are too recalcitrant, and besides it is but a small part of the message which is conceived in a form that may be expressed to the eye. Allston erred, as West did, in trying to put into a picture emotions that were not pictorial. His contemporaries had the same emotions and understood. We do not, and it is as unlikely in his case as in that of West that posterity will ever renew its interest in his works. They are, however, better than West's — not done with the same monotonous facility, but with traces of real distinction. The color is harmonious and pleasing; though all of Allston's color has faded, owing to his system of glazing, so that it has no longer the richness that surprised his Italian friends. The line is especially sensitive and sure. " Jeremiah dictating to the Scribe Baruch," even if a little empty, would still hold its own with most academic work ; but during his life the taste for such subjects had already begun to decline.

They were admired at the exhibition of his works held in 1839 after his death but rather perfunctorily. A more sincere enthusiasm was displayed toward the smaller canvases with graceful, sentimental figures or heads, which Allston himself had regarded as of little importance. To judge them fairly, we must remember how barren American art had been up to that time of anything approaching them in grace or refinement. Their sweetness was not insipid, their drawing was delicate, their color was refined. They were not strong, independent masterpieces, but there was in them the breath of a finer, more delicate inspiration than had appeared before in American art or than was to appear again for a generation. What the work and the life of Allston meant to those of his compatriots whose souls yearned for some touch of beauty and culture in their meagre and commonplace surrounding, we can hardly appreciate to-day. We get a glimpse of it, though, in a review in the *Dial* of the Allston exhibition, by Margaret Fuller. It is written in absolute ignorance of any technical standards, but is good, emotional criticism.

" The calm and meditative cast of these pictures, the ideal beauty that shone *through* rather than *in* them, and the harmony of coloring were as unlike anything else I saw as the *Vicar of Wakefield* to Cooper's novels. I seemed to recognize in painting that self-possessed elegance, that transparent depth, which I most admired in literature; I thought with delight that such a man had been able to grow up in our bustling, reasonable community, that he had kept his foot upon the ground, yet never lost sight of the rose-clouds of beauty floating above him. I saw too that he had not been troubled but had possessed his own soul with the blandest patience, and I hoped, I scarce knew what, probably the *mot d'enigme* for which we are all looking — How the poetical mind can live and work in peace and good faith! how it may unfold to its due perfection in an unpoetical society."

To-day the answer to the riddle seems to be that the mind could unfold to perfection, but it could not produce its perfect work in its uncongenial surroundings.

CHAPTER VIII

DECLINE OF THE ENGLISH INFLUENCE

PASSING OF THE STUDENTS OF WEST. — STUART'S OLD AGE. — KING. — WALDO AND JEWETT. — JOHN WESLEY JARVIS. — HIS YOUTH IN PHILADELPHIA. — BEGINS POR-TRAIT PAINTING IN NEW YORK. — SOUTHERN TRIPS. — WORK AND CHARACTER. — THOMAS SULLY. — YOUTH. — WORK WITH HIS BROTHER. — MARRIES HIS WIDOW. — VISITS STUART. — GOES TO LONDON. — STUDIES WITH KING UNDER WEST. — SET-TLES IN PHILADELPHIA. — CHARACTER AND WORK

THE venerable West died in 1820, five years after Copley. The group formed by Allston and his youthful admirers was among the last to receive his counsels, and practically the last Americans to go to England to learn the rudiments of painting. The loss of the personal aid and counsel of the ever helpful and generous President of the Royal Academy was undoubtedly a factor in the change, but also the outburst of artistic force in England was beginning to lose its first vigor and unity and to dissipate itself into divergent chan-nels. In some of these, as in landscape, the originality and talent displayed was not less admirable than in the earlier work; but por-traiture, figure painting, and most of the branches which appeal to the student showed a distinct falling away in both knowledge and feel-ing. The influence of the early school was perpetuated here both by those actually trained in it and by their imitators. Stuart died in 1828, and Charles W. Peale about the same time; but Rembrandt Peale, Charles B. King, and Waldo lived on to or through the begin-ning of the Civil War, and Morse died in 1872. Many of the men were diverted to other pursuits, or through discouragement relaxed the practice of painting; but Stuart labored to the last with a con-stantly increasing excellence. Age diminished the old restlessness, and he settled in Boston and lived there fairly contentedly. He was recognized as by far our best portrait painter, and never was entirely without sitters, though his independence and his old hot temper sometimes made his commissions fewer than men with less talent but more ingratiating manner got. His outbursts were known and

FIG. 30. — WALDO : PORTRAIT OF REV. DR. GARDINER SPRING, METROPOLITAN
MUSEUM.

dreaded. A loving husband kept complaining of the portrait of his excellent but plain wife, until the painter's patience gave way and he cried, " What a d—— business is this of a portrait painter — you bring him a potato, and expect he will paint you a peach." And when Sully was frightened at having accidentally trod on a canvas, he was told, " Oh! you needn't mind, it's only a d—— French barber," viz., — Jerome Bonaparte. He was besides kept busy denouncing the countless copyists of his portraits of Washington, who tried to pass off their works as originals. He retained, however, with his old temper, his old wit and ingratiating charm. With his huge snuff-box, his anecdotes, and his repartees, he was a character in Boston, and when he died, in 1828, he was properly mourned in the public press, and he left, if not much money, a memory which endured long after him.

Another of West's pupils, King, settled in Washington and painted portraits for forty years of all the political celebrities; a man of exemplary character and simple life, who left a handsome competence, bequeathing pictures and an endowment to the Redwood Library at Newport, his birthplace.

Waldo, a man of similar type, also stuck to his profession for over half a century after his return from England, practising mostly in New York, where there are still to be seen scores of heads by him, of dignified, benevolent gentlemen with white hair and white chokers, or of ladies in wonderful caps and shawls; the faces thinly but skilfully painted, with a suggestion of West's *technique*, but with more accuracy of drawing, as was fitting in a portrait painter. If the satin lapels of the gentlemen's coats or the leg-of-mutton sleeves of the ladies are finished with a laborious completeness, adorned with shining high lights, it is probable that the work will be signed by the firm name, Waldo and Jewett. Jewett was another Connecticut youth, who coming originally for instruction as an apprentice was kindly received and made a partner, and for many years the pair worked in unison, turning out work so quiet and unaggressive that when its really considerable technical merit is revealed on close examination it comes as a surprise.

One of the picturesque characters of the early years of the nineteenth century, almost the same age as Allston, and as well known though in a different way, was John Wesley Jarvis. Born in England in 1780, he was named after his uncle, the famous founder of Methodism, and lived with him as a child during his early years until he was five. A certain similarity may be traced in the temperaments of the two. Both were of exceptional ability, forcible, eloquent, with strong and generous feelings, and a power to hold and influence others; but the talents of the nephew were early diverted from the path of his saintly uncle. When he was five he joined his father, who had settled in Philadelphia, and unlike all the other painters of the time who attained to any eminence in America, he never returned to England or profited by foreign instruction. In fact, he had no regular training, but picked up the mysteries of the craft as he could, and his own description of his first efforts is amusing. " In my schoolboy days the painters of Philadelphia were Clark, a miniature painter, Galagher, a painter of portraits and signs; he was a German who, with his hat over one eye, was more *au fait* at walking Chestnut Street than at either face or sign painting. Then there was Jeremiah Paul, who painted better and would hop farther than any of them ; another who painted red lions and black bears, as well as beaux and belles, was old Mr. Pratt, and the last that I remember of that day was Rutter, an honest sign painter, who never pretended or aspired to paint the human face divine, except to hang on the outside of a house; these worthies, when work was plenty, flags and fire-buckets, engines and eagles in demand, used to work in partnership, and I, between school hours, worked for them all, delighted to have the command of a brush and a paint pot. Such was my introduction to the fine arts and their professors.

"About this time I first saw Stuart, who occasionally employed Paul to letter a book, for example the books in the portrait of Washington, which Jerry thought it no dishonor to execute; the two great men, however, quarrelled, and Paul threatened to slap Stuart's face, trusting, I presume, to being able to hop out of the way of his arm. Mr. Pratt was at this time, say 1790, an old man, and as he encouraged my visits, I frequently passed my out-of-school hours at his shop, making figures of what passed for men and things by dint of daubing on my part and imagination on the part of the beholder."

This gives a vivid picture of the state of the arts in Philadelphia at the end of the century. The omission of Peale's name is noticeable, but he was busy with his museum at the time and perhaps was inaccessible to Jarvis. Mr. Pratt is, of course, Matthew Pratt, spoken of before as West's first pupil, and Jarvis may have had from him some training in the English methods of work. When the time came to choose a trade, the prints in the shop windows seemed much more perfect to him than the paintings of his contemporaries, so he chose to become an engraver and was apprenticed to one Savage, " the most ignorant beast that ever imposed upon the public. He painted what he called fancy pieces and historical subjects, and they were published as being designed and engraved by him, though his painting was execrable and he knew nothing of engraving. He was not qualified to teach me any art but that of deception." The incapacity of the master was the advantage of the pupil, for it gave him greater opportunities. David Edwin, an English engraver, had come to America, and being in straitened circumstances was employed by Savage, and from him Jarvis learned to draw and engrave. The two moved together to New York, but there Edwin became better known, and no longer needing the aid of Savage returned to Philadelphia as an independent engraver, while Jarvis remained to the end of his apprenticeship and made, engraved, printed, and delivered to customers the works that were attributed to his master. When his time of service expired, to quote again from his own story: " I began to engrave on my own account; but Edwin visiting New York asked me to go and see a great portrait painter, not long since arrived, and full of employment — with of course his pockets full of money. I went to the painting room of Mr. Martin and found him overwhelmed with business. 'This,' said Edwin, 'is the best portrait painter in New York.' 'If that is the case,' said I, 'I will be the best portrait painter in New York to-morrow, for I can paint better than Mr. Martin.' And I have been at it ever since."

The foregoing quotations are from Dunlap, who knew Jarvis well up to the end of his life, and who had the details of his early years directly from him. They did not meet until 1805 or 1806, when Jarvis occupied rooms on Park Row with Joseph Wood, whom he was teaching to draw, and with whose aid and that of a profile machine which he had invented he used to draw silhouettes in black for a dollar and on gold-leaf for five. Malbone, happening to visit the painting room, was asked for some advice, and readily offered to instruct them both in miniature painting, to such effect that Wood, a farmer's boy who had been apprenticed to a silversmith, became a creditable miniaturist and practised successfully first in Philadelphia and afterward in Washington. Wood was something of a musician, and Jarvis already a noted *raconteur*. There was often a hundred dollars a day to be divided up as the receipts from the silhouette industry in addition to the painting, and life was merry on Park Row, but not, Dunlap says, "merry and wise." "The artists indulged in the excitements and experienced the perplexities of *mysterious marriages*, and it is probable that these perplexities kept them both poor, and confined them to the society of young men, instead of that respectable communion with ladies and the refined circles of the city, which Malbone enjoyed; and I have reason to think that these mysteries and perplexities caused the dissolution of the partnership of Jarvis and Wood on no friendly terms."

After the dissolution, Jarvis moved to Broadway, making a specialty of little heads on cardboard at five dollars apiece, though painting anything else that was called for. It was soon after this, in the autumn of 1807, that Sully being without work in New York offered himself to Jarvis as an assistant, and the latter, while employing him and paying him liberally, declared that it was a great shame that such a man should want work in an inferior position. The connection was only transitory, for Sully soon went to Philadelphia, and Jarvis remained to enjoy his popularity in New York, and when that showed signs of waning, proceeded to Baltimore, where his capabilities as an artist and a diner-out gave him a great success. This was the first of the visits to southern cities, which became a feature of his life. To Baltimore he went many times, but he kept continually pushing farther south. In 1810 he visited Charleston, South Carolina, and finally got as far as New Orleans, taking with him on the trip Henry Inman, who had been apprenticed to him in 1814 when fourteen years old.

FIG. 31. — JARVIS: HENRY CLAY, CITY HALL, NEW YORK.

While still making New York his headquarters, occupying at one time what had been the governor's mansion in Bowling Green, then used as a custom house, these southern trips continued regularly to employ his winters with great social and financial success. In New Orleans especially, he painted full-length portraits of Andrew Jackson and all the military and naval heroes, and was well paid. In his own words: " My purse and pockets were empty. I spent $3000 in six months and brought three thousand to New York. The next winter I did the same." At the prices current in those times (Jarvis charged $100 for a head and $150 for head and hands) this involved an enormous production. He had six sitters a day, worked an hour on each, and then handed the canvases over to Inman, who put in the background and draperies under his direction, thus enabling him to turn out six portraits a week. Inman left him and set up for himself when his seven years' apprenticeship was over; but Jarvis continued to work with much the same erratic energy until his continued excesses wrecked his vigorous constitution, and he died worn out in body and mind at the age of fifty-four.

Few can fail to regret the end of the brilliant life, for Jarvis was no man's enemy save his own. It is true he always abused Stuart and all his works, but too openly and energetically for real malice. Apart from that, throughout his life he was, in his erratic and spasmodic way, a kindly, sympathetic man. And this from his childhood, when he aided impulsively and efficiently another child who was lost, down to his latest years when during terrific epidemics of yellow fever or malignant cholera he frequented the hospitals with an Olympian indifference to danger, making pathological drawings for the doctors, and giving freely from his limited means.

As an artist his work suffers from his manner of life. He was not negligent in acquiring the *technique* of his profession, he drew from the antique, studied anatomy seriously, and especially became an enthusiast in phrenology, then a novelty; but his work shows the haste of production — not so much in lack of finish as in lack of inspiration. It is usually commonplace, without distinction of drawing or brilliancy of color. At times he rises above this, and he usually gets the character of his sitter; but his best is far from equalling Sully's. His continued success (and he had an abundance of commissions as long as he was in condition to execute them) was due as much to his social as to his artistic ability. His character was of the type termed convivial, as was also Stuart's; but Stuart's associates were on a higher plane, and he kept something of the dignity of an earlier day. He moved in the best society of Boston, and though his bills for port and madeira were larger than normal, yet Sully who knew him in his old age declares that he never saw him in the least affected by wine. Jarvis, on the other hand, remained the Bohemian, squandering money without thought of the future, eating and drinking of the rarest and costliest and living in squalor, without the comfort or decency which would have cost nothing except a little self-restraint. He was welcome everywhere, but somewhat as a licensed buffoon. His stories were innumerable, and related by himself to a dinner party well flushed with wine their success was enormous. Some were adapted to the stage by Dunlap, Hackett, and Matthews, and even when related in cold print they are amusing. There was something of the actor about Jarvis himself and much of the press-agent. He liked notoriety — *monstrari digito* — and he affected singularity in dress and demeanor. He wore a long, fur-trimmed coat, and a couple of huge dogs followed him, sometimes carrying his market basket. To his southern friends, when they passed through New York, he showed a lavish hospitality — banquets where all fluids were obtainable save water, where canvas-backs were eaten with broken handled knives and one-tined forks, and where the soap was thrown out of the shaving mug to furnish an extra glass. The result was inevitable: "he died in extreme poverty under the roof of his sister, Mrs. Childs."

The contrast to Jarvis is offered by Sully, who has been mentioned as serving him as an assistant for a few months in 1808. Like Jarvis, who was three years his senior, Sully was born in England and came to America while a child. His parents were actors of considerable reputation in the English provinces, and their children, of whom there were many, inherited talent. Thomas was the youngest son and nine years old when his parents were induced by Mr. West. the manager of the Virginia and Charleston, South

FIG. 32. — SULLY : DR. SAMUEL COATES, PENNSYLVANIA HOSPITAL, PHILADELPHIA.

Carolina, theatres, to remove to the latter city, and there in 1793 the young Sully met at school Charles Fraser, the future miniaturist and friend of Allston. The two boys mutually encouraged each other to scribble their copy-books full of drawings; Fraser, the elder by a year, being the leading spirit. This, however, only continued for a couple of years until 1795, when Sully, then twelve, was placed in an insurance broker's office, where after the manner of youthful artists of all times he neglected his work and spoiled much good paper with drawings of heads and figures until the broker finally advised that he should be devoted to art instead of business. This was easily arranged, for one of his sisters had married a French *emigré*, Mr. Belzons, who had been forced by the vicissitudes of the Revolution to leave France and to employ what he had merely cultivated as an accomplishment as a means of support; and though but an indifferent artist he managed to support his family by his miniature painting. With him Sully stayed until he was sixteen; but then Mr. Belzons, being of a hasty temper, flew into a passion over an imagined neglect, the two came to blows, and finally the boy took his hat and left the house. He suffered some hardship, but friends came to his aid and he was finally enabled to reach his brother Lawrence at Norfolk.

Lawrence Sully was but a poor painter and apparently attempted nothing more than miniatures. Thomas soon surpassed him in skill and became the main support of Lawrence's family, which consisted of a wife and numerous children, but he tired of water color. Fired with ambition by the sight of some portraits by Bembridge and one by Angelica Kauffman he attempted to paint in oil, though his ignorance of the method was so great that he mixed his colors with olive oil and was surprised when they did not dry. A sign painter gave him some knowledge of the rudiments of the craft and finally with great trepidation he visited Bembridge himself, who was good to the lad, showed him what he could, and painted his portrait, explaining his palette and the mixing of tints as he proceeded. Even this increase of knowledge was not enough to make the efforts of the artists profitable; the elder brother went back to Richmond, which promised more remunerative employment, and his family soon followed him. Thomas, left to himself, gained in a year one hundred and twenty dollars, which was enough to main-tain him in comfort. He rejoined his brother at Richmond, but feeling the need of wider knowledge he determined to visit Eng-land and started by a system of rigid economy to save sufficient money for the trip. He was on the way to success when his brother died, leaving his wife and children unprovided for and unprotected. The painter at once gave up his cherished plans, returned from Petersburg, where he was at the time, and undertook the support of his brother's family, and something over a year after-ward married his widow — a step that he never had cause to regret.

The first success of the young artist came through his friends of his father's profession. Thomas A. Cooper, a famous actor of the time, sat to Sully during a professional visit to Richmond and later, when he became the lessee and manager of the New York theatre, invited him to that city, secured him sitters, and opened to him a credit of a thousand dollars. This was greater prosperity than the artist had ever known, but he was conscious of his deficiencies and he paid Trumbull a hundred dollars for a portrait of his wife in order to learn what he could during its execution. He wished, however, to see Stuart, whom he rightly regarded as the first painter of the coun-try and for that purpose made a trip to Boston where he saw the master, who received him as kindly as Bembridge had done, per-mitted him to stand behind his chair while he painted, and finally arranged to have him paint a portrait and submit it for criticism. This was finally done, and after a long examination, which was an agony for the aspirant, he received the admonition : " Keep what you have got and get as much more as you can."

The oracle was dark but not entirely discouraging, and above all it was gratuitous, for Sully was still in need and could not afford many lessons at a hundred dollars. He had had few orders in Boston, and it was on his return to New York that he was obliged to apply to Jarvis for a position as assistant. From there he soon moved to Philadelphia, where he occupied a house with Benjamin Trott the miniaturist, a skilful and popular painter. But Sully was still in difficult circumstances. His family was large and increasing, his patronage fluctuating. He had been fully employed at fifty dollars a head; but business failing he got up a subscription for thirty heads at thirty dollars each, which tided him over the period of depression. He still nursed the desire to visit England. His friend Benjamin Wilcox finally opened a subscription at two hundred dollars for each signer, the amount raised to be given to Sully, and in return each subscriber was to receive a copy from an old master. Seven subscribed, thus raising fourteen hundred dollars, a sum entirely inadequate for the purpose. Wilcox opened his purse without restriction, and on him the artist finally drew for five hundred dollars, but even with this aid the trip would have been impossible without the most pinching economy. One thousand of the fourteen hundred he left with his family and with the rest started for London.

Fortunately the first letter he presented was to Charles B. King, who was a student of about his own age (two years younger), but who had been already four years in London and could appreciate Sully's inexperience. "How long do you intend staying in England?" "Three years if I can." "And how much money have you brought with you?" "Four hundred dollars." "Why, my good sir, that is not enough for three months — I'll tell you what — I am not ready to go home — my funds are almost expended, and before I saw you I had been contriving a plan to spin them out and give me more time. Can you live low?" "All I want is bread and water." "O, then you may live luxuriously, for we will add potatoes and milk to it. It will do, we will hire three rooms, they will serve us both — we will buy a stock of potatoes — take in bread and milk daily — keep our landlady in good humour, and (by-the-bye) conceal from her the motives of our mode of life by a little present now and then, and — work away like merry fellows." The arrangement was agreed upon and successfully carried out. The two young men were alike not only in their poverty but in their enthusiasm, their industry, and the simple integrity of their lives. King introduced Sully to West, who was to him "like a father," a phrase continually applied to West by his pupils, though the first of them, Matthew Pratt, being considerably the elder, was obliged to say "like a brother."

When it came to making the copies for which he had engaged himself, Sully found that the pictures in England were in private possession, difficult to see and impossible to work from. He managed to visit some of the collections, but it seemed that to fulfil his contract he would be obliged to go to France, where paintings were more accessible. But West when consulted said: "I understand that your object on your return is portrait painting?" "Yes, sir." "Then stay in England. You wish to fulfil an engagement and improve yourself by copying some pictures. My collection, old and new, is at your service. There are specimens of the ancient masters and of the moderns. Take them as you want them and come to me for my advice when you want it."

This is no more remarkable for readiness and capacity to help a student than for the soundness of the advice. England was still the place for a portrait painter to study, and it would have been a serious detriment to Sully to have gone to Paris for a short visit in an altogether different school. As it was he stayed in London nine months, painting by day, drawing by night, studying anatomy in the spare time until his funds were exhausted and he was obliged to return, although West wrote a letter urging that friends should furnish funds for a longer stay.

Back in Philadelphia with his family and sharing as before his house with Trott, he found the effects of his study in increasing orders and freedom from financial cares. He met Leslie now, and painted a head to show him how to work in oil, just before the talented boy left for London to join King, Morse, and Allston. He was painting some of his best work, and from these years date his portrait of Cooke as Richard the Third, now in the Philadelphia Academy and portraits of Dr. Rush and Dr. Coates in the Pennsylvania Hospital. For some years his receipts were over $4000, which was considered affluence in those days. He was paid $500 for a portrait of Decatur painted for the city of New York, which was desirous of commemorating the heroes of the War of 1812 then recently concluded. His delicacy prevented him from receiving more commissions of the series; for although he was asked to paint several others, the order for one of them had originally been given to Stuart, and through some misunderstanding with the sitter or the corporation, or through some eccentricity of the painter, work had been discontinued and Sully was unwilling to appear as casting a slight on a man who had benefited

FIG. 33.—SULLY: MRS. JOHN RIDGELY, OWNED BY MRS. JOHN RIDGELY, HAMPTON, MD.

him and whom he considered his superior as an artist. Finally, when urged further, he wrote to Stuart offering to secure the commission for him and to aid him in the execution of the backgrounds, draperies, and other accessories; but Stuart did not answer the letter, though some years afterward (when it was too late) he himself proposed a similar partnership to Sully, declaring: "We can carry all the continent." As it was, Jarvis, who had no scruples in regard to Stuart, got the commission.

Soon after this Sully's prosperity began to diminish. Sitters fell off a little, and the work which he commenced as a supplement to his portrait painting was not remunerative. A drawing to be done for an engraver from West's "Christ healing the Sick" was undertaken for $500, but when it had been proceeded with for some weeks it was seen that the price was inadequate for the work, and when an advance was refused, it had to be given up and the labor already expended was lost. Then the North Carolina legislature applied to him for two portraits of Washington, and his ambition suggested to him that he should propose to paint instead some prominent action of the hero, and he mentioned the crossing of the Delaware. This was agreed upon, but when he wrote asking for the dimensions of the space to be occupied, he received no answer and started a great canvas on his own responsibility, and the undertaking with all its infinite and unfamiliar difficulties of composition, models, and costume was a burden and expense to him; portrait painting fell off, money had to be borrowed to complete it, and finally he found that there was no place fitted for it and the labor of years was thrown on his hands. Again he was forced to pass difficult years without patronage, and in 1824 he was on the point of moving to Boston with his family in answer to invitations that had been given him; but then his townsmen stirred from their apathy and offered him commissions for portraits in order to retain him. The tide turned, and a modest prosperity set in.

Soon after he moved to a large, old-fashioned brick mansion on Sixth Street, just above Chestnut, which was built for him by Stephen Girard, with rooms suitable for painting and exhibition purposes, and which remained his home for more than forty years. Toward the end of his life, the city authorities abstained from tearing it down to make way for a proposed street, out of regard to the old painter, who was touched by the kindness. Only once did he leave it for long. That was when, in 1837, he made another visit to England for a couple of years, painting a number of portraits, and especially one of Queen Victoria on a commission from the St. George's Society of Philadelphia. The Queen, who was still very young, charmed both Sully and his daughter by her simple frankness and naturalness, and Miss Sully, who was about the same age, used to tell how when she (Miss Sully) was posing for her father, arrayed in all the regalia jewels, which weighed some forty pounds, the Queen came into the room and dropped a deep courtesy to the emblems of authority she wore, and afterward had tea with them, seeming to take a real pleasure in the simple manners of the painter.

Sully lived until 1872, and after this record of his life it seems unnecessary to say that he was a good man, courageous in adversity, helpful in prosperity. He was, moreover, a good painter, one of the best in America from the time he returned from his first visit to England until his death. He was not the equal of Stuart (he would himself have been the first to declare it), but, putting aside Stuart who is in a class by himself, it would be difficult to mention any superior. He was skilful in his handling, with a feeling for warm, mellow color and for beauty. This last sometimes degenerated into mere prettiness and "*chic*"; in fact, a looseness of drawing was his besetting fault, which was much remedied by his first trip to London, where West warned him against it, and Leslie also said, "Your pictures look as if you could blow them away." The effect of these admonitions was shown in the work that he did on his return, for nothing could be solider or firmer than the portraits of Dr. Rush and Dr. Coates; admirably posed and painted with a rich, solid impasto in the figures, they recall the more serious work of the school of Reynolds, which was already passing away. Those men had taken the solid craftsmanship of their predecessors and had built upon it a grace and charm of their own. Their successors left out much of the foundation, and for the charm depended largely on technical processes and tricks. Sully felt this influence, and stands to Stuart much as Lawrence stands to Reynolds. Some of his heads of actresses are but empty things, only fit to be reproduced in Lady's Books and Albums, a fate which befell them; but at his best he is a reflex of the good old time with its feeling for style and freedom from the prosaic rigidity of the newer men.

The portrait of Queen Victoria shows his skill in arrangement. He had to paint a short, dumpy young woman with retreating chin and protruding eyes, with no majesty, and not much comeliness except her youth. He has represented her as ascending the steps of the throne with a long cloak trailing behind her, which gives an appearance of height; the face nearly full, looking backward over her shoulder (the Queen had good shoulders). The warm brown of the shadows, the crimson of the carpet and robe, the gold of the embroidery and throne leading up to the white of the dress, the shoulders and the face, make a pleasing harmony. The whole is thinly painted with a flowing brush, the face a fair likeness but without any deep searchings for character. In short, an admirable official portrait. A half-length, possibly a study for the larger picture, but more probably a replica, now hangs in Hertford House, and holds its own well, even amidst the splendors of the Wallace collection.

CHAPTER IX

RISE OF A NATIVE SCHOOL

Social Conditions in America in the Early Part of the Nineteenth Century. — Development of the West. — Early Life of Chester Harding. — Success in London and Boston. — Francis Alexander. — Alvan Fisher. — John Neagle. — Henry Inman

THE period between the War of 1812 and the beginnings of the Rebellion was a time of profound social change in America. Its history is to the average man a blank. The Mexican War was too short and too one-sided to persist in the popular imagination after the more stirring times of the struggle against slavery, and apart from the Mexican War there were no picturesque incidents. It was a time of legal definition and interpretation of the new plan of government, of new, independent development of the land, of practical working out of certain theories of the relations of man to man enunciated with conviction in the Declaration of Independence, but never before put in actual practice.

The first manifest effect was a falling off in the dignity and graces of life among the political and intellectual leaders of the community. At the time of the Revolution there was a continuous line of cities along the Atlantic coast from Charleston to Boston, in constant communication with the mother country, and where the visitor of position from England or France was received, if with more modest surroundings, yet with a certain state and with no less dignity and courtesy than he had been accustomed to, and the people of importance whom he met were personally in touch with the circle which he had known at home. He talked with them as with his equals, and to the great leaders of the Revolution he looked up with respect and reverence. But the generation that succeeded Washington and Franklin, Jefferson and Hamilton, saw no statesmen that equalled them either in capacity or in culture. If an apologist for the later day should insist on the abilities of men like

FIG. 34. — HARDING: JOHN RANDOLPH OF ROANOKE, CORCORAN GALLERY, WASHINGTON.

Webster and Clay, it may be pointed out that those men, great as they were (and Webster was probably the equal mentally of any man the continent has seen), were yet provincial; their manners were pompous when they were not uncouth, their time was taken up with petty personal squabbles, they had no profound culture, their point of view was limited, and they could not see life sanely and see it whole with the high philosophy of their predecessors.

It may well be argued that the slavery question itself would have been settled justly and peacefully if it had been in the hands of statesmen with the calm, shrewd wisdom of Franklin and his circle, and also with their authority over the decisions of the community. But this last consideration brings up another prominent feature of the change, — the growth of democracy and the distrust of aristocratic tendencies. In colonial times, every city felt the influence of the English court, sometimes advantageously, sometimes not, but always very decidedly. Trade, navigation, boundaries of provinces, wars with the Indians, religious tolerance, all were regulated more or less by royal decree, and to carry out the royal will there came a continuous succession of commissioners and governors, soldiers and divines, who were supported or opposed by men of approximately their own rank and education among the colonists, and who thus formed a governing caste almost as much above the laborer as those in Europe. This could not endure. The theory of the equality of all free-born men was set forth in the Declaration of Independence, and the physical conditions of the time forced it into practice.

Immigration into the country diminished greatly at the beginning of the nineteenth century, but the colonists were a prolific race, and their ample families soon outgrew the narrow strip along the seacoast; they struck into the interior, into western New York and Pennsylvania, and beyond into the region back of the Alleghanies, where they found a soil more fertile than rocky New England, unlimited in quantity and unrestricted by any royal grants or special privileges. Each man took what land he could employ, and the vicissitudes and hardships of frontier life soon destroyed any pride of birth. Even on the coast the diminished social intercourse with the Old World, the fading away of the old ideals, the general turning to the material development of the country, and the pursuit of wealth had weakened the amenities of life; but in the settlements, in the backwoods of Ohio or Indiana, the last vestiges almost disappeared. The dwellings were isolated, the roads almost impassable, the struggle for existence severe, and though a few books had been brought out in the scanty baggage, and though itinerant preachers still did something for faith and morals, life was harsh and often squalid. Later, when towns and cities rose on the great rivers, they reflected the social life of the backwoods, and not of the East from which the settlers came. This was the time when the English travellers visited us and wrote books on our manners and customs, the memory whereof has hardly ceased to rankle to this day. And yet for the most part they told the truth, or as near it as they could get, in all sincerity: the uncouth manners, the narrow-mindedness, the shirt sleeves, the squalor, and the tobacco juice were all there. The tourists could not see all of the energy, the practical wisdom, the infinite kindliness and helpfulness, the high ideals, that lay beneath the surface. They recognized somewhat of this and gave praise, but it was not enough. The Westerner cared nothing for the coarseness of the environment in which he had been brought up, but he saw with the eye of a prophet the enormous future development of the country. It was inevitable, it could not fail to be, and he boasted with unabashed spread-eagleism of the greatest nation in all creation whose meanest citizen was a sovereign in his own right. It was largely this which stirred a vague hostility in our visitors, for it was the time of reaction against the ideas of the French Revolution, and that the state should in no way by special laws recognize religion nor protect the learned, the wealthy, and the well-born against the ignorant or vicious was believed to lead direct to atheism, anarchy, and the reign of terror.

This development of the West, it has been necessary to recall in order to explain the changing conditions of art, for the same democratic influence applied to the remoter parts of New England and later to the cities themselves. In spite of the increasing wealth and population of the country, most of the painters who succeeded Jarvis and Sully grew up in surroundings much harsher and averse to the muses than the early colonial society that West and Copley, Stuart and Allston, knew. There was no sharp dividing line. The older men trained by West or through his example worked side by side with their younger *confrères*, and even in some cases outlived them, but the spirit of the new generation was different. One of the best of them in his old age wrote out for his children the story of his life with a charming sincerity and humor, and the career described in his *Egistography* by Chester Harding is almost as curious as that of West.

Harding was born in Conway, Massachusetts, in 1792; but when he was fourteen his father moved with his family into Madison County in western New York, then an unbroken wilderness. The boy was of splendid physique, over six feet three in his stockings (when he wore any), and throve under the hardships of frontier life. His strength was prodigious, he was renowned as an axe-man and in all the labors of the pioneer. He even tried soldiering and marched as a drummer with the militia to the St. Lawrence in 1813; but getting no nearer to the enemy than the breadth of the river, his company inflicted no damage save upon the chicken coops of their country-men. Happening to fall behind on the march, he and a companion asked how they could regain the troops, and were told by an old woman to "follow the feathers." The soldiering would have been ludicrous were it not for the ravages of disease in the camp. Many perished of dysentery, and Harding almost died of the disease and of subsequent exposure.

When he came of age he attempted various pursuits, including chair-making, peddling, and keeping a tavern, which last got him so deeply into debt that to avoid his creditors, imprisonment for debt being still in force, he left his wife and child with his parents (for he was already married) and struck through the woods for the Allegheny River, down which he floated on a raft to Pittsburg. There he earned a little money as a house painter and went back for his family, returning with them to Pittsburg, where he set up as a sign painter and worked away for a time until the sight of some heads by an itinerant painter of the name of Nelson filled him with amazement. He engaged him to paint his wife and himself, though the ungenerous artist would not allow him to see how the painting was done or give him any information. Yet his ambition was aroused, and getting a board, with his sign painter's materials he attempted a portrait of his wife. "I made a thing that looked like her. The moment I saw the likeness I became frantic with delight: it was like the discovery of a new sense; I could think of nothing else." From that time sign painting became odious and was neglected. He painted ten or a dozen heads in which some likeness to the original could be seen and then started for Paris, Kentucky, where he boldly announced himself as a portrait painter, and where in six months he painted nearly a hundred heads at twenty-five dollars each. Being thus in funds he went to Philadelphia, where he drew industriously in the Academy and also saw some good pictures, which discouraged him mightily with his previous productions.

After two months of study he returned to Kentucky and finding no demands for art there wandered with his family to Cincinnati, Louisville, St. Louis, wherever business promised to be remunerative. He even made a trip of a hundred miles to paint a head of old Daniel Boone, then a man of ninety, still living the primitive life of the backwoodsman, surrounded by an enormous progeny, but hardly known by name or reputation to his immediate neighbors. Finally he returned to his parents in western New York and astonished his neighbors no more by the paying of his debts than by the art which enabled him to do so; and his aged grandfather felt obliged to call him aside and say: "Chester, I want to speak to you about your present mode of life. I think it very little better than swindling to charge forty dollars for one of those effigies. Now I want you to give up this course of living and settle down on a farm and become a respectable man." But Harding had gone too far to take this excellent advice. He had determined to go to England to study, and even had his trunk packed when his mother pointed out the precarious position in which he would leave his family should anything happen to him when abroad. Recognizing the justice of this, he promptly put off his trip, bought a farm, ordered a house built, and set off for Washington to raise money to pay for them. There he painted busily during the winter, and in the summer went to Pittsfield and Northampton, Massachusetts, where he was so successful that some gentlemen from Boston advised him to go to that city. He

FIG. 35.—HARDING: MRS. DANIEL WEBSTER, OWNED BY MRS. REGINALD
FOSTER, BOSTON.

went and "for six months rode triumphantly on the top wave of
fortune." He had much more work than he could do. "I do not
think that any artist in this country ever enjoyed more popularity
than I did; but popularity is often easily won, and as easily lost.
Mr. Stuart, the greatest portrait painter this country ever produced,
was at that time in his manhood's strength as a painter; yet he
was idle half the winter. He would ask of his friends, ' How
rages the Harding fever?'"

His popularity was unabated, but he was determined to go to
Europe. The farm was paid for and he had $1600 besides. He
stopped again to bring his family to Northampton instead of leaving
them on the farm, so that his children might not run wild and
deteriorate while he was mingling with a better class of society
and developing, and then sailed in the autumn of 1823.

He went to England to learn, but to learn not as a student but
as a practitioner, and he was successful beyond anything that could
be anticipated. It was largely owing to his personal charm and
the interest that he aroused. The huge backwoodsman when
he began to paint portraits was about as uneducated as it is possible
for a man to be. When a boy he had learned to spell out the
Bible with difficulty, and that was the only book that he knew until
in Pittsburg his wife brought to the house *The Children of the
Abbey*, the old romantic novel by Regina Roche. Harding had been
brought up to consider novel reading sinful, or at least unprofitable;
but when his wife read him a chapter, he demanded another, grew
interested in the plot, and finished by keeping her reading all night
until the volume was finished. His scruples against novel reading
disappeared, and he plunged unrestrained into the delights of Walter
Scott. His first book he could not read understandingly without
pronouncing the words aloud, and he confesses that even to the end
of his life he often caught himself whispering the words of a book
or newspaper. It was some time before he realized that it was considered more dignified to paint heads than houses, and the entrance
into polite society filled him with terrors unknown before. His
experience in Washington and Boston had given him more confidence, and in England he painted royal dukes and visited in the
country places of the nobility without too much uneasiness. For

he was really liked; his simplicity appealed to his hosts, and in later years N. P. Willis found his best introduction in England was as "the young friend of Harding, the artist."

His prospects were so bright that his family joined him in 1825; but a period of financial depression set in, and that together with a dislike to bringing up his family under the social conditions of England, where his profession enabled him to be received in circles in which his wife and children would not be recognized, caused him to return to America the next year. He never went abroad again, but passed the rest of his life in different cities of the United States as his profession called him, but his house and home were in Boston. He painted most of the political leaders of the country, — Webster, Clay, Calhoun, Marshall; and as Colonel Boone had been one of his first sitters, so General Sherman was his last.

Harding's career seems remarkable to-day, but it was in no way unique. Of his development we have a picturesque record, but many of his contemporaries went through similar experiences. Francis Alexander's youth, for instance, was much the same. Born in Windham County, Connecticut, in 1800, eight years after Harding, he worked on his father's farm in the summer and went to the district school in winter — as a pupil until he was eighteen and then for two years as a master, when, as he says, "I taught the small fry under my charge, the bad pronunciation and bad reading which I had imbibed from my old schoolmasters, and which I have found so difficult to unlearn since." The next summer he wore himself out so by his labors at haying and reaping that he was forced to rest and very wisely went fishing. The beauty of the pickerel and perch that he caught reminded him of a shilling box of water-colors, "such as children use," which had been left him by a boy. He produced a picture of the fish that filled all beholders, including himself, with amazement and delight. He had always drawn in school on his slate or on scraps of paper, but now he painted from nature, flowers, dead birds, and the like, and with such success that he determined to abandon farming for sign painting, which he thought would be more remunerative, and which was the highest form of art of which he had any conception.

He had heard from a book pedler of New York as the chief home of the arts, and went there to perfect himself. He finally was introduced to Alexander Robertson, the Secretary of the Academy of Fine Arts, and given some models to copy in pencil. Finally, on his insistence, he was permitted to copy in oil "two or three first lessons for girls, such as a mountain or lake, very simple"; but was told that he could not attempt heads or figures until he had been there some months. As a five or six weeks' stay had exhausted his funds, he returned to the farm and there decorated the white-washed walls of a room with rude landscapes filled with cattle, horses, sheep, hogs, hens, and chickens.

Again the beholders were amazed, but no one desired similar decorations or any form of landscape; so Alexander painted a head on a lid from an old chest. While in New York he had had access to the gallery over the schoolroom of the Academy, and now his only idea was to produce something which should be like the portraits he had seen there. The head was a success and aroused not only wonder but approval. He painted heads of two young nephews on pieces of board that were pronounced excellent likenesses. His "fame had now spread half a mile in one direction." The paying patron appeared and offered five dollars for a full-length portrait of a child; other orders followed until he had earned fifty or sixty dollars when he started again for New York, this time with the intention of learning portrait painting. Systematic instruction he could not obtain; but an old gentleman gave him Stuart's mode of setting the palette, and Trumbull and Waldo and Jewett treated him with kindness and gave him portraits to copy. When his funds were exhausted, he returned to Connecticut and travelled from town to town, getting eight dollars for a head until he reached Providence, where he was so successful that he stayed there over two years, raising his price to fifteen and finally to twenty-five dollars. Encouraged by this, he came to Boston and presented to Stuart a letter of introduction that Trumbull had given him, at the same time showing him a portrait of two sisters which he had brought with him. The old painter "said that they were very clever, that they reminded him of Gainsborough's pictures, that I lacked many things that might be acquired by practice and study, but that I had *that* which could not be acquired."

Stuart invited Alexander to settle in Boston as a portrait painter; which he did and was successful, raising his prices to forty, fifty and seventy-five dollars, and his vogue continued unabated until he sailed for Italy in 1831. There he visited most of the larger cities and spent two winters in Rome, part of the time with Thomas Cole, and after two years returned to Boston to continue his portrait painting at increased rates. In 1833, soon after his return, he, with Harding, Fisher, and Doughty, opened a joint exhibition of their works in Boston, which was extremely successful and which brought them reputation and some profit. They were all about the same age and of much the same type of character and upbringing. But the development of Alexander's personality was different from that of the others, and rather amusing. He was known at one time as the art jockey from the Yankee persistency and skill with which he obtained orders and advanced his fortunes. On Charles Dickens's first voyage to America, in 1842, while still out of sight of land, behind the pilot who boarded the ship appeared Alexander and begged the privilege of painting his portrait. Dickens, who had not as a rule much appreciation of the humor of such situations, was enough amused at his enterprise to consent, and sat for him in his studio, which was thronged with the *élite* of Boston, come to pay their respects to the great author. Later, however, after Alexander's trips abroad, the crudeness of his native land became unbearable to him. He settled in Italy and, though he planned to return, he finally died there in 1881.

Doughty was a landscapist and will be mentioned later as one of the founders of the American school. Alvan Fisher was mainly a portrait painter, though he worked in many departments. Like Harding and Alexander and many of his contemporaries, he was brought up where he could see no works of art of any degree of merit, and worked away as a clerk in a country store until he was over eighteen, decorating the margins of the account books until "they resembled the old illuminated manuscripts." Then he determined to be an artist, and, less fortunate than the others, was placed for two years with an excellent ornamental painter from whom he acquired a style of work which it took him many years to shake off. In 1814, when twenty-two, he began to paint the usual cheap portrait heads, but soon found a demand for rural scenes with cattle, portraits of animals, winter scenes and the like, and alternated these with his likenesses.

FIG. 36. — ALEXANDER: MRS. FLETCHER WEBSTER, BOSTON MUSEUM.

He travelled in Europe in 1825 and in Paris studied in a life-class and copied at the Louvre. After his return he became one of the Massachusetts group of painters working chiefly at portraits, though producing some pieces of *genre*.

These men formed what might be called the Boston group. Others of the same age and approximately the same skill belonged rather to Philadelphia or New York, though it cannot be too often repeated that portrait painting in America was still a vagrant trade, its practitioners wandering from city to city as they saw a chance of employment.

John Neagle should be credited to Philadelphia, though he was born in Boston (in 1799), his parents being there on a visit; but soon returning to the former city, the boy saw more of art than Harding or Alexander and began to paint earlier. Even at school he had for a friend Edward F. Petticolas, who was enough his senior to take the lead in their boyish drawing, and who received later some instruction from Sully in miniature painting, then began to paint portraits in oil, visited Europe several times, and finally settled in Richmond and there continued his work with moderate success. " There was a modest manner in the artist, and rather a want of boldness in his work," says Dunlap, who, nevertheless, speaks kindly of both. Neagle, when he got out of school, was apprenticed at the age of fourteen for five years and four months to a coach and ornamental painter, Thomas Wilson; but the coach painter had ambition and took lessons of Bass Otis, who from being a scythe-maker had become a portrait painter, and who was at one time in a sort of partnership with Jarvis. Neagle thus had access to Otis, and applied himself day and night, when not employed by his master, in drawing and painting " in his own way." The increasing skill of the apprentice was of value to his master, who arranged that he should have a couple of months' instruction from Otis, which was all the regular teaching that he ever had. But there were some good pictures to be seen in Philadelphia, and some good painters willing to advise, and his lot was very different from that of the backwoods aspirants. He was praised by Krimmel, a German who painted miniatures and gave drawing lessons, and whose picture of Centre Square with a crowd of figures in the costumes of the time is in the Philadelphia Academy.   He was a favorite with C. W. Peale, and Otis took him to see Sully, who was polite but formal, and who assured him that "the arts did not point the way to fortune and that, had he been a merchant with the same perseverance which had characterized his efforts in art, he might have realized a fortune."

When Neagle finished his apprenticeship in 1818, he was in his nineteenth year and had already painted portraits that were good likenesses and admired.   He thought that there might be a chance for him in some of the primitive towns farther west and travelled across the mountains to Lexington, Kentucky.   He asked at once if there was any portrait painter there, and was amazed to find that there were two.   The first one that he visited was Matthew Jouett, and he recognized him as a better artist than himself.   Jouett was a Kentuckian by birth, "a tasteful, humorous man," and a well-trained artist.   Just before this time he had been in Boston studying under Stuart, and he gained something of the style, not so much of Stuart, as of his English contemporaries.   He painted through all the country from Kentucky to the Gulf and was recognized as the best painter "west of the Mountains."   Born in 1783, he was an older man than Neagle, and the latter, feeling that it was useless to compete with him, continued on to New Orleans, finding no demand for his services anywhere and only succeeding with difficulty in raising enough money to pay his passage by ship back to Philadelphia.   If the journey seems long and useless, it may be worth while to recall that in those days it was easier though longer to go from Lexington to Philadelphia by way of New Orleans than by land.   Road travel over the mountains involved great hardship.

Back in Philadelphia, Neagle found the success denied him on his travels.   He was employed steadily, married a stepdaughter of Sully, and settled to the study and practice of his profession.   A portrait that he painted in 1826 of Pat Lyons, a blacksmith, established his fame and was exhibited not only in Philadelphia but also in New York.   Pat was a good deal of a character, skilled at his craft and had become rich by it.   One of the stories about him is that a man who had bought from him an iron chest with a complicated lock lost the key and sent for Pat, who with his tools readily picked the lock and raised the lid with one hand while he extended

FIG. 37.—NEAGLE: PAT LYONS THE BLACKSMITH, PENNSYLVANIA ACADEMY.

the other with a demand for ten dollars. This was refused, where-upon he promptly dropped the lid, and the spring lock held the treasure as securely as before. The owner was compelled to send for him again, but when the lid was up a second time Pat de-manded twenty dollars, which was paid without demur. Neagle went to Boston and there visited Stuart, had the advantage of his counsels, and painted the best portrait of him which exists, and also saw Allston, who complimented him on his work; but he lived mainly near or in Philadelphia and was known as a Philadel-phia painter. He was at one time a director in the Pennsylvania Academy of the Fine Arts.

These men whose lives have been outlined in this chapter were representative of the time and the best of its artists. From them others of similar type descended to all grades of inferiority. Whether the work of those set forth as leaders is to be considered good or bad depends on the standard of comparison. It has none of the grotesque incompetence of the early colonials nor the painful accuracy of the later ones. The great number of portraits turned out gave to the artists facility and boldness, while directly or indirectly they learned of the men trained under West how to set a palette and sound technical methods, but their work as a whole is deadly uninteresting. Its very competence condemns it. They did completely what they tried to do, and except occasionally there is no grace, no nobility, no decorative feeling or beauty of handling, but instead a petty insistence on every trivial detail. Neagle tried for a larger, more striking effect, owing probably to his relations with Sully, whose tendency was also in that direction. He forced up masses of white, like a waistcoat or shawl, against a dark shadow to obtain a striking effect somewhat in the style of Lawrence, but the effect is often unconvincing and flashy. Harding was more sincere. His heads are as solid as iron and his coats as uncompromising as tin, while his faces shine with bright lights touched into the eyes and on the forehead. Alexander shows the effect of his Italian study and long residence abroad in more grace and in a smoother handling and a softer, more pleasing color.

To these men should be added Inman, although he was not ex-clusively a portrait painter and belonged by his associations to a later development. Henry Inman (born in 1801) has already appeared as an apprentice of Jarvis, an experience which gave him a solid training in art and much picturesque experience of life, travelling with his master over the whole country from Boston to New Orleans. Later he used to recount with zest the incidents of this time. When his apprenticeship with Jarvis was out, he began painting on his own account, making New York his headquarters and entered into the artist life there. He joined the association of artists for drawing, and when this led to the founding of the Academy of Design, he was elected the first vice-president and retained the office until he removed to Philadelphia in 1832. There his success continued until his income in 1838 amounted to nearly $9000, but soon after the tide turned. His health, always delicate, began to fail; he made unfortunate investments; his work declined. He removed to New York and enjoyed again the society of his old friends; but lack of work, the cares of a large family, and repeated and severe attacks of asthma threw him into deep dejection. His friends helped him as they could, and finally James Lenox, Edward L. Carey, and Henry Reed induced him to visit England and portray Chalmers, Macaulay, and Wordsworth for them respectively, hoping that the change of air might benefit him. The expedient was a happy one. He thoroughly enjoyed the artistic circle to which his congenial disposition made him welcome. He was successful with his portraits except in a single case. He had received a commission to paint a Lord Codringham. The Lord Chancellor at the time was Cottenham, and Inman, getting the names confused, asked him for sittings. The astonished Lord Chancellor protested that he knew nothing of the gentleman who wished his likeness. " But he knows you," cried Inman, " and is a most prominent and respectable citizen," and such was his insistence and enthusiasm that Cottenham posed for him in full costume, wig, robe, and the rest. The portrait was one of Inman's best, and great was his disappointment when it was thrown on his hands in spite of the similarity of names.

He succeeded in pleasing his other sitters so well that inducements were offered him to settle in England; but his family and his precarious health obliged him to return to America, and a few months after he died of heart disease. One of the most touching incidents in the history of the Academy of Design is the meeting called to amend the constitution so that assistance could legally be given to the family of deceased members from the funds of the society. It was difficult to get a quorum together, and there had been several failures from that cause. Finally a desperate effort was made, Miss Hall, the only lady Academician at the time, was induced to come, although it seems to have been considered an extraordinary act, and yet one was lacking to a quorum. The meeting accordingly adjourned to Inman's sick room so that he, on his death-bed, made up the number necessary to pass the resolutions that kept his family from destitution.

Inman's portrait work was about in the same class with that of Harding, competent but commonplace, more likeness than character in the heads, and the door-mat painted with the same insistence upon all the facts as the face. His work was very unequal, but that applies to all the portrait painters of the time, and it is hard to give a short and accurate judgment on any of them. Their productions varied greatly according to the conditions under which they were produced, and while the worst are hopeless, all of the artists have at times, when favored by fortune and a congenial sitter, produced work which may still be seen with pleasure. Inman had a wider scope than the others; he painted miniatures, *genre* scenes, and also landscapes and excelled in all. But these branches of art are for a later chapter.

CHAPTER X

NEW YORK BECOMES THE ART CENTRE OF THE COUNTRY

New York takes the Lead in Wealth and Population. — The American Academy of Fine Arts. — The New York Drawing Association. — Trumbull's Character. — Founding of the National Academy of Design. — Early Struggles and Successes. — Decline of the American Academy. — Social Organization of the Artists. — The Sketch Club. — The Century Association. — Early Members of the Academy of Design. — Works displayed

THE men described in the previous chapter, with the exception of Inman, lived and worked but little in New York, yet it was during their lives that the development of New York City as the principal art centre of the country took place, — a development which was slow, but which is the principal fact in the history of American painting in the second quarter of the century. The city had taken the lead in population early in the nineteenth century, passing Philadelphia at a time when they each had a little over a hundred thousand inhabitants. But it was far from taking an equal importance in the intellectual life of the community. In material things it had ever held its own: men ate and drank, were clothed and housed as well there as in any of the other cities; but the things of the spirit were less served. As early as 1758 West had felt unpleasantly its busy commercialism as compared with the quiet, refined, and thoughtful society he had known in Philadelphia. During the Revolution it had been long occupied by the British, and both the city and state were much accused of lukewarmness, indifference, and Toryism, though when listening to the fervid eulogiums of other states uttered by favorite sons, it is permissible for the New Yorker to recall that during the Revolution his state honored every call upon it by Congress for both men and money.

At the close of the war the seat of the government was soon removed from New York City to Philadelphia, and later to Washington. It was not even a state capital, with politicians desiring

FIG. 38.—INMAN : MARTIN VAN BUREN, METROPOLITAN MUSEUM.

their likenesses handed down to posterity, and the artists that visited
it, after exhausting what custom they could get, usually went
elsewhere like Stuart, suffered like Vanderlyn, or simply made it
headquarters while scouring the country for commissions.   Nevertheless the harbor was the best on the coast and the merchants were
keen and enterprising.   The population more than doubled with
each twenty years, and the city swelled in wealth and importance.
Finally a movement was made in the direction of a recognition of
the arts, but later than in the other large cities.

Philadelphia, under the influence of Charles Wilson Peale, had
already its Academy of Fine Arts, which had been preceded by the
art school which he had founded with the aid of Ceracchi the sculptor, and where, for the want of a better model, he had posed himself.
This was in 1791, and though the school was discontinued, out of
it grew the Columbianum, under whose auspices was held, in 1795,
the first exhibition of paintings in Philadelphia.   The Columbianum
also failed after a few years, but the unwearied Peale still persisted
until, in 1805, the Pennsylvania Academy was founded, and the next
year chartered.   Peale's Museum, with its portraits and natural curiosities, was continued; his son Rembrandt had started a similar
museum in Baltimore; Newport had had, since 1750, the Redwood
Library, founded by Abraham Redwood and enriched by various
donations of pictures and books; Boston had Pine's Museum, where
Allston got some inspiration and the collection of portraits belonging to Harvard College; and if it was not until 1826 that the
Athenæum opened to artists a room with plaster casts and a few
portraits, there was already at the beginning of the century the
Columbian Museum, where was to be seen John Adams in wax,
with "on either side of him Liberty with staff and cap, and Justice
with sword and balance," and, in a lighter vein, "The New York
Beauty" and "The Boston Beauty."   This was probably not dissimilar from the Museum of Curiosities, which the Rev. Joseph
Stewart, forced to retire from the ministry by ill health, set up at
Hartford in 1800.

But New York had little or nothing at the beginning of the century.   It was not until two years later, in 1802, that the first step
was taken, and it was proposed to found an institution for the pro-

motion of art, under the title of " The New York Academy of Fine
Arts." Officers were elected, but the institution was not actually
incorporated until 1808. The charter fixed the name as the "American Academy of Arts," set the number of stockholders at one thousand, the price of the shares at twenty-five dollars, and limited the
income to five thousand dollars per annum. The officers elected
were the most prominent men in the city, with Robert R. Livingston for president, Trumbull for vice-president, and DeWitt Clinton
and David Hosack among the directors. Before the charter was
obtained Livingston, who was then minister to France, purchased
for the society a number of casts from the antique, and they were
shown in the winter of 1803–1804, at a hired building originally built
for a circus on Greenwich Street, near Morris. The exhibition did
not pay, and the casts were packed and stored until the charter was
granted, when they were shown in the upper part of a building on
Broadway, once intended as a residence for the President of the
United States, subsequently set apart for the governor's house, but
finally devoted to use as a custom-house. It was in this building
that Jarvis lived, about 1815, when Inman was with him as an
apprentice, and the casts were stored there at that time.

Soon after, DeWitt Clinton, who was now its president, made an
attempt to revive the Academy. The old almshouse, a long building
facing on Chambers Street, where the County Court-house now
stands, was vacant (Dunlap explains that the paupers had been
transferred to "a palace at Bellevue"), a part of it was appropriated
by the Corporation to the American Academy of Fine Arts, money
was borrowed to fit up the galleries, and an exhibition was held.
The display was a good one for the time, including the " Lear,"
" Ophelia," and " Orlando," by West, which were the property of
Fulton ; many of Trumbull's best pictures, some works presented
by Napoleon, and the full-length portrait of West, by Lawrence.

It was at this time that the building, "a plain range of brick
near the City Hall," was visited by John M. Duncan, an ingenuous
English traveller, who had a kindly word to say for most of the
occupying societies, including the Lyceum of Natural History and
the Historical Society, as well as the Academy, but who felt obliged
to declare that the wax works in " Scudder's Museum " upstairs were

" prodigies of Absurdity and bad taste."   He had previously visited Peale's Museum and the Academy in Philadelphia, in the latter of which he saw, besides Allston's " Dead Man Revived," a collection of old masters, including a Raphael, a Correggio, and three Titians, which disappeared during the succeeding more sceptical years.

The receipts at first from the New York Academy exhibition were far beyond expectation, and the institution seemed entering on a career of prosperity.   On October 23 of 1816, Governor Clinton delivered an address and resigned.   Shortly after that the by-laws were altered so that twenty Academicians were to be elected from the stockholders, the board of directors was to consist of five, of whom not more than three were to be Academicians, which board was later enlarged to eleven, though the number of Academicians in it remained the same.   In 1818 Trumbull was elected president, and the artist members among the directors were Archibald Robinson, Waldo, and Dunlap, who was also keeper and librarian.   The directors, misled by the results of the first exhibition, launched into large expenditures, the most serious being the purchase of a number of the president's pictures, including " The Woman taken in Adultery" and " Suffer Little Children," at $3500 each.   These he had completed a few years before in London and were in West's worst style. But the exhibition remaining the same with few new pictures, attendance fell off, there were no funds and no means of payment, and the pictures had to be returned to the artist.   An attempt to obtain subscriptions by solicitation was without permanent success, the stockholders became discouraged, and the daily attendance was not enough to pay the doorkeeper's salary.

There had been an attempt at the time of moving into the new rooms to open a school where students might draw from the antique, but the hours (from six to eight in the morning) were inconvenient, and the scheme soon fell through.   The whole Academy lapsed into torpor until 1824 or 1825, when the school was again reopened and the hours extended from six to nine.   There were students even at these hours, but the curator was an old Revolutionary soldier who had " crossed on the ice from New York to Staten Island " in the " memorable winter," and who in virtue of that fact was insolent and arbitrary even beyond the ordinary of the tribe of doorkeepers.

He opened the gallery when he saw fit, and finally one morning when
Trumbull came about eight Dunlap made an appeal to him in behalf
of a couple of students who had been excluded up to that time.   The
curator asserted that he would open the doors when it suited him.
The president sustained him, saying : " When I commenced to study
painting there were no casts in the country, I was obliged to do as
well as I could.   These young gentlemen should remember that the
gentlemen have gone to a great expense in importing casts, and that
they (the students) have no property in them," concluding with these
memorable words, in encouragement of the curator's conduct, " they
must remember that beggars are not to be choosers."

The incident is related by Dunlap, who may have strengthened the
case a little, but it agrees perfectly with Trumbull's character.   He was
at heart a kindly man enough.   He was deeply interested in art and
again and again aided beginners with counsel and money, but he had
an exaggerated idea of his birth and importance.   Insistent on having his own way and absurdly sensitive to any imaginary slights which
he resented with a pig-headed stubbornness or unreasoning invective,
his whole behavior was that of a spoiled child.   He threw up his
commission as colonel in a pet on account of an alleged error of
date ; afterward when he was a student in London and Reynolds
said of a picture he submitted to him " that coat is bad, sir, very bad.
It is not cloth — it is tin, bent tin," he admits, " the criticism was but
too true, but its severity wounded my pride.   I bowed and withdrew
and was cautious not again to expose my imperfect works to the criticism of Sir Joshua."   Jefferson had been his friend, had aided him
in every way, and received him repeatedly into his house in Paris ;
but he broke with him permanently because when one of his guests,
after the manner of the time, attacked religion, Jefferson nodded and
smiled, which seemed to Trumbull a personal attack or slight.   His
animosity even extended to inanimate nature, and surely no one else
before or since ever felt obliged to speak of " the filthy water of that
peculiarly stagnant, muddy lake," referring to Lake Champlain, the
camp on the shores of which was not to his mind.   These personal
peculiarities of Trumbull had far-reaching consequences and make
him appear as the malicious genius of the Academy of Design — its
one invincible, implacable foe.

FIG. 39.—INMAN: MUMBLE THE PEG, PENNSYLVANIA ACADEMY.

The two students who had been snubbed in this uncivil style were F. S. Agate, afterward a painter of some merit, and T. S. Cummings, also a painter but leaving a more permanent record as the annalist of the Academy of Design. Cummings was studying painting at the time with Inman, who took up his cause and consulted Morse, who became warmly interested, calling a meeting of artists at his rooms where the propriety of petitioning the directors was discussed and abandoned and the plan formed for a drawing school managed by the artists themselves. This was organized at another meeting held on Nov. 8, 1825, with Durand in the chair and Morse as secretary. The name was the New York Drawing Association, Morse was chosen to preside, and there were thirty members enrolled. Rooms were loaned them by the Historical and Philosophical Societies, which were, like the American Academy, quartered in the old almshouse, and work was begun at once. But the school had scarcely been running a month when a characteristic interruption occurred, thus described by Cummings: "On one of the drawing evenings in December, 1825, Colonel Trumbull, President, and Archibald Robinson, Secretary of the American Academy, entered the room in which the associated artists were drawing, and going directly to the President's seat, took possession of it, and looking authoritatively around, beckoned to the writer, who was in charge of the room, to go to him — producing the matriculation book of the American Academy, he requested that it should be signed by all, *as* students of that institution. That the writer, as one, declined, bowed to Mr. Trumbull and left him, and reported to the members. The Colonel waited some time, but receiving neither compliance nor attention, left in the same stately manner he had entered, remarking aloud, that he had left the book for our signatures, with the additional request that, when signed, it should be left with the secretary of the American Academy!"

The only result of this visit was a specific declaration of the independence of the Drawing Association from the American Academy, though the artists were still willing and even anxious to unite with the older institution. Conferences were held between delegates, and it was finally agreed that the Academy was to let six artists into their board of directors, and the insurgents were to return.   This was accepted by the younger men, six candidates were chosen, the American Academy was notified, and as only stockholders could be represented on the board and only two of the six were so qualified, shares of stock were bought by the other four and peace was expected to reign; but when the election was held six artists were indeed made directors, but only two from the list furnished by the Drawing Association.   These immediately resigned in wrath. War was openly declared.   " There was not only a breach of faith, — an injury inflicted by taking the money of the Association (which was never returned), — but at the time of the election the most con- temptuous expressions were used by members of the directory.   The artists were declared unnecessary to the institution, and one of the directors, whose name is spared, proclaimed that 'artists were unfit to manage an Academy' — 'that they were always *quarrelling*,' and concluded with the words, ' Colonel Trumbull says so.' "

Morse now took the lead of the opposition, and on his suggestion fifteen members of the Drawing Association were elected by the members, and these were to immediately elect ten more professional artists in or out of the Association, who were to constitute the National Academy of the Arts of Design, a title carefully selected on the ground that the " arts of design " were painting, sculpture, architecture, and engraving, while the " fine arts " also included poetry, music, landscape gardening, and the histrionic arts.

The fifteen Academicians thus elected by the Association were : —

S. F. B. Morse.	Peter Maverick (Engraver).
Henry Inman.	Ithiel Town (Architect).
A. B. Durand (Engraver).	Thomas S. Cummings.
John Frazee (Sculptor).	Edward Potter.
William Wall.	Charles C. Wright (Engraver).
Charles C. Ingham.	Mosely J. Danforth (Engraver).
William Dunlap.	Hugh Reinagle.

Gerlando Marsiglio.

These elected a second fifteen : —

Samuel Waldo.	John W. Paradise.
William Jewett.	Frederic S. Agate.

Rembrandt Peale.	John Evers.
James Coyle.	Martin E. Thompson (Architect).
Nathaniel Rogers.	Thomas Cole.
J. Parisen.	John Vanderlyn.
William Main (Engraver).	Alexander Anderson (Engraver).

D. W. Wilson.

The first fifteen all consented to serve; from the second fifteen there were no formal acceptances and some altogether declined, among whom was Vanderlyn, who published a bitter letter against the presumption of the new Academy in publishing his name without his consent.

As soon as the organization was effected, Morse published an address to the public, and a committee was appointed to arrange for an exhibition in the spring, which eventually took place in " a room on the second story of a house on the southwest corner of Broadway and Reade Street — an ordinary dwelling, and not covering an area of more than twenty-five by fifty feet, with no other than the usual side windows." The display was preceded by a reception, where the Academicians with white rosettes in their buttonholes received the invited guests: — " His Excellency Governor Clinton and suite, his Honor the Mayor, the Common Council of the City ('then a respectable body,' adds Cummings), the Judges of the Courts, the Faculty of Columbia College, the members of the American Academy of Fine Arts, and the persons of distinction at present residing in the city." The next day, May 14, the display was opened to the public. It consisted of "copies, originals — Oil Paintings and Water Colors, Drawings for Machinery, Architecturals, Engravings, — etc. etc., to the unprecedented number of one hundred and seventy productions." Morse and Dunlap wrote appeals to the public in the catalogue; the rooms were opened in the evening and lighted by six gas jets. But the exhibition closed with a deficit which the Academicians taxed themselves to pay.

And it was not financial trouble alone that the new Academy had to face. There was a strong social feeling against them fostered by the eminently respectable, conservative gentlemen connected with the rival institution. There were attacks and defences, threshed

o

out in long articles in the *North American Review* and in letters to the daily press. Morse was the chief spokesman for the National Academy of Design, fighting in the open over his own signature, and he shows to advantage, keeping his temper, which others did not, and using argument rather than invective. The squabbles which caused it to be formed and the principle of artistic management upon which it rested were gone over with much recrimination, insult, and charges of bad faith, and in the end no one was convinced. During the fight the National Academy had continued its drawing schools, with lectures on anatomy and perspective, held its second exhibition of works of living artists only (which paid expenses), became incorporated, and voted that thereafter "none but original works shall be exhibited," and finally, May 5, 1828, held its third exhibition preceded by a private reception, with a committee in attendance to receive the company, and a collation on the table during the whole day and a carpet on the floor during the whole exhibition.

The new society had established itself and as it gained strength the old American Academy fell behind, its schools were closed, its exhibitions small and poorly attended, and the friends of the National Academy ceased to be apologetic and became aggressive. Shortly after the opening of the exhibition a series of letters appeared in the *Evening Post* signed "Denon," and comparing the two institutions decidedly to the disadvantage of the older one. The letters were ascribed to Morse, though he did not write them, and drew out bitter answers and finally a personal attack from Trumbull, which was answered by Morse. More joined in until everything had been said that it was possible to say and the discussion died away and was not renewed, although it left a train of animosities behind it.

There were other efforts made to unite the two Academies, the most important in 1833 when conference committees were appointed, and a joint report agreed to by them, so that it was supposed that the matter was settled; but at the critical moment when it was to have been laid before the directors of the American Academy, Trumbull arose, drew from his pocket a paper, which he proceeded to read, praising the nobility and liberality of the founders and inveighing against union with any other institution. His paper

FIG. 40. — INGHAM : FLOWER GIRL, METROPOLITAN MUSEUM.

was ordered printed and his views were followed, the report of the committee not even being presented.   Trumbull's action was said to have been due to the fact that he had ascertained that he was not to be elected president of the consolidated Academy.   There were some sporadic attempts made later, but nothing was done and the fine old conservative American Academy slowly sank into a moribund state until in 1841 its remaining property was sold for debt, and it ceased to exist even as a name, the National Academy profiting by its fall to purchase its collection of casts, which same casts, originally purchased by Livingston, were used in its schools until they were almost all destroyed by fire in 1905, a little over a century after their arrival in the country.

In the meanwhile the National Academy continued, with some difficult periods and some falling off of the youthful energy that had started it, but with a steady advance that made it on the whole the most important influence in American painting until well after the Civil War.   It was an influence not only artistic but social.   It brought the artists together in an organized body, and from their personal intercourse came a vaguer, less formal, but more potent influence.   Most of the early Academicians were men of exceptionally high, pure character, and their friends represented the best culture of the time.   The list of honorary lay members was a roll of honor.   When with time the painters outgrew the reproach of youth which fell so heavily upon them at first, the artists exercised an indirect power in New York, not to be compared with that of their *confrères* in France or Germany, but greater than in any other American city.   This influence was felt from the beginning.   Whether all of those set down on the notable list of dignitaries invited to the opening reception of the National Academy attended, is doubtful. The members of the American Academy, for instance, would be apt to find the surroundings uncongenial ; but it was an attempt (possibly the first made in the country) to give the followers of the fine arts a standing not only as individuals, but as a body.

Soon after a further effort was made to unite artists, authors, men of science, and lovers of art by congenial intercourse among themselves, and the Sketch Club was founded, "the *old* Sketch Club," so called to distinguish it from later organizations of like nature.   It had its rise in the second year of the Academy, when the professors of the school — Morse, Durand, Cummings, and Ingham — were regretting the demise of a previous club, the "Lunch." Ingham suggested a new society. But as a rivalry in expenditure had been fatal to the "Lunch," which had met at a hotel to be entertained by the host of the evening, it was determined to make the Sketch Club as inexpensive as possible; meetings were to be held in rotation at the homes of the members, and as they proposed to fleet the time carelessly as they did in the golden world, so the refreshments were limited to blameless and inexpensive food — dried fruits, crackers, milk and honey, and the like.

The first meeting was held at Thomas Cole's, and the diet of figs, and milk and honey was entered upon with enthusiasm, but after comparing experiences the next morning the diet of the golden age was somewhat amended out of respect for the weaknesses of the modern man. The club, however, still maintained its simplicity, in spite of repeated attempts to introduce luxurious living, and a tendency of the milk and honey to develop into oysters and champagne. It long remained an honored and envied organization. The meetings at the members' homes and the rule that a single blackball excluded kept the membership down and rendered it almost impregnable to new aspirants, and about a score of years after its foundation the members added more to their number, rented permanent rooms, and founded the "Century Association," though the Sketch Club still continued its existence as a separate body.

This, however, is of 1847; in 1826, when the National Academy began, the members were a weaker body. Of the original members some were fairly established in their profession, and some, like Morse, Dunlap, and Waldo, belonged to the earlier generation that studied in England with West, but most of them were younger men. Prominent among them was Henry Inman, whose career has been given among the Philadelphia artists. He had encouraged Cummings, who was his pupil, in his revolt against the American Academy and was influential in forming the "New York Drawing Association," and when this led to the founding of the Academy of Design, he was elected the first vice-president, and retained the office until he removed to Philadelphia in 1832.

Almost equally active and prominent with Inman in the beginnings of the new Academy was Charles Cromwell Ingham, who lived to be one of its leading members. He was born in Dublin, Ireland, in 1796, but was as may be conjectured from his middle name of English stock. He was precocious, drawing from his earliest childhood, and his taste was encouraged by his family, who saw that he had the best instruction available from the time he was thirteen. At eighteen he received a premium for a composition in oil of the "Death of Cleopatra," which Dunlap pronounces "a wonderful specimen of skill, considered as the production of a boy." When two years later he came to New York with his father's family, he brought the picture with him and it was shown at the first exhibition of the old Academy and much admired. Although only twenty years old and looking scarcely sixteen, he established himself as a portrait painter and continued a successful practitioner until his death in 1863.

Ingham's painting was of a style little known in America, neat, laborious, elaborate, every detail minutely drawn and finished by successive glazings. The result of such labor is apt to be hard and shiny, but the high finish made him popular as a ladies' portrait painter, and the careful *technique* gave a wonderful purity and brilliancy to his coloring. He could draw flowers, for instance, with the painstaking accuracy of the Dutch still-life painters of the seventeenth century; and if he lacked their strength and fine decorative feeling for line and composition, yet his color surpasses them in brightness and richness, and has endured without the slightest alteration.

Another Dublin man was William G. Wall, who, born in 1792, came to New York in 1818, and though of no particular importance as an artist still had some reputation for his views of the Hudson and other American landscapes, done mostly in water-color and with much facility. G. Marsiglia was also a foreigner who came from Italy in 1817, and whose coloring had something of the crudeness of the Italian school of the time.

The American-born were further represented by Agate, a promising young pupil of Morse who went to Italy in 1835 and studied there, but who died before he had reached full maturity; by John

Paradise, an older man, much esteemed among the Methodists, to which sect he belonged and whose paintings furnished the subjects for the engravings in the *Methodist Magazine;* and by Huge Reinagle, a scene and landscape painter who died in New Orleans of cholera in 1834.

Most of these men exhibited with fair regularity in the annual exhibitions. In fact, a law was soon passed by which an Academician who failed for two years to show work became an honorary member and lost his active right to vote. In the first exhibition, besides members, Jarvis, Allston, and even Trumbull were represented, presumably by pictures borrowed from their owners without the painters' consent. So in later years, Gilbert Stuart, G. S. Newton, and Leslie, also Chester Harding, Alexander, and others appeared; but the bulk of the exhibition was furnished by men living in or near New York. Morse was an important exhibitor, Dunlap apparently turned out all of his old as well as his new work, and Cummings, Agate, Marsiglia, Ingham, Inman, sent eight, ten, even eighteen canvases at a time. At first portraiture largely predominated, in fact of the pictures painted in America before this time very few except portraits have been preserved. We know that while both the demands of their patrons and the difficulties of doing other work tended to confine the artists to that branch, yet from the earliest times they painted many other things. Tempted thereto by engravings or remnants of Old World tradition or training, many essayed the grand style, — religious, allegoric, or historic. Familiar *genre* was also tried, and landscape and sign painters sometimes made still-life studies to be hung on the inside instead of the outside of houses; but the demand was uncertain, the itinerant craftsman, if fortunate, got orders for portraits but rarely for anything else, and the piety of descendants which preserved the likenesses of their forebears had no interest in retaining other uncouth canvases of like date after they had once lost their freshness. Occasionally one appears in some old house or on the dusty walls of a local " Historical Society," more undoubtedly lie forgotten in old garrets, but even if brought forth they would gratify little save an archæological curiosity. Nor did " the grand style " ever resume its sway. There was some demand for huge canvases like Rembrandt Peale's

"Court of Death," and Dunlap painted a "Christ Rejected" in 1822, the "Bearing of the Cross" in 1824, "Death on the Pale Horse," from an outline engraving of West's work, a "Calvary" in 1828, and exhibited them in halls and schoolhouses throughout the country; but his success was not great. The public taste was still for portraits; Inman blazed away to a questioner, "I tell you, sir, the business of a few generations of artists in this country as in all others is to prepare the way for their successors — for the time will come when the rage for portraits in America will give way to a purer taste."

The change which came was perhaps not to a "purer taste," but the growth of a large merchant class in the cities, with no high ideals or feeling for art, yet well housed and comfortably rich, created a demand for small pictures, familiar *genre*, costume pieces, still-life and the like, and the annual exhibitions of the Academy gave an opportunity for their display and sale; moreover, this showing of their works together, and the intercourse of the artists, tended to raise the execution to a certain respectable degree of skill. From these conditions there arose a new class of painting, trivial and rather crude, democratic as the old colonial work had been aristocratic, yet with all its faults adapted to the taste of the country.

CHAPTER XI

FIGURE PAINTING IN NEW YORK IN THE MIDDLE OF THE NINETEENTH CENTURY

CHARACTER OF LIFE AND TASTE IN NEW YORK. — GEORGE W. FLAGG. — JARED B.
FLAGG. — W. S. MOUNT. — R. CATON WOODVILLE. — THE ART UNION, ITS RISE
AND FALL. — LUMAN REED. — INTRODUCTION OF FOREIGN WORK. — SPREAD OF TASTE
FOR PICTURES. — TUCKERMAN'S "BOOK OF THE ARTISTS"

THE English influence founded on colonial ties and on the splendid
short-lived outbursts of English portrait painting was fading out.
The students of West were dead or growing old, and the younger
ones among them had wandered more or less from London to Paris
and Rome. A new period of development in American art was
beginning — a period in general of less lofty aims, owing less to foreign tradition and training, more native in feeling and justifying in a
way its modest character by the increased public to which it could
appeal. Of this movement New York was the centre. Other cities
still continued to have their painters, notably Boston, which has
always had an important local school from Pelham's time down to
to-day; Philadelphia, Baltimore, Charleston, all had their practitioners,
but their influence was not widespread. It was to New York that
the rising artist came; it was from New York that artistic influence
went out, and this rather in spite of the spirit of the place than on
account of it. As has been said at the beginning of the last chapter,
it was from purely commercial reasons that New York took her position as the undisputed metropolis of the Western world. She had no
political importance, she was the centre of no intellectual or religious
movement, but she had a good climate, the best harbor on the coast,
and the easiest access to the interior. Her leading citizens were
merchants and successful ones, and with wealth and population there
came in time a leadership for which she had never consciously
striven.

When in 1830 Mrs. Trollope reached New York after contemplating the *Domestic Manners of the Americans* in the South and West, she gave it unstinted praise, declaring it one of the finest cities she ever saw and much superior to any other in the Union, Philadelphia not excepted.   But while she visited and admired the collections in the Academy in the latter town, and even has a good word to say for Rembrandt Peale's Museum in Baltimore, and a picture of "Hagar and Ishmael" by Chapman at Alexandria, she found nothing to admire in all the exhibitions of New York except the pictures

FIG. 41. — MOUNT: THE GOOSE RAFFLE, METROPOLITAN MUSEUM.

by Colonel Trumbull; and when, about the same date, Fenimore Cooper, writing in the guise of an intelligent foreigner, explained the domestic economy of the New Yorker and described typical interiors with the minutest detail, omitting not even the fire irons nor the window curtains, there was no mention of a picture anywhere.

The fact is that during this time there prevailed in trade the "hungry philosophy" of *Poor Richard's Almanac ;* economy was the basis of wealth, a penny saved was a penny earned, and while the rigor of the rule was relaxed for the material comforts of life, a man who fooled away his money on such things as pictures was looked at askance by his business associates and his credit and capacity doubted. Moreover, there was little knowledge. Few even of the wealthy had any experience of art except as something of which they read in books. Mrs. Trollope, after declaring that "the Medici of the Republic must exert themselves before they can become even respectable," goes on to say: "The worst of the business is that with the exception of about half a dozen individuals the good citizens are more than contented, they are delighted. The newspaper lungs of the Republic breathe forth praise and triumph, nay, almost pant with ecstasy in speaking of their native *chef d'œuvres*. I should hardly be believed were I to relate the instances which fell in my way, of the utter ignorance respecting pictures to be found among persons of the *first standing* in society. Often when a liberal spirit exists and a wish to patronize the fine arts is expressed, it is joined to a profundity of ignorance on the subject almost inconceivable," and elsewhere the good lady records her indignation at fellow-travellers who insisted that Chester Harding was a better painter than Sir Thomas Lawrence.

This was the public to which the National Academicians had to cater; but they had the advantage of being in sympathy with it and on much the same plane of culture. It is surprising that they did so well. Portraiture, of course, in all its phases, from miniatures and silhouettes to life-sized full-lengths, was a standard article and nearly all turned their hand to that as occasion offered; but apart from portraiture the chief demand was for small pictures. For religious painting in the old ample sense there was no opportunity, but a certain type of Bible illustration and pietistic allegory flourished. Sentimental figures and heads of orphan girls and Italian boys were furnished by men like George W. Flagg and his younger brother Jared B. They were nephews of Allston, had received his counsels, and strove to reproduce in historical scenes and single figures the mild sentiment and grace of his smaller canvases, with enough skill and feeling to give them success during their lives, but not to interest posterity.

A robuster type of figure piece was produced by W. S. Mount, the youngest of three brothers, Long Island farmer boys, who all practised art, entering through the humble door of sign painting. The others devoted themselves mostly to portraits with some success ; but the youngest, who began in New York with a scriptural composition of the " Daughter of Jairus " and portraits of children, was forced from the city by ill health and is now known for his series of pictures of the everyday farm life that he saw about his home. These are of astonishing merit and have hardly been surpassed since. Allston, who saw some of them, advised him to study Ostade and Jan Steen, though how he was to do so except through engravings is not clear ; but whether he followed the advice or not it is the Dutch naturalists that his work suggests. He saw the farmers, field-hands, tavern-keepers of Long Island, he understood and enjoyed their life and painted it in its uncouth simplicity. He had no such *technique* as his great prototypes, but he painted better than almost any one else about him. His figures are well drawn and well constructed, and hold their places in their respective planes. The faces are well characterized without exaggeration, and the attitudes of the little dancing, fiddling, or fighting figures are natural and original.

The only one of Mount's contemporaries who can compare with him is R. Caton Woodville, who was his junior by some ten years. But Woodville's art was no such distinctively native product as Mount's. He was born in Baltimore about 1820, of good family, a graduate of St. Mary's College, and had access to the pictures of Robert Gilmore, then one of the best collections in the country. His first efforts had hardly been favorably received when he left for Düsseldorf to study, and from that time until his premature death in London, in 1855, he spent most of his time abroad, though making two short visits to his native land from which also he drew the subjects of most of his paintings. Educated thus, Woodville's workmanship was practically that of the Düsseldorf school and need fear no comparison with the best of it. It was without weaknesses, the composition, drawing, and color all being thoroughly competent. In color especially he is often stronger and purer than his German contemporaries and much better than Mount, who was no colorist in the strict sense, though his pictures often have a pleasant brown tone. But Mount's pictures have the charm of real groups sympathetically

rendered; they carry the conviction of the thing seen, whereas Woodville's compositions seem to have been worked up mentally with
constant reference to their story-telling effect.

Few of the other painters of the life of the time were above
mediocrity. Bingham produced rustic scenes in the style of Mount,
and his "Jolly Flat Boat Men," engraved by the Art Union, may
still be found hanging in old tavern barrooms; but his skill was
not great, and the same may be said of the humorous *genre* of John

FIG. 42. — MOUNT: MUSIC HATH CHARMS, CENTURY ASSOCIATION.

W. Edmunds, who added the practice of art to his duties as bank
cashier.

Contemporary with these men, and in fact preceding them somewhat, were the early painters of American landscape; but while the
early figure men are in a way in a class by themselves, and Mount,
for instance, had no successor, the landscape school has had a steady,
unbroken development from its first beginnings down to the present,
and its most notable successes were in the latter half of the cen-

tury. Before this, in the forties, just as the National Academy of
Design was affirming itself, special influences were brought to bear
on art. The first was purely material, but important — the founding
of the Art Union. This was begun in 1838 and first called the
Apollo Association, the meetings and exhibitions being held in
the Apollo Gallery. It was modelled after similar societies abroad,
and the principle was, in brief, to collect five dollars from each member, to expend the money on works of art likely to please the popular
taste, and after holding an exhibition to distribute them among
the members by lot. The scheme was a success from the start.
The Union was energetic and efficient. It had engravings and
medals made for its subscribers, it published a paper, the *Bulletin*,
which was well written, and contained some sound criticism on the
art of the day. Its exhibitions were so successful that the Academy
of Design, which was at first inclined to look on it favorably, discovered that it was a dangerous rival. It distributed annually from
five hundred to a thousand works of art. Its subscriptions increased
to a hundred thousand dollars a year, and then it was discovered
that the scheme violated the statute against lotteries, and after a
dozen years' existence it was dissolved in the moment of its greatest
prosperity. How much more widely it would have developed it is
impossible to say ; but it had already accomplished an important
work when the law cut short its career. It had popularized art, as
nothing else could have done, by its appeal to the gambling instinct.
The fee was but small and included as certainties free entrance to
the exhibitions, a subscription to the *Bulletin*, and a copy of a pretty
good engraving. All sorts of people subscribed, who would never
have considered the outright purchase of a painting — business firms,
literary societies, and even the volunteer fire companies ; but when
the possessor of a lucky number hung on the wall the canvas that he
had won, it became to him a source of pride and pleasure. It must
be said, too, that the Union catered wisely to the popular taste.
The list of their purchases and the prices may still be read in the
Bulletin, and few artists of the day were unrepresented. It was
particularly serviceable as the patron of rising talent, though the
prices given were not large.

When the Art Union no longer existed, its former patrons turned to the Academy of Design or to the artists themselves to gratify their new-found taste. Even before its time one patron of American art had appeared, Luman Reed, whose name is never mentioned in the annals of the time without respect and admiration. He was a merchant, rich, but not exceptionally so even as riches were rated in the thirties; but he loved art and the society of the artists. Inman, Mount, Morse, Durand, Cole, Flagg, and many others were aided by him. He not only bought their works at liberal prices, often higher than was asked, but he cultivated their friendship, and helped them in their troubles. His paintings were displayed in a gallery in his house in Greenwich Street, and after his death in 1836 it was endeavored to continue the collection as the New York Gallery of Fine Arts, but the receipts from admission were less than the cost of maintenance, so the pictures were finally deposited with the New York Historical Society, in whose galleries they still remain.

Luman Reed's younger partner, Jonathan Sturges, was also a patron of American art until his death in 1874, but as a rule there were no such important individual collectors. There was, however, from many sources, a steady demand for pictures not only native but also foreign, and it is from this time that New York commenced to be a market for European work. There had been already some sporadic dealing, mostly in " old masters." In 1839 the Abraham collection was brought over, later came that of Cardinal Fesch; while for a score of years "old Paff" had a shop under the Astor House, where he dealt in darkened, damaged canvases by Titian, Correggio, and Raphael. He was a grotesque old man, of whose amazing enthusiasm and ignorance many stories are told. We laugh now at the sort of canvases that were offered to the early collectors and at the critical insight that accepted them as genuine; but some good pictures drifted over from the revolutions and unrest of the early part of the century, and there were some collectors capable of judging of them, as many of the canvases buried in the galleries of the New York Historical Society (and haply to be resurrected when the new building is completed) can testify.

It was later, however, that the modern foreign invasion began. Just before the Art Union was dissolved, Goupil, Vibert & Company of Paris established a branch in New York, mainly for the sale of prints, but also of oil paintings; and an International Art Union was started which the native one fiercely combated until the law put a stop to both. About the same time the Düsseldorf Gallery took up its quarters on Broadway, and was for a while an important item in

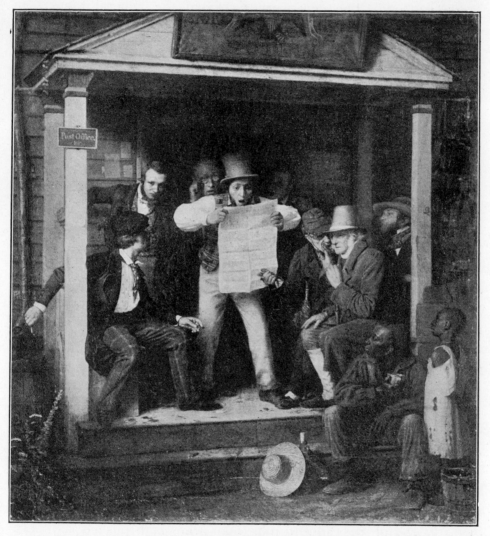

FIG. 43.— WOODVILLE: READING THE NEWS, NATIONAL ACADEMY OF DESIGN.

the art life of the city. That was intended to be carried on as an exhibition and sales gallery, in which work by the best men of the school were to be seen. Their first catalogue shows the names of Hasenclever, Schrödter, Camphausen, both the Achenbachs, besides some old paintings. From now on the importation of foreign can-

P

vases steadily increased. The opening exhibition of the Brooklyn
Athenæum in 1856 had many works by English and German
artists, and two pencil drawings by Ingres. Everywhere art dealers
multiplied. The effect of all this was on the whole beneficial to
American art. The new work increased the general interest in
painting, and the growing wealth of the community was sufficient
for the patronage of both schools. The native artists learned
much from the foreign *technique*, nor was the comparison too
humiliating to them. In figures, in costume pieces, and all the
varieties of *genre* they were certainly inferior; but the German
work, careful, thorough, laborious, still lacked distinction of conception, color, or drawing; and even against the French figure work
(and the best French work did not come at first) the local painters
with their personal reputation and their knowledge of the buyers'
taste could successfully compete, while in landscape they held themselves inferior to none. Sales increased, prices rose, the demand
seemed inexhaustible.

The third quarter of the nineteenth century is still looked back
to as the golden age of American painting. The artists were an
important element in the social life of the city. The population
had increased enormously, but there was no leisure class, and those
who cared for art or culture were few, and more or less in touch with
each other. There were no such general means for gratifying taste
as at present. Photography was still imperfectly developed, and its
copies of pictures were bad, and usually made from engravings
rather than the originals. Art books and art magazines, as we
understand them to-day, were utterly lacking. There was much
writing about art; but the woodcuts with which the theories were
illustrated were incapable of conveying any just idea of the originals. Foreign travel was still a serious undertaking and confined
to a few, and the adventurous man who had pushed as far as
Munich or Rome was listened to with interest and respect when
he recounted his strange experiences.

The early artists had mostly travelled and studied abroad, and
had a touch of cosmopolitan culture. The business man who cared
for something beyond mere trading thought it no slight privilege
on his way up town after the day's work to be able to stop at the

studios in Tenth Street or the old University Building, and pass an hour in a congenial atmosphere; and when those buildings gave a general reception, the streets in front were blocked with private carriages — and private carriages were less common in those days than now. Nor was this friendship of the merchant an empty thing. He aided the beginners, he bought his friends' pictures, spread their merits, defended their renown against all comers, took their advice in art matters, and was liberal toward their institutions. It was provincial, undeveloped, unsophisticated, the New York of Civil War times; but it is not surprising that the old artists look back to it through the mist of years as to an Eden, the like of which cannot occur again.

The annalist of this period is Tuckerman, as Dunlap was of the earlier colonial time, but the *Book of the Artists*, published in 1867, is not the equal of the *History of the Arts of Design in America*. It is badly arranged, without sense of proportion or clearness of statement, long-winded, and stuffed through and through with purple patches of fine writing. There are interminable descriptions of scenery, analyses of emotions, reflections on morals, on science, on history, and a wealth of poetic quotation, original and selected, most blameless and unreadable, while over each artist is poured the same buttery vial of praise of his blameless character, his sensitive mind, his perfect work. In short, the whole thing savors strongly of *Godey's Ladies' Book*, in which portions of it first appeared, and the reader longs for old Dunlap's clear narrative and frank admissions of poor work, unreliability, bad temper, and excess. And yet Tuckerman, when the tawdry ornament is cleared away, has the pith of the matter in him. He knew the artists well, enjoyed their society, admired their works, and revered their characters. He had looked much at art and thought much about it in a rather hazy, sentimental way. He knew his surroundings, the social and business life about him, and he felt the need for a nobler, ampler culture to balance the spreading commercialism. He knew the difficulties of the artists, their isolation, the uncertainties of patronage, the lack of just appreciation, the material difficulties of studios and models, and all the machinery of art, and for all he had ample sympathy. He was not an advanced critic. His judgments were the judgments of his time, and many of them have been reversed; but for us it is rather a merit, for he voices the contemporary point of. view, and if we wish to know the manner of men for whom our artists worked in the sixties, their enthusiasms, their sentimentality, their limitations, we can find it all reflected in the pages of Tuckerman.

DURAND : LANDSCAPE, LENOX LIBRARY.

CHAPTER XII

BEGINNINGS OF LANDSCAPE PAINTING

THE GROWTH OF A LANDSCAPE SCHOOL. — EARLY WORK. — THOMAS DOUGHTY. — ASHER
BROWN DURAND. — HIS YOUTH — CHARACTER OF HIS WORK AS AN ENGRAVER. —
BEGINS PAINTING PORTRAITS. — TRIP ABROAD. — LANDSCAPE WORK. — THOMAS
COLE. — EARLY LIFE. — COMES TO NEW YORK. — SUCCESS. — LATER YEARS. —
CHARACTER OF HIS WORK. — CHARACTER OF DURAND'S WORK AS A PAINTER

THE noteworthy characteristic of the period just described was
the new development of landscape painting. It had always been
practised. There is a record that Smybert left landscapes among
his other pictures when he died; it was a landscape that the artist
Williams showed to West, and the youthful Benjamin himself tried
his hand in the same direction. Constantly we find mention of other
examples, but practically all these have disappeared. The landscapes which Allston painted while an undergraduate are about the
earliest which survive and probably resemble their precursors in
being ideal in character, at least to the extent of being constructed in
the mind in accordance with ideas gained from pictures and prints
rather than from any immediate study of nature. Allston later
painted other landscapes with more skill, but always in accordance
with European tradition, and by that time the native American
school had already begun, its chief characteristics (forced on it by
necessity rather than adopted by choice) being its ignorance of
European composition and handling and its literal study of the
scenery about it. The earliest of this school was Thomas Doughty,
born in 1793 and who lived until 1856. He began painting rather
late in life, giving up his business as a leather manufacturer for it,
and has been mentioned already as one of the quartette (Harding,
Alexander, and Fisher being the others) who held an exceptionally
successful exhibition in Boston in 1831. Doughty's pictures are
transcripts of the nature he saw, small and unassuming, with no
trace of foreign models, but their luminous, milky skies and violet

distances have a peculiar personal charm. One would think that
he must have enjoyed painting them, but we know that his life was
unhappy and that his lack of pecuniary success rendered him mor-
bidly despondent.

Fisher and Alexander also had painted landscapes until the want
of patronage drove them to portraits and so had Inman and others,
but the real founders of the school (for Doughty was but a precursor) were Durand and Cole, who stand to it in much the same
relation that Copley and West do to the early portraitists. Durand,
born in 1796, was the elder by five years, his father of old Huguenot
stock being a farmer in New Jersey and his mother a daughter
of one of the Dutch families of the neighborhood. The elder
Durand managed his small farm on the slope of Orange Mountain,
but was in addition a watch-maker and silversmith, and had a
mechanical ingenuity that enabled him to turn his hand to anything. He could build an oven or plaster a well, and he made a
brass gun unaided, inventing the necessary tools. He is credibly
reported to have manufactured from the rough, nineteen barrels in
a single day, and when Washington, reconnoitring on Orange
Mountain behind the farm, broke his field-glass, the skilful farmer
was called on and successfully repaired it.

Much of this industry and ingenuity the son, Asher Brown
Durand (the eighth of eleven children), seems to have inherited.
His father and two of his elder brothers were accustomed to engrave
monograms and devices on the objects manufactured by them, but
the boy, excited by his admiration of the woodcuts in his school
books, attempted more ambitious subjects, inventing his own
gravers and beating out copper cents for his plates. These efforts
led to his being apprenticed to an engraver. W. S. Leney, the most
prominent practitioner in New York, demanded a premium of $1000,
which was far beyond Durand's means; but arrangements were
finally made with Peter Maverick, son of Peter R. Maverick, also an
engraver, who lived near Newark, only some seven miles from the
Durand farm, and he served him five years as an apprentice, at the
end of which time he became of age and was taken into a partnership. His first engraving from a painting (a head of an old
beggar by Waldo) was seen by Trumbull, who was seeking an

FIG. 44.—DOUGHTY: RIVER GLIMPSE, METROPOLITAN MUSEUM.

engraver for his "Declaration of Independence." James Heath of London demanded $6000 for the plate. Durand was glad to undertake it for half that amount, and when Maverick wished to be joined in the commission, Trumbull demurred and the partnership which had lasted three years was dissolved. The next three years were devoted to this plate, which was finished in 1823. It was a daring experiment to intrust so large and difficult a subject to so inexperienced and young an engraver, and Durand was always grateful to Trumbull for his confidence ; but the result justified it.

Although the plate was hardly remunerative and the sale of the prints was slow, it was an artistic success and finally established Durand's reputation as an engraver. For the next dozen years he was fully employed. Much of the work was purely commercial ; business cards, lottery tickets, diplomas, and especially bank notes, for the production of which he formed a partnership with his elder brother and designed many graceful vignettes ; but he also produced a great number of other plates, chiefly portraits of divines and actors, heroes of the War of 1812, and race-horses, ending with a "Musidora" and the "Ariadne" of Vanderlyn. In these Durand shows himself a thoroughly competent engraver ; he had studied diligently the best prints he could procure and had mastered a variety of *technique* from the cross hatching of the school of Raphael Morghen to the stipple of Bartolozzi. Mezzotint he attempted but once and then did not finish the plate. His drawing is good, his line clear and strong, and faithfully reproduces his models. That his work has so little interest is due mainly to this last virtue. If fortune had given him the compositions of Reynolds or Lawrence to work from, his prints might now be disputed by collectors in the sales ; but the heads by Waldo or Neagle which were for the most part his portion, were calculated neither to increase his fame nor his skill. On the few occasions when he had an opportunity for better things he acquitted himself honorably. His plate of the signing of the "Declaration of Independence" has no such delicacy or refinement as the "Battle of Bunker Hill" by Müller, but the comparison with the mature work of one of the most skilled European practitioners is not overwhelming to the American novice. The "Musidora" is filled with work of exquisite delicacy, but the design, made by Durand himself, probably without a model, is a boneless, impossible thing; the "Ariadne," on the contrary, his latest work, gives admirably the character of the original with much subtle varying of handling, while a certain coarse literalness of form is inherent in the picture itself and is mitigated rather than enhanced by the engraver.

With the "Ariadne," finished in 1835, his work as an engraver practically stops. He had already painted a number of heads, but in that year received commissions from Luman Reed and Charles Augustus Davis to go to Washington and make portraits of General Jackson and Henry Clay, and he acquitted himself so well that he received an order from Reed for heads of all the Presidents, done when possible from nature, the others copied after Stuart and others. From now on he was a painter producing portraits, figure pieces, and some landscapes until 1840, when he made his only trip abroad, visiting London and the principal continental cities and passing the winter in Italy, studying the galleries, copying Titian, Rembrandt, and the other old masters, and doing some original work. On his return the next year he abandoned more and more figure work to devote himself to landscape, which he practised continuously until in his eighty-third year he said, "My hand will no longer do my bidding," and laid down his brush forever, passing the last seven years of his life on the Orange Mountain farm where he was born, in peaceful communion with the nature that he loved.

The early life of Thomas Cole is in contrast to the steady, quiet tenor of that of Durand. He was born in England of a family partly American and did not cross the ocean until he was in his nineteenth year, but he became in after life so good an American that he declared that he would give his left hand to be identified with the country by birth. Cole's father seems to have been a gentle, high-minded man, without much energy or business capacity. He was unsuccessful in England and transported his family to Philadelphia, where he set up a small dry-goods store; but failing at the business or tiring of it, he moved westward again to Steubenville in the Alleghanies.

In this migration Cole was left behind. He had already worked at wood engraving in Liverpool and had found employment in Philadelphia, so he remained there with the exception of a trip to the West

FIG. 45.—DURAND: JAMES MADISON, CENTURY ASSOCIATION.

Indies until the following summer, when he set out on foot and rejoined his family at Steubenville and remained there nearly two years, helping his father in a wall-paper manufactory that he had established. His ambition for higher things was aroused by the visit of an itinerant portrait painter to the village, who talked with him, showed him his work, and loaned him an English book on painting, very likely, from the description, of that same Richardson, which had been potent with so many beginners. When the artist left, Cole procured colors from a chair-maker, manufactured some brushes, and proceeded to turn out the usual early efforts. In his case they were at first landscapes, but these being unremunerative, his family were pressed in as models, a few recognizable likenesses were made, and in February of 1822, when Cole was just of age, he started out on foot, with his materials in a bag on his shoulder to emulate the other wandering artists of whom the country was full. It was too full of them for his profit, for at the villages where he stopped he found he had been preceded by a German who had exhausted the available patronage. Cole succeeded in surpassing him to such an extent that he was called in to improve his rival's work, and when they met a truce was arranged on the basis suggested by his rival: " If you will say notink apout ma bigtures, I will say notink apout yours."

Finally the German saw a new opening and deserted art for preaching, but even this did not bring prosperity to Cole. There was little work and that badly paid, the hardships of travel were great, and the company he was forced to keep uncongenial. He ran into debt at a tavern, was in danger of imprisonment and returned to Steubenville, owing money which he strove vainly during the winter to repay. The next spring he followed his family to Pittsburg and aided his father at his new occupation, the making of floor cloths, working also at painting, but now resuming landscape and making careful drawings from nature. In the autumn he determined definitely to be an artist at any cost, and set out for Philadelphia, where he passed a fearful winter alone, living on bread and water, almost frozen by the cold, sleeping on the floor wrapped in a cloth table-cover, which served him also as an overcoat, and suffering from a severe attack of inflammatory rheumatism. Under these conditions he drew at the Academy, painted landscapes from drawings he had made, and was especially productive in comic scenes.

The next winter, though trying, was not so severe, and in the following spring of 1825 he came to New York and his privations were at an end. He had borne them courageously, yet he had suffered acutely under them, and in his future prosperity did not refer to them as one who rejoices to remember past woes, but rather in a tone of self-commiseration; for Cole was of a delicate temperament, abnormally sensitive and bashful, a being of sensibility who wrote poetry, and solaced his griefs by playing the flute. When he first came to Philadelphia he grieved over "the rudeness and indelicacy of his employer, who called him a woodcutter, speaking lightly of his craft and wounding his sensitive mind;" and the drunken teamsters and barroom loafers whom he was forced to meet in his travels tortured him. A more strenuous type of character is at present popular; but Cole's emotional nature and the singular purity of his mind made him friends, and his shyness forced him into a more intimate communion with nature.

On his arrival in New York he showed five small canvases, which were promptly bought for about ten dollars each; and shortly after three others, displayed in Paff's window, were seen by Colonel Trumbull, who bought one of them, sought out the young painter, and introduced him to Dunlap and Durand, who bought the other two and welcomed the newcomer with generous enthusiasm. From this time, as Durand says, "his fame spread like fire," and he entered on an era of uninterrupted prosperity. He at first passed his winters in New York (to which one more removal had brought his family), going into the country to sketch during the summer. But he wished for foreign study and went abroad in 1829, remaining over three years, nearly two of which were spent in England, where he worked industriously and mourned over the way his pictures were hung in the London exhibitions. Afterward he went to Italy, first to Florence, where he lived in the same house with Greenough, the sculptor, and then to Rome and Naples, sketching and painting everywhere, and studying the old pictures, but seldom making a copy. He married most happily in 1836, and in 1841 made his second trip to Italy, staying a year and leaving his family in New York.

FIG. 46.—DURAND: IN THE WOODS, METROPOLITAN MUSEUM.

He seems to have had some hopes of obtaining the Roman consulate;
but they came to nothing, and he never went abroad again, dividing
his time between New York, various trips that he made in search of
landscape, and the Catskills, where he had had a studio from 1827,
and where he finally died in 1848 at the age of forty-seven. Thus
he did not see the fortunate days that followed; while Durand, an
older man by five years, both saw and survived them. The old
White Mountain, Hudson River school had been born, had flourished, and had fallen out of fashion, the new taste for foreign work
had arisen, the young men had deserted to the new gods of Paris
and Munich, had studied, returned home, and finally established
their new views, struggling not against their native predecessors, but
against their foreign masters before the veteran went to his rest in
1886.

These long lives, traversing so many stages of development, often
make it difficult to put each man in his proper place, but Durand's
position is that of founder of the landscape school. Joined with him
is Cole, who, although a younger man, preceded him in landscape
work, for Durand was still an engraver when Cole came to New
York; and even when ten years later Durand turned to painting, he
did not devote himself to landscape until a few years before Cole's
death, and then in a style and with a feeling not at all resembling
that of his friend. The pair have already been compared as founders
to West and Copley, and like them they represent the contrast
between the emotional and literal temperament. Like West, Cole
strove to achieve high moral objects through his art. It was to suggest profitable musings on the grandeur and decline of nations, the
transitoriness of human life, the rewards of virtue after death. The
plot of his best-known pictures can be related like that of a play, and
like a play usually required several acts for its exposition. The
series of the " Course of Empire " represented the same harbor surrounded by mountains, and followed its fortunes through five scenes,
as a city was built up, grew to wealth, was sacked by the enemy, and
sank into ruins. The " Voyage of Life " gave in four canvases
infancy, youth, manhood, and old age, drifting on an allegorical
Stream of Time. The " Departure " and the " Return " represent a
knight leaving his castle in the morning with floating banners and

Q

prancing steeds and brought back at night dead. There were series of " Life, Death, and Immortality," of the " Cross and the World," and such like, which he planned but did not live to complete.

These allegories were in the taste of the day and were enormously popular. Luman Reed, for whom the " Course of Empire " was painted, generously doubled the agreed price of fifteen hundred dollars, and when the " Voyage of Life " was secured by the Art Union, its subscriptions increased amazingly; but in all these Cole was studying to find visual symbols for ideas better expressed in words. Like West, he was studying for edification, and pure painting was neglected. In the *Crayon* of 1856 there is (probably by W. J. Stillman, to judge by the Ruskinian touches) a sound criticism of the "Voyage of Life," *à propos* of the engravings just published by James Smillie. " As landscapes the pictures are false, artificial, and conventional, and far below the standard he aimed at in his pure landscape painting. There is not, we believe, in the whole series, one object in which we can find that Cole was reverent toward those truths which it is made the duty of the landscape painter to tell us (which in fact he never was, even when he professed only to paint a landscape); rocks, trees, and shrubs fall alike under the censure of a student of Nature."

This is true enough, and the " Course of Empire " was worse painted than the " Voyage of Life." If these were his only works, his position would be quite different from what it is; but he really loved the wild, untamed country, the mountains, forests, and streams of New York and New England, and he painted them with a truer feeling. His work even then is thin and dry and painted in his studio from sketches; but he was the first to give the character of our landscape, the hills wooded to the top, the clear lakes, the crystalline air. His smaller pictures, both American and Italian, are his best; but his big canvases, like the " Oxbow," with its winding river in a wide-stretched plain filled full of minute detail of trees and fences and houses, with its coming thunder-storm and its Salvator Rosa trees in the foreground, are original and impressive, and had a great influence on his successors. It is a pity that he did not develop in that direction. Perhaps his foreign travel was a detriment. His *technique* was sufficiently formed when he went abroad, and his effort there seems to have been not to paint better,

FIG. 47.—COLE: EXPULSION FROM EDEN, METROPOLITAN MUSEUM.

but to find nobler subjects. Already on his return some of his old admirers complained of the change, and there are indications that before his death a considerable body of the judicious were alienated by his growing insincerity to nature. What was lacking in that respect in his work they could then find in Durand's.

Sincerity is not the greatest of the artistic virtues, but no great work is without it, and it goes far to redeem what otherwise would be mediocre. It underlies all of Durand's work, as it did Copley's, as a firm foundation. The portraits with which he began as painter are unlike any by his contemporaries. They suggest some of the early Dutchmen, men like Moreelse, in the thoroughness of their workmanship and their lack of display or seeking for attention. They are all of men, the whole interest thrown on the head, which is modelled with infinite delicacy, his training as an engraver standing him in good stead. They are the best work of the time, far better than his figure pieces. The "Wrath of Peter Stuyvesant" is amusing now only because it is old-fashioned, and the interview between Washington and Harvey Birch is stiff and wooden. There were difficulties in the way of figure composition, but it seems strange that he should have deserted portraits for landscape. The success of Cole probably influenced him, and possibly what he saw abroad of Constable, Turner, and Claude opened his eyes to its possibilities, for he devoted himself almost entirely to it on his return. He had painted landscape before that. Even in his engraving days it had been his solace to go to the Elysian Fields and study from nature, and his *technique* was formed from the first and hardly changed during his long life.

Like his portraits, his landscapes were his own, and not to be mistaken for those of another man. He was too good a craftsman to tolerate any of the slipshod work of Cole — everything is finished clearly and definitely. His canvases have a silvery gray tone, very true to what the eye sees on a clear summer day, after the bright light has dulled its sensitiveness to strong color. His wood interiors are naturally richer; but his shadows are true to the local color and not of the warm brown used both by Cole and by many of his successors, and this in spite of the fact that from the way some of his pictures have cracked he must have painted on a foundation of bitu-

men or something of the sort.   The silvery tone must have come
from the fact that he worked largely out of doors, not making studies
only, but painting directly on his final picture, a practice exceptional
at the time.   The earlier men, Claude for example, had occasionally
done so, and Turner made infinite water-color sketches in the open
air; but his great oil paintings were essentially studio works, as were
landscapes generally before Constable.   Constable himself, independent as he was, and painting much out of doors, yet was influenced
by the old masterpieces which surrounded him and which he studied

Fig. 48. — Cole: Roman Aqueduct, Metropolitan Museum.

and copied, and also by the strong and rich coloring of the English
portraits of his day, beside which his own were hung in the
exhibitions.

Durand had no such knowledge of the great traditions of art to
fall back on.   He had no feeling for the balance of line and spot
and, without any desire to be an innovator, his surroundings and
his study from nature forced a new composition on him if that may
be called composition which is principally lack of it.   His pictures
are largely great sketches or studies from nature.   A fine view, a
pretty fall in a brook, perhaps only a rock or a great tree, is taken in

its most favorable aspect and enough of the contiguous detail added to fill up the canvas. The composition never perfectly fits the frame, and sometimes it does not fit it at all. The charm is in the detail. The acute engraver's eye and unhurried hand has gone over every object, not perfunctorily, but with loving interest. The wooded hills, the silvery lakes, the rocks with their twisted veins and gray lichens, the leaves of the trees, the corrugations of their bark, the pebbles in the brook — there is enthusiasm for all. There is no such deep emotion as broods over Inness's work, or that of some of our later men, but there disengages itself the feeling of peace and rest which came to a strong, simple mind from the intimate communion with nature.

CHAPTER XIII

THE HUDSON RIVER SCHOOL

DEVELOPMENT OF THE HUDSON RIVER SCHOOL AS ILLUSTRATING A CITATION FROM
GOETHE. — ALL STUDIED MORE OR LESS ABROAD. — KENSETT. — CASILEAR. —
BRISTOL. — CROPSEY. — T. ADDISON RICHARDS. — WILLIAM T. RICHARDS. — WHIT-
TREDGE. — MCENTEE. — SANDFORD R. GIFFORD. — F. E. CHURCH. — BIERSTADT. —
MIGNOT. — MORAN. — BRADFORD. — PHILADELPHIA AND BOSTON ARTISTS. — GEORGE
L. BROWN. — CHARACTERISTICS OF THE SCHOOL

DURAND came late in life to landscape work, and the men who
joined themselves to him were much younger: Casilear, born in 1811,
served a preliminary apprenticeship as engraver with Maverick and
later with Durand before taking up painting, and John F. Kensett,
who was the first to begin as painter, was born in 1818, and was
consequently twenty-two years Durand's junior; two years later came
T. Addison Richards and Whittredge and then Cropsey, Bristol,
Sandford R. Gifford, George Inness, F. E. Church, Bierstadt, Mc-
Entee, in the order named, the last two in 1828. The younger men
saw the light in the thirties, — William Bradford, Mignot, Samuel
Colman, William T. Richards, Homer D. Martin, Wyant, Thomas
Moran, and last, in 1840, R. Swain Gifford. Some of these men had
direct instruction from Cole or Durand or from each other. More
commonly there was no relation of master and pupil; but they all
more or less knew each other intimately, worked together, aided
each other, exhibited their works together, and appealed to the same
public.

One section of them formed what is called the Hudson River or
the White Mountain school. A school in art has been defined as
"a combination of traditions and methods, a *technique*, a particular
feeling in design, a particular sense of color also, all united together
to express a common ideal followed by the artists of a given nation
at a given time." Put for "traditions and methods" a common lack
of them, and the definition would fit this group sufficiently well.

FIG. 49.—KENSETT: WHITE MOUNTAIN SCENERY, LENOX LIBRARY.

They were the primitives, the men who followed most closely the ideals of Cole and Durand. They had like ideas and aspirations. They all worked much out of doors and had a great faith in nature literally and minutely copied. They had a great personal delight also in the American country. Apart from their work it was a joy to them to walk in the woods, climb the mountains, and breathe the clear, dry air. They gloried in the boundless views of the Hudson Valley seen from the Catskills. They accompanied the first explorers into the wilds of the Rockies and the Yellowstone. They thought that the size of the great lakes, the mighty rivers, and the boundless prairies must reflect itself in the greatness of the national art. They were patriotic, boasted themselves to be the first really native school (which was true), and spared an incredulous Europe not one jot of the blazing vermilion of the autumn foliage.

Some of the men as they matured and attained wider knowledge and greater skill followed ampler ideals, some remained true to the simple early faith and frowned at the laxity and heresies of their successors. The development of American landscape art as a whole follows with absolute exactness the principles laid down by Goethe in regard to the imitation of nature. " If an artist turns to natural objects, uses all care and fidelity in the most perfect imitation of their forms and color, never knowingly departs from nature, begins and ends in her presence every picture that he undertakes — such an artist must possess high merit, for he cannot fail of attaining the greatest accuracy, and his work must be full of certainty, variety, and strength.

" But man finds usually such a mode of proceeding too timid and inadequate. He perceives a harmony among many objects, which can only be brought into a picture by sacrificing the individual. He gets tired of using Nature's letters every time to spell after her. He invents a way, devises a language for himself, so as to express in his own fashion the idea his soul has attained, and give to the object he has so many times repeated a distinctive form.

" We see that this species of imitation is applied with the best effect, in cases where a great whole comprehends many subordinate objects. These last must be sacrificed in order to attain the general expression of the whole, as is the case in landscape; for instance, where the object would be missed if we attended too closely to the details instead of keeping in view the idea of the whole."

This evolution American landscape went through, but not entirely unaided. Foreign influence helped and hastened. There seems to be an impression that the young men of the seventies discovered modern European art and that since then we have been in bondage to it, while their predecessors of the fifties were a free, unperverted product of the soil; but in fact foreign experience was more indispensable then than now. All of the painters mentioned above with the single exception of Bristol visited Europe for travel or study and many of them made long stays there. When Durand went abroad in 1840, Casilear, Rossiter, and Kensett went with him, and while the first two returned the next year (though Casilear made another trip in 1857), Rossiter and Kensett remained six and seven years respectively. Rossiter was a figure painter and consequently to be spoken of elsewhere, though it may be remarked that he too made a second visit abroad. Casilear was a landscapist, showing clearly the influence of Cole and Durand and especially his training as an engraver under the latter, in the careful, minute finish of his views of Lake George or Swiss scenery. Kensett also had tried the engraver's trade which his father had practised before him, but broke away from it early and took up painting, influenced partly by Rossiter, who was of the same age and knew him in New Haven.

The other men, too, visited Europe and, naturally, in widely different ways, according to their tastes and opportunities. Sandford R. Gifford and McEntee were there but little; Church went only late in life and in search rather of subjects than of knowledge of painting; Inness made several trips of from one to four years' duration. Bierstadt, born abroad, was brought to America as an infant and in early manhood returned to Düsseldorf, his birthplace, for study, which place was, next to Rome, the principal objective point of the young artists. Whittredge spent some five years there and nearly as much in Rome, where Bierstadt also came. Wyant, too, tried the Düsseldorf instruction, but had little enthusiasm for it as compared with the Constables and Turners that he studied in London. Cropsey made two visits abroad, and on the second stayed for seven years in England; there, too, William T. Richards

FIG. 50. — WHITTREDGE: THE BROOK.

got much of his inspiration, and there Mignot went, though his visit was rather from political than artistic reasons. He was from South Carolina and well established in New York; but at the outbreak of the Rebellion he left for England and never returned to America. Colman, and later R. Swain Gifford, not only studied abroad but were among the first to seek subjects in Spain, and the countries south of the Mediterranean.

All of these men (and they are but the representatives of a much larger body that it is impossible to enumerate by name) differed from a later generation in that they were already practising artists before they left America; some were fully mature in skill and reputation; some at the very outset of their career, but even these last had already painted and sold pictures, though it might be only some little canvases disposed of to the Art Union for twenty dollars or so. They had already some idea of what they wanted to paint and how to paint it. The influence of whatever foreign academy they went to was less overwhelming (some would say less thorough) than it became later. They started in sympathy with the ideals around them and never got entirely out of touch with them. They differed greatly among themselves in character and feeling, nor is each man's work harmonious with itself. The advance, however, may usually be followed from the specific to the general, from the minute rendering of detail to a larger handling.

Of those who accepted Durand's point of view and painted American scenery as they found it, Kensett is the most prominent. He, too, tried to give nature exactly, without reference to the way it had been arranged by other artists, striving in Rome to unlearn what special school training he got in Germany. Unlike Durand, he worked mainly from drawings and sketches instead of directly from nature, thus missing the closer truth of the earlier man. Kensett's shadows are usually all of a warm, transparent brown instead of the varied and subtler colors of nature, and his rocks and trees are often made brilliant by high lights touched in with a drawing-master's facility but without absolute faithfulness to the objects represented. His handling is never large and ample, and his painting is apt to be thin. In all of these respects, though better than Cole, he compares unfavorably with Durand. His superiority lies in his wider scope, for Durand is most at home in the full light of a summer day, while all seasons and hours have their charm for Kensett. If he has preferences, it is for autumn and for sunset light, and these changing lights and colors are represented with effect and unity. In copying the multiplicity of details of nature out of doors the relative place and importance of the objects is apt to be forgotten; but with a canvas begun and finished in the studio the first object is to get it into harmony with itself. This harmony most of Kensett's canvases have; and often, in spite of sharpness of handling and smallness of detail, the skies are very beautiful and luminous and the rest of the landscape very true to them. They never quite reach the heights of some pictures of Homer D. Martin's middle period, where the contrast between the execution and the conception is the same; but like all of the work of the school they breathe a feeling of intimacy with nature at first hand and a reflection of the serene and kindly character of the artist.

For even beyond his fellows, Kensett had the gift of forming deep and lasting friendships. He was not a ready talker, his disposition was rather reserved; he often sat mute, but when he spoke it was with understanding, and even his silence diffused an atmosphere of friendliness about him. He had endured much of poverty and ill health during his student years in Europe, and in his later life this experience of his gave him a special friendliness and helpfulness to beginners in their troubles. When wealth came to him, he aided them generously, for he was prosperous and successful even beyond the standards of that prosperous time. Probably none of his contemporaries received so ample a pecuniary reward, nor any of his successors who have done their work in America. Church and Bierstadt may have sold pictures at as high or higher prices, but Kensett produced more freely, he had buyers for everything that he was willing to sell, and after his death the canvases remaining in his studio realized over $150,000 at public auction in 1873.

Bristol, still working to-day with undimmed eye and unwearied hand, was another of the men who kept to the early spirit of the school, and more than Kensett retained and developed the silvery tones of Durand. He began with portraits and did not study at all in

FIG. 51.—CHURCH: CAYAMBE, LENOX LIBRARY.

Europe, yet he has qualities which are supposed to be best if not exclusively developed by academic study. No one constructs a landscape more firmly than he; the solidity of the earth, the level of the lake, the plane of the distant hills, the enveloping of all by the summer sky with sunlit clouds — all are given with an absolute sureness which seventy years have not diminished. The work of Casilear, who like Bristol found in the steep, wooded mountains and clear waters of Lake George a favorite source of inspiration, has already been mentioned. Cropsey belongs in the same class, although his later years did his reputation injustice. There is danger that the thin, crude autumn scenes of his old age, with glaring yellows and reds, may make his earlier and better work forgotten. He was trained as an architect, but soon deserted to painting, though at least once he returned to his first profession long enough to design the stations for the elevated road and probably did no worse than any one else would have done who tried to add beauty to that utilitarian structure. His first work showed the ordinary characteristics of what was being done about him; but during his long stay in England, beginning in 1857, he painted many important pictures not only of the warm, brilliantly colored American autumn, but of the cool, green English landscape which were of merit and found purchasers in London.

T. Addison Richards added to the views of Lake George and the White Mountains, which were visited by all of his associates, studies of the richer, half-tropical vegetation of Georgia and the Carolinas, where his early years were passed, although he was English by birth. His work is sometimes confounded with that of William T. Richards, though only from the similarity of names, for otherwise there is no great resemblance, nor were the artists related. William T. Richards was born in Philadelphia and is interesting as one of the very small group of artists who tried to put Pre-Raphaelite principles into actual practice; but these principles as transplanted into American soil brought forth fruit hardly to be recognized by the P. R. B.'s.

Ruskin's writings had an enormous sale (mostly in pirated editions), and they stirred up great waves of emotion and aspiration, but there was hardly any one in America at this time, who had any knowledge of the works on which his theories were based. He could denounce Michael Angelo and the Dutchmen, he could praise the early Italians and Turner; but his readers knew little more of these names than what he told them. They believed in the prophet; his eloquence, his sincerity, his nobility of character inspired them; but the inspiration was vague. It is on record that an exhibition, mostly of Pre-Raphaelite paintings, was organized in New York in October of 1857 and created "an immense impression." Material, however, was entirely lacking with which to construct the curious mixture of mysticism, toryism, high church, and *pastiche* of fifteenth-century Italy. The best the painter could do was to go out and copy nature leaf by leaf, with a loving fidelity, and that was what the other painters had been doing for a generation with no impulse from Ruskin. Richards's wood interiors are hardly more minutely exact than those of Durand. The weeds and wild flowers are instantly recognizable as botanically correct, and each leaf is insistently brought forward; but this is a defect rather than a merit, for the general harmony of the canvas is often lost, and the foreground and distance do not hold their places. Of late years Richards has confined himself mainly to marines, and the same accurate knowledge which he earlier displayed in vegetation is now turned to every form of rolling wave and breaking surf, and the pictures are now both firm in construction and harmonious.

Whether Whittredge should be mentioned in the same class as the preceding men is a little doubtful. His experience was greater, his scope wider, and yet he seems to belong with Kensett among the followers of Durand rather than of Cole. He was born in Ohio in 1820, only two years later than Kensett, and went through the usual preliminary experience of portrait painting before he turned to landscape. In Cincinnati, where he worked at first, there were some good pictures and considerable pride in the local artists, and there he remained until 1849, when he had accumulated money and orders enough to justify a trip abroad, which trip prolonged itself until it was ten years before he returned to America. The first half of the time was spent mostly in Düsseldorf, where he studied three years under Andreas Achenbach; later he travelled and spent several winters in Rome. While abroad he painted a number of landscapes, some with figures, and on his return he also painted some figure pieces. His admiration for the German school had not been without limitations, but he had adopted its methods and its thorough, accurate, but dull and uninteresting, execution. This style he slowly grew out of.

In 1866, with Sandford R. Gifford and Kensett, Whittredge made a trip to the far West, accompanying General Pope on a tour of inspection, and like his friend Bierstadt he produced a number of pictures of the unknown country between the Mississippi and the Rockies, which still show something of the Düsseldorf handling and the Düsseldorf conception of a picture; but from this time the influence grows weaker. The charm of the hills and streams and woodlands of New York and New England possessed him, he ceased to seek strange or wonderful subjects, and studied with sincerity the nature around him, working out of the conventions he had learned, getting a truer, more varied, richer color than Düsseldorf knew, a less conventional composition, and above all that sentiment, that wholesome love of nature which runs through the whole school. He has perhaps a deeper, graver note than the rest, and the old training remains in the severeness that keeps the construction solid through all complexity of detail. Some of his forest interiors with great trees, mysterious depths of shadow and light trickling down on masses of rock and fern and moss, are among the best things of the Hudson River school.

Much of the same grave feeling is found in the works of Jervis McEntee (born in Rondout, 1829), but he had not the thorough training of Whittredge. Church gave him some instruction, but for some time he wavered between trade and art, and it was not until he was thirty that he finally decided on the latter. He then made a short trip to Europe with Sandford R. Gifford, but he had no thorough training, and his works sometimes show the lack of it. His autumn and winter scenes are his best productions and have a very personal character.

Sandford R. Gifford, who went to Europe with McEntee in 1859 and made the western trip with Whittredge in 1866, is in a way a connecting link between them and the men next to be described. The dividing lines of the different groups must not be drawn too strictly.

Most of the painters lived long and produced steadily. Their canvases are countless, with constant interchange of subject and style among themselves. An idea of the personal idiosyncracy of each could only be given in the presence of their works, and that in sufficiently large numbers. A verbal analysis, however long and complete, would only be confusing and wearisome. And yet under the similarity of handling and feeling there is a real difference in the point of view, the eternal difference between the realists on the one

FIG. 52. — BIERSTADT: YOSEMITE VALLEY, LENOX LIBRARY.

hand and the idealists and romantics on the other. The one paint their actual surroundings with some selection, but faithfully and literally as they are, the others seek strange scenes and try to infuse into them poetry or mystery. It may be objected that the preceding men all more or less painted European views, but they painted them because they were in Europe for travel or study, and there was nothing else to paint. But Gifford painted Venetian sails and the Acropolis because he preferred them to the Catskills.

The marked difference in this respect between Durand and Cole has already been spoken of, and it is noteworthy that Gifford was much influenced in his youth by Cole. As a boy he had instruction from John Rubens Smith, a painter of water-colors, an Englishman by birth and son of John Raphael Smith, the well-known engraver who had worked much for Boydell. His son had painted portraits and exhibited in the Royal Academy and had, moreover, known personally the group of artists that illustrated the Boydell Shakespeare, — Reynolds, Fuseli, West, and the others. His stories of them may have inclined Gifford when, after two years at Brown University, it was necessary to decide on a profession, to turn from the paternal iron works to painting. A stronger influence, however, was his acquaintance with Cole, whose Catskill studio was near his home and from whom he got much of his inspiration. Soon after he had decided to be an artist, he made a trip to Europe; but he found nothing in the schools there that made him wish for their training. He was a peculiarly independent, self-centred man, and Whittredge, who met him on this trip and went up the Rhine with him, recounts how curiously direct and uncompromisingly personal were his remarks on the scenery. He worked for a while in Rome and then returned to New York and took a studio in the old University Building, which he retained to the end of his life. At the outbreak of the Rebellion he joined the Seventh Regiment and served in the ranks through the campaigns in 1861 and again in 1863 and 1864. In 1866 he made the trip to the West with Whittredge and Kensett, but the offer of a horse made him desert his sketching for exploration. Again in 1868 he went to Europe and then made a trip around the Mediterranean, not again returning there.

Gifford had never lacked for money, but the impedimenta of civilization were irksome to him. He lived contentedly in his small studio, which soon became well known to a large circle of friends; he was generous; he was kindly and particularly chivalrous in his attitude toward women; but luxury, *Persicos apparatus*, he abhorred far more than Horace. Even in social intercourse he avoided more than the strictly essential. When he left for Europe he said "good-by" to his friends with no word as to his destination, and when two years later he returned, he entered his studio and set to work without vain salutations or explanations. His sole baggage on this trip (as on others) was a satchel hung by a strap over his shoulder and from this the lining had been removed as a useless incumbrance. New apparel was purchased as the old was cast away, and in emergencies his ingenuity found a remedy, as when he appeared at an evening reception in the dress suit of his hotel waiter.

His pictures do not suggest this asceticism, there is in fact more of a sensuous note in them than in those of any of his contemporaries. Kensett he resembles most, but his color is in a higher key, richer, softer, sweeter. Like him he painted in his studio often from very slight sketches, keeping his pictures long, retouching and glazing until they were brought into harmony. He is the first to base the whole interest of a picture on purely artistic problems, such as the exact values of sunlit sails against an evening sky. It is this idealizing and poetizing temper that brings him into affinity with Cole.

But Cole's real pupil and disciple is F. E. Church. He is the only one who in a literal sense can be said to have been his pupil, for when Church decided that he wished to be an artist, his family made no opposition but arranged a meeting with Cole, who took him into his own house in the Catskills and he worked under the counsel and influence of the master until Cole's death. The effects of this teaching were not direct. While Church's methods of painting were probably influenced by Cole, yet he was infinitely more skilful, and of Cole's story-telling, moral, allegorical subjects, he made no use; but it was probably from Cole that he got the idea that a picture should be grander, more ennobling than a mere transcript of everyday nature, and that the way to produce this effect was not by deeper feeling expressed through the artistic means of line, color, and composition, but by a choice of nobler subjects. The idea is unsound, but it has not always been as universally rejected as to-day. It has had many followers, but in landscape none has carried it out to its ultimate conclusion with the industry, the intelligence, and the brilliancy of Church. What the world offers of natural marvels to delight the eye and amaze the mind he sought out: the falls of Niagara, the forests of the tropics, icebergs and volcanoes, the isles of the Ægean and the Acropolis of Athens. He arranged all the beauties of each in a sort of panoramic combination and added every conceivable adjunct of light

FIG. 53.—MORAN: SOLITUDE.

and atmosphere, rainbows, mists, sunsets, eruptions; and the result is not absurd, but on the contrary always interesting and, in some of the later work like the Parthenon, noble and beautiful.

Even Church's South American scenes, in spite of their fundamental unsoundness, are fine. The execution is amazingly clever. There is probably no man to-day who could do the same thing. The tangled mass of tropical foliage in the foregrounds — ferns, vines, orchids, palms — is put in with a wonderfully minute yet brilliant handling. It does not always connect perfectly with the distance, but the distance itself makes us feel as if we really knew what a tropical lake or a volcano were like. It is no wonder that they awoke the wildest admiration not only in America but also in Europe, and especially in England, where he was enthusiastically praised by the critics, even Ruskin commending. Besides his public comments the latter wrote to Charles Eliot Norton in 1865: "Church's 'Cotopaxi' is an interesting picture. He can draw clouds as few men can, though he does not know yet what painting means, and I suppose he never will, but he has a great gift of his own." This is not enthusiastic, but it comes near being so in comparison with his ordinary attitude toward America as a home of the arts. Nine years before (in 1856) he justified himself in calling America ugly. " I have just been seeing a number of landscapes by an American painter of some repute; and the ugliness of them is Wonderful. I see that they are true studies and that the ugliness of the country must be Unfathomable," which is all the more amusing because the painter was probably Kensett, who was fondly supposed by certain of his friends to illustrate Pre-Raphaelite principles.

Associated with Church in these successes was Bierstadt, who did for the Rocky Mountains what Church attempted for the Andes; but Bierstadt's work, while inspired by the same desire for stupendous subjects, is heavy and inert. He was born in Düsseldorf, a cousin of Hasenclever, whose *genre* paintings were one of the staple articles of export of the school. When he came to America he was two years old, and when he finally determined to be a painter his first object was to get together enough money to enable him to return to his birthplace and pursue his studies there. He acquired thoroughly all the faults of the school, and unlike Whittredge, who was his fellow-pupil, never succeeded in shaking them off. His smaller pictures are interesting and clever, but the huge canvases which made his reputation are but a sort of scene painting, superficial, exaggerated, filled with detail imperfectly understood. Every ingredient of the work, composition, color, mountain peaks, waterfalls, clouds, sky, rocks, trees, underbrush, are all done with an exasperating, a monotonous ability up to a certain degree of excellence beyond which nothing goes. There is a dulness, a mechanical quality about it all. The leaves seem of painted tin, the rocks of pasteboard, the mountains themselves seem rather reminiscent of the Alps than possessing the actual characteristics of the Rockies. But the great superficial canvases impressed the popular mind (and some of the critical too) both at home and abroad, and great prices were given for them. Their success, though, came at a time when other influences were becoming potent with the younger men, and Bierstadt and Church had fewer imitators than might be supposed.

Louis R. Mignot (only five years younger than Church) worked much in the spirit of Church, and some of his smaller tropical scenes are deceptively like his model. He was born in South Carolina, and his southern sympathies forced him at the outbreak of the Rebellion to leave New York for London, where he remained, painting with success until his death.

Another extremity of Church's realm was occupied by William Bradford, a Quaker born and bred, who made repeated trips to Labrador to study icebergs, but who also painted many marines. One is also tempted to add here Thomas Moran, whose long series of views of the Yosemite and the Yellowstone, painted with a wonderful facility of hand, give him a certain relationship with Bierstadt and the other seekers for natural marvels; but he is a later man, has a wider knowledge of painting, and draws his inspiration quite as much from Turner as from the Hudson River school. In fact when that school was at its zenith he was still settled in Philadelphia, and the Hudson River school was always intimately connected with New York, influencing the other cities only remotely. If some Philadelphian artists seemed more closely allied to it, it was largely owing to the group who strove to follow the Pre-Raphaelite faith with which it had many ignorances in common, and which, as in the case of Richards, also a Philadelphian, produced very similar work. Besides him there were Henry Farrer, Henry Newman, Charles Moore, and some others who worked laboriously and aspiringly, but whose enthusiasm was not able to escape from the conditions of their environment.

Boston held still further aloof—the best-known landscape painter there being George L. Brown, who had little connection with the native school. He was born in the city in 1814 (which makes him

FIG. 54.—JAMES M. HART: THE ADIRONDACKS, OWNED BY J. L. CRAWFORD, ESQ.

the senior of most of the New York men), and though he lived at one time in the latter place, yet his connections and sympathies were with Boston. He first showed his genius in some scenery for a dramatic club; then practised wood engraving until almost with his first effort in painting a patron appeared and gave him a hundred dollars with which sum he promptly started for Europe. He endured hardship as a matter of course but he managed to make a short stay and soon after went back for a long sojourn in Italy, where he painted Venice and Naples and more or less of the intervening country rather well, according to the methods practised around him but with little specifically American either in his handling or sentiment. On his return in 1860, after a residence abroad of twenty years, he continued his Italian views, but also made some paintings of New England scenery much in the same manner, until his death in 1889. His works are no worse than most of those of the White Mountain school, but they are no better and have not like them a native flavor of the soil. That is the saving merit of the school.

All of the men cited and many more, like R. W. Hubbard, Bellows, William and James McD. Hart and Brevoort, did at their best good work — work which would show without discredit beside that of their European contemporaries, but to have its full effect it must be seen sympathetically, from their own point of view, and with allowance made for their limitations. Their worst work, which is far commoner than their best, no sympathy can save. Thin, dry, crude without being bright, niggling in execution and puerile in composition, they hung on the white walls of the houses in lower Fifth Avenue above the haircloth-covered furniture, and may still so hang in some belated cases, but the canvases are as antiquated as the haircloth. Even at their best they lacked the indefinable quality of style, inseparable from great painting. Whittredge and McEntee are exceptions, so is Gifford, and some would even exempt the later works of Church; but as a rule no breath of inspiration, no mastery of noble traditions is found. Under the circumstances it could not well have been otherwise. There is a charming story of Durand, at the end of his long life, full of years and honors, after he had given up painting, sitting in the studio of a younger painter and comparing the spare surroundings of his own youth with the congenial associations and ampler culture of the later day and saying quite simply how much he regretted that he could not have done other and better work. It was a more practical appreciation of the same difference that made Inness study and take out sketching with him, engravings of landscapes by the old masters, that he might discover the secret of the sentiment that he found in them and not in the paintings produced about him.

INNESS : AUTUMN OAKS, METROPOLITAN MUSEUM.

CHAPTER XIV

CULMINATION OF THE EARLY LANDSCAPE SCHOOL

GEORGE INNESS. — WYANT. — HOMER D. MARTIN. — COMPARISON OF THEIR WORKS WITH THOSE OF THE LEADING FRENCH LANDSCAPISTS. — SHURTLEFF. — GEORGE H. AND JAMES D. SMILLIE. — SAMUEL COLMAN. — R. SWAIN GIFFORD

THE time was now ripe to build a loftier structure on the foundations painfully laid by the earlier men, and it was with Inness, Wyant, and Homer D. Martin that the early school culminated. George Inness was the earliest of the three; born in 1825, he was contemporary with some of the most indurated and limited of our landscape painters, but he felt instinctively the weakness of the school, and his foreign study and personal genius led him to an ampler, completer art. He was born in Newburgh, New York, but his family moved to Newark, New Jersey, where his boyhood was passed. He was delicate as a youth, and after trying storekeeping without success was obliged to give up a position with a firm of map engravers, the confinement telling on his health. He went back to Newark, made some studies and sketches from nature, and when about twenty had a few lessons from Regis Gignoux, his only direct instruction in painting. His small canvases sold readily, the Art Union being a steady customer; but he was dissatisfied with his work, which was like that done about him, — thin, smooth, meagre. It was then that he studied prints of old pictures, but he soon had an opportunity to see the originals, for in 1847 a friend offered to send him to Europe, and after stopping at London, he passed fifteen months at Rome. He came back with his style still unformed, yet struggling toward perfection. The sight of the foreign pictures which were then beginning to come to the country sent him again to Europe; but instead of going to Düsseldorf, like most of the students of the time, he spent a year in Paris.

When he got back again to America, there followed a long

period of assimilating what he had seen and developing not only his art but his character; for Inness was a deeply spiritual nature, who was not content to put aside the great mysteries of life as vain speculation.   He took counsel of men and books.   For seven years theology was almost his only reading.   Finally he accepted the doctrines of Swedenborg, which seem to have a peculiar attraction for some men of exceptional ability, and whose temperaments combine the mystical with the logical.   In 1871 he went abroad again for four years, spending them partly in Paris and partly in Rome.   It will be seen that many men had more of foreign experience than he, but no other drew so amply and so wisely from the great store of European art, both old and new.   There is no man whom he can be said to have copied or even imitated.   He felt nature too immediately and sensitively to accept another man's point of view; but he was a meditater and reasoner on theories of art, and sought out in great work the qualities that made it so and developed them for himself. His art philosophy was admirably sound.   When he reasoned, as he loved to do, with a congenial listener on the mysteries of life, death, and the world to come, his talk as befitted his subjects was lofty but obscure; but when he spoke of painting, he was admirably clear.

"The purpose of the painter is simply to reproduce in other minds the impression which a scene has made upon him.   A work of art does not appeal to the intellect.   It does not appeal to the moral sense.   Its aim is not to instruct, not to edify, but to awaken an emotion. . . .   It must be a single emotion if the work has unity, as every such work should have, and the true beauty of the work consists in the beauty of the sentiment or emotion which it inspires.   Its real greatness consists in the quality and force of this emotion.   Details in the picture must be elaborated only enough fully to reproduce the impression which the artist wishes to reproduce.   When more than this is done, the impression is weakened or lost, and we see simply an array of external things which may be very cleverly painted, and may look very real, but which do not make an artistic painting.   The effort and difficulty of an artist are to combine the two; namely, to make the thought clear and to preserve the unity of impression.   Meissonier always makes his thought clear, he is most painstaking in his details; Corot, on the contrary, is to some minds lacking in objective force, . . . but Corot's art is higher than Meissonier's."

The quotation is rather long, but it is worth giving, not only as illustrating the spirit of Inness's work, but as supplementing the preceding extract from Goethe. The painter does not fall below the philosopher either in soundness of thought or clearness of expression, and when it comes to practical application far surpasses him, for the Sage of Weimar admired some fearful things in landscape painting.

Inness's painting never became rigid. It was altering and developing to the last, even at the same date he worked in different manners to suit his subjects and said himself that he "seemed to have two opposing styles, — one impetuous and eager, the other classical and elegant." He painted both small canvases and also large works like the " Barberini Pines " or the " Peace and Plenty " of the Metropolitan Museum. His variety was great. All seasons of the year, all times of the day, all tempers of the sky, were represented not mechanically, but with a new formula discovered for each. He preferred the rich tones of autumn and sunset; but he could take a bank of June foliage on a gray day when there were no strong shadows, when grass and leaves were alike of the same brilliant, uncompromising green, and without mitigation of the brilliancy nor laborious drawing of detail make the whole mass firm, yet soft and dewy with infinitely delicate gradations of tone and shadow. His earliest work shows much minuteness, and there is sometimes a shock of surprise at finding his signature on a canvas with a blue mountain, hard and sharp against a bright sky with a group of anemic trees in the foreground. But he soon gained richness of tone and breadth of handling, and there are not wanting those who prefer pictures of his middle period, like the small thunderstorms painted at Medford, Massachusetts, with their brilliancy and their enamel-like texture, to the looser, freer work of his later years. They have not the same mastery, however. The structure is not so solid, the harmony is not so true. In his middle period, frequently a light spot, a group of cattle, a sail on a river, is out of value, strikes the eye with too great insistence. His late work holds together flawlessly.

s

His method of painting was to cover the whole canvas with a thin glaze of Indian red, to touch in the main masses of shadow in black, and then to work on this foundation, gradually bringing the whole picture forward by constant working over. As a reasoner and theorizer on his art he had many maxims for his work, the most important being that the sky should be given as a half-tone against which both the lights and darks of the picture should con-

FIG. 55.—INNESS: DELAWARE VALLEY, METROPOLITAN MUSEUM.

trast. This is one of the reasons why his canvases seem richer and more decorative than those of the White Mountain school, who usually strove to key the sky up to the brightest possible tone. Inness's practice was also that of Ruysdael, and Fromentin has noted how admirably it makes the pictures of the latter set in the gold of the frames, though it was probably only indirectly through the French landscape painters, the so-called Fontainebleau school, that Inness received the Dutch tradition. It is with these last that he is affiliated, and his pictures hang harmoniously with theirs and hold their own in the company. In some of his later work there may be

FIG. 56.— WYANT : BROAD SILENT VALLEY, OWNED BY GEORGE A. HEARN, ESQ.

a vagueness, a lack of firmness. Some of the things sold from his studio after his death he might have worked on more, but it is probable that he found, as he said about Corot, that more objective force meant weakening or loss of that sentiment which was to him the reason for the picture. Like the Greek, he felt the God in the stream or grove, the immanent presence of superhuman powers, and it is his crowning merit that he does succeed to a certain extent in "reproducing in other minds the impression which the scene made upon him."

Inness had less popular vogue than most of the men around him. Until the end of his life his larger pictures sold with difficulty, and the newspapers served him no such adulation as they gave to Church or Bierstadt. It is curious therefore that Wyant should have heard of him and should have made the journey from Cincinnati in the early sixties to see him rather than another. Wyant was born in a little Ohio village and had the usual early experiences of the boy with a desire for painting in such a place. He worked on signs, but it was not until, at the age of twenty, he moved to Cincinnati that he saw any meritorious paintings. He may have found there something by Inness which pleased him or have had some special knowledge of him. In any case, he made the journey to Perth Amboy for advice and aid, which were freely given and then returned to Cincinnati and worked there until 1864, when he came to New York and the next year sailed for Europe, though his stay there was short. He got some German training, but disliked the work of the school and preferred the English work of Constable and Turner. On his return he settled in New York until in 1873 he joined a government exploring expedition to Arizona and New Mexico, in hopes of benefiting his health, which was beginning to fail; but the hardships which he endured, caused partly by the brutality of the leader of the expedition, so far from improving his condition resulted in paralysis, and he was never able to use his right hand after. He however learned to paint with his left hand with no diminution of skill.

As an artist Wyant makes no such varied and ample appeal as Inness. Much of his work consists of variations on a single note. His typical picture is a glimpse of sunny, rolling country seen between the trunks of trees that have grown tall and slender in a wood, usually birches or maples. This he painted with sure, firm brush work, which enabled him, when he would, to model the summer clouds and give the foreground detail with exactness yet without losing for an instant the unity, the sentiment and silvery shimmer peculiar to his work. In a certain delicate refinement none of our other artists have equalled him. Both Inness and Wyant altered and matured their style with age, but it was a steady, subjective development. The work of each is perfectly harmonious with itself.

The alterations of manner of Homer D. Martin are far more abrupt and confusing. Born in Albany in 1838, he was the same age as Wyant. He turned naturally to painting, and after two weeks' instruction from James Hart began to produce pictures, exhibiting in the Academy of Design before he was of age. He went abroad first in 1876, then in 1881, when he stayed five years, and again in 1892 for several months. His early work resembles that of Kensett. The shadows are of warm brown, the outlines are sharp, and brilliancy is given by crisp lights touched in much in Kensett's manner. But Martin studied nature more intimately and more profoundly. His Adirondack views have Kensett's qualities in a higher and more artistic development. The composition is less commonplace, better both in line and mass, and more characteristic of the country. The edges of the mountains against the sky and the shores of the lakes are sharp and fine as they show through the clear mountain air, but drawn with infinite delicacy; while the masses of the forests and hills are kept simple and strong in spite of the multiplicity of detail with which they are filled. The painting is thin but finished, with a smooth, rich, transparent surface, like a piece of old lacquer.

From this style he developed until his later work is in the strongest contrast with it. It was the sight of the works of the French landscapists of the Fontainebleau school, then just beginning to be imported, which gave the impulse for the change. Martin felt the effect of their greater unity, their deeper sentiment. At the very beginning of the seventies he was a fervent admirer of Corot, then hardly beginning to be recognized even in France. It was not an admiration that led to direct imitation, but which served rather as an inspiration to show how much of feeling a

FIG. 57.—MARTIN : LAKE SANDFORD, CENTURY ASSOCIATION.

landscape could be made to express.   His first short trip abroad in 1876 only strengthened this endeavor, which culminated during his five years' stay.   Martin was much older than the others of his school when he made his long visit abroad, and he came in contact with a different spirit in landscape painting than the others had known.   In the eighties the Fontainebleau school had triumphed and had been accepted so indisputably that argument about them had ceased.   It was a different group — Monet, Sisley, Pissarro, and their like — who were in fullest activity, challenging attention.   The high-keyed pictures, the disintegration of color to give the brightness of sunlight, the spotty brush work, all the insistent innovations of the school did not influence Martin ; but he recognized in each canvas the unity of impression which gave the school its name, and their great power and carrying force.

The lack of this power had been the failing of the old American school and to obtain it Martin changed his whole manner of painting and produced a series of works which seem at first glance scarcely the work of the same man.   The paint is laid on heavily, sometimes with the palette knife ; the drawing, while true and subtle, is generalized and simplified to the last degree ; the sky and water instead of smooth, thin, single tints are a mass of heavy, interwoven strokes of different tones.   Even the subjects — the Normandy churches and farms, the roads and meadow streams lined with tall, trimmed poplars — have small relationship to the gaunt, burnt mountains of the Adirondacks.   At base the change is not so great — hardly more than the use of the palette knife, larger brushes or more fully charged with color, and a looser touch.   The real essentials (the feeling for the relations of mass, for the exact difference of tone between the sky and the solid earth, the sense of subtle color) are the same, and under every change of surface remains the same deep, grave melancholy, sobering but not saddening, which is the keynote of Martin's work.   After his return to America he painted with the same handling many of his old subjects, mountain and coast views, and these, his latest canvases, may well be considered his crowning achievements.

With these three men — Inness, Wyant, and Martin — the early American landscape school culminates.   If we insist on unprofitable comparisons and claim for any of our art an equality with what was best in contemporary Europe, — a real equality, not one hedged and bolstered up with apologetic references to the limitations of our position, — it is these men that we must put forward, for the long period between the death of Stuart and the rise of the present school. The essentials of greatness they seem to have had, — deep feeling which took a pictorial form, ample knowledge, complete mastery of their material, and for each a style, personal and distinguished, which burst through that commonplace which fetters us all.

FIG. 58. — MARTIN : VIEW ON THE SEINE, METROPOLITAN MUSEUM.

The unprofitableness of comparison has been admitted, yet appreciation of the standpoint from which they should be regarded and of the grounds on which supremacy is claimed for them is best gained if they are regarded in connection with the trio of great Frenchmen, Corot, Rousseau, and Daubigny. Thus it is possible in a way to get their bearings, to put them in proper perspective with the great world. It is noticeable that the comparison can only be made with the very best men like those above named. With the ordinary excellent Salon landscape painters, even (to take names at random) with men so good as Français or Pelouse, they are absolutely incommensurable. The obvious mastery of the French, the knowledge of great traditions, the perfect drawing, the skilful brush work, the sound construction, approve themselves at once to any beholder. The great mass of the work of the Hudson River school would look thin, weak, and amateurish beside them, and even Inness demands a different point of view — as does equally Corot. It is only with time and companionship that this very obviousness of skill, this insistence on external form, becomes wearisome or at least loses its power to interest and refresh. The endurance of charm is the mark of the greater men, and this is the common possession of both of the groups under consideration. Their pictures on the walls of a room make no insistent appeal to attention, but their presence is felt half unconsciously like that of old and sympathetic friends whose real value can only be comprehended after long acquaintance. In the effort to express these deeper emotions, natural and obvious methods of the schools, however sound, must be discarded or developed to suit the individual genius. The resultant work is difficult to judge by fixed critical standards. The French painters show the effect of their nationality and surroundings in a greater completeness of expression and a more even excellence. The work of the Americans, while at its best it leaves nothing to be desired in construction or finish, yet often, as in the case of Inness's later work, is so loose, so vague, that a European critic even though an admirer of Corot might refuse to consider it on account of its insufficiency. Yet the charm is there also, subtle and not to be reproduced. The world to-day cares less for elaboration in painting than it did and more for charm. Perhaps posterity may delight in all of the work equally, in any case the position of the best of it seems assured.

With these paintings we are brought into the immediate present, far from the beginnings of the old White Mountain school. They are even more in accord with the taste of the day than when Martin died in 1897. Who else should be added from the older men, alive to-day and painting with unabated vigor, to round out this first culmination of our landscape art is a difficult question that few would answer in exactly the same way. Shurtleff, born in 1838, probably has more affinity to Whittredge than to the younger men if only because our native forests are more to him than all the oaks of Fontainebleau or beeches of Burnham. He did not, however, begin to paint until 1870. There had been some drawing and illustrating after his graduation from Dartmouth College, and a short but severe experience of soldiering. He volunteered in the naval brigade at the outbreak of the war, rose to be adjutant, and is said to have been the first federal officer to be wounded and made prisoner. When he took up art, he began as an animal painter and only later produced the clear, broadly painted sunlit forest interiors for which he is now known.

They are as far from the grave note of Whittredge as the land-scapes of George H. Smillie are from the melancholy of Martin. Both he and James D. Smillie are sons of James Smillie, a Scotch engraver who early emigrated to America, first to Quebec but soon after to New York, where he was long active and was the authorized interpreter of the works of Cole, Durand, Kensett, and their friends from the days of the old Art Union, for which he executed several plates, down to comparatively late times. James D. Smillie, who was the elder son, began in his father's profession, etching his first plate at the age of eight and collaborating with his father in most of his important work until 1864, when he turned to painting. George H. Smillie studied with James M. Hart and painted from the first, though his work shows little trace of the influence of his master. Both of the brothers are skilful executants, but there is in the paintings of the younger a special note of gayety and brightness which is personal and recognizable. There is nothing in the work of either that is antiquated or out of date, and it is something of a surprise to learn how long they have been practising their profession.

It gives an even greater shock to learn that Samuel Colman exhibited his first picture in 1850. To be sure, he was young, only eighteen at the time, and had been favored in his surround-ings. His father was a publisher and bookseller, a man of excep-tional culture, and his store was a resort for artists and those who loved books and prints, a little centre of light and learning, and prized after the manner of the time when the material of culture was rare and enjoyed with a zest which we have lost. Colman studied under Durand, but his work shows affinity with that of Sandford R. Gifford, if with any one.   He travelled abroad in 1860–1862, in 1867 he founded with James D. Smillie the American Society of Painters in Water Colors, now the American Water Color Society, and was its first president.   In 1871 he again went abroad for four years, travelling extensively.   His work shows the effects of these travels, for he loved the picturesqueness of foreign lands and the warm, rich light of Italy, Spain, and the East.   Both in the choice of these subjects and in mellowness of tone he resembles Gifford,

FIG. 59. — R. SWAIN GIFFORD : LANDSCAPE.

but he paints with a solider impasto of color and a larger, stronger draftsmanship.

Another artist who sometimes resembles in subjects and in love of warm color Sandford R. Gifford is his namesake (though the family relationship, if any, is extremely remote), R. Swain Gifford. The resemblance is, however, less strong than in the case of Colman. R. Swain Gifford had his first instruction from Albert van Beest, a Dutch painter of no great talent, but thoroughly trained, a man of education, an ex-officer in the Dutch navy, and the master and collaborator of Bradford.   Him Gifford as a schoolboy used to take out in a sail-boat when he went sketching, and possibly he got from him something of the gravity of the old Dutch painters, which shows even in his Algerian and Egyptian scenes, and still more in the canvases which are most characteristic of him, — the long brown sweeps of moorland or seashore under a sky of broken gray clouds, thoroughly constructed, solidly painted, and with a fine, virile sentiment.   But here the list of living landscape painters must stop for the present.   There are many more whose work is in entire harmony with that of those last named, but all of these latter were painting and exhibiting before the end of the third quarter of the last century.   They may have broadened and matured during the last thirty years, but they laid the foundations of their art in a different time than their successors, whose achievements are of the present and who will be spoken of later.

CHAPTER XV

FIGURE AND PORTRAIT PAINTING IN THE YEARS PRECEDING THE CIVIL WAR

THE PORTRAIT AND FIGURE PAINTERS. — ELLIOTT. — LE CLEAR. — GEORGE A. BAKER. — HEALY. — HUNTINGTON. — WILLIAM PAGE. — HENRY PETERS GRAY. — J. G. CHAPMAN. — ROSSITER. — ROTHERMEL. — LEUTZE. — MAYER. — LANG

THE American landscape school was in truth a school, as far as such a thing is possible, under modern conditions. Its development was logical, consecutive, so that it may be followed closely. The characters of the men, the changing social surroundings, the influence of foreign schools, developed not only individuals, but the school as a whole. With the portrait and figure painters of the same period it is different. There is no unity. They could not start, as the landscapists did, from a common basis of inexperience, to learn by painfully representing everything what could with advantage be omitted. There were already plenty of portrait painters, Trumbull and Vanderlyn, Jarvis and Inman, and Sully and Harding, all working vigorously and each breaking further away from the English tradition of Reynolds and West, which was pretty nearly dead even in England. To replace it there was a multitude of influences of every nation and of every age; but no sufficient number of artists following the same illumination to form a clearly defined group. There was not even a pious error as to the artistic importance of our national characteristics to inspire them, and the heads of American statesmen and burghers were painted with none of the rapt enthusiasm which was lavished on the contemporary " Autumn in the Catskills," or " Views on Lake George."

Inman died before the middle of the century; Morse had abandoned painting by that time; Sully still worked in Philadelphia, but was growing old and rather out of fashion. The English tradition, or some transmogrified development of it, was carried on by Charles

Loring Elliott, who was a skilful portraitist and about the best of his time. He was born in Auburn, New York, in 1812, his father being an architect, and the usual tales of precocious talent describe him as first showing mechanical genius by the construction of windmills and water-wheels. It was envy, or rather emulation, of a schoolmate, who could draw a horse and who was greatly admired for the accomplishment, which first turned him to art. He got all the pictures of horses that he could, and struggled over them until at length he took to looking at real horses, and finally, in a set competition, vanquished his rival and succeeded to all his honors, because the vanquished one could only draw a horse standing, whereas Elliott could draw it in motion. This success turned all his energies to art, until, at the age of ten, he made his first effort in oil painting, which came near being fatal to him. He had procured with difficulty the necessary materials, and retired to a vacant room, where he might work in secret, taking with him a pail of lighted charcoal for warmth, from the fumes of which he was rescued just in time to escape asphyxiation.

Elliott's father disapproved of the painter's profession, but employed him during his school days to make architectural drawings, and finally allowed him to go to New York with a letter to Trumbull. It was perhaps because he himself in his youth had been advised by Burke to study architecture as a more promising profession than painting that Trumbull urged the same course upon Elliott, citing his own case to show how inadequate were the returns from a painter's career. Yet when the young man insisted, Trumbull gave him access to the casts in the American Academy, instructing and aiding him; but always insisting that he should become an architect, until Elliott finally broke away from him and the old Academy, and went to study under Quidor, who had been a fellow-pupil with Inman under Jarvis and who painted signs, fire-engines, and very bad pictures. Here he worked away for two or three years doing anything and everything, until he finally produced a couple of pictures, " The Bold Dragoon " and " A Dutchman's Fireside," which he exhibited in a shop window, and which gained him some renown and a sort of official consecration besides. For one day there appeared at his studio Colonel Trumbull, whom he had not seen

FIG. 60.— ELLIOTT: GOVERNOR BOUCK, CITY HALL, NEW YORK.

since he left the Academy, and who, removing his hat with old-time dignity, solemnly said: " You can go on painting, sir. You need not follow architecture. I wish you good day, sir," and so departed, and Elliott never saw him again.

Instead of remaining in the city to follow up this first success, Elliott returned to the centre of the state, and there painted portraits, for small prices, in the regular itinerant way. He did an enormous amount of work, and his skill increased greatly. Tuckerman relates with much detail how he became possessed of a particularly fine Stuart, which he studied profoundly and which had considerable influence on his style. This Stuart was admired and coveted by a local dignitary, who, when the painter would not part with it, had it seized for debt and sold by the sheriff, and then bought it in at a trifling cost — or, rather, he would have done so if the painter, forewarned, had not removed the original and placed in the frame a copy quite good enough to deceive the local critics. It was not until the new owner bragged of his prize that the truth came out, and then there was a lawsuit, which resulted in Elliott's paying his debt and retaining his picture.

After ten years of this life he, in 1845, returned to New York, and from then on until his death he had constant work. He was happily married, of a bright, sunny nature, with many friends and sufficient financial prosperity. The only cloud on his life was an excessive indulgence in drink, records of which crop up in the old annals, and which was commoner then than now. It is mentioned here only because he broke the habit, in the old manner (also rather out of fashion at present), by taking a pledge drawn up in legal form, witnessed by a friend, and signed on the bar after a valedictory drink.

This career, as will be noticed, is simply that of Chester Harding or Francis Alexander in a more settled community with another quarter of a century of development. There is one marked difference, however, in that Elliott apparently never went abroad. In spite of this and of his limited training, there is nothing provincial or uncertain about his *technique*. He was for his time the most skilful portrait painter in the country, and his work shows an even level of excellence, and a mature and unchanging method of work. He painted with a brush well charged with freely flowing paint, without fumbling or working over.   The drawing is firm, the color fresh and clean, the likeness well caught, very much like the contemporary work of Winterhalter and his contemporaries in France and, like that, rather lacking in personal feeling and poetry; but yet a distinct advance on Harding and Inman.   Elliott after his early days painted portraits exclusively and mostly heads, which were excellent.   When he attempted full-length figures the result was much inferior.   The costume of the time was inelegant and most of his sitters ungainly, and he had little idea how to compose a large canvas, painting the boots and the table-cover with the same insistence as the face.

FIG. 61.—HEALY: WEBSTER REPLYING TO HAYNE, FANEUIL HALL, BOSTON.

Working with Elliott in New York were a number of skilful practitioners.   Like him Thomas Le Clear was born in the centre of the state with a taste for painting, and led the itinerant portraitist's life in his youth there and in Canada, coming to New York in 1839. George A. Baker was a native of the city itself, whose father, said to have been an " artist of merit," instructed him in miniature painting, and he also studied in the schools of the Academy of Design. Both of these men painted some figure pieces, but their works are mostly portraits and very good.   Their *technique* has nothing of Elliott's sure, facile handling; it is much more uncertain, more variable; it will not average as good, but each at times produces a head which has finer qualities than anything of Elliott's.   Baker and Le Clear made short trips abroad, but these do not seem to have had much effect on their painting.   All three made New York their home, exhibited in the Academy, and formed part of the artist life of the city.

Healy, who had a greater reputation than any of them and probably painted more portraits, — even though Elliott is said to have executed over seven hundred, — had curiously little connection with the metropolis, executing some commissions there as he did in almost every great city, but residing mostly in Boston, Paris, or Chicago.   He was born in the first city, his father being a midshipman in the English navy, who settled there in his youth, married, and became captain in the merchant service.   He was Irish, and the Celtic strain runs bright and lovable through the temperament of his son.   In the father it was shown in the lack of business capacity which left his family practically without resources on his death, and George Peter Alexander Healy, the eldest of the five children, was chiefly occupied as a boy in trying to earn what he could to help his mother.

He made no attempt at drawing or painting until he was sixteen, and only then like Elliott because some of his schoolmates showed him their work and said that he could not do the like.   He succeeded beyond expectation and was fired with ambition to perfect himself.   He made the acquaintance of Miss Stuart, Gilbert Stuart's daughter, who was herself a fair painter and who helped him by advice, by the loan of an engraving of Guidos "Ecce Homo," which he copied in color and sold, and especially by introducing him to Sully, who after seeing his work advised him to become a painter and aided him with a kindly sympathy which Healy never forgot, but as long as the old painter lived, whenever he passed through Philadelphia, he called on him and paid what courtesy and honor he could to his not too prosperous declining years.

Encouraged by Sully's approbation and when only eighteen, Healy hired a room, put out a sign as portrait painter, and waited for clients.   Quarter day came before the clients, and he was forced to go to his landlord and explain the situation, but the latter was a

kindly man and instead of ejecting him gave him orders for portraits
of his son and son-in-law.   These were satisfactory and, other sitters
following, a modest prosperity commenced; but his sitters were all
men, and a portrait of a lady by Sully had given him a consuming
desire to paint a similar subject.   Finally one of his sitters advised
him to go to Mrs. Harrison Gray Otis and ask her to sit for him.
Healy was at this time nineteen, abnormally sensitive and shy, but
with that high courage which sometimes goes with such a temperament.   He needed it all, for Mrs. Otis was then in the full force
of her youth, a beauty, a social leader, and in every way an appalling
apparition for the youth of nineteen, who blurted out his message
after the manner of his kind and was surprised to find that the great
lady after the manner of her kind was rather favorably impressed by
his embarrassment in her presence.

She sat for him, got him other sitters, introduced him, and his
prosperity increased until, in 1834, he got together enough money
to start for Europe and insure his mother against want during his
absence.   The spirit in which he went is shown by his colloquy
with Morse in New York just before he sailed.   "So you want to
be an artist?   You won't make your salt.   You won't make your
salt."   "Then, sir, I must take my food without salt."   He managed
to do better than that and never knew real want, but his returns were
modest for a long time.   He had intended to stay a year or two in
Paris; he made it his home for sixteen, when he removed to Chicago
in 1855.   There he remained until 1867, when he went back to
Europe and remained in Paris and Rome until in 1892 he returned
to Chicago to die there three years later.   These were his chief domi-
ciles, but he made continual trips to England, to all parts of the Continent and to America when he was in Europe, to Europe when he
was supposed to be settled in America.   The number of his portraits
was enormous; he did not know it himself.   It is doubtful if any of
his contemporaries painted as many, or of more variously distinguished sitters.   Webster and Clay, Louis Philippe and Guizot,
Lincoln and Grant, Thiers and Gambetta, and many hundreds more
all passed before his easel.

As to the way in which he improved his opportunities, there
is not much to be said.   He had entered the studio of Baron

FIG. 62. — HUNTINGTON: MERCY'S DREAM, METROPOLITAN MUSEUM.

Gros on his arrival at Paris and worked there for two or three years. Couture passed through the studio at the time, but Healy did not know him until later when he became intimate with him and gave him his unqualified admiration. He was never his pupil, but his work is mostly according to the simple, effective method that Couture taught by word and example, strong firm outlines, warm transparent shadows, the lights built up with solid opaque color retouched and finished with transparent glazes. It is a good method enough, though like all methods, unless relieved by genius, apt to become monotonous when applied to a mass of work. It has the advantage when once thoroughly learned of relieving the painter of any doubts or hesitancy of what he is to do next, each stage of a canvas toward completion being clearly defined. In this style, using if anything a heavier impasto, Healy painted his numberless portraits, with sound drawing, pleasing color, and a resemblance which satisfied his sitters and their families. At his best his heads are strong, dignified, and characteristic; at his worst they are insipid — not badly executed, but heavy and uninteresting. There is no subtlety, the sentiment is apt to be commonplace, and the picture is held together in no harmony of artistic composition, his full-length figures being about as ungainly as the average American production of the time.

Besides his portrait groups he painted two huge compositions, " Franklyn urging the Claims of the American Colonies before Louis XVI " and " Webster replying to Hayne." Both were executed in France and shown at the Paris Exhibition of 1855 with a dozen or more portraits, and the Webster gained Healy a gold medal, a rare distinction then. It hangs now in Fancuil Hall in Boston, a valuable historical monument (the heads are all from life studies), and a testimony to the value of thorough French training and French surroundings. No other American artist at any cost of time and energy could have produced the huge canvas which does not seem to have required any special effort from Healy, who as far as schooling and *technique* go was entirely Parisian.

Healy lived to be eighty-two, painting up to the last. Another artist of the old portrait school only three years his junior has surpassed him both in length of years and in hale and vigorous old age. It gives a vivid measure of the brevity of our national art to recall that when Daniel Huntington was born in 1816, West was still alive and working.   The long and prosperous life had a fitting idyllic prelude when a pretty Tory girl sat on a Peekskill wall to see the Revolutionary army go by and General Jed Huntington, promptly and profoundly smitten by her charms, returned to win her for his bride in spite of royalist and high church prejudice, quite in the style of the popular romantic plays of to-day, although the opposition of the family was hardly fierce enough to be dramatic.   This pretty girl was Huntington's grandmother, her daughter marrying another Huntington (apparently no relation) and having three sons, of whom the artist was the second.   All three showed early talents for drawing, but the others finally entered the ministry.   Daniel's early efforts were considered so remarkable by his mother that she showed them to Trumbull, who was her kinsman, and got the opinion, " Better be a tea-water man's horse in New York than a portrait painter anywhere," which recalls the Colonel's gloomy attitude toward life and the fact that the ordinary water of the city was, before the opening of the Croton Aqueduct, considered so bad that a superior quality from certain favored springs was habitually peddled about the streets.

While still a boy Huntington went to New Haven, where he prepared for and entered Yale, but after about a year left it for Hamilton College in central New York.   Here Elliott came on one of his itinerant expeditions and painted heads of ten of the students at a reduced rate (five dollars instead of eight dollars), in consideration of their taking a quantity.   Huntington was one of the ten, and a lasting friendship sprang up between him and Elliott, who encouraged him to try painting and gave him some instruction.   On his graduation he entered the short-lived art department of the New York University recently founded by Morse, and also studied with Inman. In 1839 he went abroad, painting in Florence and Rome for a couple of years, and from 1851 to 1858 was in England; since then his work has been done in America.

For prolific production of portraits, Huntington fairly vies with the men just described.   Whether he or Elliott or Healy produced the greatest number, is probably an insoluble riddle; but Huntington, unlike the others, attempted every branch of painting, landscape,

FIG. 63 — PAGE: PORTRAIT OF MRS. PAGE, OWNED BY G. V. PAGE, ESQ.

with the ... lliputians ...... one olie ...... s ...... and retire *genre,* allegory, and still-life.   One of his first excursions was into the Catskills, and through his early life he was in sympathy with the Hudson River school, producing landscapes in their manner, includ-ing a huge Chocorua Peak.   He painted also figure pieces, pietistic allegories like " Mercy's Dream " or " Christiana and her Children," illustrations of Irving, comic, sentimental, and historical composi-tions, culminating in sixty or more figures of colonial times gathered about Martha Washington and representing the " Republican Court." Many of these have been reproduced in engraving and have enjoyed a wide popularity continuing even down to the present day, yet all together they are almost inconsiderable beside the long series of portraits — divines, bankers, merchants, pillars of society generally, with their wives, children, and other relations near and remote — that has appeared in an unbroken sequence for nearly seventy years.

Besides these purely professional labors, his high character, his intelligence, his social talents, his long life, gave the painter a lead-ing position among the artists of the city.   The people who posed to him for portraits (and as said, they were the best that the city or he country at large could show) held him in the highest esteem and 'ooked up to him as an oracle.   He was for years president of the Century Association and of the National Academy of Design; and such other honors as the country afforded were freely and deservedly his.   In view of all this it is an ungrateful task to define the limitations of his art, but it may be pointed out that he was unfor-tunate in his epoch and in his early surroundings.   Born a quarter of a century earlier, he would have gone naturally to London and West, and got something of the sound workmanship and large inspiration of Reynolds and his school ; a quarter of a century later he would have been brought in contact with the influx of good Continental work and would have had a cosmopolitan standard of excellence. As it is, his early activity corresponds with the lowest ebb of taste in the country, when thought was most platitudinous and when concep-tion of real distinction in art was smallest.

The causes for this have been already argued at length ; the fact remains that Huntington could not fail to be affected by such surroundings.   Talented, intelligent, industrious, he embodied the popular ideals in forms that are unexpectedly artistic under the circumstances. "Mercy's Dream" for instance, done on his return from his first trip abroad when he was but twenty-six, is well composed, solidly modelled, and with a pleasing color scheme. It was so popular that several replicas were made, and in general his work was enthusiastically accepted by the public. He did not have to struggle through long years of neglect and isolation to perfect himself, he only had to produce as rapidly as possible. Even when higher standards were slowly introduced, his host of friends still remained true to praise and purchase. Moral considerations, too, had something to do with the matter. He said himself, and not entirely unjustly, *à propos* of the Centennial Exhibition, that many of the French pictures were "evidently intended to pamper the tastes of lascivious men," and surely it were better to have "Martha Washington" in the house, however painted, than such things as that.

This attitude of mind manifests itself in his portraits: his men show capable and benevolent; his women, dignified and well-bred. The goodness displayed in their countenances might be conventional and rather insipid — the goodness of the Sunday-school books which formed so much of the reading of the time; but there were those who reviled them in the galleries for their commonplaceness who would yet have preferred them for family portraits in their own home to the brilliant work that was adorned with more meretricious graces. The weight laid on these moral qualities probably caused the purely artistic ones to be more neglected. The portraits are "like" but with no profound likeness, and while some are solid and strongly painted, especially among the earlier ones, the great majority are woolly in texture and of an unpleasant gray tone.

The public demanded nothing more than this, and anything further would have meant all manner of difficulties, doubtful success with small general recognition; and yet there were some who struggled with these unsympathetic surroundings, too sensitive to the higher beauty to sink to the commonplace admired of the general public, and yet unable to find in the uncertain maze of their admirations and aspirations any sure path to the expression of what was in them. Allston was the earlier type of this spirit, but Allston at least had the school training under West.

William Page, a mind of almost equal distinction and refinement, and with greater energy and perseverance, was driven from one of the great masters to another as the gusts of enthusiasm struck him, glowing with their inspiration, experimenting with their methods, and leaving a mass of work most various and unequal, and even at the best tentative and imperfect.   He was born in Albany in 1811, and was consequently the senior of Huntington by five years.   At nine he came to New York with his family and at eleven took a prize at the American Institute for an India-ink drawing.   In spite of this early inclination to the fine arts he was at first put in the law office of Frederic De Peyster, but his inaptness for the legal profession promptly showing itself, he turned to painting.   He had been presented to Colonel Trumbull as the accepted oracle in such matters, received his usual tirade on the unprofitableness of the painter's career, and then took employment under one Herring, who painted " portraits, banners, transparencies, etc."   After a year in his employ he became a student under Morse, entered the drawing school of the Academy of Design when it was founded, and his name appears on the list of prizes given on the first anniversary as the recipient of a silver medal.

This was in 1827, when Page was only sixteen ; but the next year he broke from art for a while, his whole mind occupied with the mysteries of religion.   He entered the Andover Theological Seminary, and though he persisted only some two years in his study of divinity there and at Amherst, yet the religious temperament endured with him to the last.   On giving up the idea of entering the ministry, he returned to portrait painting and found ample occupation in Albany, New York, Boston, and elsewhere. He married, not happily, was divorced, married again, and it was not until 1849 that he could make the long-desired trip to Italy.   There he entered into that chosen circle so charmingly described by Henry James in his recent life of Story, and which with its friendship, its atmosphere of culture, its stimulation of all beautiful emotions, its freedom from all cares, made the Rome of the fifties an Armida's garden to the sensitive American deprived in his native land of every soft, caressing touch of art or poetry.

After eleven years he returned to America and painted there

with varying popularity until his death, with the exception of a visit abroad in 1874 to study the alleged death-mask of Shakespeare. He had a home and studio at Eagleswood near that of Inness, with whom he was in peculiar sympathy.   One artist friend says of them, "With the single exception of George Inness I know of no man in whom the religious sentiment is so strong as in Page or who has so vivid and logical an apprehension of spiritual things," and like Inness he

FIG. 64. — GRAY: GREEK LOVERS, METROPOLITAN MUSEUM.

finally found contentment in the Swedenborgian faith.   That the landscapist left a more enduring work than the figure painter may be due somewhat to the fact that he was the younger by fourteen years and so of a more favored epoch; but more that he was a landscapist with a group of sincere fellow-workers about him and an acquaintance with the not too numerous examples of the Fontainebleau school, whose excellencies he was quick to detect and to adapt to his own work.   With the figure painter it was different.   His master, Morse, worked in widely varying manners, and the other contemporary portraitists resembled each other mainly in their mediocrity.   Any knowledge of higher art had to be worked out mainly from prints and books, aided by copies from the old masters, and perhaps an original or two.

On this shifting and insufficient foundation, Page produced some remarkable work.   He was naturally of an investigating and inventive mind.   He published later a *New Geometrical Method of measuring the Human Figure* and patented various improvements in guns and boats.   The processes of painting interested him enormously, and to the end of his life he was experimenting with all sorts of mediums and methods, greatly to the detriment of his pictures, which have almost invariably faded or darkened.   Some of his earlier work, like the "Governor Marcy" in the New York City Hall, is unlike any-thing that he was likely to have seen at the time, and must have been evolved from something read or heard about the methods of the old masters.   It is done in a heavy impasto, very forcible, strong in color and in contrast of light and shade, well drawn, fine in character, and with a real sense of composition and subordination of detail.   It stands out from all the surrounding portraits, even from Page's own "Governor Fenton," painted twenty-five years later.   If at this time he could have had access to a few good paintings of the Venetian school, it is possible that his style might have formed and he might have followed a single path to success; as it was, he went from experiment to experiment, and when he finally reached Venice, by way of Rome, it seems to have been too late.   His admiration for the Venetian work was unbounded, but he had accumulated too many tricks and crotchets on the way.   His work shows this mental dissipation.   He painted in every conceivable manner: from the most summary sketch to the most minute finish, from the roughest to the smoothest surface; but in all there is the struggle for something beautiful and noble.   There is distinction in his drawing, there is character in his heads, and more than a perfunctory echo of Venetian color in his "Venus."   There are portraits of his, rich, sumptuous, and mellow; there are others low in tone, subtle in tint, that have the delicate refinement of a Whistler.

A kindred spirit to Page, less profound, less energetic, but with the same admirations and the same ideals, was Henry Peters Gray,

U

some eight years his junior.   But Gray, after some preliminary study under Huntington, went to Italy when he was twenty for a stay of five years and frequently returned there.   He was spared, consequently, the struggle over the manner of expression, and his *technique* was simple and not greatly varied.   He had a liking for mellow color, for classical beauty, and for the balanced composition of the school of Poussin.   His allegorical and *genre* figures still retain not only charm but vitality.   Toward the end of his life he devoted himself largely to portraits of a soft, warm tone, an even smoothness of finish and with an Italianate echo in the style, very difficult to define, but perfectly recognizable in front of the canvas.

Another worker in Italy at this time was John Gadsky Chapman. Born in 1808, he was older than either Page or Gray, but he survived them both.   His talent for drawing manifested itself when he was a boy, and he was enabled to go to Italy to study, so that he began producing pictures of serious merit when he was very young, his " Hagar and Ishmael," admired by Mrs. Trollope, being executed just as he came of age.   Besides painting he made and engraved innumerable designs on wood and copper for Harper Brothers and the American Tract Society, and also published a drawing-book which went through many editions, and which, setting out with the principle that " any one who can learn to write can learn to draw," gave clear and sound advice of a modest sort.   His own drawing is shown in his etchings, which at their best are remarkably good for the time. Some of his little landscapes have a clean, neat execution resembling that of later men like Lalanne, for example.   A loftier achievement was the decoration of one of the panels of the Rotunda of the Capitol with the " Baptism of Pocahontas."   In 1848 he returned to Italy, and from that date he made Rome his home, though he revisited America twice, dying in Brooklyn in 1890.

Chapman was a skilful practitioner, whose Italian landscapes and whose groups (whether of " Pifferini " or of " Israelites spoiling the Egyptians ") followed so well the taste of his time that they have not for us to-day the interest of the more personal efforts of Page or even Gray.   Both of these latter painted figure subjects, but like Chapman they painted them mostly abroad and there was a constant tendency to lapse into portraits or single allegorical figures on their return to their own country. In fact, historical painting was almost impossible in America. Durand had intended to devote himself to such compositions when he came back in 1841, but he found the material hindrances too great. There were no suitable studios, no models, no costumes, no means of supplying the backgrounds or the hundreds of accessories needed. A historical scene could only be constructed with infinite pains, involving heavy expenditure, much time, and doubtful success. Domestic *genre*, the reproduction of the immediate life of the time, requires a perfection of workmanship to relieve the commonplace subjects, and Mount and Woodville had had no successors.

Some figure painting there was to satisfy the romantic and emotional demands of the day, heroines from Shakespeare and Byron, scenes from popular authors and from history, sacred and profane, but it was all pretty shallow. Any sentimental head was labelled with any sentimental heroine's name, and the settings of history in painting were on the same genial, uncritical level as in contemporaneous drama or opera. A hat with a plume, a long cloak, and a pair of tights did well enough for any character from the fall of the Roman Empire down to the Revolution. There were few artists of merit. Huntington's work has already been mentioned. Thomas P. Rossiter, who was born in New Haven in 1818 and who studied there under Jocelyn, went abroad with Durand and Kensett in 1840, and after a year and a half in London and Paris went with Cole to Rome and spent five winters there. He came back to New York and occupied with Kensett and Lang a studio building on Broadway, which was built for their accommodation. In 1853 he went to Paris again for three years, returning with a gold medal won at the exposition of 1855. Rossiter's work is facile, rapidly done, and was popular in its day, and for that very reason is antiquated now. The very titles tell the story, — " The Last Hours of Tasso," " The Parting between Ruth, Orpha, and Naomi," " The Return of the Dove to the Ark," " Morn, Noon, and Evening in Eden." He would have been a mighty man indeed who in the fifties could have infused enough vitality into such subjects to carry them unimpaired through half a century.

His contemporary, P. F. Rothermel of Philadelphia, was about a similar case. He got his first instruction from Bass Otis (the master of Inman), passed the usual years abroad, and sought fame with his canvases of "De Soto discovering the Mississippi" and "Saint Paul on Mars Hill," and also by some more modest classical groups in the taste of Coomans, which retain yet something of their prettiness; and there were many, many more whose names and achievements the curious may find detailed in Tuckerman's *Book of the Artists*, and elsewhere. They may even discover here and there a picture of real merit, but such finds will be rare. The fact is that the skill of the time was too small, the ideals too inartistic for good work. More skill, more knowledge, came through the Düsseldorf connection already spoken of in connection with the studies of the landscape painters and of Woodville, whose short life relegated him to an earlier epoch, though born about the same time as the men now under consideration.

The strongest exponent of Düsseldorf training is Emanuel Leutze who is counted as an American artist, though, as in some other cases, there could be argument adduced in support of an opposite opinion. He was born in Würtemberg in 1816, but his family moved to the United States soon after his birth and settled in Fredericksburg. The father was a mechanic whom political discontent led to emigrate, and the boy had the usual bringing up of a small inland town with rather more education than the average. He did not turn to art until he was twenty-two, and as soon as his portraits and figure pieces got him enough money and orders, he moved to Düsseldorf and stayed there nearly twenty years, marrying and making it his home, though with some visits to Italy and Munich and one to America in 1851. Here he painted a long series of historical compositions, many of American subjects, — "The Landing of the Norsemen in America," "Columbus before the Council," "Washington crossing the Delaware." In 1859 he returned to America and made it his home for the rest of his life. The next year he received a commission from Congress to decorate a stairway in the Capitol building and painted the "Course of Empire," being conscientious enough to make a trip to the Rocky Mountains for his scenery and another to Germany to consult Kaulbach on the best methods of fresco painting.

FIG. 65.— LEUTZE: WASHINGTON CROSSING THE DELAWARE, METROPOLITAN MUSEUM.

He continued the series of historical works, "The Settlement of Maryland," "First Landing of Columbus" and the like, and also executed a considerable number of portraits.

In all his works Leutze shows himself a typical Düsseldorfian, with the enthusiasms and admirations of the German romantic period expressed in a smooth, dull *technique*. He was not in the advance guard of the school. Younger men like Knaus were to put more brilliancy into the handling and more sincerity into the sentiment. Leutze clung to the earlier idols and was a sort of Teutonic Paul Delaroche, but without the finer French taste. His taste in fact now seems lamentably commonplace, and though greatly admired at the time, it was inferior to that of many of his American associates; but in knowledge of his craft as a figure painter he was far in advance of them. He could put together a complicated composition of many life-sized figures, all soundly drawn, in fairly accurate costumes and surroundings, and do it easily and without too much effort. It was a common accomplishment in France and Germany, but Leutze was skilful even among the Düsseldorfians. His works, like similar productions of the epoch in Europe, have not shown as great artistic vitality as that of less learned men with more feeling, but from some of his American historical compositions a generation of youth largely formed their ideas of history, and one at least, the "Washington crossing the Delaware," has fairly entered into the national consciousness and not unworthily. It is a good picture of its kind, well drawn, well composed, with the details of the scene realized by the imagination until it carries conviction of its reality. Above all, the sentiment of the subject is there rendered in such a way as to be understood by all. It has taught to successive generations of school children, as text-books could not, the high fortitude and faith of Washington amid discouragements and dangers. There is something of German rather than American in the faces, showing where his models were obtained; just as the ice-filled river was painted not from the Delaware but from the Rhine. The coloring is cold and there is the smooth, monotonous finish of the Düsseldorf work. The picture succeeds by its story-telling rather than its artistic side, but it still is the most successful of Leutze's works. The others are all less convincing in conception and rarely any better painted.

Leutze represents the culmination of a certain type of historical painting in America. Pictures like his are still produced in Germany and, with modifications for national taste, everywhere in Europe, but they have practically ceased here for causes which have been already suggested. Their execution demanded a training that was not to be had in America, and the painter that came nearest to equalling Leutze's productions was not only educated, but born abroad. This was Constant Mayer, who was born in Besançon, studied in Paris under Cogniet, and did not come to America until 1857. He was a younger man than Leutze by sixteen years and no way his equal in ability; but in spite of Mayer's French birth and training their ideals were much the same. Mayer's " Captain John Smith and Pocahontas " is manifestly of the same epoch as Leutze's " Settlement of Maryland." With all this Mayer was a thoroughly competent painter with a tendency to commonplaceness both in workmanship and taste. He painted not so many great historical compositions as smaller canvases of one or two figures, reflecting a mild sentimentality.

To complete the list of foreign-born artists working in New York at this time, mention should be made of Louis Lang, who was born in Würtemberg at about the same time as Leutze, and after studies in Stuttgart and Paris came to this country in 1838. His works, mostly small pictures of a sort of historic *genre*, are hardly good enough to require notice; but Lang himself was a cheery, bustling little figure in the art world for many years, a constant exhibitor at the Academy, active in the clubs and in social circles, and trying to infuse into the life of the day something of the Düsseldorfian *gemüthlichkeit.*

CHAPTER XVI

INCREASE OF FRENCH INFLUENCE

SUCCESSORS OF LEUTZE. — STUDENTS IN FRANCE FOR THE MOST PART. — THOSE THAT STILL WENT TO ITALY. — VEDDER. — COLEMAN. — MAY'S WORK IN PARIS. — WILLIAM M. HUNT

THE works of Leutze and his school, in spite of their knowledge and industry, are become old-fashioned and strange to us, and the same may be said of the productions of Page and Gray. Exceptions might be made in regard to some few canvases, but as a rule they lacked either inspiration or skill, and interest in them is dead. They are recognized as hopelessly of another age, with other methods and other ideals. But another generation of artists was rising not much younger than Leutze, and who exhibited with the men described in the last chapter, but whose work is living and modern to-day. Some of the men themselves are still alive, their powers unimpaired, their enthusiasm undiminished, their influence on the increase. They are not thought of as old; they may be in the fullest maturity of their powers, exercising their greatest influence, but they form a class by themselves.

There is a clearly appreciable difference between the men who were of age when the Civil War broke out and the more numerous group that studied in Europe in the early seventies, and who for a quarter of a century endured to be called "the younger men" and who are at times so referred to still, although the imputation of youth has lost something of its accuracy. Their predecessors of the sixties had a different training. Studying abroad had not been simplified then as now, there were more difficult surroundings, a greater struggle, and it would seem, as a result, a higher and more personal success. This impression may be largely due to the longer lapse of time which has permitted the dross to fall out and be forgotten while each year has confirmed and strengthened the works of the masters,

and given to them an assurance of merit to which newer productions
cannot at once attain. Something of the kind has happened to landscape, and the men under consideration were contemporary with and
rank beside our great landscapists, — Inness, Martin, and the rest, —
but these latter in spite of their differences of temperament were a result
of an orderly evolution; they were bound together by certain similarities of aim, they belonged, in short, to a school. With the figure
painters it was otherwise; their training was as dissimilar as their
characters. Whether they went abroad, as most of them did, or
stayed in America, they took as their fancy moved them whatever
they found desirable in the whole range of painting and adapted it to
their wants, and yet in them all there was a greater sanity, more
knowledge of the conditions of painting, and of what was possible
and what not, than their predecessors like Allston and Page had.
Their emotions were not less noble, but they were better adapted
for pictorial expression.

Naturally they do not divide readily into groups. Each man
was a law to himself. Paris had become the favorite place for
study as it was the best. There May and Hunt and La Farge
sought each in his own way the principles of the grand style,
and there Whistler perfected his delicate talent, while Wylie and
Mosler studied *genre*. England was practically deserted, and even
Germany suffered a temporary eclipse, though Eastman Johnson,
older than most of the others, studied a year or so at Düsseldorf
before going to The Hague. In Italy there was no instruction worth
seeking, but the old inspiration was still there. The charm of Rome
and the ample classic dignity was still potent with men like Eugene
Benson, Vedder, and C. C. Coleman.

These last-named men have a certain bond among themselves if
only in their common renunciation of aims held by nearly all their
co-workers. It was not methods of work which they sought in Italy;
they had not been charmed by the glowing color or the beauty of
surface of the Barbizon school, still less by the more accurate representation of nature by its followers. What they sought, consciously or
unconsciously, was a deeper sentiment, a larger inspiration. It was
the old thirst for the fulness and beauty of intellectual and emotional
life which had mastered Allston and Page and Story and so many

FIG. 66.—VEDDER: ECLIPSE OF THE SUN BY THE MOON.

others, and beside which all that America had to offer seemed poor and meagre. It is noticeable, however, that the men mentioned reached Rome in the sixties, and that they have had few followers since. Changed conditions in Italy largely account for this, but something is also due to an improvement at home. It is true that the exodus to Paris still continues, but the charm of Paris, subtle and wonderful as it is, is still not comparable to the spell that Rome cast upon her visitors fifty years ago. Paris is modern, and for Paris it is possible to develop an equivalent on this side of the Atlantic; but the old Roman society of fifty years ago is as irrevocably a thing of the past as the *douceur de la vie* in pre-revolutionary France. At the same time, at home the old narrowness and bareness of American life, that by contrast gave such fascination to the soft, cultured, rather degenerate Italy, has been replaced by a culture broader and more liberal even if it still lacks mellowness.

The most important of these later emigrants to Italy was Vedder, as he was also the oldest, having been born in New York City in 1836. He had a childish love of art, and produced work of "decided promise," even at the age of twelve. From Tompkins Matteson, a prolific *genre* painter of the days of the Art Union, he received some instruction; but before he was of age he went to Paris, where he studied under Picot, but soon moved from there to Rome, where he spent five years, returning for another five years to America; and finally, in 1866, settling in Rome, which has been his home ever since, though with visits to America numerous enough and long enough to keep him still a "good American."

This long stay in Italy has been for no training that the schools had to offer, nor for any inspiration that he gained from work being done there. In fact, he has rejected both. Even during his first visit when he was still learning the principles of his art he frequented no academy, followed no teacher, and his work at no time had any resemblance to that done by living Italian masters. The affinity was rather with the great men of the past, with Raphael or Michael Angelo, but that came later. Its early characteristic was its classical quality. While the whole trend of art at this time was toward a more accurate and minute study of nature, a careful discrimination of slight differences of form and tone, Vedder has consistently held

to the old simplicity and has sought, not the infinite transitory details that differentiate the individual, but the eternal type that lies
beneath them.   This point of view is shown in his earliest work produced during his stay in America during the sixties.   Technically
it is painted much like other work of the time, but there is a tendency
to minimize detail, to accent the characteristic lines, and to exalt and
dignify the subject.   A notable instance of this is the " Lair of the
Sea-Serpent," where the monster of the deep, stretching his interminable coils along the barren sand-dunes, was in fact copied, and for
the most part literally copied, from a dead eel cast up on the shore,
but transfigured by the painter into a type of the terror and mystery
of the sea.   This note of mystery, this recognition of the infinite and
unknowable, forms, with his classical feeling, the other characteristic
of Vedder's work.   It is not classical, but still less is it mediæval or
of the modern neurotic type.   There are no vague terrors, no emotional hysterics, no murky shades populated by malignant or beneficent spirits.   It is calm, virile, intellectual, a mystery of which Darwin
and Huxley might well approve, recognizing the immovable barriers
set to our knowledge, and that while we may conjecture what is beyond we can have no certitude and yet are forced continually to ask
the question to which we know there is no answer.

This idea, not in itself a pictorial one, was expressed without any
of the romantic expedients of blurred outlines, misty backgrounds, or
forced effects, but with a classical clarity and simplicity.   It appears
in a number of small pictures of about the same date as the " Sea-
Serpent," such as the " Questioner of the Sphinx," the " Lost Mind,"
" Recognition," which were accompanied by landscapes and by several subjects from the *Arabian Nights*, realized with a grave humor.
After his return to Rome his art developed along these lines, sometimes in canvases whose sole object seemed to be arrangement of
dignified, simplified form, sometimes with a deeper meaning as in the
" Cumæan Sibyl " or the " Marsyas," with its underlying pantheism.

It was, however, in 1884 that he published his illustrations to
the *Rubaiyát* of Omar Khayyám, his most important work up to
that time, and the one which confirmed his reputation.   It was not
that the artistic advance was so great.   A limited number admired
him before, but his pictures were few, mostly in private possession,

and moreover their point of view was so personal that it was not readily seized in a few scattered examples. The *Rubaiyát* revealed him to the world. The charm of the work is very great. The drawings were made on gray paper in black and white crayon, and reproduced by a photographic process which was faithful, but which had no special charm of surface or tone. The compositions, as was inevitable in such a series, varied in merit, yet the general effect was of a unity profoundly and nobly simple.

Never before had a book of poems received a pictorial commentary so sympathetic, so beautiful, and so illuminative, for it is not too much to say that the illustrations deepen and illumine the sentiment of the quatrains. It took no effort to fit them together. The philosophy of the verses was Vedder's own, and one might almost say that the form would have been his also had he expressed himself in words. They bring up again the great, simple problems of life which have run through all variations of men and manners. The art to match them must be intellectual, not sensuous, depending for its interest on something other than richness of color or texture of surface. It must be literary in fact, and literary art is at present much denounced in theory and little followed in practice. A picture which does not contain within itself all the elements necessary for its enjoyment is false in construction — a principle true enough in its way, but which must not be pushed too far. The greatest art has always had in it something beyond an appeal to the eye, and to make that appeal intelligible to the spectator has always been the task of the artist. Vedder has struggled with it like another, aiding the meaning with symbols and emblems; sun-dials and rose leaves, hour-glasses and nightingales taking the place of the scrolls with inscriptions of a more primitive art; but the main point is that he has been successful.

The man of ordinary intelligence feels the thrill which is the test of a work of art. It is a triumph of Invention — that quality which Richardson puts first in the list of parts in which the whole art of painting consisted, though it has fallen from its leading position in these days of realism. But there are other artistic qualities besides invention in Vedder's *Rubaiyát*. The drawing has an ample, synthetic charm, the figures have an appealing dignity or grace, and the composition, constantly varied, constructed on the most different plans.

is ever drawn into original and charming harmonies of mass and line. The lack of color and of rich surface is not felt. It was the idea that occupied the artist and the clothing of the idea with a form which should make it intelligible. It is this which gives him his affinity to the fresco painters of the Renaissance, and it is worthy of remark that like them this knowledge of form enables him to turn his hand to sculpture or goldsmith work, creating a bust, a piece of jewelry, or an elaborately decorated memorial cup with equal facility. Some of his early works were rich in color and surface effect, but he seems to have distrusted brilliancy as a disturbing element, and even before the time of the *Rubaiyát* he had begun to use opaque color in his shadows until his works had something of the tone of paintings in gouache, with no strong contrasts of light and shade. This method he still uses and with peculiar effect in the decorative painting which he has mainly produced of late years, but this is so recent that it must be discussed later under the general subject of recent decorative painting.

Associated in a way with Vedder in Italy, with something of his temperament and something of his execution, is Charles Caryl Coleman. One of the earliest of his pictures was a study of Vedder's studio with the artist in it, and he painted in the early part of his career a number of figure pieces and portraits; but of late he has turned more to landscapes and architectural subjects, with their characteristic lines strengthened so as to give a decorative, almost monumental, quality. This is particularly recognizable in the studies of blossoming branches of apple or plum, which are his most characteristic works, and where the flowers, studied directly from nature, are yet arranged with such a balancing of mass, such a delicate choice of color in the background and accessories, and so firm an accentuation of their outline, that the canvas has a charm of decorative unity. Coleman has not made his permanent quarters at Rome, but has lived elsewhere, and even at one time had a studio in London; but of late years his home has been in a villa at Capri, never to be forgotten by its guests, with its orange trees, its vine-clad terraces, and its white walls leaning against the steep hill.

Eugene Benson also has the echo of the classic feeling in his landscapes; but of late years he has painted little, and he was never

FIG. 67. — COLEMAN : TWILIGHT AND POPPIES.

[From a Copley Print. Copyright, 1899, by Curtis & Cameron, Publishers, Boston.]

very productive in pictures, turning quite as often to writing as to painting for a means of expression.

Besides these there were other artists in Italy. The visits, more or less long, of the landscapists have already been recorded. There was always a changing group of visitors admiring the marvels of old art and occasionally stopping to work, and there were some permanent residents left over from an earlier day; but after the war few chose it for their home or as a place for learning their art. Paris had become the art centre of the world. Leslie writes in his memoirs after seeing the exhibition of 1855, "The enormous collection of pictures and sculpture confirmed what I had before thought, that these arts have gradually declined in England and advanced on the Continent since the peace of 1815." But France had had for a couple of centuries a sounder tradition and a more thorough training than any other country. It was only the brilliant group of English portrait painters that challenged her supremacy at a time when the exaggeration of classical authority had chilled original genius. When these influences weakened, she resumed her old leadership, which even the subsequent fame of Munich hardly affected. The great influence for good which her rising school exercised in American portraiture and landscape has already been mentioned. Outside the White Mountain school there were many that felt the inspiration. As far back as the early forties, Winckworth Allan Gay was working under Troyon, less than a dozen years his senior.

Gay was born in Massachusetts, and while quite a boy his taste for painting had led to his being taken into the family of Professor Weir at West Point, and receiving from him a sound foundation. His art life, after his return to America, centred around Boston, where most of his works are. His career has been long and honorable, and deserving of greater fame than it has received. His painting is better than that of most of the New York men who were his early contemporaries, but perhaps on that account he never had the same pecuniary vogue; for even in New York it was not the best painters whose pictures sold for the highest prices. Most of the men who broke away from the dry, thin manner of the early landscape school suffered for it financially, appreciation coming to them not so much from New York, where prices were highest, as from Boston.   It is no small honor to the latter city that men like Rousseau, Troyon, Millet, and Corot, and such American painters as felt their inspiration and assimilated their spirit, found there cordial admirers and purchasers while the new movement was still but vaguely understood or accepted even in France.   This was owing largely to the influence of men like Gay, and more especially of later men — Babcock, Hunt, and others,— who were not (as in New York) opposed by the authority of other painters, older, more respected, and bound together by contrary dogmas.   One figure painter went to Paris from New York in those early days, Edward Harrison May, born in 1824, the same year as Hunt.   But May was of English birth and came to America as a boy of ten, when his father was called to the pastorate of one of the Dutch Reformed churches.   It was a cultivated, talented family.   His sister had some reputation as a writer of both prose and poetry, and painted besides, and May had an aptitude for the exacter sciences of mathematics and engineering.   He studied under Huntington, and his early work met with fair success in New York in the days of the Art Union; but he soon left for Europe, and after that most of his life was spent abroad. He was working in Couture's studio in 1851 and subsequently made several trips to Italy to study the old masters; he came back to America for visits and finally died in Paris in 1887.

May was an excellent painter of the academic type.   He had mastered the methods of work taught by Couture, which, in spite of Couture's position as an outsider, were the generally accepted methods of the time.   To these he added a sound, large draftsmanship, a feeling for warm, rich color of the Couture type, and a sense of composition gained perhaps from the many copies that he made of old paintings.   These copies were highly praised for their faithfulness, and his portraits were also commended; but his reputation now is mainly connected with his figure pieces.   These were good-sized canvases with life-sized figures, — "The Death of a Brigand," "The Magdalen," "Jewish Captives at Babylon," the regular Salon picture in fact, but thoroughly well done.   The French critics of their day, including Théophile Gautier, praised their sterling qualities, and they are not yet antiquated or out of fashion.   They would still make a good show in the old Salon and win medals and decorations, but there is no intensity of personal emotion nor of personal expression, least of all is there any national character about them. May should probably be considered an American artist, but from his work he might have been a Frenchman or even a German.

In all these respects William Morris Hunt, who preceded May by a few years in Couture's studio, was in strong contrast to him. In the first place, he was an American by birth, race, and training, having been born in Brattleboro, Vermont. The family had some wealth and more than usual intelligence. The father was a member of Congress, and the sons all followed professional careers. Besides the painter, his brother Richard M. Hunt was an architect of exceptional training and influence, and two other brothers were respectively a doctor and a lawyer. William Morris was sent to Harvard when he was sixteen and enjoyed the life there more than he did the studies, which seemed to him tedious and barren. He succeeded in getting rusticated, and imprudence during the period of his suspension resulted in a cold which threatened to become consumption and which rendered a warmer climate necessary. His mother therefore moved with her family to Europe, and after visiting several cities finally settled in Rome long enough for Hunt to begin work with H. K. Brown the sculptor.

The idea of returning to Harvard was given up in favor of a life devoted to art. Hunt is said to have worked for a short time in Paris under Barye, in 1844, but soon went to Düsseldorf to study painting. He found school discipline there as little to his taste as at Harvard. The school was conducted "upon the principle that the education of art genius, of a mechanic, and of a student of science were one and the same thing — a grinding, methodical process for the accumulating of a required skill," and he determined to go to Pradier in Paris and recommence sculpture. The sight, during a flying trip to America, of the " Falconer," by Couture, changed his mind again, and he entered the latter's studio. There he found instruction to his taste — an art feeling that he could enter into, and there he stayed some five years, becoming a favorite pupil, working in the private studio of the master, and praised and put forward by him.

But the study of some of the old masters caused him to doubt
the adequacy of Couture's method and, soon after, an introduction by William Babcock to Millet caused him to transfer his
allegiance to the Barbizon master in spite of the jeers of the
Atelier Couture.   He went to Barbizon to gain a greater intimacy
with Millet, studying his works and buying them as far as his
means permitted, going on long walks with him and doing all
that he could to enter into his spirit; for Millet never taught any
pupils except indirectly by example and casual talk.   After two
or three years of this life, in 1855 he returned to America, settling
first in Newport, but working much elsewhere in New England,
especially in Boston, where he finally took a permanent studio in
1862.   He painted many portraits, many figure pieces, was prominent in art circles, executed two remarkable decorations for the
Capitol at Albany, and was an active, artistic, and social influence
up to the day of his death, in 1879.

It is not easy to give a satisfactory appreciation of the work
and influence of Hunt.   He belongs to the class of which Allston
was the type and precursor, ardent young Americans, intelligent,
enthusiastic, feeling the charm of the accumulated art of the Old
World with a freshness and an intensity to which the native mind,
dulled by constant familiarity, rarely attains.   Nor was it all vague
emotion.   The men produced work full of promise, but the promise
was never quite fulfilled.   When they returned to America there
was something in their surroundings or in themselves that checked
their development.   In the case of Hunt, it was not the lack of
sympathy.   If the great mass were wholly indifferent and the
majority of the artists rather hostile, yet the people with whom
he came in contact were his friends and admirers, comprehending
and encouraging him.   Few artists have had surroundings more
sympathetic.   What he lacked was professional criticism, a few
intimate friends — or enemies — who were of the craft, knowing of
what the art was capable, understanding his aims, and insisting on
their complete achievement rather than taking the intention for
the accomplishment.   Such criticism was peculiarly necessary
to Hunt, for he was not completely master of his craft.   He was
right to reject the drudgery of Düsseldorf, which would certainly

FIG. 68. — HUNT: THE BATHERS.

have limited his development; but though later he worked hard under Couture, who was an excellent draftsman, his drawing lacks some of the prosaic but necessary Düsseldorfian qualities. He was just emerging from the student stage when he broke away to follow Millet, and a dozen years of the severest self-training should have followed. Something of the kind there was but not enough, and he remains to the end an amateur, not only in the sense of loving his art, but also in lacking the sure professional mastery.

His first exhibited work, a portrait of his mother done in 1850, is purely a work of Couture's *atelier*, and the same may be said for the " Prodigal Son," though there the handling had become looser and freer so that it was not very well received. His other early figure pieces mostly show the same influence, though yielding to that of Millet in his "Sheep Shearing" and some smaller canvases. It was after his return to America, when he had forgotten or assimilated the example of his French masters, that his most personal and original work was produced, figure pieces like the "Boy and the Butterfly," his many portraits, his landscapes and still-life studies, culminating with his decorations in the Albany Capitol.

The work is most varied and most unequal, but it leaves an unsatisfied feeling in the mind. It was so promising, so promising to the end, but somehow it never culminated into masterpieces, rounded and complete, where the painter could be said to have given the full measure of his temperament. The Albany decorations approach nearest such a standard, but done under unfavorable circumstances and in almost impossible time limits, they were still tentative and incomplete. It might have been otherwise if the scheme for the complete decoration of the Capitol had been given him, as proposed, and his life had been spared to complete it.

This regret for what might have been should not belittle Hunt's actual achievement. His was a strong, artistic temperament, personal and not to be turned into a mere echo of Couture or any other master. He had not only the emotional delight in beauty common to so many young Americans in Europe, but his emotional perception was artistic. He saw form simply, nobly, and in those great masses that give character, and he was besides a colorist. There is a certain ability to give a warm, rich tone to a picture which the competent student gets in a good school.   In this sense May has just been called a good colorist, but Hunt was something different and beyond.   He was a colorist as Inness was, and felt naturally the delicate harmonies and contrasts of nature ; he remembered them and recorded them in all their strength or subtlety.   Coloring was not a kind of varnish to be spread over the picture; it was the picture.   Canvases like the " Bathers " or the " Boy and the Butterfly," his landscapes or still-life studies, are simply records of his delight in beautiful tones.   Even some of the earlier figure subjects are relieved from commonplaceness by the luminousness of a neck or a bit of dress against the sky. This feeling for color united with that for large, simple form made Hunt impatient of minute handling and forced him into a freer *technique* than had been previously used in America, and it is through this large handling and the feeling for texture involved with it that he exerted his greatest influence.

We have to recall the opposition and abuse which so conventional a thing as his " Prodigal Son " aroused when exhibited at the Academy of Design and at New Haven to understand how universal was the laborious, inartistic *technique* evolved from Düsseldorf and an untrained native taste.   In landscape, Inness and Homer D. Martin broke away from it, bringing down upon themselves the reproaches and ridicule of their *confrères*, but in figure painting Hunt was the first.   He was hardly master enough of his craft to lead the way with absolute authority.   He could draw accurately enough in the Couture manner if he set himself seriously to the task, but in the swift, dashing work that he loved he was not sure enough to do with certainty what he would.   When, for instance, he painted a larger version of the " Bathers," he neither corrected the faults nor retained the freshness of the original sketch, and his portraits were generally left unfinished.   He worked on them impetuously for a few hours, striking in the broad general masses, and then his interest would die out.   He shirked the labor of carrying the sketch to completion ; but when his enthusiasm lasted to the end, he produced canvases like the " Chief Justice Shaw," admirable in character and workmanship, — and much derided in Boston when first   shown.   His   message   was   that   nothing   but   the   essential should be painted, and nothing unless the artist felt an immediate, personal enthusiasm in his work. It is this that gives vitality to his paintings, and he taught it equally in his life.

Hunt was a personage in Boston. His irrepressible energy, his magnetism, his outbursts of praise or blame, his picturesque phrase, his catholic taste, so independent and sure that he was an apostle for Japanese art as well as for the Barbizon school, all gave him a power which he exercised nobly. At Newport, in the early days of his return, he greatly influenced La Farge and later, when J. Foxcroft Cole and Bicknell and other early students in Paris came back, he bought their pictures and did what he could to make their path easy. At the sight of some of Vedder's pictures he wrote to the artist, whom he did not know at all personally, and organized an exhibition of his works in Boston, which was successful in every way. Special fame has been gained by the class of young ladies that he taught, and his incisive admonitions to them have been garnered in a book. It is not recorded that any of his pupils gained great distinction in art, but one envies them their excitement, their loyalty to their master, their illusions. Hunt made them share his emotions, which was an education in itself; he could not make them share his work, and even in his own case the emotions were probably finer than the work. He may have thought so himself, for one of his sadder sayings is, " In another country I might have been a painter." Perhaps with more encouraging surroundings his art might have been more complete, but his influence could hardly have been greater for good. He was of his time and helped to shape it, and as he retorted to some one who spoke to him of Allston, feeling perhaps a sort of parallelism in their lives, " Well, there is one thing they can say of me : that I have seen something of what has been going on around me."

CHAPTER XVII

LA FARGE AND WHISTLER

THIS French influence culminated in two artists almost exactly
contemporaries by birth, and who, though dissimilar in character, in
training, and in almost all the circumstances of their lives, are yet
approximately equal in achievement; and who, moreover, are united
by a peculiarly intense refinement of artistic perception. John
La Farge was the younger of the two, being born in 1835, a year
later than Whistler; but his work connects with and carries on, in
a way, that of Hunt and May, while Whistler's formative influences
and surroundings were exclusively foreign. The career of La Farge,
is part, and a large part, of the intellectual development of America.
It may be claimed as indisputably our own, and yet the fact that he
was of undiluted French blood seems to help to explain it.

His father, an officer in the French Marine, came to this country
in 1806, by way of the West Indies and Louisiana, finally reaching New York, and there marrying a daughter of one of his compatriots, an *émigré* of the Revolution. From plantations in
Louisiana and purchases of lands elsewhere, the elder La Farge
became rich, according to the standards of his day, and his son grew
up surrounded not only with material comforts, but with means
of culture, which French influence made completer and ampler
than common. There were books, there were pictures, and
his maternal grandfather, M. Binsse de St. Victor, who himself
painted miniatures, taught him drawing. When, after some study
of the classics and some of law, he visited Paris, his father advised
him to take up the study of art as an accomplishment, and he

WHISTLER: PORTRAIT OF ARTIST'S MOTHER, GALLERIE DU LUXEMBOURG, PARIS.

entered the *Atelier* Couture, moved thereto by the advice of May,
who recommended his own master. He entered simply as an amateur and did not remain long, though Couture was sympathetic and
approved his work, fostering his individuality and advising him to
study the masters in the Louvre; so he made drawings from them
and afterward copied the sketches of the old masters in Munich
and Dresden, and, during a trip to England, saw and studied the
works of the Pre-Raphaelites.

All of this was combined with personal and social intercourse
with the artists and critics, to whose inner circle his family connections gave him admission. Paul de St. Victor was his cousin,
and he met men like Théophile Gautier, Charles Blanc, Puvis de
Chavannes, and later Rossetti and Millais. With all this he was
continually testing the work that he saw, the theories that he
heard, by his own reasoning, by his own emotions. He was not
grubbing at the drudgery of a profession; he wished to appreciate,
to understand, to enjoy, but not to become a painter; and so, his
travels over, he returned to New York and entered a lawyer's office.
The study of the law was not likely to prove entirely congenial to
him, and it is on record that he combined it with much miscellaneous reading, thinking, and dreaming.

But the final break seems to have occurred when Hunt returned
from France. His nature, so frank, so enthusiastic, so buoyant, so
appreciative of what was beautiful or noble, impressed the younger
man, who deserted the office and followed him to Newport, and
there worked under his influence and counsel. He painted everything — landscape, figures, still-life — until 1866, when there came a
severe illness, from which it took him several years to recover, during
which time he made drawings for illustrations. In 1873 there was
another short trip abroad; in 1876 came the decoration of Trinity
Church in Boston, the next year that of St. Thomas in New York,
and other decorative work followed, but he now became especially
interested in stained glass. His attention had first been called to it,
in 1873, by the defects which he saw in the work done in England;
and experiments that he made upon his return aroused his interest,
until finally his chief energy was given to the new development of
the art, though there was time, also, for the direction of decorative

work in marble or wood, with additions of ivory, mother-of-pearl, and the like.   Then in 1886 came failing health again, and a trip to Japan, followed by one to Samoa and the South Sea, and after that more stained glass, writing, lecturing, and painting taken up again with enthusiasm and increasing power, gaining in strength and ripeness up to the present time.

If any one acquainted with the history of American art could know the career of La Farge without knowing his works, the conclusion would be inevitable that here was another Allston, with less brilliant promise in his youth, and less complete failure at the end, but still a man whose inspirations and emotions must wither within him for lack of adequate means of expression and a comprehending public.   The training is so manifestly insufficient, the New York of the seventies was so hopelessly material in its interests!   That the achievement, in spite of difficulties, has been so high, that the appreciation, though limited, has been so sincere, after all honor has been given to the artist, yet leaves a feeling of satisfaction that such a life, if not fostered by its surroundings, has at least become possible in America.   Granted the exceptional quality of the talent, yet there must have been culture to recognize it, wealth to employ it, and some surroundings of beautiful works of art to foster it, and all of these he found somehow in his own country.   Certain great traditions of the masters he possesses as no other of his compatriots; but of actual study in Europe he has had less than any of them.   His training, in fact (granting, as before, his talent), casts grave doubts on the methods of education for artists now universally adopted.   He made no long series of laborious studies of weary, ungainly nude models, years of which task work are now considered the unavoidable prelude to a painter's career.   He seems to have rarely done anything where the result was not intended to be in itself beautiful or interesting.   Difficulties did not deter him.   Of all things for a beginner, the copying of sketches by the great masters would seem to be the most impossible and impractical.   They are either the hasty record of some conception, careless of accuracy, the lines running helter-skelter at the instinct of the hand, and the result gained, the artist himself hardly knows how; or else they are careful notation of details, a head, a hand, a cast of drapery, to take their place later

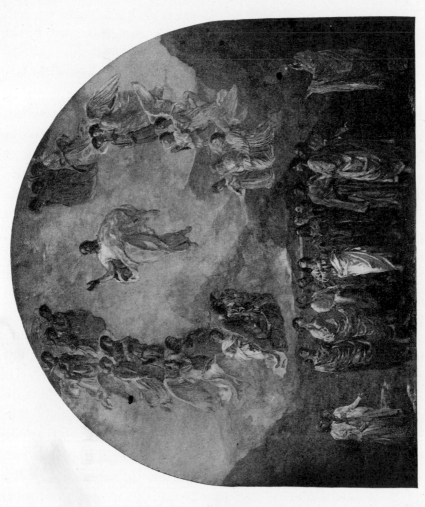

FIG. 69.— LA FARGE : ASCENSION OF CHRIST. CHURCH OF THE ASCENSION, NEW YORK.

in a larger work. They but supplement an unexpressed conception in the artist's mind. They are the most intimate revelation of his nature and admirably adapted to enlarge the insight and enthusiasm of the amateur, but apparently most unsuitable to teach proportion, construction, and the other fundamentals of the craft.

Yet it is through this sympathetic insight not only into the appearances but into the spirit of things that La Farge's art has developed. The association with Hunt was fortunate for him, not only in finally turning him to art (if indeed it was the deciding influence), but because it gave him a friend and counsellor, sympathetic, enthusiastic, and peculiarly qualified to correct the defects of his training and temperament; for the natural tendency of La Farge seems to have been toward an over-interest in detail, a supersubtle discrimination of tones and forms which gave him sympathy with the Pre-Raphaelites in England, and made Hunt dispute with him for " paying too much attention to refinements which not one artist in a hundred would understand." This intense perception of minutiæ was always retained, so subtle, so characteristic, that it can hardly be appreciated except from his own works or words. The following illustrates it as well, and no better, than a hundred other extracts that might be made. He is speaking to a pupil who is trying to paint a dull gray sky: —

" The sky that we are now looking at is not only modelled by what we call light and shade, so delicately that we find it difficult to trace, but it is modelled by varieties of color.

" As you will see, toward the horizon, I mean our horizon, because the tops of the houses are over the horizon, it is a little yellower. The clouds that float in it, of which we mainly see the shadows, are more violet; the upper sky, where the clouds are thinner, is greener, meaning that there is the faintest suggestion of blue, and, if you will watch a little, you will notice that all this mass of low cloud where it is thicker and makes shadows as it comes nearer to the brick buildings, seems to harmonize with them and you feel that there is a little pink or rosy hue more or less everywhere.

" Were the sky to appear suddenly, you might see these fog-clouds — those that are low down, at least, look reddish; but as you have no contrast to help you, your eye is not very sensitive to this. Only if you do not feel it and give some suggestion of it, you keep

Y

on wondering why your painted sky is so cold and tea-boardy."
The reader wonders what the young lady pupil made of such
advice.   It contrasts strongly with Hunt's *Talks on Art*, where the
counsel is always of simplicity, boldness, unity, so that it is fair to
suppose that La Farge owes much to him in that direction, as well
as in color, texture, and handling, the influence in these latter qualities being clear in many of the earlier pictures.

Of La Farge's work as a whole, there is not space to speak ade-
quately.   It is not so great in quantity, considering the long life, the
constant labor, but it is so varied in subject, in feeling, in scale; it is
executed in so many different mediums, employed in such unexpected manners that it does not lend itself to generalizations.   Each
work has its own mood, its own message, its own charm, so individual and appealing that it seems impossible to pass it over without
description and analysis.   Take the earlier work at random, the
" Portrait of a Boy with a Dog," the " Paradise Valley," the little
" Venus Anadyomene," a gem that might have been made in Bel-
lini's studio by some young fellow-student of Titian or Giorgione,
the " Saint Paul."   These are the more important, but there were also
little things remembered vividly after thirty years, — a small gray
panel that seemed perfectly blank until suddenly the eye penetrated
into it to see through the fine, soft fog a line of headlands above
a smooth, swelling sea, a study of azaleas with their fragile delicacy
rendered in little square dots of color to serve as a pattern for cross-
stitch embroidery, a large water-color with an iridescent Spanish
mackerel, and a branch of apple blossoms done in broad, transparent
washes.   What unity of subject or execution is there in all these!

The " Boy with the Dog " or the " Saint Paul " show traces of
Hunt; but they are not like Hunt's work, nor like each other, the
rest have not even that in common.   Their many-sidedness extends
to the *technique*, which matches the subject and scale of the work
with absolute fitness, from the enamel-like smoothness of the " Venus "
to the broad brush work of the " Boy and Dog " or the rough, crumbly
surface of the " Saint Paul," and the same may be said of the inspiration, of the inner quality of his subjects which the artist has stripped
of the unessential, giving their very spirit so that we feel the immanent personality of goddess or saint, of landscape or flower.   The

amount and intensity of mental effort involved in this only artists
can know; but thought is lavished everywhere in a way that often
seems entirely out of proportion to the work in hand. The drawings are full of it and it gives them a persistent vitality. A dozen
or so illustrations made for a juvenile magazine or for poems, some
of them unfinished and unpublished, are not likely to be an important item in an artist's work; but no critic of La Farge fails to notice
them at length, their quality is of such distinction. And this is
gained by taking infinite pains. There is a bit of background in
one of the Enoch Arden series (utterly destroyed by the wood-
engraver), the study for which, about an inch square, is monumental in line and mass; while in the best known of all, the "Wolf
Charmer," apart from all more obvious merits, the fringe of
woods in the extreme distance is most interesting in the varied
character and grouping of the tree trunks, while every line and spot
continues and strengthens the composition.

These qualities of inspiration, of handling, of drawing (and something more might be said of this last), have been insisted upon
because the great reputation of La Farge has been as a colorist, and
rightly so; but color with him is not an external grace added to the
picture, nor is it the subject-matter as sometimes with Hunt; it is
like the composition or the brush work, a means of conveying the
emotion. Fine color is probably no rarer than fine draftsmanship,
— and yet perhaps it may be so now, for the French who have been
the leaders of modern art have always leaned toward form rather
than color, — but draftsmanship that is not fine can still save itself by
a literal fidelity that satisfies the intellect; while color, like music,
makes a direct appeal to the emotions and can be judged only by
them. If they are unmoved, it is naught.

The drawings of La Farge have no "color," as the term is used
with reference to black and white work, but his painting vibrates
with it. It is of the structure, there is no relapsing into a convenient
undertone of black or brown any more than in nature. How a gray
sky appeared to him the quotation from his works has shown; but
his power is more striking in the richer effects to which he tended
more and more until they culminated in his stained glass — probably the richest color creations that have yet been fashioned. There

is a glory, a radiance in light streaming through glass that cannot be given by paint on canvas; but even on canvas in combining the purest, strongest colors into a harmony that lifts the spectator for an instant out of himself and into an enchanted world no man of his generation has equalled him. There is beneath it a science of complementary colors, of light vibrations and the like, which has been profoundly studied and which has undoubtedly aided in practice, but which has no more made the painter than a knowledge about sound waves makes the musician. Fine color in the end comes through feeling, and it must be appreciated in the same way and not by science, though La Farge's color responds remarkably to some material tests. Its carrying power, for instance, is surprising, and one of the little Samoan water-colors will sparkle and glow like a sapphire or opal on a gallery wall eighty feet away, making the other pictures look dull and lifeless.

All of La Farge's earlier work, however, and the easel work generally, admirable as it was, still left for the most part a somewhat disquieting feeling. It was not that it was defective in technical qualities, though at times the mind failed perfectly to triumph over the recalcitrant material; the trouble was that here were qualities of the very highest—qualities akin to those of the great masters, displayed for the most part in studies, in momentary impressions. The masters produced such things, but they were a by-product. Their characteristic achievements were ampler, more synthetic. Here the talent seemed to be scattered over too wide a field and nowhere to give its full measure. The larger opportunity needed came with the commission for mural paintings, which began with Trinity Church and culminated for a time with the great composition in the chancel of the Church of the Ascension, New York. With this came purely decorative work, tinting of walls and ceilings, designing of borders and arabesques, work in ivory and mother-of-pearl, and rare woods or metals, grave monuments carved in marble by him or under his direction, mosaics in all materials, and above all the colored glass. In all this varied mass of production there was nothing that did not have interest and charm, nothing that was not original with that "strangeness in its proportion" without which Lord Bacon tells us "there is no excellent beauty."

FIG. 70.—LA FARGE: WATSON MEMORIAL WINDOW, TRINITY CHURCH, BUFFALO

[Copyright, 1898, by John La Farge.]

With the opalescent glass he may be said to have given the world a new and splendid art, and yet there were those who regretted the neglect of pure painting just when achievement culminated and who welcomed with peculiar enthusiasm the return to mural compositions of the past few years. This last work, such as the decorations for Bowdoin College or the St. Paul Court House, are the ripest and completest productions of a talent which shows no signs of declining.

It is not yet time to estimate critically the painting of John La Farge. It is too varied and too far apart from the ordinary categories. Something of its quality shows in the mere description of his life and production, and a special word of respect is due to the artistic probity of that life. In a land where art is comprehended by an infinitesimal minority, and where it gains small pecuniary reward and no public honors, he has followed his ideal, and neither uncertain health, business complications, nor the expostulations of patrons have made him waver from the completest expression of which he was capable. His influence has been great, not so much as a teacher of pupils, but as a master with assistants. A notable list of men have worked under him at various times, Saint Gaudens (then just beginning his career), Francis Lathrop, Will H. Low, J. Humphrey Johnston, Wilton Lockwood, none of whom reproduces closely his style, but each of whom shows in a different way the effect of his inspiration.

La Farge is surely an American artist by every conventional test. He was born here, he developed here, his work is here; across the Atlantic, in spite of some displays of sketches or glass, he is hardly more than the shadow of a great name, and yet there is something in his painting, a sanity, a clarity, a delicacy of perception, that proclaims his French blood. As for Whistler, he spent his boyhood (from eight to fifteen) abroad and at twenty-one went to Europe, never again to return to his native land; but though he for years mingled in the life of London and Paris, it was always as a sort of envoy *in partibus infidelium*. He remained an American to the last, and while his Americanism was certainly not of a common type, especially in its developments, yet as an Englishman or a Frenchman he was inconceivable. If another race can justify a claim to him, it is through his Irish grandfather. The imaginative, combative Celtic strain, passionate, warm-hearted, illogical, was in him to the last, making his manners those of a fascinating but thoroughly spoiled child.

Whistler was born in Lowell, Massachusetts, on the 10th of July, 1834. The place and date are set down at length because, as it suited his fancy, he made contradictory statements about both, giving to Baltimore, St. Petersburg, and other cities the honor. He was christened James Abbott, which he subsequently changed to James Abbott McNeill at about the time of his final departure for Europe. The Whistlers were, many of them, connected with the army. His grandfather, of an English family long settled in Ireland, had fought under Burgoyne, but afterward entered the American service, and his father was a major and, moreover, a distinguished engineer. It was in this latter capacity that he was called to Russia in 1842, and there he died in 1849, his wife and children returning to America.

It was natural that the boy should have turned to the army as his career, and he was appointed to the Academy at West Point in 1851, his diminutive stature probably being overlooked out of regard to the martial record of his family. He followed the course for three years, without much distinction as a student, and finally was discharged for deficiency in chemistry in June, 1854. As one of his contemporaries at West Point recalls the incident: "The subject given him to discuss in chemistry before the Academic Board was 'silica,' which constitutes eight per cent of the solid matter of our earth. Whistler, it is said, in perfect innocence of the subject, but with his characteristically charming manner, described silica as an 'elastic gas' or a 'saponifiable fat.' The young ladies in the audience smiled approval, but the stern Academic Board dispensed with Whistler's further valuable services at the Military Academy. He found employment for a time in the United States Coast Survey at Washington, but finding that his compensation 'hardly paid for his gloves,' he went to London, and years afterward made a reputation as a painter."

His employment in the Coast Survey lasted three months and five days. He had stood at the head of his class in drawing at West Point and had a knack at scribbling heads and figures, but the laborious topographical work of the office was unpleasant to him and he absented himself with such regularity that he was finally

dismissed to the perfect satisfaction of both sides.   Immediately
after this he seems to have gone abroad, first to London and then to
Paris, where he entered the studio of Gleyre and remained two years.
That, with the exception of what instruction he got from Weir
as a cadet at West Point, constitutes all his school training.   He
continued awhile in Paris after leaving the studio and then moved
to London, where most of the remainder of his life was passed with
some returns to Paris and some travelling about the Continent, and
even, in the sixties, a voyage to Valparaiso for his health; but
though he often planned to do so, he never revisited his native
land.   There is no clear chronological record of his movements,
nor, what is much more important, of the production of his pictures.
A head of himself in a broad-brimmed hat is one of his earliest
paintings and must be about contemporary with the " Normandy "
etchings which were published in 1858, and were really done
almost everywhere except in Normandy.   " At the Piano " is given
as of 1860, a " Coast of Brittany " is dated 1861, and the next year
produced the " Blue Wave," the " Building of Westminster Bridge,"
and the " White Girl."   These were followed by other studies of
the Thames, by compositions of small figures in classical costume
inspired by Japanese prints, which got no further than sketches
but whose spirit influences the " Princesse du Pays de la Por-
celaine" of 1864.   Then comes the " Little White Girl " and the
" Music Room."   Of about the same time are the Thames etchings,
published as a set in 1871, but executed earlier, and the Japanese
influence culminates in the " Balcony " and in some landscapes.

A little later the series of large portraits begins with the " Artist's
Mother," sent to the Royal Academy in 1872, the " Thomas Carlyle," and the " Miss Alexander."   These continue on through the
" Rosa Corder," shown at the opening of the Grosvenor Gallery
in 1877, the " Yellow Buskin," and the rest.   This brings us
nearly into the eighties, and from there on it becomes increasingly
difficult to date or place Whistler's work.   His effort was scattered
more in a multitude of small things which he kept long by him,
sometimes wishing to bring them to a higher perfection, sometimes simply unwilling to turn the children of his fancy out into
an unsympathetic world.   He sent irregularly to the great annual

exhibitions or showed his works by themselves in the gallery of some dealer.

From now on the subject, in the prosaic sense, became less and less important; he had always called his pictures "Harmonies," "Symphonies," "Arrangements," and the like, and many of them now were little else. Among the earliest in this new manner were the "Nocturnes,— Black and Gold," and "The Falling Rocket," which was exhibited in the Grosvenor Gallery in 1877 with the "Rosa Corder," and which aroused the wrath of Ruskin and gave rise to the famous libel suit. In 1880 came the first series of Venice etchings, in 1886 another series of twenty-six was issued, and in the same year he became president of the Society of British Artists, a position which he did not long hold. The series of views of the sea, of the Thames, of bits of old buildings, or of little shops in dim twilight streets is innumerable. He employed every medium, oil, watercolor, etching, lithography, each in accord with its special fitness. There were no large works except a few full-length portraits, and these as a rule were far below his earlier achievement, though single heads, like the "Blacksmith" or the "Little Rose of Lyme Regis" showed all his old power. Toward the end of his life he became dissatisfied with England and tried to settle in Paris; but finally returning to London, died there in 1903 and was buried in Chiswick graveyard beside his mother.

At his death Whistler's position among the leading painters of his time was firmly established. He was not a member of the Royal Academy,— a dignity which, however well merited, would yet have been rather incongruous,— but all the other honors of medals, decorations, praise in print and from the mouths of adoring disciples were his, and among his admirers were wealthy men ready to buy his pictures at his own prices. It was not always so. In the beginning he failed utterly of comprehension by the public and endured much hostile criticism. Almost the only drop of gall in all of Tuckerman's great agglomeration of sugar and butter is his paragraph on Whistler.

"A son of Major Whistler, U.S.A., who is also from Baltimore, has made some curious experiments in color, and some of his sketches are singularly effective. A critic of the Paris Exposition

FIG. 71.—WHISTLER : THE LITTLE ROSE OF LYME REGIS, BOSTON MUSEUM.

[From a Copley Print.   Copyright, 1897, by Curtis & Cameron, Publishers, Boston.]

of 1867 thus describes and estimates Mr. Whistler's somewhat numerous contributions to the American Department. ' Mr. Whistler's etchings attract a good deal of attention, and differ from his paintings in meriting it. They display a free hand and a keen eye for effect. Three of the oil pictures are blurred, foggy, and imperfect marine pieces. The fourth is called the " White Girl," and represents a powerful female with red hair, and a vacant stare in her soulless eyes. She is standing on a wolfskin hearth-rug, for what reason is unrecorded. The picture evidently means vastly more than it expresses—albeit expressing too much. Notwithstanding an obvious want of purpose, there is some boldness in the handling and a singularity in the glare of the colors which cannot fail to divert the eye, and to weary it.' "

This is stupid and coarse without the slightest comprehension of what Whistler's art contained or what it lacked, but so almost without exception was all early criticism of him in England. In France it was different. There were French critics who praised the " White Girl " with intelligence and enthusiasm, not only at this exhibition, but earlier in 1863, when it had been one of the most prominent canvases of the famous *Salon des Refuses*, and this gives in a way the keynote of his position throughout life. He belonged artistically to the little group of realists who succeeded to Courbet in France, — men like Fantin-Latour, Manet, Degas, and Legros, — men of the greatest ability who threw over the whole mass of academic tradition and set themselves to interpret the visible world before them, each as his own personality led him. They received abuse in plenty, some of it as stupid as anything lavished on Whistler; but some of it intelligent and just, and from the beginning they never lacked a circle that understood and encouraged. Even those who failed to comprehend were not indifferent. For intelligent French people, art was a serious matter, and innovators who strove to degrade it were miscreants and outlaws of course; but still, just on account of their " bad eminence," not persons to trifle with or ignore.

Out of this little group of artists among whom he had perhaps the most immaterial, subtle perception, it suited Whistler to go and settle in mid-Victorian England, among a stolid race in one of its

most stolid moods.   Legros lived with him at first and he wrote
to Fantin-Latour, begging him to join them; but he never came,
except for short visits, and Whistler drifted more and more away
from his earlier friends, and his work and character were more and
more shaped by the British Philistia about him.   What ferment
there was in the inert mass came from the leaven of Ruskin's teaching, and that unfortunately was the exact opposite of Whistler's
practice.   The Pre-Raphaelites built up their pictures out of painfully observed bits of detail, the figure subjects first conceived in
the mind, and then laboriously wrought out with all the explanatory
or symbolic accessories that would reënforce the idea, the artist
ordinarily being more anxious to convey a literary than a pictorial
emotion.

In this atmosphere Whistler struggled for forty years and more.
Even Ruskin, who had the passionate moral conviction of the Hebrew
prophets (as well as their lack of humor), and who expressed himself
with an eloquence unmatched in his time, was for the mass a sort of
jest, and as for "Jimmie" Whistler, with his diminutive stature and his
queer clothes, his absolute disregard for proprieties, and all "the sort
of thing that makes us English what we are," he became a licensed
buffoon.   When these two joined in a lawsuit, really *c'était a se
tordre*.   Ruskin pleaded ill health and did not appear in person, but
"Jimmie" descended into the arena and fought with the beasts at
Ephesus, and for two days the utter obtuseness of the whole English
nation to any conception of art was displayed to their own enormous
amusement.

A somewhat similar display had taken place nearly a century
before in another lawsuit in which an American artist resident in
London was one of the parties, but the temper of the trial was
entirely different.   West was president of the Royal Academy, a
favorite of the King, and when, called as a witness in behalf of Copley,
he explained that there really could be a difference in the copies
made by a good engraver and a bad one from the same picture, the
judge treated him with the greatest deference, insisted upon calling
him Sir Benjamin (although West protested against the title), and
finally, after hearing his evidence declared to the jury: "I suppose, gentlemen, you are perfectly satisfied.   I perceive that there is

much more in this than I had any idea of, and I am sorry that I did not make it more my study when I was young." But the jury vindicated the national temperament, and promptly brought in a verdict against the painter.

That with all the world open to him Whistler should have persisted in dwelling in this uncongenial land may seem strange, but there were personal reasons besides the fact that most of his near relatives were in England, and that (what is not generally recognized) he had found patrons there to buy his work from the first, although no critic gave it anything except ridicule. Paris would seem to have been his natural refuge, but it is doubtful if he had any deep comprehension of or liking for French culture and manners. In Paris he could have known familiarly no such large circle of distinguished people as at London, and above all he would not have been so prominent himself.

Many excuses have been made for his egotism, his delight in notoriety, his disregard of the general standards of behavior. His friends have attributed it to a proud consciousness of the merit of his work, or to his passionate devotion to art, all slights to which roused him to indignant fury. His apologists have conjectured that he may have been forced to it by the need of notoriety to enable him to sell his pictures. His enemies have said it was just inordinate, inborn, unrestrained self-conceit, and the mass of the public are generally taking that view. All of the accounts of his early life agree with the description of his West Point experiences, given some pages back, in showing his personal idiosyncrasies clearly marked long before he had anything to do with art. No word seems too harsh to apply to him after reading some of the amazing lives and reminiscences and tributes with which his alleged friends have recently rushed into print, but the impression left by these is certainly false. Those who have come under his personal charm can never judge him harshly. He had such an amazing fascination and a brilliancy so entirely his own that his claim to be treated as an exceptional person seemed justified.

This claim was strengthened in England by his art, which stood absolutely alone both for reviling and adulation. There he had no rival, which is possibly the main reason why he preferred it to

France, where he would have been compelled to stand alongside of men like Corot or Degas, whose point of view was not far different from his own, and where the *Ten O'Clock* would have been considered as a clever exposition of views held by a large school. This desire for prominence, this overestimation of his own importance, is frequently an element of strength in an artist. If some form of beauty appeals with peculiar force to a man, and for years he studies it and the means of expressing it, he is not to blame, when he succeeds, if he delights in his own work or even if, not possessing an eclectic taste, he misjudges the works of others. Whistler's faults, if faults there were, lay in overshooting the mark. Carried away by the joy of fighting and the delight in stinging epigram (was it the Celtic blood?), he loses sight of the main object. He was for the most part right in the squabbles reported in the *Gentle Art of Making Enemies*, but all of its shrill, nervous brilliancy carries no such assured conviction of the right of the artist to be a law unto himself as the courteous note with which John La Farge interrupts the current of his *Impressions on Art* to inquire: "Has it ever occurred to you how excusable are the misapprehensions of many literary critics of art?" and then goes on to show that those unhappy men can have no assured basis for judgment and consequently are obliged to promulgate a mass of negligible opinions.

The art of Whistler manifestly was not English nor yet American but in its derivation purely French. Gleyre, with whom he studied, was not so insignificant as most of the biographers make out; the "Illusions Perdues," if a trifle frigid, has sentiment and charm; but to have mastered either Gleyre's method or his point of view would have taken more time than the two years spent in his *atelier*. At that time, however, instruction was not confined to work from the model, but included also study of the masterpieces in the Louvre, and thither Whistler went often. He looked and lounged more than he worked, though he is known to have copied Boucher's "Bath of Diana" very badly and the "Angelica" of Ingres, as well as the "Group of Cavaliers" by Velasquez. It was the Whistler of that period that Du Maurier knew and afterwards sketched as Joe Sibley in the unexpurgated *Trilby*, and it was then also that Whistler made the acquaintance of Fantin-Latour, who was a diligent student of the old masters and who became for a while his most intimate friend.

Fantin has never been properly appreciated in America, but a study of his early portraits of his family or his friends, with their grave harmonies of blacks and grays, their enveloping atmosphere, and their quiet, profound feeling, would help to explain the formation of Whistler's art. It was not to him, however, but to Courbet, the peculiar detestation of Gleyre (who refused to send again to the Salon after his enemy's pictures had been received there), that Whistler acknowledges obligation. They met in Fantin-Latour's studio, and there must have been a good deal of personal intercourse between them, for they were both at Trouville during one or two summers, and of the Irish girl, Joe, who was Whistler's favorite model, and who posed for the "White Girl," Courbet painted two portraits.

There is more resemblance between the two men than might be supposed. Apart from their colossal egotism which was in both of the aggressive, shameless type, neither had the education nor the temperament to understand the classical or the romantic point of view. It may be said of Whistler as of Courbet, "Nothing that he read or heard or thought left a pictorial impression on his brain." But Courbet was the founder of a school and twenty-five years older than Whistler. When the latter came to Paris, in 1855, Courbet was at the height of his power. He had shown eleven works in the exposition of that year, and had organized outside a special exhibition of thirty-eight more, which was considered at that time a scandalously unprofessional act and gained him great notoriety. Such a shining mark would naturally appeal to Whistler and awake emulation, but none of the followers of Courbet equalled him in direct, simple vision and in strong, rich handling — Whistler least of all. What might have happened if he had had the physique of the peasant of Ornans is open to conjecture; but his diminutive body and nervous temperament is reflected in his work, as also his refinement — the fact that he was an aristocrat and throughout his life associated with the people of intelligence and social position. He attempted Courbet's heavy impasto in the early head of himself but not successfully, and made tentative essays in different direc-

z

tions before he began to find his proper expression in " At the Piano." Even here the massing of each color as a spot by itself may have come from the influence of Fantin-Latour, and the brush work of Manet appears now and then as in the rug of the " White Girl," or much later in the hat in " Rosa Corder," which might have been picked out of the heap of garments in the " Déjeuner sur l'Herbe." The " Coast of Brittany " and the " Blue Wave," strong in color with brown shadows, have an echo of Courbet and are thoroughly uncharacteristic, but with the " White Girl," exhibited in the same year as the latter, he comes into his own realm. It must have been painted before he was twenty-eight and is not only a beautiful work in itself, but contains all his characteristic qualities: the luminosity, the delicate differentiation of almost similar tones, the melting together of the figure and background, the feeling for pure, sweet color, the composition by spots and spaces, the strange pathetic charm of the face.

The portrait of his mother, the " Thomas Carlyle," the " Miss Alexander," are usually considered the height of his achievement, and they with works of their class are likely to be the corner- stones of his future fame; but their very strength, their completeness, their comprehensibility, render them less characteristic than the " Little White Girl," for instance, which is all his own, with a com- position apparently accidental but in reality very perfect, and an exe- cution so personal, so complete, so flawless, that it vies with the blue and white porcelain and the azaleas represented in it. Of equal work- manship is the " Music Room " of the same date, but that stands quite by itself. It seems like an effort to show some of his Pre-Raphael- ite contemporaries how to do artistically, what they, with much labor and many protestations of high principles, were doing other- wise. The subject was the same as many of theirs, an English interior of the sixties. The whiteness of the room and the black- ness of the lady's riding habit are given with no attempt to mitigate the contrast, the red and green pattern of the chintz hangings is unsoftened, but the canvas sparkles with color that has no touch of crudeness.

He never worked again in the same way. Perhaps the effort was too irksome. Certainly as he advanced he cared less and

less for the definite realities; it was the spirit of things which he
wished to give, but expressed beautifully. He himself declared
that he had no desire to reproduce external nature at all, but only
beautiful combinations of pattern and tone which would logically
land him in combinations, like the spotting of tortoise-shell or the
glazes of Chinese potters. He must not be taken too literally, however. The message was probably made overstrong that it might
penetrate somewhat into unresponsive minds. In reality he never
forgot his subject, whether it was his mother, or Battersea Bridge
at twilight, or a huckster's barrow in Whitechapel, the spirit of the
person, the place, or the hour as he felt it is most exquisitely and
accurately rendered, even if the exact joints of the timbers of the
bridge or the price cards on the apples are not entirely comprehensible.

Some of the work (the pastels, water-colors, lithographs, and the
like) is slight in execution, nearly all is delicate. It demands that it
be treated with particular regard, and looked at only under special
conditions, something like those that the Japanese connoisseurs
have formulated for enjoying works of art. It must be hung in
harmonious surroundings, in its own special light, and be viewed
with a receptive and tranquil mind. These conditions are not so
easily fulfilled in these days of strenuous life; but if a man will
make the effort, he will have his reward. There is in Whistler's
work a sentiment of beauty most delicate, subtle, rare, almost
impalpable and like that of no other man. He has been much compared to Velasquez, but the comparison (apart from all questions
of proportion) is not felicitous. There is in both accuracy in values,
a sense of atmospheric depth, a preference for grave harmonies in
white or black or brown, rather than in gaudier tints; but the
Spanish master stands alongside of Rubens as an illustration of the
strength and sanity of genius, with even a loftier dignity and a
craftsmanship if not greater at least more restrained and sure. No
mists of sentiment dim Velasquez's eyes, for him no factory chimneys
turn to campanili. It is truth, not painting that he seeks, and there
is nothing in all Whistler's work, not even the portrait of his mother,
that would not show faded and nerveless beside the weakest of his
canvases.

If a comparison must be made with one of the great dead, it would be far more suitable to choose Giorgione — provided that the critics will grant him the authorship of the works that are called Giorgionesque. There will be found the same tranquil figures gazing out of the canvas, with quiet, shadowy eyes, the same enveloping air, the same love for polished surfaces reflecting the light or for tranquil water, the same turning of commonplace into poetry and mystery, the same sensitive, loving perfection of *technique*. The spirit is the same, even though one produced harmonies in brown and the other symphonies in white; but while the spirit is similar, the achievement is far different. For all his delicacy, Giorgione is strong. His work is rich and full, and while few may fathom its depths, all may find delight in its glowing color and beautiful forms. Whistler's is elusive, not readily yielding its secret. The endurance of his fame depends on whether posterity, which is apt to be indolent, will think the return worth the effort which it demands; but this is of small importance to us. He had his message for those of his own time and in the end it was accepted.

CHAPTER XVIII

FIGURE PAINTERS OF THE SIXTIES AND SEVENTIES

Eastman Johnson. — T. W. Wood. — Guy. — J. G. Brown. — Boughton. — John F. Weir. — E. L. Henry. — Wordsworth Thompson. — Winslow Homer. — His Originality. — His Subjects. — Character of his Work. — His Water-Colors.

The consideration of French influence on one or two exceptional men led naturally to the art of Whistler, which was its final culmination, — an abstract, subtle refinement in painting, despising the commonplace, and appealing to a select and limited public. Between it and the work produced by most of his fellow-craftsmen in America during the sixties and seventies there is no bond of sympathy possible. They were the companions of the old landscape school, and to them Hunt and La Farge stand in much the same relation as Inness and Martin to the landscapists. They did not lack foreign training. Like Kensett, Whittredge, and the rest they had made their studies abroad, but like them they appealed to the popular taste which in America, as elsewhere, demanded anecdotic subjects and reproductions of real life. This does not of necessity imply inferior work, and in fact some of the men under consideration were admirable painters, displaying in their simple themes the best qualities of their art.

This is perfectly illustrated in Eastman Johnson, who, born in 1824, is one of the earliest of the group as he is one of the most important. He turned to art early and almost before he was of age began painting portraits in Washington and Cambridge, but finally went abroad in 1849, sharing the studio of Leutze at Düsseldorf, travelling in France and Italy, and afterward settling at The Hague, where he worked five years with such success that he was offered the position of court painter if he would remain. He returned to America, however, and finally settled in New York in 1860.

Eastman Johnson's technical training is both sound and complete. It shows in the slightest of his sketches. He knows how to draw and he knows how to paint, but he escaped the deadly monotony of the Düsseldorf training; there is no trace of his association with Leutze in his work. His first success was made as a portrait painter, and he has always remained one. His heads, of

FIG. 72. — JOHNSON: OLD KENTUCKY HOME, LENOX LIBRARY.

men especially, are fine in characterization and have both dignity and distinction. The execution is luminous and rich in color, with a firm certainty of drawing and construction rare at the time; but his greatest interest is as a painter of *genre*. He took up, not the traditions of Mount, for there were none, but something of his subjects of rural life, and rendered them with a greater knowledge and more artistic qualities, and yet kept the sincerity and naturalness of the older man. As early as 1867 he painted the "Old Kentucky Home," a charming picture, which makes its apology for the easy, kindly side of slavery more potently than a dozen volumes. This was followed by other subjects less "literary," more direct, and taken usually from the country life of the Northern states—the "Husking Bee," the "Cranberry Pickers," children playing in a barn or around an old stagecoach, the quaint characters of the village or the farm. In all is the same wholesomeness and delight in the simple, universal things, — the sunlight, fresh air, the play of children, or the mellow humor of age. Moreover the subjects were far better painted than ever before in America and with a varying handling. Many of the smaller canvases have a finish that suggests the contemporary French work of Edouard Frère, but in the larger paintings the brush work is freer and looser, becoming in the lights of portraits a sort of granular impasto, while the shadows are a warm transparent brown. The brown shadows persist also in the out-of-door scenes ; but in spite of that they have the true sparkle of the bright New England autumn while the Nantucket interiors with their white-washed walls, and the old squire and his cronies in black have something of the quiet charm of the little Dutch masters.

Genre pictures similar to these were painted by T. W. Wood, who in his early days was a pupil of Chester Harding, and who after a couple of years' study in Paris returned to America to paint portraits in Kentucky and Tennessee until 1867, when he settled in New York and has since, like Johnson, painted both figure pieces and portraits in somewhat the same manner.

A distinctly different style of painting was brought to the country by Seymour Joseph Guy, who was born in England the same year as Eastman Johnson, and who got all his training there, not coming to America until he was over thirty. His painting was of the smooth, enamel-like type, which Ingham had also practised, its minute finish approaching that of Düsseldorf, but with a brighter, purer coloring and a less monotonous draftsmanship. He has painted portraits, landscapes, and ideal heads, but especially subjects with children — something like those of Meyer von Bremen, but with a greater variety in the compositions and in the faces.

But if Guy has a claim as a painter of childhood, his compatriot, J. G. Brown, who, seven years younger than Guy, came to America a couple of years later, has made boyhood his own special province. He painted a few portraits both in England and America ; but he soon

began the series of his newsboys, bootblacks, and street urchins generally, which instantly suited the popular taste. Since then his reputation has been inextricably connected with such subjects. They
touched the humor or the sentiment of the great public, which felt
itself defrauded if they failed to get just what they had got before.
The artist has tried other subjects and painted them rather better than
his newsboys, one an important composition of laborers taking their

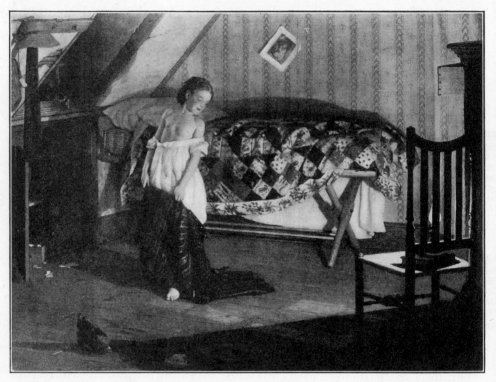

FIG. 73. — GUY: MAKING A TRAIN, OWNED BY MRS. GEORGE W. ELKINS, PHILADELPHIA.

noonday rest along the docks, with the different nationalities and
characters well observed and discriminated, and latterly types of
country life; but they are received distrustfully by his old admirers.
For them he is the painter of newsboys, and any desertion to other
models savors of disloyalty. His workmanship has the minute and
careful finish resulting from the English training, which shows also
in Ingham and Guy, though he lacks their pureness of color and
transparent enamel-like surface; but from the torn cap to the copper-
toed shoes every detail is given with untiring thoroughness; the
well-scrubbed faces shine, and the eyes gleam with well-placed high

lights.   These details may not delight all, but they have a large and faithful circle of followers.

There is still a third English artist to be noted, but the early life of George H. Boughton was English only by the accident of birth. He came to America when three years old and all of his training was received under distinctly American auspices.   Not that he profited much from any systematic teaching.   He began drawing and painting when a boy in Albany, without much help from any one, but succeeded in selling his early productions to the Art Union on such favorable terms that when he was seventeen he was able to make a six months' sketching trip in England.   His success continued after his return.   He left Albany for New York and a year or so later, in 1860, went to Paris.   There he entered no *atelier*, but got what counsel he could from different French artists, especially from Edouard Frère of whose kindly helpfulness he kept a grateful memory.   He worked in Normandy and Brittany and in 1861 went to London, took a studio, and remained there until his death.   Born in England and returning there so young, Boughton may fairly be claimed as a British artist, and yet he belongs to America rather more than the exact chronology indicates.   Long after his final departure he continued to send his pictures to American exhibitions and to find many of his patrons here ; and even his art itself was, as to its spirit, largely formed before he went abroad, and his subjects, with the exception of his studies of French peasants, were usually taken from the life of the early colonists.   Even his Holland pictures, when they came, seemed to be a reversion to the old Dutch traditions of Albany and Knickerbocker New York.   It is a pity that a still stronger plea for his Americanism cannot be made, for Boughton's art is of a sort so sweet and wholesome that one would willingly annex it if one could.   It is true that his maidens, whether Puritan, English, or Dutch, have a more than family resemblance, slender, blond, with dreamy eyes and dewy lips; but their charm is unfailing, and the coloring, pale, soft, and sweet like them, is delicately varied, but always, even in pure landscape, showing the same feeling and individuality.

Another figure painter, a few years later in date, is John F. Weir, son of Robert W. Weir already mentioned as the painter of one of

the compositions in the Rotunda of the Capitol and also long the instructor in drawing at West Point. It was from his father that John
F. Weir received his first instruction, and its efficacy is proved by the
sound workmanship of his early pictures. There were some imaginative subjects like the "Christmas Bell" and the "Culprit Fay,"
pleasant and fanciful; but far more important were the purely realistic scenes. The "Gun Foundry," studied at Cold Spring, opposite
West Point, was finished in 1867 (the same year as Johnson's "Old
Kentucky Home"), and the "Forging the Shaft" the year following.
They are remarkable achievements to have been done at that time
by a young man who had had no foreign study. Not only are they
well drawn and well composed, with a clearly conveyed sentiment of
the enormous power of machinery as compared with human strength,
but the varying relations of daylight and the glowing metal are felt
and rendered in a way that is novel and in advance of the time.
Soon after this Weir made a short trip abroad and on his return
became director of the newly founded Yale School of Fine Arts, a
position which he has retained ever since. His duties as director
and professor have undoubtedly diminished his artistic production,
but he has never ceased to work and to develop, and his later landscapes, cool, green, and fresh, would look strange beside some of his
earlier efforts inspired by the Hudson River school. Deserting the
smaller figure subjects, he seems to have turned at present to these
landscapes and to some admirable portraits as his main work, although he has also attempted sculpture with success.

Born in the same year as Weir was E. L. Henry, and a comparison of the work of the two men shows how deceptive internal
evidence as to schools and influence is apt to be. Weir's training,
although he has visited Europe several times, was exclusively American, yet his *technique* seems clearly the result of foreign teaching.
Henry, on the contrary, when he was nineteen, was a pupil of Gleyre
and he has been often abroad since, but his work has a peculiar, distinctive, native quality, and this not alone from the subjects. They
add no doubt to the effect. No one else knows as well as he the
manners and customs of an age which has become old-fashioned, but
hardly as yet historic; the first half of the last century, when travel
was by stagecoach or packet-boats on the canal, when railroads were

FIG. 74.— BROWN: SYMPATHY.

strange innovations of doubtful merit, when women wore hoops
and carried reticules and bandboxes and the men were stately in
swallow-tailed coats and hats of real beaver fur.   He knows besides
the country of the time, the construction of the houses, the corduroy
roads, and the bridges.   Apart from all this local interest of his subjects, however, he paints them as they might be painted in England
but hardly on the Continent, minutely, with all the funny, quaint
details given so that the eye wanders amused among them ; but in

FIG. 75. — BOUGHTON : PILGRIMS GOING TO CHURCH, LENOX LIBRARY.

some cases this very multiplicity of interest weakens the carrying
effect of the picture at a distance.

Wordsworth Thompson, who was a fellow-pupil with Henry
under Gleyre, paints the same epoch, or the revolutionary one just
preceding, if without so intimate and curious a knowledge yet more
broadly and with a smoothness and skill of handling recalling that
if he worked under Gleyre, he was also a pupil of Pasini.

Besides these men were many others whose names appear regularly in the Academy catalogues : Henry A. Loop, who was a student
of Couture ; and animal painters like William Hays, who painted dogs
and deer, but especially some western landscapes which with their
great herds of buffalo have now a historic interest.   There were also
J. F. Tait with his shining trout or his well-groomed deer, and
W. H. Beard, whose groups of bears or monkeys imitating the

weaknesses or vices of mankind delighted a large and uncritical public. From all the other figure painters, however, one man stands out quite by himself. American landscape, in spite of its native origin and spirit, reached its highest point by assimilating and adapting something of foreign methods. No one of the men with whom the school culminates worked out for himself a point of view and a method of expression in indifference to foreign models any more than did figure painters like La Farge or Eastman Johnson; but such independence may fairly be asserted of Winslow Homer. Of itself there is no particular merit in it. A painter takes his inspiration and his methods where he finds them, and he stands or falls by his work; but originality has an interest of its own. It does not necessarily involve strangeness nor queerness. There seems nothing strikingly novel about Homer's subjects or methods; both are on the contrary perfectly simple and straightforward, and yet there is no man or school that can be said specifically to have influenced him.

Homer was born in Boston in 1836, but when he was six the family moved to Cambridge, then so small a town that he had the life of a country boy, and got a delight in the open air that never left him. He drew as a small child, and his skill developed so that when at nineteen he went into a lithographer's office he could undertake the more artistic part of the work, making titles for sheet music and a series of portraits of the Massachusetts Senate. After a couple of years he set up for himself and made drawings for *Ballou's Monthly* and for Harper Brothers — the latter offering to employ him on a regular salary, but this was declined. In 1859 he first came to New York and two years later took a studio in the old University building. He studied in the night class of the Academy of Design, and also took a few lessons in painting from Rodel, who taught him how to set a palette and use his brushes. With the breaking out of the war he went to the front as special correspondent and artist for the Harpers, and later made a second and independent trip to the Army of the Potomac.

It is at this time that his paintings begin with a series of army scenes, including the "Prisoners from the Front" of 1865. Then came studies of negro life and character, followed by subjects taken from the life of the country and the little villages. Later he went into the Adirondacks and found there congenial matter in the rugged landscape and the equally sincere and unpolished guides, but more and more he gravitated toward the sea. He was at Gloucester in 1881. The next year he made a trip to England, where he had already been for a short visit in 1867, and he went several times to Bermuda. Most of all, however, he has been drawn of late years

FIG. 76.— JOHN F. WEIR: FORGING THE SHAFT, METROPOLITAN MUSEUM.

to the austere and rugged grandeur of the Maine coast, of which he has become the recognized interpreter.

This sequence of subjects is roughly given and should not be regarded as exhaustive nor, still less, as having been followed consecutively. The " Visit from the Old Mistress," one of the best of the pictures of negro life, was painted as late as 1880; " Snap-the-Whip," with its line of schoolboys racing down a grassy hill, is of 1876, and it would be difficult to say when the sea first appears, but certainly very early. The mere naming of the subjects shows the feeling for the open air, the strong, simple types of soldier, farmer, and seaman that have persisted through all the ages; but the subjects themselves do not tell the whole story. Eastman Johnson painted almost the same themes, but in a way more trained, less bare and elemental.   Homer's experience as an illustrator perhaps aided the clearness and directness of his vision.   The sketches of "Our Special Artist at the Front," in 1861, had to be indestructibly clear to withstand the clumsy way in which they were transferred to the wood block.   Whether from this cause or another, when he began to paint, his pictures were from the first firmly constructed, well

FIG. 77. — HENRY: ON THE WAY HOME.

drawn, and with an amazing power of striking the mind.   They were manifestly true.   The conviction of their veracity, of their absolute reproduction of a thing seen, is overwhelming; and yet they never reproduce a subject as the spectator would have imagined it.   Johnson's "Old Kentucky Home" has but to be seen to be appreciated. That is what every one imagined an old Kentucky home ought to be; but when Homer's Old Mistress, stately in black silk, visits her former slaves who sit embarrassed but grateful, or when a negress with the sad seriousness of our simian relatives in her face sews scraps of red and yellow flannel on the ragged coat of her equally serious spouse that he may shine in the carnival, we recognize that thus and not otherwise the reality must have been.   But we would not have thought of it that way unless we had seen it.   The perfectly-honest would probably admit that even if they had seen it they would not have painted it just that way. They would have arranged the scene a trifle more, they would have accented the humor or the pathos or the beauty, and by just so much they would have lessened the carrying power.

It was probably this lack of arrangement, of prettiness in his pictures, that made Mrs. Van Rensselaer detest them when a small child, as she confesses in an article on Homer; but even a small child's dislike could not prevent their making an indelible impression on her mind. They are remembered when most of their companions in the old Academy exhibitions are forgotten, even the little things, the interior of a country schoolhouse with one small boy kept in, a couple of children turning to look at a dead fish on the beach, or even two or three pencil drawings, made on gray paper and touched in with white, of a half-grown, long-legged girl with a crook and knots of ribbons on her ill-fitting dress, standing out in the sunlight among the mullein stalks, a New England conception of a Boucher shepherdess. Any one else would have rendered her with some recollection of the grace of the prototype if only by way of caricature; but Homer in a few firm strokes draws her exactly as she was, with no more suggestion of the court of Louis XV than if she had been a lumberman, and yet the child with the funny attempt at finery, finishes by being more charming than any attempt to resuscitate the eighteenth century.

This ignorance of or indifference to what other men have done before leads Homer to attempt things which have been generally accepted as impossible of representation, as when he draws out against the dark background the scarlet threads made by the darting sparks of a campfire with a result not only novel but fine; but his independence shows still more in the treatment of the subjects themselves, of which such technical innovations are but incidents. The hunting of the deer has occupied the attention of artists continuously since the days of the cave-man; but no one else ever painted a guide sprawling on his stomach over the edge of a rowboat holding a struggling buck by the horn with one hand and trying to cut his throat with the other, while the fool hound who

2 A

has run the beast to water does his best to upset the boat by trying
to clamber in.   It is not a sportsmanlike method, and moreover it is
out of season, for the horns are still in the velvet, a stray cut from
the knife bleeding red; but there was a lot of deer meat got that
way in the woods in the bad old days when game laws were not
enforced — and some is got that way still.

"Winter" calls up many images, but scarcely a red fox, running
over white, drifted snow, under a dark gray sky and chased by two

FIG. 78. — HOMER: THE LIFE LINE.

black crows; yet when the picture is seen it approves itself as the
very incarnation of winter.   These as well as all other pictures of
Winslow Homer's representing motion suggest another and a very
personal characteristic — his exact feeling for weight and force.   In
the "Winter" the snow is soft and dry, and offers no resistance to
the fox who leaps heavily through it; the struggle between the guide
and the deer gives just the effort that each can put forward under
the unfavorable circumstances they find themselves in, and the boat
is pulled down to just the proper point.   When a man carries a pack
it settles on his shoulders and he rounds his back, so that we can gauge
its weight accurately, and we feel the momentum that in "Snap-the-

Whip" hurls the youngsters at the end over on the grass.   No other artist has so felt the weight of water, its buoyancy, and its enormous force.   When his boys sail a cat-boat, it settles into the waves and tips to the exact force of the wind and pull on the sheet, and when he renders the power of the sea no one else approaches him.   The "Wave" of Courbet, for instance, is an excellent picture, with one of the most beautiful skies ever painted, but the wave itself is exaggerated and unconvincing; but when Winslow Homer's great swells roll in out of the fog, and slowly heap themselves up against the granite coast without foam, without effort, until with the ebb the thousands of tons of clear green water grind crashing down through the crevices of the rocks, we feel the awful, elemental force; and when his bathers are rolled dazed and helpless in the undertow, they will be saved no doubt, but it will give two strong men a struggle to do it.

More stress than usual has been laid upon the subjects in treating of Winslow Homer's work, because the execution is intimately wrapped up with them.   His *technique* in oil differs from that in water-color, and while it has gained ease and breadth it still remains substantially the same as at first.   The figures are put in with firm, large outlines, well detached from the background, with the highlights (and it seems as if almost all of his early figures were in sunlight) blocked in crisply and simply.   The brush work is direct with little working over and no glazing, and while he is capable of elaboration of detail when it is of the essence, as in the clearing across whose tangle of weeds and vines his "Two Guides" tramp, yet as a rule he simplifies it as much as possible.   His color is strong and sure, sometimes a little harsh, but always true.   The writers who confuse tone with values should study his works.   The values are impeccable, not subtle, not overrefined, but sure, every bit of light and shadow holding its place; of tone, however, of a pervading color note which draws the whole picture into a harmony there is no trace except in pictures like the "Lookout," where Nature has charged herself with the task of providing it.   For this reason the pictures are not decorative in the generally received sense.   They do not unite with a wall as an ornament on it apart from their meaning as pictures, as Inness's or Whistler's do.   Time adds a certain mellowness, but they will

always be windows opened in a wall rather than squares of brocade
stretched upon it.

In water-color the handling is much more varied.   In his oil
paintings he seems never in a hurry.   His picture is finished as he
would, and we cannot imagine that longer time would have changed
it a particle; but in the swifter, more summary medium we feel the
hurried inspiration of the sketch.   The early water-colors approach
more closely to the completeness of the oils, the later ones come for
the most part in series; records of trips to Gloucester, to England,

FIG. 79. — HOMER: WINTER, PENNSYLVANIA ACADEMY.
[Copyright, 1898, by The Pennsylvania Academy of Fine Arts.]

to Bermuda, or the Adirondacks, each set having a character of their
own.

The English series done about 1883 stand a little apart.   They
are pictures, not sketches, and are grayer, subtler, better composed
than the others.   The English fisher girls are comely in a large, open-
air way, and their poses have something of classic rhythm.   They
brought him praises from critics that had hitherto been recalcitrant,
and there seemed even danger that he might be moved toward prettiness rather than beauty; but if there was such a danger, it came to
nothing.   He painted the English girls as he saw them, and he strove
to give the delicate mists of the English coast, as in Bermuda he

tried to give the full strength of tropical color, a sea of blue incredible to the untravelled, fruits that glow in the leaves and whitewashed walls that blaze with sunlight, while to support their strength of color the shadows are painted as dark as possible.

The Adirondack sketches and those made at Gloucester have somewhat the same forcible contrasts, but along with sunsets and purple mountains we are not spared the gray skies and blackish shadows. Wherever the subject is taken, however, the treatment is pure water-color. There is little or no gouache. Even in the English series the pencil marks show through the covering washes. In some of the earlier pictures from the woods which the color hardly more than tints, this underlying drawing is still more evident, and is often masterly, with all the accidental felicities of a trained hand driving furiously to get somehow the effect of rocks or trees or the jam of driftwood across a trout stream without stopping to draw it carefully. In much of the later work, and especially in the Bermuda sketches, there is little of this preliminary drawing. It is color and light that is sought for, and the strongest pigments in the box are put on in broad sweeps. The result is often rather crude, but sometimes again there are felicities like the " Land-locked Salmon " in the Boston Museum, where a thin wash of gray, a touch or so of pure black, and a patch of untouched paper give all the silver gleam of the leaping fish. It is a wonderful bit of painting, but like many another similar bit in Winslow Homer's work it appeals as such only to those curious in such matters, and even to them only secondarily. The first interest goes to the fish, and is so great that we forget to ask how it was done.

It is this absorption in his subject that makes it so difficult to compare Homer with other artists. To step from a dealer's gallery into a room filled with his water-colors, is as if one left pictures for reality; you like them if you like the things represented,— the mountain lakes, the dark, spruce-lined shores, the clear, thin air. It is only by making a special effort that his very great artistic merits are recognized, his draftsmanship, his composition, his color, and even when that is done the tendency is to revert again to the indwelling spirit, the love for the strong, free life of men who fight in the open air against man, beast, or the elements, the life that his great namesake sang in the days before history.   They are Homeric, and if some of the end-of-the-century subtleties seem too much of an Armida's garden, we can look into Winslow Homer's pictures and find again

"like surf-beat on a western shore
The surge and thunder of the Odyssey."

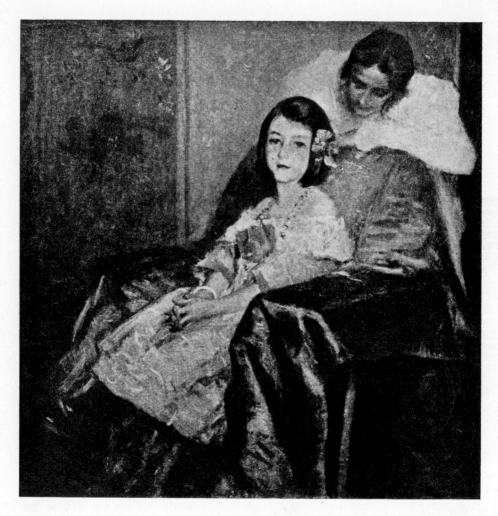

CHASE : PORTRAIT.

CHAPTER XIX

THE NEW MOVEMENT

Of all the men hitherto described none was born later than 1841, and only one or two in that year. The decade of the forties was probably as prolific as that preceding it in American painters, but few seem actually to belong to it. They were either belated members of earlier groups or precursors of later ones. They reached maturity at the close of the Civil War, a time of changes and developments even greater than followed the Revolution. The West had been opened, the work of the pioneers had been largely done, the wilderness had been subdued to the use of the farmer and lumberman. There were trade and manufactures in the new cities, but they were still on a small scale and intercommunication was difficult. Great fortunes were rare and wealth was in perspective rather than in possession. Life was still simple, and there was no attempt to equal the luxury of Europe.

There were signs of a change even before the war. The fears of the South for the growing wealth and population of the North had had much to do with precipitating the conflict. Just as it was beginning Cornelius Vanderbilt sold out the ships that had given him his title of Commodore and put the proceeds into the railroads that were still in their trial stage, and a few years later the satirists ridiculed the dollars gained from striking oil as well as those from shoddy contracts; but the war held back the rising tide of prosperity until with its close the flood swept on with redoubled force. Compared with later developments the wealth of the seventies and eighties seems modest indeed, but still many people had money far beyond their ordinary necessities which they felt obliged to spend, and did with some difficulty manage to spend. They gave more than generously to charities and all pious uses; they gratified themselves with fast trotters, diamonds, and champagne; they built big and amazingly ugly houses and filled them with furniture whose only excuse was its cost. And with the other things they bought pictures generously and blindly. Some from personal friendship or from real liking for the work clung to the native artists of the Hudson River school. It was in those days that Bierstadt and Church received the prices which seem incredible to-day, and the lesser men were proportionately prosperous. There was patronage for all, but already a dangerous rivalry had started, and foreign work was brought in to compete with the native product.

Pictures had always been imported from the earliest colonial days, and the influence of this importation of foreign work on the native school was constant; but such importation had been modest in quantity and not overwhelming in quality. With the seventies it became an important business exploited with all the energy of the other newly found methods of gaining wealth. As a rule the dealers were men of commercial integrity, making large profits, but making them by perfectly honorable dealing; one or two of them, however, were much more than that, — connoisseurs in the best sense of the word, understanding and loving good painting, recognizing the great merits of some men still unappreciated in France, counselling and educating their patrons — men like Cottier and Samuel P. Avery, to whom the culture of the country owes much. They forced upon the hesitating purchasers the works of Corot and Millet and Daubigny, and with others brought over also the more readily comprehensible Meissoniers and Gérômes and Bouguereaus. These were for the wealthier and more enlightened patrons; for the others there was the whole school of Parisian *genre* painters with their brilliancy, their manifest skill, their deceptive imitation of textures, their amusing modern anecdotes or reconstruction of old fashions and costumes; and to them was added the new German school of Munich with its shiny bitumen and bold brush work beside which the old Düsseldorfian favorites seemed faded and prosaic.

The new pictures went naturally into the new houses with the new furniture and the new clothes. The invasion was inevitable and on the whole beneficial. The growing prosperity forced a departure from the older, simpler mode of life. Men of ability and character found their wealth increasing far beyond their expectation or even their desire; but having the wealth they had to spend it — merely to hoard it would have been a confession of weakness. *Richesse oblige* as well as *noblesse ;* taste had to be formed which could only be done by trying all things and cleaving to that which was good. The dealers' galleries were an education in painting to which the Philadelphia Exposition of 1876 added a wider knowledge of the decorative arts also.

Against this rising tide of foreign work the native painters struggled manfully, but for a while it was a losing battle. When in 1856 Cropsey had an auction sale of his studies and sketches, the editor of the *Crayon* wrote, "We believe that in no other country will the same class of pictures bring so high prices as here, especially if they are painted by American artists;" but twenty years later he would hardly have added the last clause. The purchaser with a few hundred dollars usually preferred Baugniet or Toulmouche to Cropsey at the same price and not unreasonably. The old landscape school had at bottom appealed to a very trivial sentiment, the delight which the average man takes in the minute and literal reproduction of familiar objects. The better men had by their own personal feeling for nature or beauty lifted themselves to a higher plane, but by just so much had they alienated their patrons until, in the case of men like Inness and Homer D. Martin, their pictures were unsalable not only in spite, but because, of their merits. It seems ludicrous now that when they forsook the thin, minute handling of their earlier work for a broader style their fellow-craftsmen argued, protested, and vituperated against their folly, but at the time it was a serious matter. It cost the innovators dear in personal friendships and public patronage, for they were not greatly benefited by the education of some of the wealthier buyers to the beauties of breadth, tone, and color. The joy in purely artistic qualities was of so late a date and so uncertain that it had to be confirmed by foreign approval of the artists. It was only after a generation of struggle and when even second-rate Barbizon pictures had been forced up to prohibitive prices that it became generally admitted that some Innesses might be as good as some Diazes.

The other landscape painters who were unmoved by the new influences and painted on unchanged, retained to a certain extent their old friends and patrons; but death and the dealers made heavy inroads upon them, and besides many of the artists themselves were growing old — they painted the old subjects, but without the old enthusiasm. In Cropsey's later work, for instance, it is difficult to find any trace of his earlier skill and feeling. The average of workmanship at the Academy exhibitions in the seventies was lamentably low, not worse perhaps than it had been before, but seeming so because it was contrasted with the clever, well-executed canvases in all the dealers' galleries. The claim was put forward for the pictures in the old Venetian palace on Twenty-third Street that they represented the national art, but the bulk of them represented nothing of the kind. To be sure, the traveller saw nothing like them in the Munich or Paris salons, but if perchance in the latter city he got into the club exhibitions of the *Mirliton* or the *Cercle de La Rue Volney* where the members could display whatever they pleased, unhampered by juries of admission, he felt himself at home once more. There was the same still-life of a skull, a book, and a meerschaum pipe or a bunch of flowers, the same woolly landscapes, and the same saccharine ideal heads. It was amateur work, weak and trivial in conception, fumbling and incompetent in execution. In both cases there was a minority, an "unsubmerged tenth" which was of a different quality, and between the works of the professional members of the Paris Clubs and the best things in the National Academy of Design there was a difference of spirit as wide as the Atlantic, but no such great difference of merit.

They are pleasant to look back on, those old Academy exhibitions, which were an event in the city's intellectual life. The poorer things are forgotten and only the best are recalled, whose very rarity gave them an importance which no picture has to-day. The public was not surfeited with pictures. Those that cared for them had leisure to study thoroughly even the lesser ones and extract what good there was in them, and the artists themselves had something of the same thoroughness. When the inspiration was trivial, it was at least rendered laboriously and completely; but when it was noble, as it occasionally was, the absorption of the artist in his work, with no desire to make an appeal by some single cleverness or amusing quality, but rather to put into his picture all that he could, gave them a personal and enduring interest. Like the Barbizon work, they wear well and do not become tedious and empty when some single effect of handling or color is fathomed, as happens in some of the more brilliant canvases that succeeded them.

It was not possible, however, for the new generation to develop as the best of the men who exhibited in the sixties and seventies did. American painting has always been sensitive to the general development of art in Europe, taking what it could assimilate and adapting it to its use. The romantic movement in France it had received mainly through the landscapists of Barbizon; the part of it which the new *technique* of Delacroix represented with its revolt against the opaque shadows and hard, dry modelling of David and Ingres they knew only through the mitigated and almost academic methods of Couture. The new impulse, which may be said to have started in England with the followers of Reynolds, finally spread to Germany and was taken up by men like the younger Kaulbach, who painted on grounds of the brownest, warmest bitumen, with broad, sweeping brush work, and achieved a fascinating effect of dashing mastery. Munich was the home of the new school, and to Munich consequently went a troop of young American students so that the city succeeded to Düsseldorf as a place of study, with all the kindly, genial tone of the older city, but on an ampler scale and with a newer, more aggressive inspiration.

David Neal was the first to go, in 1861, followed by Rosenthal in 1865, and then with the beginning of the seventies Shirlaw and Chase and Duveneck and the followers of Duveneck, Vinton, Alexander, Bacher, with Carl Marr, Currier, Fitz, and many more. Paris even was displaced for a time in popular favor, and those who did not go to Munich were apt, like Millet, Minor, and Maynard, to go to some place like Antwerp, where the instruction was excellent, the life quiet and simple, and the methods taught, if without the dash and brilliancy of Munich, yet richer in coloring and texture than in France.

For in the schools of Paris as a rule the old French feeling for form was in the ascendant. Recent developments had modified it somewhat, especially as to the subjects for pictures, but accurate, unrelenting drawing from the nude was the basis of all instruction. The enthusiastic and enterprising might win the acquaintance or the friendship of Millet or Daubigny or Diaz, but these men kept no schools, and the students went for technical training to the École des Beaux Arts, or the academies of Julian or Colarossi. It was Gérôme who taught Bridgman and Eakins and Thayer and Alden Weir and Wyatt Eaton; Boulanger and Lefebvre in the *Atelier* Julian taught Dewing and Vonnoh and the rest. Bouguereau and Robert-Fleury had classes in the same *atelier:* Bonnat had an *atelier* of his own much frequented by Americans, and there were many more; but in general it may be said that these masters, whose names still call up grateful memories to hundreds of old pupils, were above all, draftsmen, — a fully rendered impeccable charcoal drawing of the figure was the basis of all their teaching. One alone, Carolus-Duran, based his instruction primarily on painting; but he admitted few pupils, though a large proportion of them were Americans, including Low and Beckwith and Sargent.

About this multitude of students (and only a fraction of them have been mentioned by name) it is impossible to generalize absolutely, but it may be pointed out that as a rule they were by no means so far advanced in their art when they went abroad as the earlier generation. Something of this may be attributed to the war, which turned the aspirations of boyhood to military glory rather than to the arts; but more was due to the greater development of the country. The careers of Chester Harding or of Alvan Fisher were no longer possible. The old type of itinerant portrait painter was a thing of the past. Paintings, engravings, and photographs were to be found even in the remote villages. The boy with a knack for scrawling heads in his school-books no longer in an ambitious moment borrowed the sign painter's colors and started with the courage of ignorance to paint the portraits of his relatives. Those men rushed straight to the goal and produced pictures from the first, bad pictures, weak or crude or grotesque, but still a completed product which reflected something of the joy that the artist had had in their creation and which suited the

taste of the artists' acquaintances so that they bought them for a few
dollars. With more practice and more thought the pictures grew better
and the prices higher, until by the time that the thousand dollars or so
that justified a trip abroad had been saved, the artist was a skilful
craftsman in his way and produced works which pleased his compatriots; and it was to this foundation that he adapted what further
knowledge he received in Europe.

For the new type of student the surroundings were different.
Such courageous ignorance was impossible. There were people

FIG. 80. — DUVENECK: TURKISH PAGE, PENNSYLVANIA ACADEMY.

everywhere to point out his deficiencies so that the necessity of
sound technical training was felt at once. Such training was difficult to get in America; for though drawing-masters were plenty,
and there were some fairly efficient schools like those of the Pennsylvania Academy and the Academy of Design, yet even in these
instruction was given on rather old-fashioned lines and by men of no
great skill or wide reputation. The result of this was to send the
young aspirants abroad to the schools whose pupils had turned out
the works seen in the dealers' galleries, the skill of which seemed won-

derful to them.   It was in Europe that the famous government establishments were to be found with up-to-date methods and professors
known and honored throughout the world, and the obstacles to
frequenting them had diminished.   The old difficulties of travel
had disappeared.   Railroads led from every town to the seaports,
and thence regular lines of steamers made the voyage across the
Atlantic with less discomfort and danger than the trip from Boston
to New York had involved a generation before.   There was also
more money in the country, and besides pictures were being sold as
reputable merchandise at prices which seemed to give a good profit
to the producer.   Many parents whose sons showed no aptitude for
other employments but, like Trumbull, "pined for the arts," were
willing to support them a year abroad, at the end of which time it
was supposed they would be able to command a handsome income
from their skill.   The young enthusiasts presented estimates from
which it appeared that life could be lived with comfort and even with
elegance in Paris or Munich for a trifling sum per day.   It was cheaper
than starting in business or learning a profession, and so a multitude
of youths, some of whom had never even attempted to draw and
whose sole equipment was a distaste for ordinary work and a vague
enthusiasm, gained from reading Ruskin or *La Vie de Bohême*,
descended upon Europe with the conviction that they were to become masters in painting.

Not all were like this, not the majority even; the description
applies better to the men of a decade later.   Of the men of the
seventies many had painted or illustrated or worked at some form
of applied art, and most had some knowledge of drawing, but even
of them very few were as yet full-fledged painters.   They found
the opportunities for study excellent; but art, as understood in the
ateliers, was longer than they had expected.   A year passed and
even two, and yet to their surprise and to the indignation of their
families there was much to learn before they could produce a picture.
Some were forced to make an untimely return, but some stayed on
until they had learned what the schools had to teach them, not the
classical tradition with all its literary association, but the *technique*,
the methods of work, which were mastered, in some cases surprisingly well.   Their enthusiasm, their intelligence, their hard work,

made the Americans good students. They felt that their time was precious, and diligence in the study of the model seemed to be the way to make the most of it, and in this they made rapid progress, winning the school prizes and the encouragement of their masters. In the other branches of art education, in composition, anatomy, perspective, they took less interest, and practically none at all in theories of æsthetics or general culture.

Even the works of the old masters, though enthusiastically admired, were seldom seriously studied. They wanted to learn how to paint and were convinced that their natural genius would supply the rest. Individuality was to be preserved at any cost, and the copying of Titian or Raphael might weaken the precious personal quality, and so the student obtained the desired originality by imitating the innovations of those among the younger painters of the day who seemed to them most original. But by this time they had got what they sought in Europe, and most of them returned to America. The art which they brought back with them was something of a novelty here. As was natural, apart from the personality of the painters who were usually extremely American in temperament, it was a purely foreign product, formed by foreign training on foreign models, with no reference to, or understanding of, American tastes. It even appealed less to the average man than the imported pictures by foreigners. They, at least, took his point of view and were for the most part amusing, or pathetic, or anecdotic in a way that was as easily comprehensible as the completeness and skill of their workmanship. When they rose to higher flights and more purely artistic qualities, they had behind them a weight of European approval in medals, decorations, and titles that carried conviction of their merit with it.

The American student on his return had none of these qualifications. He was rarely able to paint a clever *genre* picture, nor as a rule did he desire to do so. His ambition as well as his real feeling directed him to more purely artistic qualities, to refinement of drawing, beautiful color, skilful handling. His ideals were incomplete and savored of the school which he had so recently left, where a well-constructed figure or a bit of strong, sure handling had been enough to win the praise and admiration of his fellows.

He had not yet learned the necessity of unity, the higher composition that makes of a picture the rounded expression of an artistic idea, and yet his workmanship by all school standards was so manifestly superior to that current in America that immediate recognition of its merits seemed to him inevitable.

The Academicians, the "older men" as they were called in the controversy that followed, did not abdicate so readily as was expected. The innovators had been received with civility, even welcomed at first. The artistic side of art, as distinguished from the popular, had always been represented at the Academy of Design. Landscapists like Inness had developed within it; La Farge had been a constant exhibitor since 1862. Hospitality had even been shown to foreign artists and works by Meissonier, Cabanel, Couture or Troyon, loaned by amateurs or dealers, had appeared on the walls. In 1870 the H. W. Derby collection of foreign paintings formed part of the regular winter exhibition, and in 1873 there was a collection of English water-colors and sketches. The works of the students abroad began to come in, too. As far back as 1864, David Neal had sent his first study from Munich, and in 1871 there were paintings by Bridgman and Bunce sent back from Europe. Chase, Wyatt Eaton, Low, and a number of others appear about the same date for a single exhibition or so; but in their case it meant their departure for Europe, not their return. In 1875 Brush, Maynard, and Alden Weir sent work, the next year Lathrop, Sartain, and Francis D. Millet were added to them, and the new movement began to be talked about and written of in the newspapers; but it was in 1877 that it appeared in full force.

There had been some complaint in previous years about the placing of the works of the younger men, but that year the hanging committee was sympathetic; a lot of new men appeared, — Beckwith, Appleton Brown, Montague Flagg, Gilbert Gaul, Eakins, Duveneck. A special effort was made and their pictures were well placed. For the first time in the history of the Academy an illustrated catalogue was issued, the exhibition was a great success, and the air was filled with enthusiasm over the future of American art. But the older Academicians were not pleased. They neither understood nor approved the new movement. There is no book on the artists of the time as complete or as pretentious as Dunlap's or Tuckerman's, but a good idea of the situation may be gained from G. W. Sheldon's *American Painters*, published in 1879. The text was written merely to accompany a series of woodcut reproductions of paintings so executed, according to the methods of the time, that every scrap of individuality has disappeared; but the lives are well done. There are no raptures nor any philosophizing about art; but dates and details are accurately given, and the artists' views about art in general, and especially about certain foreign pictures just imported, are taken down in their own words.

Inness's opinion has already been quoted, but he stood almost alone in his admiration for the French landscapists. The general opinion agreed that " Half the foreign stuff that is sold here is a swindle on the public. . . . I can't think anything of Corot. I can't understand him. . . . Beauty in tone, in harmony, we can all recognize at a glance, but I can't see where Corot's 'Orpheus' has it." Corot was naturally the chief stumbling-block. He was "incomplete and slovenly. His landscapes are ghosts of landscapes. They have neither technical nor literary excellences." Millet's pictures are declared to be "coarse and vulgar in character; they are repulsive. He shows us only the ignorant and the base peasant; he suggests nothing noble or high, nothing that is not debased," and the whole matter is summed up: " Indeed French art in my opinion scarcely rises to the dignity of landscape — a swamp and a tree constitute its sum total."

It must in fairness be declared that these opinions are mild — almost flattering — compared with those expressed by the French Academicians about the same men. When a lifetime has been spent in the pursuit of " beauty of tone, of harmony," and it has been achieved to the satisfaction of the painter in one way, it is difficult for him to recognize it when it is arrived at in an entirely different and novel way. Much odium has been heaped upon Academicians in all lands for their inability to recognize the originality of rising genius, but unjustly. Such a criticism ignores the fundamental character of an academy, which is — to be academic. Its function is to preserve the methods and principles of the masters of the past, to apply them

2 B

to present needs, to teach them to pupils, and to use them as *criteria* for judging new work. Thus study is made more easy, taste is improved, and extravagances repressed; but in the face of a movement to develop new methods for a new situation, an academy can only exercise an indirect influence offering to the choice of the innovators the treasures of the past, and inclined to think harshly of them if they do not accept everything at the traditional valuation.

This is the excuse and the justification of the French Academicians, but it hardly holds with those of the Academy of Design.

FIG. 81. — SHIRLAW : FIGURES.

They had no such knowledge or practice as would make of them the conservators of the great traditions, although having for so long been at the head of all the art there was in the country, some of them honestly thought they had. Their attitude toward the younger men was absolutely human; they had received and hung the first pictures offered by them, and though the tendencies displayed seemed unsound, they were ready to welcome the painters in their proper rôle as modest beginners, and allow them with time to work up to a proper position, so that on the death of the older generation art might not perish from the land. To their surprise they found

the returning students unwilling to accept any such position.   With
more than the average self-confidence of youth, considering themselves full-blown artists and the mass of the Academicians as futile
old duffers whose work was incompetent or trivial, they did not
hesitate to say so and even found critics to echo their sentiments
in print.

Even so, a *modus vivendi* might have been patched up if it had
not been for the limitations of the old Academy building.   With its
great staircase surrounded with Gothic arches on granite columns, it
had a rather effective interior, but it was a poor place to hang pictures.   The south gallery was the only good one, the smaller ones
were almost all bad, and in the corridor around the staircase there
were shadowy depths that the eye could scarcely penetrate.   High
on the wall in these remote retreats, invisible to all, were hung pictures from Munich and Paris upon which their authors had depended
to win fame and fortune, and great was the indignation thereat.   But
it was only a trifle compared to the rage when in 1877 certain of
the Paris and Munich pictures occupied eligible places on the line
in the south gallery, and some works of the Academicians were
"skied" or relegated to dark corners.   They were insulted in their
own house.   Their vested rights were in danger.   It was "most
intolerable and not to be endured," and so at the next meeting a
law was passed giving to each Academician an absolute right to
"seven feet on the line" at all exhibitions, which transferred the
weight of indignation back to the other party once more.

More was involved than a mere question of wounded pride;
there were practical considerations.   The new men were unknown,
they had to gain patrons to purchase their pictures, and the chief
stage whereon rising talent might display itself had been the exhibitions at the Academy.   With their pictures rejected or, worse yet,
hung so that they could not be seen, there was no way of reaching
the public; and moreover their work was branded as inferior by the
majority of the Academicians whose opinion still carried weight.
There was much indignation and hard language on both sides, and
finally the opposition movement culminated on June 1, 1877, when
in Miss Helena De Kay's studio, she with Saint Gaudens, Wyatt
Eaton, and Shirlaw met and organized the Society of American

Artists, encouraged thereto possibly by an exhibition held a couple of years previously in the rooms of Cottier & Co. to which Miss De Kay, Miss Oakey, Francis Lathrop, Thayer, and Albert Ryder contributed. It was a more courageous act than it seems now when new groups of artists are being formed continually. Then the Academy of Design stood alone and was a powerful body, with ample means, owning its own galleries and possessing a social influence more important still. As has been said, the old Academicians were men pleasant socially, and of unexceptionally high character; for a generation the men of wealth or position who cared for art had sought them out, received their counsel, and prized their friendship. They had grown old together, and that a lot of young fellows hardly of age, fresh from the schools, should try to supplant them was unmannerly and indecent.

In spite of opposition, however, the new society persisted, and in March of the next year opened its first exhibition in the Kurtz Gallery with a membership of twenty-two. Of these nearly half were of the old Academy, and of its best: La Farge, Inness, Thomas Moran, Homer D. Martin, Tiffany, Samuel Colman, Swain Gifford, and some others of like quality. Four new members were added the next year, the following year three; but as two old ones dropped out the net gain was only one. After that, however, the growth was rapid, the membership rising to fifty-two in 1881, and passing the hundred mark in 1888, which number has never been greatly exceeded. At its beginning the new society was not a powerful organization. It had no money nor any efficient backing. It had no rooms, but met in the studios of its members and held its exhibitions when and where it could; in the Kurtz Gallery, in the American Art Galleries, in the Yandell Gallery, one year, during the summer, in the Metropolitan Museum, one year in the Academy of Design itself, and one year (1885) there was no exhibition. The longest use of any one place was at the Fifth Avenue Galleries, which were occupied by four exhibitions from 1889 to 1892. Such wanderings might make an active association, but hardly a dignified one.

The Society had all the struggles of a new organization that strives to replace an old and honored one, and its sole valuable possession was a grievance. It had not even unity among its members nor a single aim. But the grievance was a valid one. The Academy as a body was not fair either in selecting pictures, in hanging them, or in electing new members. They were unduly moved by personal friendships and dislikes, and by a taste in art which, though honest and inevitable, was yet too narrow for the times. The Society of American Artists started with the principle that there should be no limit to its membership, that any artist proving himself competent to do good work of any kind should be elected and given equal powers in the management of the Society, but that the members should have no favors shown them in public exhibitions. There was even a law passed that all pictures submitted to the jury of admission should have their signatures covered, but this law, which was rather a manifestation of principle than a practical measure, was soon repealed. There was no rule requiring that pictures should be sent exclusively to the Society, and most men sent also to the Academy whose rule giving seven feet of space on the line to its members was also withdrawn. Many of the Academicians returned the compliment and showed their work with the younger association, but there was a decided difference between the two exhibitions.

The Society was composed of men not long removed from the student state, its rapid increase in membership being caused by the influx of men returning from Europe after learning more or less thoroughly their trade. Their admiration was especially drawn to displays of the skill which they had just been striving to gain so that the exhibitions were full of "Studies" and "Sketches," with occasionally a big "Salon Picture," wherewith, as with a sort of thesis, the young aspirant graduated from the *atelier*, and demonstrated his ability as an independent artist. These latter works, however, were sent quite as often to the Academy, the fact of their having been accepted at Paris or Munich (possibly with an "honorable mention" besides) being supposed sufficient to impress even the Academy hanging committee.

The work represented the very latest ideals that had swept through the foreign schools and aroused the enthusiasm of the transatlantic students, who were embarrassed by no art traditions whatever, and

who were eager to gain distinction in the shortest way. Nor were
the ideals alike. At the first the Munich men and the Paris men
were in striking contrast, and each year sent back new enthusiasts
possessed of a new and infallible view-point. Whether it was the tonal
picture or the open air study, the minute realism of Bastien-Le Page
or the dots of the impressionists, the latest novelty in art appeared
promptly on the walls of the Society's exhibition, to the pride of the
practitioner and the amazement of the simple-minded. In this way
the Society fulfilled its mission and was a means of enlightenment
to many that dwelt in darkness. The scoffer who came to ridicule
the remarkable landscapes with the blue shadows or the broadly
smeared pictures (he knew that he could paint better than that
himself) sometimes remained to declare that there was something
in them; but the Society itself profited less than might have been
expected. It was never a social power like the Academy, nor did
it or its members ever taste the financial prosperity that the older
institution enjoyed at one time. It began when the old type of
American art was outworn and when the new was still crude and
unformed, and it had to face the strongest competition with foreign
work and the greatest prejudices and timidity of native taste. Even
those who applauded the new movement usually spent their money
for foreign pictures or photographs of old masters, and of the epoch-
making Academy exhibition of 1878 it is recorded that though
admission fees increased sales diminished. When the "younger"
men went abroad to study, painting was a lucrative profession; when
they returned, they found that it was not possible for a man to live by
it, even if he were talented, well taught, and hard working. Hardly
one succeeded in supporting himself by painting, and the rare exceptions were mostly portrait painters. The rest were forced to treat
painting as a sort of self-indulgence and to turn to illustrating, teaching, or writing to get ready money. But for these latter vocations there
was ample demand. Not in the great cities alone but still more in
the smaller towns the nation was educating itself to a higher standard of taste. This was due partly to the increasing wealth, but
there were many contributing factors. There was the leaven of
the old New England "high thinking," there was the national pride
that demanded that everything from a rolling-mill to an etching

should be the best in the world, and the corresponding individual pride that was unwilling to be inferior in any of the forms of culture. Photography had been perfected so that the spirit of great masterpieces could be reproduced with a verity unknown to the engravings or lithographs of an earlier date. Travel was becoming general, and pictures and works of the applied arts as well were being imported not only from Europe, but from Japan and China, and to this must be added the natural desire for novelty and for new fashions in place of the old.

These new interests were fostered and catered to by the three magazines, *Scribner's*, *Harper's*, and the *Century*. *Scribner's* took the lead (the old *Scribner's*, now the *Century*), but the others were soon drawn into the movement. There were articles critical and descriptive of the new arts and artists, a new school of wood-engraving grew up to answer the new-found appreciation of texture and tone, which with improved printing made possible a new and better class of illustrators. There was a public which delighted in these things, much the same public that had read Ruskin, — and still read him, — for the most part in absolute ignorance of what the masterpieces that he praised or blamed were like, but filled with vague emotions from his perfervid eloquence. They felt that they " ought to be able to talk about art," and they were greatly interested in the new movements which the improved methods of reproduction gave them better means of judging than they had had before; but even so it was the emotional and anecdotic side which appealed to them. They adored Millet much more because he was a peasant painter than because he was a good one. They were eager to learn the details of artist life, they rejoiced in the articles descriptive of the meetings and excursions of the Tile Club, they strove to take the artist's standpoint, admiring the slightest sketches that showed any technical quality; they wanted instruction, lectures, articles in the magazines, illustrations, but there their desires stopped. They did not want American paintings. Those who had much money to spend bought foreign work, those who had little contented themselves with photographs of it, and the American painters were encouraged to write about their art or teach it, or even to exhibit it, but rarely to sell it.

The clash between the old and new has been described as it

happened in New York; it was strongest and most personal there.
No other artist societies compared in importance with the Academy
of Design and the Society of American Artists, and the great majority of the returning students made the city their headquarters; but
the same movement was felt everywhere, not, however, with the same
strong animosities. The more common manifestation was a revived
interest in art and increased facilities for its study or display. The
Philadelphia Academy moved into its new building in 1876 and resumed its spring exhibitions there. Boston, whose Art Club was
founded as far back as 1855, under the influence of Hunt and the
new movement generally, was moved to new enthusiasm. Chicago
and other western cities followed until over the whole country
there were art schools, societies, and galleries. The course of instruction in the " Art Institutes " was sometimes limited to twelve
lessons in china painting for ten dollars, and the taste displayed was
often crude or trivial. There was little knowledge of art, and the
lack of any real standards of appreciation was responsible for the
production of much sloppy literature and amateurish work, but
the interest in art was awakened and went on with a continuous
development.

The last quarter of the century saw a marvellous development
of the nation in the direction of culture. It was preparatory, and its
actual achievements were so tentative and unsatisfactory that we are
apt to miss its importance. Even to-day the actual visible work has
hardly begun, but the taking of a whole nation, whose ideals hitherto,
although high, had still been purely material, intellectual, or moral,
and endowing it with some perception of the beauties of art, is an
accomplishment probably without any parallel — at least on such
an enormous scale. If the future historian traces to it as a cause
the noble monuments and higher culture which haply he may have
to chronicle, he may, perhaps, also find a kindly word for those
" younger men " who with talent and enthusiasm struggled to bring
to the country the higher foreign workmanship and adapt it to our
uses, and who as a rule got little praise and less profit for it.

CHAPTER XX

THE SOCIETY OF AMERICAN ARTISTS

MEMBERS OF THE SOCIETY OF AMERICAN ARTISTS. — THE MUNICH MEN. — NEAL. — MARR. — ROSENTHAL. — DUVENECK. — SHIRLAW. — DIELMAN. — CHASE. — ANTWERP AND THE SMALLER SCHOOLS. — THE PARIS MEN. — SARTAIN. — WYATT EATON. — J. ALDEN WEIR. — WILL H. LOW. — OTHER SCHOOLS. — LATHROP. — GEORGE FULLER. — RYDER. — GROWTH OF THE SOCIETY OF AMERICAN ARTISTS. — THE AMERICAN FINE ARTS SOCIETY

STRESS has been laid on the fact that the founders of the Society of American Artists were but little beyond the student stage of their development. With each year this condition changed. Their art broadened and fitted itself as best it could to its surroundings. The Munich section, which in the beginning was the most important, had the greatest difficulty in adapting itself, nor did it as a school long persist. The men trained there showed its influence to the end, but they altered their workmanship in its more apparent features and they were not reënforced by younger recruits — the city in a few years almost ceasing to be a resort for American students. Of the earlier men, some (mostly of German blood, though born in America), after trying their own land with small encouragement, returned to Munich and are now properly counted as of the German school. David Neal was born as far back as 1837, Toby Edward Rosenthal in 1848, and Carl Marr a decade later. These men not only mastered the Munich *technique* and mastered it thoroughly (some heads by Neal, for example, would have done honor to any of his professors), but they also assimilated the Munich ideals, the whole mental and emotional view-point of the school, so that we search their works in vain for a trace of anything distinctly American. They have executed numerous figure compositions which take high places among the productions of the contemporary German school and which like the others only fail from a certain lack of distinction.

There is something heavy in the best of them. When Rosenthal sent his " Elaine " to the Centennial Exhibition at Philadelphia, a critic characterized it as "a good loud translation of our household Tennyson into the dialect of Munich," and the phrase gives a fair idea of the picture.   Well drawn, well painted, well composed, with a sort of pathos and a sort of picturesqueness and a sort of richness, it was sure of popular admiration, for it expressed the popular conception of the scene as the public would have expressed it if they had had the training, and as a dozen other Munich painters would have done had they chosen the subject.   Neither in conception nor in execution is there any trace of a lofty or subtle insight for beauty personal to the artist.   The merits and the faults of the slightest of Whistler's etchings would be equally impossible to it.   The same thing may be said of Marr's work, though the huge canvas of the "Flagellants" is more seriously painted, with traces of real feeling, but not enough to make the higher artistic qualities dominant in a picture depending for its interest on its dimensions and on the strangeness of the scene represented.   The workmanship is more sincere than Rosenthal's.   The canvas was the labor of years, but after all it is only the recounting of a rather repulsive historical anecdote in a way and on a scale which, while it makes it the delight and wonderment of the great international exhibitions, renders it unfit for any other surroundings.

Another of the Munich students of quite a different type, but who equally failed of appreciation in his own country, was Henry Muhrman, whose water-colors were broadly executed with rich, flowing brush work, very beautiful in tone and suggesting the recent work of Holland quite as much as of Germany; but though the critics praised, the buying public held timidly aloof, and he has been obliged to seek in London the success denied him here.   With him might be mentioned J. Frank Currier, who with something of the same breadth of handling failed likewise for a long time of the appreciation that he merited, though he is now receiving a tardy recognition.

This immediate appreciation that was denied to most of the returning artists was still gained by a few, but by none to an equal degree with Duveneck, though it came from Boston rather than New York.   He had sent a single picture there that was so novel, so striking, that in 1875 the Boston Art Club specially invited him to display his work.   The five canvases that he sent created a sen-

FIG. 82. — J. ALDEN WEIR: ROSE PINK BODICE.

sation, the critics hailed him as a master, he was urged to leave Cincinnati and come to Boston, and a dozen commissions for portraits were promised him there ; but he was not yet willing to forsake the training and surroundings of Europe. He went back to Munich and afterward to the little town of Polling, where he worked surrounded by a group of students who looked up to him as their master and who accompanied him to Venice and Florence and elsewhere in Italy on painting trips. Finally when he returned to make America his home the new movement had advanced and his work was less of a novelty.

The canvases that so electrified Boston seem to-day typical of a school rather than of a distinctly original artist. They are the very essence of Munich in the seventies with their rich, bituminous backgrounds, their unctuous brush work, and their resemblance to darkened, time-stained old masters; but it is the Munich of a young and greatly daring man who had got the trick and who executed it with a slap-dash *bravura*, delighting in his strength and without too laborious or profound investigation. Whether it be a Turkish page or a professor or a *schusterbub*, the face is wiped in with warm brown color in facile brush strokes whose breadth is unimpaired by subsequent "repentances" and which give a characterization no more profound and no less amusing than the illustrations in *Fliegende Blätter*.

Even in Munich itself Duveneck was looked up to as a leader, and his brilliancy and dash found many imitators and were important factors in shaping the style of the school. Extraneous circumstances have prevented his art from developing naturally and completely. There has been ill-health, there has been domestic sorrow, there has been a turning aside for a while to the study of sculpture, and the noble monument to his wife contains those deeper emotional qualities that are lacking in his youthful work. The time devoted to teaching and perhaps also the fact that he has lived out of contact with his old comrades has combined with the other factors to make his recent production smaller and less important than was to have been hoped. His painting has changed in character also, and bitumen and darkness have been abandoned to some extent for light and even cool, gray shadows.

The Munich handling generally had to be changed to fit it to American surroundings or to suit a taste formed by the later open-air school. The influence of the training was permanent, but showed indirectly. Almost the only man who has retained consistently the old manner is Shirlaw, in whose works the Munich style is usually immediately recognizable. It is rather curious that it should be so, for he was not of German stock. Though brought to America when only two years old, he was born in Scotland, and his early training came through an apprenticeship to learn bank-note engraving and afterward by study in the schools of the Academy of Design. He had practised painting and exhibited and was over thirty when he went to Munich, but the six or seven years he spent there removed all traces of the earlier training. " Tuning the Bell " (done in 1874) and " Sheep Shearing in the Bavarian Highlands " (1876) are typical Munich pictures and good ones ; and so also was the " Marble Quarry " of 1880, but the quarry was in New England, and the work-men and the oxen native-born Americans. The other men had confined themselves mostly to painting bric-à-brac or portraits, and it was something of a shock to see an actual New England scene " translated into the dialect of Munich," so that, though admirably done, the public failed somehow to encourage the venture as it deserved. It was the decorative side of Shirlaw's work which was the more successful rather than the realistic, not only in his designs for stained glass or similar work, but also in his easel pictures. The handling is broad and flowing, the drawing large and simple, the color, even when light in key, still keeps the warm tones of Munich, and the whole canvas has a sort of decorative unity of tone and texture very different from the minute dependence on the model which was taught in France. Even in Munich and in Dietz's studio other manners of work could be learned. Dielman, who was in turn treasurer and secretary of the new Society of American Artists, as Shirlaw was its first president, drew from the beginning with minute care the *genre* pictures or the graceful heads, showing with almost monumental dignity against the leafy back-grounds which are characteristic of him, and he has kept his original manner with no great change.

Of all the Munich men, however, the one who exerted the greatest influence upon American painting both by his instruction and his example was William M. Chase. He was born in Indiana, and there found a portrait painter to give him his earliest instruction. When he was twenty he came on to New York and studied a couple of years in the schools of the Academy of Design, and then in 1871 started practising art in St. Louis, painting mostly still-life. There he saw the studies made in Munich by John Mulvaney, which determined him to go to Germany himself. He studied under Wagner and Piloty, and was one of their most brilliant pupils, but rather intractable to advice, the main trouble seeming to have been that he had no desire to compose the regular exhibition pictures, but preferred to work at still-life or subjects which were largely excuses for brilliant execution. Toward the end of his six years' stay he painted a number of such canvases as the "Broken Jug," the "Apprentice," "Ready for the Ride," and others; and the next year at Venice the "Portrait of Duveneck," the unconventional attitude of which, the head only showing above the back of a chair, shocked some critics as a sort of indecorum.

Duveneck may have exercised some influence on Chase's painting at this time. They were certainly in sympathy, and their work had much resemblance; but from the time when he left Venice to take charge of the painting classes of the Art Students' League, Chase's art has developed along independent lines. Unlike Duveneck and too many of the other Munich men, there has been no retrogression or falling out of the battle even temporarily. For thirty years he has been on the firing line, painting, teaching, lecturing with amazing and unconquerable energy. In the early days when the similitude of a battle was more apposite than at present, he was counted among the most prominent and aggressive leaders of the new movement; for ten years he was president of the Society of American Artists, and his studio in the Tenth Street building served for its meetings and as a rallying place for its friends until, in fact, their cause was practically gained.

During this long time his production was continuous and very varied, — still-life and *genre*, landscape and portrait; done in oil, in water-color, in black and white, and in pastel. He has tried all branches of painting and all mediums, and has used all in constantly varying manners. The old bituminous shadows of Munich soon disappeared from his work, to be but seldom reëmployed. The general tone became bright and luminous, the color pure and sparkling, the handling always suited to the material, whether oil or pastel or charcoal. Through all the varied works, however, there runs the same spirit, the same individuality, sometimes almost hidden, sometimes breaking out in a new form, a spirit delighting in the external aspect of things, with all their infinite variations, and also in all the cleverness and skill of craftsmanship.

This accounts for his variety of subject; everything seen makes its appeal, — the clouds drifting over the sand-dunes, the children at play, the pots and pans and old stuffs of the studio, anything that the eye can see the hand can render with a dexterity that is a joy of itself; but, as with Whistler or even more than in his case, the object must be before the eye. The interest is not in general types but in those subtle and momentary differences of appearance which no mind could retain or divine. This would explain why Chase has not attempted decorative painting (if his activity in the other branches were not a sufficient explanation), and also account for a certain externality in some of his work as a portrait painter; for though many of his portraits are excellent, there are others where he seems to have treated his sitters as bits of still-life to be brilliantly reproduced, but with no more attachment to their personalities than if they were brass pots or Kennebec salmon. But this is only to say that he has the defects of his qualities. Among our painters there is no other who is so purely a painter. He delights in the technical exercise of his art, and it is in this direction that he has influenced his many pupils. They have been taught to use paint with freedom which has probably been an excellent addition to the ordinary instruction conducted, as at Paris, mainly on a basis of drawing.

The Munich methods were the most strikingly novel among those displayed by the returning students. They may be said to have dominated the early exhibitions of the Society of American Artists. They even created more interest than the French work, which was the next most important factor. Between these two clearly divided groups there were all degrees of difference. The men who had studied in Belgium or Holland stood as far as train-

FIG. 83.— FULLER: NYDIA, METROPOLITAN MUSEUM.

ing went about midway.   They had no reckless dashing brush work, their draftsmanship was accurate, even laboriously so; but their shadows were warm and brown, and they took more pleasure in texture and surfaces than the austerity of the French training usually permitted.   It was, in fact, sound academic training, with no very distinguishing local characteristic.   Much the same might have been given by the more conservative of the Munich professors, and though his own work had a special dexterity and firmness, Couture's teaching had been practically the same; but in Munich and Paris there were enthusiasms and innovations in the art atmosphere which carried the pupil beyond the instructions of the schools.   Probably Antwerp was the most patronized of any of the intermediary places; but the American student was unsettled in his search for knowledge, wandering from one school to another.   Percival De Luce, who was perhaps the first American to work at Antwerp, went afterward to Brussels and finally to the *Atelier* Bonnat in Paris, while Robert C. Minor left Paris and Diaz for Antwerp.   Bunce even studied at Düsseldorf (he was a little older than the other men); but if he was influenced by any master, it must have been by Clays in Brussels. Maynard and Francis D. Millet remained faithful to Antwerp during their student years, and their workmanship testifies to the thoroughness of the training in the Academy there.

There was no such sureness nor unity of work among the original members of the Society of American Artists who studied at Paris, and yet the proportion of them and of the other Paris students of the seventies and eighties that have developed and continued to work as established artists of repute is notably larger than among the Munich men.   This very continuance of production, with the development and alteration of their styles, keeps their careers from being history as yet, and their very merit relegates them to a later and briefer notice.   Of the foundation members themselves William Sartain might almost seem to belong to the earlier American school.   To be sure, he studied under Yvon and Bonnat and at the École des Beaux Arts, but he was the son of John Sartain the engraver, long a venerable figure in the art life of Philadelphia and New York and who vied with James Smillie in reproducing for art books and annuals the works of the older men.   The son, too, travelled in Europe and Algeria, like Colman and the Giffords, and his canvases like theirs are executed without any special brilliancy of handling; but there is in Sartain's work a delicacy of tone in the simple masses not striking at first, but whose absolute justness is recognized on longer acquaintance. Some of his Moorish street scenes have a depth of luminous atmosphere enveloping the little figures in a way comparable to that of Pieter de Hooge.

Wyatt Eaton was another of the French contingent who, though born on the Canadian end of Lake Champlain, may yet be fairly claimed as an "American," for his parents were there only temporarily and he came early to New York and studied in the National Academy schools before going abroad. There he worked under Gérôme, made the acquaintance of Millet, and lived for a while near him at Barbizon and even found room for admiration of the rising star of Bastien-Le Page, but none of these is copied in his works if exception be made of his "Hay Makers," which was a sort of combination of Millet and Bastien, and a not very successful attempt to do something strong. His characteristic note was not strength, but rather delicacy of feeling: feeling for tone and color in his "Reflection," feeling for grace in his little classic figures, feeling for character in the crayon heads that he did of Emerson and Holmes and Whittier and others. The feeling was sincere and personal and has made his work last well, so that the few things done before his early death are more appreciated now than ever.

This same refinement of perception, but of a robuster type, was characteristic of J. Alden Weir, like Eaton, a pupil of Gérôme, but who was far from imitating his master's style, even further from it than Eaton. Weir had a more vigorous handling; less feeling for classic grace of form and more for subtle harmonies of color, but there is yet a certain unity in the point of view of both. Weir's style has developed and had its phases, but the "Green Bodice" has a clear relationship to the earlier "Reflection." Weir, however, though he was a friend of Bastien-Le Page and an admirer of Millet, has yet been more influenced by Manet and Monet (or rather by the spirit of the time of which they were manifestations), trying their methods and adapting them to American portraiture and landscape. He belongs really among our impressionists, men like

Twachtman or Hassam, and is one of the ablest and most original of the group, with a peculiar feeling for delicate browns and grays and silvery tones. He has gained strength steadily so that now his canvases are complete and harmonious, with no trace of effort in their execution. Each has its own particular character of beauty or picturesqueness. He has simplified the masses in his portraits, composing them almost in flat spots and with delicate and unusual groupings and color schemes. In the same way he has transcribed our landscape, surrounding it with an enveloping atmosphere and working its roughness and unkemptness into patterns of delicate, decorative quality.

Like Weir working at the Beaux Arts under Gérôme and visiting Barbizon with Eaton was Will H. Low, but the distinguishing character of his Paris work came from neither of these frequentations, but from the *atelier* of Carolus-Duran. The broad unctuous brush work of the master can be clearly traced in the " Portrait of Madame Albani," and especially in the " Lady of the Empire," but this was but a passing phase. Already in Barbizon he had started a " Jour des Morts," and soon after his return he began to paint figure pictures with the light tones of the open-air school, which were then a novelty. They were at first taken from our own country life and infused with a delicate sentiment or pathos which culminated in an ambitious illustration of " Skipper Ireson's Ride," after Whittier's poem ; but soon Chloes and Daphnes began to replace the New England maidens, and sunbonnets and gingham dresses gave way to antique draperies. The classical traditions of French art appealed to Low ; and though he used modern formulas, his constant struggle was to express something of the grace of their line and balanced composition. His first considerable success was his illustration of Keats's *Lamia*, and his later development in painting and in decoration has been in this direction.

These three men represent fairly well the variety and quality of the results of French training at this time. They have been mentioned here for the purely arbitrary reason that they were among the founders of the Society. During the next four or five years other students returned from Paris by dozens and scores, making individual mention impossible. From England there came very few. The schools there were not calculated to tempt the stranger, and many of the English went to Paris to learn their trade. Almost the only one of the early members of the Society of American Artists with English training was Francis Lathrop, who had studied as a boy under Farrer in New York and later at the Dresden Academy, and who, just as he came of age, went from there to London, Whistler having invited him and promised to teach him more than all the art schools could.

The counsels of Whistler were admirable but rather unsystematic, and so he procured a place for Lathrop in the studio of Madox Brown, who had a young friend of about the same age as a student. There Lathrop met the Pre-Raphaelite circle, including Morris and Burne-Jones, and knew them more or less intimately. It was an unusual experience for an American student at the time. If the ordinary school training often diminished imagination and feeling while insisting on the mechanical side of art, association with the followers of Rossetti was likely to err on the other side. But imagination and feeling are so rare that something may well be risked for their sake. His English training shows in Lathrop's portraits and ideal heads, but especially in the decorative work which soon took up a large share of his energies and which, though influenced by American needs and by collaboration with La Farge, is still related to the English decorative school of Burne-Jones and Morris as very little of the other work done here is.

The remaining three painters from among the founders received what was practically an American training, though all visited Europe and have been profoundly though indirectly influenced by certain moods of European art. Helena De Kay (now Mrs. R. W. Gilder) showed a charming feeling for subtle color in her ideal heads and especially in her flower studies; but after a few years she gave up her career as an artist and ceased to exhibit. The other two (Fuller and Ryder) count among the most original and important of our native painters. Their place is with the landscape group that had Inness at its head, but they manifested themselves later.

This is true of George Fuller, although, as far as age went, he was an older man than Inness, having been born in 1822, but his career was a curious one. He began, like so many others, as an

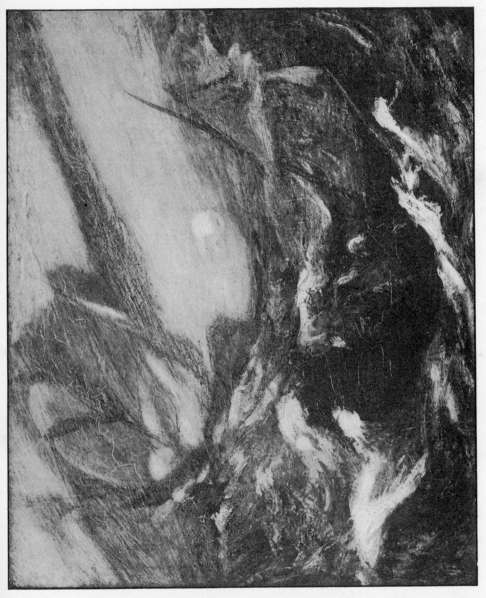

FIG. 84.— RYDER: THE FLYING DUTCHMAN, OWNED BY JOHN GELLATLY, ESQ.

itinerant painter, making likenesses for a few dollars each, and after some study in Boston and New York succeeded in painting portraits and landscapes in a way not greatly differing from the average work of the time. He was made an associate of the Academy of Design in 1857, but his painting was unremunerative. It might have sufficed for his own wants, but in 1859 his brother and father died, and it seemed to him his duty to take the old mortgaged farm in his native Deerfield and try to win from it a livelihood for the family. He did not give up his painting, but no longer tried to sell his pictures, working only for his own amusement and solace. He labored at his canvases as his mood moved him, drawing them into more perfect harmony. At length when, after nearly a score of years, he began to show his pictures once more, they bore no relation to his previous careful, prosaic work. They were filled with a brown enveloping mist that swallowed up the figures and dulled their outlines; there was little positive color, there was little positive form, and what there was was not absolutely accurate. They were what many men could very nearly do by messing over old canvases.

But in painting it is just such slight differences that distinguish between good and bad, and Fuller was no ordinary man. His heart was sound, his mind was clear, and his taste was sure. He had been trusted and loved by his fellow-workers in the early days, and had the strength of character which enabled him to develop in solitude. Just before he went back to the farm, as if to pay him for his renunciation, he made a six months' trip through Europe, visiting all the great galleries and admiring the masterpieces. In the long years afterward the memory of them must have been an enormous refining influence. There are delicate but sure variations of color in his landscapes, there is individual charm in his ideal heads, and in both there is the feeling, subtle, intangible, of poetry and mystery. When in 1876 the failure to make farming pay forced him to send a dozen of his pictures to a Boston dealer, their success was instantaneous, and for the remaining eight years of his life he had purchasers for whatever he did. It cannot be maintained that all of his works are on the same level, but the best of them, like the " Turkey Pasture," " She was a Witch," or the " Winifred Dysart," are of the greatest distinction; the latter especially, like the best of his ideal heads, making a peculiar personal appeal, like some of the portraits of Gainsborough.

If the work of Fuller is better judged by the emotion it produces than by more literal and prosaic tests, that of Albert P. Ryder has even more need of such leniency. Its strangeness is greater. It not only does not respond to the usual technical standards, but it sets up others of its own. It will not do to say that it is not literal, not exact; for it is very varied, and there are bits of still-life or landscape that are as minutely truthful as any one need desire; but in general, nature is seen through his temperament and much altered in the process. More than Fuller, he is a seer of visions and even less bound by literal fact. For Fuller saw with poetic insight the world about him, softening or obliterating prosaic details; but Ryder constructs a world of his own, mysterious and often illogical, with all the vividness and incoherence of a dream. He belongs with men like Monticelli and Blake, whose faults are manifest to the most casual and obtuse critic, but whose fascination is felt only by the peculiarly receptive.

This effect is heightened in Ryder's works by his execution, by his manipulation of paint and varnish as substances capable of being made beautiful in themselves, as well as in pattern and color. Some of them suggest the lacquer work of Korin, as when a red stag flees through dark depths of varnish beneath a streak of yellow sky, or patches of silvery, moon-lit cloud spot against the deep blue behind a brown tree. The "Flying Dutchman" is a swirl of delicately matched old ivory and violet grays, and most of his pictures are, as Whistler insisted pictures should be, beautiful simply as patterns in delicately graded colors and tones. But Ryder's pictures differ from Whistler's as well as from Fuller's in being not transcriptions from nature, but creations of the imagination, and in striving to convey ideas, vague but poetic. As in the case of Monticelli, with whom he has the closest affinity, his worst is very bad; but his best, to those to whom his symbols appeal, give a delight unlike that from any other source.

Of such varying elements as these the Society of American Artists was at first composed; but although it never became so homogeneous a body as the old Academy of the sixties, yet as time went on the differences became less than at first. Some of the older men thought they were treated with scant courtesy and soon resigned, there were fewer men who had received an exclusively American training, the Munich school lost its vogue, and the great bulk of the new members had passed through the French *ateliers*, even those who had worked in Germany or elsewhere usually making some sort of a stop at Paris; so that in a dozen years when the membership had increased to a hundred, there were very few who did not owe allegiance of some sort to French masters.

About this time the Society had become a firmly established institution, and a permanent home of some kind was a necessity, but the difficulties in the way of obtaining it were great. The Society was not at all a social institution, and the members were bound together but loosely. Its sole function was to hold an exhibition once a year, and there were none of those informal reunions which in the early days of the Academy united the artists and amateurs, and made a portion of the solid business men of the city friendly to the institution and willing to subscribe to its funds. On the contrary, this same loyalty to the old Academicians was a detriment to the members of the Society who were regarded as interlopers, and some few of whom even disquieted the minds of serious people by certain remnants of studio manners and of Parisian peculiarities in costume. It was consequently not easy to raise money; but the Art Students' League, an independent school run by its own members, needed working quarters and the newly organized Architectural League, exhibition galleries, so that a combination was made with them. Between fifty and a hundred thousand dollars were raised by subscriptions and fellowships, fifty thousand more was paid by the three societies and their friends for stock in a new company, — the American Fine Arts Society, which was to erect a building affording accommodation to the three constituting societies and to be governed by trustees elected by them. With this narrow margin, (not much over a hundred thousand dollars), land was bought on Fifty-seventh Street, running through to Fifty-eighth, and a building started. The planning and management of the affair was mainly due to Howard Russell Butler, who triumphantly refuted the idea that business capacity is incompatible with the practice of painting. Even as it was, there came a time when failure threatened, but the situation was explained to George W. Vanderbilt, who bought in the Fifty-eighth Street front with the understanding that he was to resell to the Society when it got sufficient funds. Instead of this, however, he erected the Vanderbilt Gallery and presented land and building to the Society, a gift nearly equal in value to its original resources. The completed structure was opened in December of 1892, with a special retrospective exhibition of the best works shown previously, and the Society took its place as a settled institution.

CHAPTER XXI

AMERICAN PAINTERS LIVING IN EUROPE

IN the years following the foundation of the Society of American Artists, American painting becomes more and more a part of immediate contemporary life and less and less a matter for history. Its achievements are so recent and so complex that the perspective is lacking for definitive judgment, and little more can be done than to attempt some generalities on its dominant characteristics and to notice in some way the schools or personalities that have influenced it, without pretending to make accurate or final decisions on their relative importance. The natural method is to treat of each of the branches of art, figure, portrait, landscape, and the rest by itself, and show how it stands related to the others and to the main body; but at once an initial difficulty arises, — the painters as a rule have confined themselves to no special line, but have tried all things from illustration to mural decoration and from landscape to miniature. Their work does not at first follow the old accepted divisions, for the French studios qualified their followers to paint anything that they saw, with the same facility and in the same way; though with time the young painter, after incursions into various realms, usually found his own province and settled permanently within its borders.

These studios at the time of the influx of Americans had undergone a change from the old traditions. Painting, owing to the great demand for French pictures not only from America but from England and Germany as well, had become a profitable and honored trade, and there was a great rush of youths of all sorts to learn the desirable art. Previously pupils had been received into studios in a sort of patriarchal fashion after introduction by some friend of the family, or else the beginner sought out a painter whom he admired and asked to be received as a pupil. It was always considered a favor. The master as a rule accepted no payment but exercised despotic authority and expected implicit obedience. The pupils were no more in number than he could know intimately, and it was quite within his office to criticise, if he saw fit, their morals, their literary taste, or their politics, and in matters concerning art his word was not to be questioned — the subjects to be painted, the preparation of the canvas, the handling, must all conform to the traditions of the *atelier*.

When the great influx of pupils came, it swamped these old schools. Even the government *ateliers* of the École des Beaux Arts, which were conducted in much the same way and where admission was not easy, were crowded beyond their capacity, and to accommodate the overflow there sprang up a new class of academies which charged definite fees for instruction and where any one could enter without introduction and usually without any proof of his capacity. Some of these were started by artists, some by managers who engaged the artists and undertook the responsibilities of the enterprise. The financial arrangement was like that of any drawing school, but the men who went to the academies intended to make painting the occupation of their lives and demanded the very best instruction, and in fact among the professors were the most distinguished of French painters.

The numbers that flocked to these schools, however, were so great that anything like the old personal care was impossible. The Carolus-Duran *atelier* was almost the only one that held to the old personal relations. In the others, classes of over a hundred were common, and in some cases a single man had more than two hundred pupils. The system of instruction had to be simplified and concentrated so that it could be applied in the minute or two twice a week, which was all the time that the " Professor " (which the " Master " of earlier days had become) could devote to each pupil. This reduced the course practically to drawing from the nude figure. The study of the

FIG. 85.—STEWART: HUNT BALL, ESSEX CLUB, NEWARK.

antique was practised only long enough to gain admission to the life class, and even for that casts from life tended to supplant those from classical masterpieces. The professors were members of the Institute, steeped in the cult of the grand style with its repose, dignity, and calm beauty; but in their hurried intercourse they could not inspire like views in the great mass of their pupils, who often while accepting their instruction reviled their ideals as antiquated. While a few remained true to the classical tradition, the trend was all toward naturalism. The movement had been started by Courbet and Manet, but these had been above all painters, and no such brush work was to be taught in the schools. A more popular and more readily imitated leader was Bastien-Le Page, whose minute and accurate draftsmanship appealed to students struggling to do the same and whose gray, open-air coloring was an innovation. Monet's sunlight and mist effects were hardly adaptable to the school study of the models though some attempted them, and Puvis de Chavannes' Pantheon decoration had enthusiastic followers.

The American students were moved by the same enthusiasm as their fellows, and their work was undistinguishable from that which was done around them. Like the others, when they had gained sufficient skill they took studios of their own and there produced a portrait, a study of the nude or a group, and sent it off to the Salon, where it was much discussed by their fellow-students and possibly noticed by the critics or honored by a " mention." At about this point in his career the average American had to return. He left the most beautiful city in the world, where art and artists were glorified; he left the old *atelier* crowd, so sympathetic and amusing, and the easy student life, without restraints or duties, and he came home to an unsympathetic land, indifferent to his work, where life seemed colorless and filled with all manner of irksome obligations. The Salon picture on which he was to found his fame received no attention or else was criticised in a manner so unintelligent that praise was even more maddening than abuse. The pursuit of his art was hedged with petty annoyances. Models and costumes were hard to find, studios were scarce and absurdly dear, and, worst of all, it was commonly at this inopportune moment that his friends expected him to become self-supporting. This sudden

2 D

deprivation of the art-fostering atmosphere of Paris was in some ways regrettable.   Many of the men were forced to leave with their training incomplete, others, and those among the better ones, needed the discipline of a public criticism severe but intelligent.   Too many men, satisfied with a bit of charming, subtle color or drawing,

FIG. 86. — DANNAT : QUARTETTE, METROPOLITAN MUSEUM.

left the rest of the canvas in a shape which they would hardly have dared to present to a Parisian Salon jury.

A certain proportion of the students, however, small as compared with the whole number but yet sufficiently numerous when taken by itself, was spared this untimely return.   They were enabled thus not only to acquire but also to practise their art under the guidance of their masters and in the surroundings in which it was formed. Their development has been unbroken and they have become admirable workmen, exhibiting regularly in the great European Salons, winning medals and decorations for themselves and much credit for their country. Their names are honored in all the art magazines, and photographs of their pictures are in all the shop windows from Constantinople to Lisbon.

The artists living in America seldom sent their works abroad for exhibition; it was expensive and difficult to do so, and there was nothing to be gained by it. Even if successful, foreign praise and honors were useless to them. They neither increased the price of the pictures nor the standing of the painters; besides, apart from other reasons, the small size of the canvases, made as a rule for private houses, rendered them unfit for display in the great exhibition halls. It was natural, therefore, that the work of the expatriates should have represented to foreign critics the sum total of American art and equally natural that they should have declared that it was only a branch or a copy of the art of France. This reproach (if it be one) cannot be well denied, but it applies equally to much of the best European art and even to some of the best British work.

For the past thirty years Paris has been the art-school of the world, and a multitude of painters have studied there or — what is much more important — have worked with the requirements and standards of the French Salons in their minds. Many Germans and Belgians and Italians and Spanish canvases have mingled there with the native product, and for the most part have been indistinguishable from it, — the Americans perhaps even more indistinguishable than the others, for their long distance from their home and the generally received conviction of the unpicturesqueness of their country prevented them from painting any subjects which might betray their nationality. The nationality may be traced here and there, however, by a careful observer, not in the workmanship or the subject but in the point of view, in the temperament of the painter. They have none of them become French, they all belong to some branch of the American colony. A few have become Parisians, which is a very different thing from becoming French, but as a rule there has been surprisingly little assimilation. They have their own

alien ideas on manners and morals, and these affect their works.
For instance, take a well-known picture, and one that seems at
first glance peculiarly French — the " Hunt Ball " by Julius L.
Stewart.   What French painter would catch just the spirit of
frank enjoyment of the young girls without a trace of either
shyness or coquetry?   Or, again, what French painter, at the time
that it was executed, would have conceived an " Arcadia " so free
from school traditions, so frankly naturalistic, as that of Alexander
Harrison?

But at best these traces are slight and often undiscoverable.
The American Salon painters are above all Salon painters and
of a high average merit.   The portraits and Dutch pictures
of McEwen, the figures in old costumes of Pearce, the peasant
girls of Ridgeway Knight, the scenes from humble life by Walter
Gay, are all excellent of their kind, well drawn and well painted.
A special word should be given to some of the later work of Gay,
bits of old eighteenth-century rooms, with their polished floors,
their gilded woodwork, tarnished mirrors, and old porcelain.   The
touch is brilliant and sure, the coloring very delicate and true,
and the sentiment of inanimate things exquisitely given.   No
figures are introduced, but the spirits of an earlier time are felt to
haunt the places.   Modern elegance as displayed in the life of the
American colony in France is given in a series of pictures by
Stewart, such as the " Hunt Ball " already referred to, while another
side of his talent is shown in a series of studies of nudes in the open
air, lighted by reflected sunlight.

These subjects do not in the least exhaust the productions of the
artists, but are simply the ones which occur as most characteristic
of each.   All have painted portraits and landscape and many other
things.   Like Stewart, Mrs. MacMonnies has painted nudes in the
open air with something of the charm of the old bric-à-brac of Gay,
but more frequently groups of modern figures in the sunny paths of
her garden at Giverny.   MacMonnies himself has latterly deserted
sculpture for the sister art and has produced work so amazing in its
boldness and breadth that it seems incredible that it should be the
work of a beginner.   There is no sign of weakness or uncertainty in
the execution, and the lack of the customary long apprenticeship to

FIG. 87. — MELCHERS : PORTRAIT.

the craft shows itself, if at all, in a certain superficiality and lack of nobility (to put it mildly) in the conception. Such skill, applied to ends so trivial, creates a feeling of repulsion and drew from one critic of the MacMonnies paintings, when they were shown in New York, the remark that probably no painter in America was able to do such work, and certainly none would be willing to. This unpleasant view-point is probably due to the exigencies of the Salon exhibitions, which demand that pictures shall be aggressive if they would be noticed, for some of the portraits painted during his visit in America were dignified and quiet.

Another man excelling in pure painting is William T. Dannat, whose early work showed clearly his training in Munich and under Munkacsy. One of his first works, the "Quartette," now in the Metropolitan Museum, was declared by Albert Wolff to be the best piece of painting in the Salon of 1884, and Wolff, if no very subtle critic, knew his trade and voiced accurately the current opinion. This first method was followed in a number of studies mostly Spanish and then it changed to a quite different handling, where refinement of enveloping tone was sought for and the means of obtaining it were obscured, as in the "Woman in Red," the "Woman in White," and the "Sacristy in Arragon"; and then another change came, and the canvases were keyed up to the brightest, lightest tone like the "Otero." All of these methods have been used not only consecutively, but interchangeably, and brilliant work has been done in each, the main reproach of the critic being that of late years there have not been as many as were to be desired. Another portrait painter who also began with something of the Munich training is Julian Story, who was one of Duveneck's pupils, and though he afterward went through the Paris *ateliers*, there remains still, as with Dannat, some trace of the earlier influences in broader, more dashing brush work, though there has been added an elegance and sprightliness not at all Teutonic.

These men painted as a rule the life of Paris or of France; the aristocrats or the poor of the great city, the peasants or bourgeois of the provinces. Another group travelled and recorded in their work the strange or picturesque sights that they had seen. Many were tempted by the atmosphere, the picturesque costumes, and the artistic traditions of Holland. McEwen had been there, and there among others went George Hitchcock and Gari Melchers. The first painted the tulip fields, glowing in the soft, bright sunlight with a brilliancy that has almost obscured the variety of his later work. Melchers has interpreted the daily life of the seafaring folk of the little villages in all its bare simplicity, — the labor, the courtship, the church-going, — but it is done with a peculiar insight and sympathy. The life is hard and unadorned, but it is neither sordid nor unhappy. The people are of the same race that Winslow Homer delights in, used to the open air, sturdy and self-reliant; and they are painted with something of Holbein's sincerity, not prettified but not degraded or caricatured either. The young girls have the grace of their youth, the mothers the tenderness of their maternity, and the old men the rugged dignity of sailors who have faced danger unafraid. The painting is also excellent as painting, largely in the cool, grayish, open-air tones, with no dark shadows or brilliant light, but with each mass of color kept flat and pure, the outlines firm and characteristic, and the masses "spotting" into an interesting composition.

In contrast to this search for the quiet life, Edwin Lord Weeks has pushed through semi-civilized lands as far as India and has given to those who know only the gray western world some idea of the sunlight, the color, and the strange, curiously wrought structures of the East, and his clear, sure interpretation carries conviction of the accuracy of the reproduction, not only of the places but of their light and atmosphere, and the strange and varied life which circulates through them. Charles J. Theriat, too, has reported in delicately drawn, minutely finished canvases the wandering life of the herdsmen in southern Algeria and especially the country around Biskra. But the authorized painter of Algeria and all the south shore of the Mediterranean is Frederick A. Bridgman, who after each incursion into outside territory returns again to its sunlight, its blue sky, its white housetops, or its darkened rooms. He was one of the earliest of American students to settle in Paris, going there in 1866 and sending back work to the Academy exhibition in 1871. He was represented in all the early exhibitions of the Society of American Artists, and probably were it not for his absence abroad he would have been one of the foundation members. From the very first his painting was facile and sure, with no indication of effort or of difficulties struggled with in vain. Pictures like the "American Circus in France," or even a life-size group of two girls in a boat, which seems even earlier, show none of the hesitancy of a beginner, but have the sureness of long practice. There were Breton and Normandy subjects among these early pictures, but in 1873 he visited Egypt and Algeria and began the work by which he is best known. There were some reconstructions of ancient life—the "Funeral of a Mummy," the "Procession of the Bull Apis"—natural in a pupil of Gérôme and showing some of the best qualities of the master; but there were more reproductions of the actual life, the receptions in the old palace of the Beys of Algiers, the gathering of the women in cemeteries for

FIG. 88.—ALEXANDER HARRISON: THE WAVE, PENNSYLVANIA ACADEMY.
[Copyright, 1898, by The Pennsylvania Academy of Fine Arts.]

mourning and gossip, the trading in the bazaar, the life of the harem, and the bargainings of the horse-dealers.

The record seems less exact than that of the India of Weeks, or at least the latter seems to have sought picturesqueness by literally copying all characteristic details in their completeness, while Bridgman looks for prettiness and selects what appeals to him from that side and lets the rest go. Surely there are old and skinny ladies in Algeria as elsewhere, but they are rigorously banished from the assemblage of plump and youthful forms with which his pictures are so fully supplied. He lavishes upon them the same grace that he gives his classical figures in his poetic or imaginative compositions, for almost alone among the Americans in Paris he has painted a considerable number of purely ideal subjects. His production has been very great, but it has not affected the execution. There is no slovenliness or neglect in any of them. If a reproach is to be made, it would be the one hinted at above of an excess of prettiness, the line, the color, the composition, and the figures have all a sweetness that is at times a trifle cloying, but it is accompanied by qualities rarely found in work open to such suspicion. Above all, the drafts-manship, though facile, is sure and sensitive; the Algerian women, though lovely, keep their racial type as well as the men and children, the settings, whether of landscape or architecture, are flawless in con-struction, and a special praise is due to the drawing of the barb horses with their delicate heads, smooth round bodies, and clean trim legs.

Like Bridgman, Alexander Harrison was also a pupil of Gérôme; but unlike him there is no trace even in his earlier pictures of his master's classical tastes. From the first he felt the fascination of the open air. His student days came at a time of enthusiasm, when for a group of the younger men, Bastien-Le Page was a name to conjure with, and when they were striving, like him, to look at nature out of doors with eyes unblinded by old traditions. Some of the older masters, from the Holland school down to Millet, had given the enveloping quality of the atmosphere, though they had retained the warm studio tones; but it was discovered that shadows under the soft, misty sky of France were not of any one fixed color, but infinitely varied with the varying light, and the "*Plein airists*" insisted that the truth should be given in all its complexity. Something of this had been rendered by Courbet and his successors, Manet and Monet; but they had tried for broad, general effect with a disregard of detail and with eccentricities of brush work disconcerting to the uninitiated. Bastien and his friends applied to outdoor nature the minute, sensi-tive draftsmanship that they had gained in the *ateliers*. There were no formulas, no traditions for the new school; everything had to be discovered by the artist and translated by him somehow into paint. In all these explorations Harrison was a leader. He looked at nature with an eye unclouded by recollections of the old masters and wonderfully responsive to the delicate variations of color. He gave the gray, soft tones of flesh in the open air with only the slightest modelling and entirely without the strong, dark shadows formerly employed, and he blended figures and landscape into an intimate unity.

All of this Bastien had also done in soft, diffused light, but the " Arcadia " of Harrison was an original and important innovation, for in it the most brilliant sunlight in all its strength and changeableness was analyzed as it had never been before. The golden light struck through the trees and lay in great patches on the grass, and its reflection lighted up the bodies of the nymphs with tints rarely, if ever, used for flesh before, but whose accuracy was manifest. And the effect was not alone of accuracy but of beauty. The drawing of the nude figures was realistic, and it seemed as if a touch of academic idealism would have done them no harm, but apart from that the canvas shone with the joy of light and air. Finer yet were the marines that followed, the long waves rolling in on the sandy beach in the early twilight with the infinite variation of their toppling crests or foamy ebb lighted with every subtle tint of rosy iridescence. The wave of " La Crepuscule " has been painted by hundreds since, as has its moonlit successor, but no one has yet reached, even approximately, the charm of the originals.

These marines were the admiration even of those recalcitrants whom the " Arcadia " had outraged. Harrison's position is assured and he has received the honors and recompenses that are his due. The open-air school has been accepted, and is now " understanded of the people," but it is well to recall, so rapidly has public taste changed, that many of the men whose work now seems to us good, but good along conventional lines, were at first considered eccentric and dangerous innovators. The only school of thirty years ago that has not been generally comprehended by the average art lover is that of Manet, which still finds many insensible to its merits. The whole training of the big studios was in another direction so that, though some admired, yet it found only a single follower among the Americans, but that a notable one, Mary Cassatt.

The school of Manet is not a large one, nor do the works of the different members closely resemble each other, for one of the fundamental requirements was a distinct personality. There might even seem to be some doubt about placing Miss Cassatt in it, for her taste was formed by the study of Velasquez in Spain before she settled in

Paris; but the classification is sufficiently close to give an idea of her affiliations. Like Manet she sees the world with no desire to alter it to ideal pre-conceptions, she sees it also in large spots of local color, not as contrasting masses of light and shade; these spots she does not weaken by elaborate modelling as Bastien-Le Page did, and unlike him and his followers, she insists that the paint shall be spread in a solid, fine impasto, not broken up in a multitude of small, thin touches.

To do work of this kind requires insight of a peculiar kind, a synthetic mind for form, grasping it instinctively in its simplest, most characteristic mass; and at the same time a most delicate perception of all the refinements of color and tone, for there is no elaborate drawing to hold the picture together, and if the great masses are not perfect in value it falls to pieces. Over these difficulties Miss Cassatt has triumphed, her drawing is sure and characteristic, her coloring subtly harmonized, and she has, moreover, a fine feeling for arrangement, placing the masses of her figures so that they form agreeable patterns; but her painting is painters' painting, and makes its strongest appeal to members of her own craft. By them and by the more enlightened amateurs she is appreciated and honored; but the great public stands aloof, indifferent or hostile. She has never catered to it or given it that obvious prettiness that it loves. Even her color, which is her greatest charm, is made up of subdued whites and grays and pale, sad tones, rarely a touch that is bright and strong, and the drawing is uncompromising in its search for character rather than grace. The average mother and child of real life resembles but remotely the creations of Bouguereau; but the versions by Bouguereau come much nearer to the popular ideals of what babies should be. Miss Cassatt is not to be diverted by such ideals from reality, which has its own beauty, — a beauty which so appeals to her that she seems rather to avoid nature when it runs to a more popular comeliness and so continues to paint stubby toes and pudgy noses, to the delight of the few and the bewilderment of the many.

This appeal to a restricted few is not a position forced upon Miss Cassatt by repeated rebuffs. From the first she has refused to exhibit in the great annual salons, but in her indifference to their applause and honors she stands alone. All the other Paris-American painters

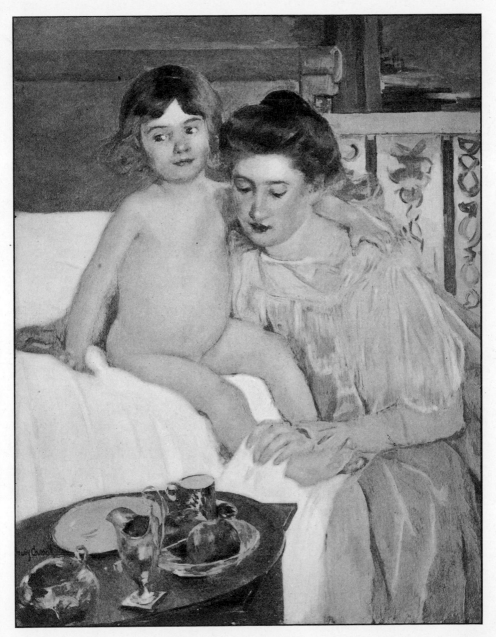

FIG. 89. — CASSATT : MOTHER AND CHILD, OWNED BY DURAND–RUEL & SONS.

mentioned (and many more, whose omission is unavoidable from lack of space for even the slightest notice) have regularly displayed their works in the great competitive exhibitions, and each boasts after his name a long string of honors won therein. Such a grading is any-thing but definitive, yet from the medals and decorations a suffi-ciently accurate general idea may be obtained of the artists' standing, not only among themselves, but as a part of the great cosmopolitan body. The result is flattering to our national pride. In proportion to their numbers, they have more than the average share of rewards, and deservedly so. There is something in the stability of their position, with its steady accumulation of vested rights, to arouse the envy of the artists who came back to America at the end of the seven-ties, and who have been practically forced to remake their reputation every year since.

But there have been drawbacks to the expatriate life also. Closely united as they were to French training and conditions, it is natural that the career of the men who remained abroad should have agreed with that of their French contemporaries. Now the most striking fact in the recent development of art has been the failure of the French painters, who came to the front in the ten or fifteen years succeeding 1875 to sustain their reputation. They triumphed aggressively in the exposition of 1889, and declared that art was to be rejuvenated by them; but at the next great international fair, eleven years later, their boast was wofully unfulfilled. It was not that they were grown old, they were in the strength of their age; their seniors, the old academic group that had been denounced for a quarter of a century by them as worn-out, empty formalists, were still in their places turn-ing out work strong and masterly that hardly showed a trace of the burden of their years. But the enthusiasm of the innovators seemed to have weakened, their inspiration to have vanished. Many of them were forced to go back eight or ten years to find works that would fitly maintain their reputation, and the critics lamented that the popularity of a painter lasted no longer than that of a tenor. Some-thing of this transitoriness was due to the search for novelty rather than beauty, the desire to be the first to represent some special effect of light or to put upon canvas some unusual subject; but even more to the exigencies of the annual Salon and of Parisian criticism. The works were placed in incongruous surroundings and judged by their ability to arrest for an instant the eye, wearied by the sight of four or five thousand other pictures equally clamoring for attention.

These conditions have not been favorable to the steady development of the highest qualities either of imagination or of execution, and these conditions — or others — have affected the American painters in France. At the exhibition of 1889 their section was clearly in advance of that occupied by works sent from America; in 1900 it cannot be said that the situation was reversed. The foreign American section, buttressed by the works of Whistler and Sargent, was an admirable display; but the native American section was approximately equal to it, preference for one above the other depending largely on the personal view-point. Of the Paris painters, however, who were the strength of the exhibition in 1889, only one or two had advanced, more had distinctly retrograded; but most were about where they had been before, doing the same work in the same way with a slightly increased facility and a somewhat diminished enthusiasm. With the men who had worked alongside of them as students, but had been obliged to return to America, the case was very different. They had been forced to paint not for the Salon, but for private houses, to modify the workmanship learned in the schools, to make experiments, to change their style and their subjects in order to find something that they were willing to paint and the public was willing to buy. Many were doing better work than in 1889; some were doing worse, but hardly one was doing the same work. There had been development, and though it was easy enough to see where most of the men had got their training, and though certain pessimistic critics still repeated the old cry that Americans were only imitators of the French, yet there were evident to the unbiassed observer certain distinct characteristics of workmanship and of feeling running through the whole which constituted a school quite as individual as most of the Continental ones.

These characteristics had been of slow growth and slower recognition. Serious and competent critics were few in America, and their views were swamped in the great mass of emotional or reportorial writing, one man's opinion being held to be just as good as another's, and better if he proclaimed it more loudly. Few foreign critics had a chance to see what was being done, and most of them found it more convenient and patriotic to follow the accepted opinion; but if a man oᶠ wide culture and open mind came to the country, he was apt to be surprised at the lack of appreciation of our painters' achievements. Some of the more prominent (artistically rather than financially) of the visiting portrait painters spoke strongly on the matter, and Dr. Bode of the Berlin Museum, writing of the Chicago Exposition in the *Zeitschrift für Bildende Kunst*, for his own people and not for America, expressed the most enthusiastic and generous admiration for the beauty and originality of the American school of painting, and declared that the American section was not only the largest, but the best in the exhibition.

In addition to the older men in Paris, whose position is now well assured, there have come forward in the last dozen years a group of painters allied to Frenchmen like Cottet or Simon, and representing the reaction from the type of Salon picture, whose laborious and unimaginative painting produced something of the effect of a colored photograph. These demand a deeper sentiment, a richer color (it is apt to be darker than seems necessary), a bolder handling of paint, a more decorative composition. The tradition of Manet reappears, but modified, less eccentric and less strong.

Among their works, to choose a few names from the mass, are the scriptural subjects of H. O. Tanner painted with all the Oriental surroundings, but with strong, religious feeling, the mellow landscapes of Van der Weyden with their antique grace, the fishing boats of Fromuth and Koopman, dark and rich in tone with their sails and reflections patterning strangely against the sky or in the water; and the arrangements of Maurer, where the subject is often nothing but an excuse for displaying a perfection of brush work and ringing the changes on exquisite gradations of white and black. These men are no longer beginners, they have achieved a position for themselves, but yet it is permissible to expect from them a further advance, completer work, and especially an excellent influence on the rising school.

CHAPTER XXII

AMERICAN ARTISTS IN LONDON

LONDON AS A RESORT FOR AMERICAN ARTISTS. — F. D. MILLET. — ABBEY. — HIS ILLUS-
TRATIONS. — HIS PAINTINGS. — J. J. SHANNON. — J. McCLURE HAMILTON. — SARGENT.
— YOUTH AND TRAINING UNDER CAROLUS-DURAN. — HIS WORKMANSHIP. — THE
CHARACTERISTICS OF HIS PORTRAITS. — HIS OTHER EASEL PICTURES. — HIS
LIMITATIONS

MENTION has been made of the older colonies of painters, formed
in Italy or Germany; but of late years these have had few additions,
Paris has been the headquarters of Americans who remained on the
Continent to practise their art, and that whether they lived in the city
itself or passed most of their time elsewhere, in Brittany like Alexander
Harrison, or in Holland like Melchers. The only place that could
be considered at all her rival was London, which held out entirely
different inducements. It is not a *ville lumière* — least of all in matters of art. As a training place for painters, even its own artists
are apt to consider it inferior to Paris; but it is the greatest and
richest city in the world, and an inexhaustible market for anything
that can minister to its comfort or luxury, including painting.
Pictures are sent there from all Europe, but as a rule the foreign
painters who settle there are portraitists. This is also true, as a
rule, of American artists, though the language and the life, the
similarity of moral and intellectual standards, render it a pleasanter
dwelling-place than the Continent for some whose subject-matter
renders residence in America difficult or impossible. Joseph Pennell, for instance, could hardly produce his delicate records of the
picturesqueness of English cathedrals and old French towns in
New York, and it would be almost as difficult for men like Millet
and Abbey, trying to reproduce the charm and quaintness of old-time
life, to live permanently in America.

Of these two, however, Francis D. Millet is much less firmly
anchored to England then Abbey. He has made it his home, but

SARGENT: MRS. IAN HAMILTON.

with long periods of absence in other lands (including his own), as his multiple activities and occupations have led him. For Millet has the old American versatility, the abounding energy that can be turned at will to whatever task most insistently demands it, and the intelligence and temper that can push it through to success. He has been a war correspondent in many lands, he has been an illustrator, he has written travels, criticism, fiction, he has acted as an expert on old pictures, he has raised carnations; it is even reported that in an emergency during the Turco-Russian War he successfully amputated an arm at the shoulder.

All of these varied activities, and the list is far from complete, he has exercised not as an amateur or a tyro, but as a professional, asking no odds and holding his place with the best; but his painting shows no signs of his multitudinous distractions. It is complete, thorough, carried through to the end, with no trace of haste or neglect. In the completeness and perfection of his finish, he suggests Alma Tadema, who, like him, studied at the Antwerp Academy before he fixed his home in London; but Millet's work is more varied in subject and execution than Tadema's minute and charming reconstructions of antique life. These, too, he has done but more, apparently, because the antique draperies set off a comely girl to advantage than from any intimate sympathy with the time. It was England of the seventeenth and eighteenth centuries that most appealed to him, not in its monumental aspect, but in its quiet, human side, — the country parlors, the libraries of the scholars, or the cheerful roomy kitchens with their whitewashed walls, peopled with far-travelled adventurers, puritans, or buxom serving maids. The scene of one of the best is laid in New York itself, where the legendary Cornelius, the trumpeter, basks in the admiration of a surrounding female circle before his untimely death in the dark waters of Spuyten Duyvel.

All of these groups are skilful in arrangement and natural and unforced in attitude and expression. They do not savor of the costumer and the hired model. The execution is solid and the color clean and sweet. The only reproach that can be brought against them is that their very completeness, their smooth and enamel-like quality, is too uniform and does not differentiate textures as a more

varied handling might do.   Besides these comparatively small easel
pictures and his large decorations, Millet has latterly turned his attention to portraits, adapting his handling to life-size works with his
customary facility.   He has also done a few portraits on a much
smaller scale, the heads only two or three inches long.   These have
not been exhibited, and consequently are not well known by the
public, but they are charming in character and distinction.

Allied with Millet not only as friend and neighbor in the little
village of Broadway in Worcestershire, but also by similar tastes
and view-point is Edwin A. Abbey ; but though Millet's work is
well known and popular, Abbey's has a still greater public.   He
began with illustrations in the widely circulated magazines to which
countless enthusiasts looked forward from month to month, and
bought eagerly when they were afterwards published in book form.
Later the photographs of his decorations in the Boston Public
Library had an almost equal vogue.   It would be difficult to name
another living artist who has given so much delight, and a delight
so keen and so wholesome.   To hundreds of thousands he has
renewed the charm of the old poems that had grown hackneyed by
constant familiarity.   He enters perfectly into the sentiment both
of the poet and of the modern reader toward him, which latter
is curiously compounded half of admiration of the verses and half
of amusement at the odd turns of phrase and thought of a past age.

Abbey renders perfectly the conscious affectations of Herrick and
the real tenderness and feeling that shines through his conceits.
He disentangles the mingled inspiration that makes of *Sally in
our Alley* at once a lyric and a humorous poem.   He understands
the social charm of the old vicar, Guglielmus Brown, "*Vir nulla
non donandus lauru*," and the irresistible fascination of the unprin-
cipled Irishman of Athlone, and he embellishes them with a wealth
of detail, quaint, unexpected, and amusing.   Thus did the porters
carry the sedan-chairs over the cobblestone streets, in such latticed
bowers was tea or syllabub served at the fair, a sword knot was tied
like this, and thus the ample petticoats of the eighteenth century
puffed out when the indwelling lady sat down.   The ballad of the
Leather Bottel was imperfectly comprehensible until he showed the
construction of that friend of the simple life, and all was done

FIG. 9c.—MILLET: BETWEEN TWO FIRES, NATIONAL GALLERY OF BRITISH ART.

[Copyright by F. D. Millet.]

with apparent unconsciousness. The initiated recognized that this enormous mass of minute and curious knowledge could only have been gained by infinite research, united with an imagination of wonderful constructive power; but there was no hint of effort in the work. The odd doorways or casements, the old iron work, the formal gardens, were touched in as Charles Keene would put a bit of London street or Scotch moor behind his figures — such were the surroundings which he saw, and he added them to fill out the pictures; but your attention was not solicited in the least. So Abbey's knowledge of his Old World detail was so complete, so assimilated, that he was not curious to display it. He hid it behind his figures, he sketched it in the slightest and most fugitive lines; but it was impeccable, without a false or disquieting note.

His execution is as complete as his conception, at least in his pen-and-ink drawings, which are, as a rule, better than those in wash. The etchings and drawings of Fortuny, which reached the country about the time that he began working on the staff of Harper Brothers, aided in forming his *technique* and for him they proved excellent models. He did not get the vigorous contrasts, the dashing spotting with pure blacks of Fortuny. He shows less "temperament" (as the word is employed in the studios), but he has the same skill in using a multiplicity of crossing lines, retouched and perfected endlessly and yet not losing their freshness, the tone remaining transparent and brilliant. Everywhere the line is sympathetic, sensitive, never degenerating into mere caligraphic facility. This unflagging interest is amazing, not an end of ribbon, not a shoe lace, not even the leg of a stool but is understood and rendered with enthusiasm.

Under the circumstances it was inevitable that Abbey should be encouraged to illustrate Shakespeare. Having done such marvels with the lesser poets, how much more wonderful things would he do with a great one? The argument is logical but fallacious. In the first place, so great an undertaking, no matter how congenial, is bound to have its moments when it becomes a piece of task-work to which the artist forces himself, — and such moments are not favorable to genial invention, — but the main difficulty lies deeper. For those who read, the characters of Shakespeare have become intimate personal friends; we are not to be put off with a jewelled stomacher or an Italian terrace. We know Rosalind and Beatrice, Falstaff and Jacques, and we care nothing about their clothes. If, maddened at the Venetian parody of justice, Shylock had removed to Amsterdam and been painted there in his old age by Rembrandt, or if, in defiance of all chronology, Velasquez on a diplomatic mission to the northern courts had made a portrait of the young Prince of Denmark, we might have had satisfying likenesses. Titian might have painted Benedick and Giorgione, Romeo; but, lacking such works as these, has any one ever seen a satisfactory portrait of a Shakespearian character? Abbey did as well as any one has ever done and gave a series of graceful figures in quaint or beautiful settings. Technically many of them are among his best works, though they should be seen in the pages of the magazine (or better yet in the originals) rather than in the smaller photogravure reproductions.

This illustrative work is beyond the strict limits of a history of painting, but an account of it is necessary in the case of Abbey, whose work grew out of it and was formed by it. His first paintings were in the same style — water-colors with body color rather freely used — and they had all the skill and charm of his work for the magazines. His beginnings in oil were less assured, the drawing was firm, but the values were disquieting. The faces or the marble terraces were often as light as the sky and seemed translucent. The fault was a natural result of much pen-and-ink work where the white of the paper does for all vacant spaces, but it shows in his decoration of the old Bowling Green of New Amsterdam in the Imperial Hotel and in some other works of the time. It was only temporary, however. In his first great success in oils, the "Richard the Third and Lady Anne," there is no trace of it, nor does it reappear. The "Richard" and the succeeding Shakespearian subjects, "Hamlet," "Macbeth," the "Trial of Queen Catherine," apart from the unsatisfactoriness which is inherent in all attempts to render such subjects, are admirably done, solidly and minutely painted, filled with all the old wealth of costume and detail, and harmonized into a unity of tone, so that they have something of the effect of old tapestry. The same may be said of his latest achievement, the "Coronation of King Edward

FIG. 91. — ABBEY : MARIANA.

[From a Copley Print. Copyright, 1897, by Curtis & Cameron, Publishers, Boston.]

the Seventh."   It is a curious coincidence that the generally accepted picture of the coronation of Queen Victoria was done by Leslie, like Abbey an American, brought up in Philadelphia and receiving his first instruction at the Academy there, and that both artists have succeeded beyond hope in vivifying with some artistic interest subjects which by their very official nature seem doomed to be wooden and frigid.

More important even than these elaborate dramatic and historical paintings is the series in the Boston Public Library, but these will be treated of in a chapter especially devoted to decoration.   It is pleasant to be able to add that these theoretically loftier works have not obliterated the skill in black and white, and that Abbey has recently shown his ability to illustrate Goldsmith with all the old freshness and grace.

Among the portrait painters who flock to England for patronage, America has never failed to be represented, though at present in far smaller numbers proportionately than a century ago.   It might almost be claimed that the number was actually greater then than now, and though that would be an exaggeration, yet the number is small of those who have become permanently established in the British capital.   They are, however, among the best, and so strongly have they enrooted themselves that their position as American painters is more questionable than might be wished.   J. J. Shannon, for instance, came to London when a boy of sixteen, got his training at the South Kensington school, and a year or two before he was of age exhibited portraits that brought him into prominence.   His work is admirable, broad and sure, full of beauty and of character; but there is little in it that betrays the American unless it be this same breadth and dignity which differentiates it from the great mass of English work.   Even so there are plenty of English artists whose work is free from the niggling prettiness of the majority of the pictures at the Royal Academy, and the underlying temper of Shannon is rather British.   His color is more varied, his composition is less academic, but his work reverts in a way to the standards of Reynolds.   He loves handsome women and pretty children and fine, healthy men with fine figures and fresh complexions.   He enjoys them with the same direct delight in their beauty or grace.   " Miss Kitty " is entirely in the spirit of the older master, and while we may have a certain pride that so excellent an artist was born in Auburn, New York, yet there is little cause to include his work in a History of American Painting.

The case is not quite the same with J. McClure Hamilton. He was older when he went abroad, and he studied with the rest of his compatriots in Antwerp and Paris. In spite of the series of portraits of distinguished Englishmen, — Gladstone, Manning, Tyndall, Watts, and the rest which constitute his best-known work, — he belongs rather to the American branch of the cosmopolitan school. His little portraits (they are as a rule less than half the size of life) give the sitter in the familiar surroundings of his books or papers, with more of the intimacy of actual life and less of official pose than is usual. The painting is thin, the background just covered by a warm glaze on which the lights are touched in cool gray tones, without much body, but so surely that they give a solid modelling. It is not at all an English manner of work but has something of the French accuracy of drawing added to the warm shadows of Antwerp, which eclecticism of workmanship ought to constitute him an American.

A more complicated problem of nationality is involved in the case of John S. Sargent, and a more important one from the standpoint of those who are jealous to exalt their country by displaying its famous sons. Born in Florence of American parents, he received his artistic training in Paris and has since lived in England, though with much travelling on the Continent and two or three trips to the land of his allegiance. His pictures have been shown wherever pictures are to be seen, and he has received for them all honors that a painter can receive. For a dozen years Continental juries have solved the problem of conciliating American jealousies in the matter of awards by giving to him and Whistler a medal of honor apiece. If another had been added to them, it would have unchained a furious discussion of relative altitude; but by common consent of the men who exhibited in Europe, these two stood above the rest, each secure on his own eminence.

The argument for Whistler's Americanism is based partly on his temperament, but Sargent's private life is not displayed to the world. His opinions, epigrams, and animosities are not exploited in the daily press. The public know of him only a few dates and statistics and what they can divine from his works. These show his artistic development clearly enough, if to outside influences is added an exceptional inborn talent. His first studies were made at the Academy at Florence when he was very young, and just what permanent influence he received there is not clear. The Carolus-Duran *atelier* is rightly credited with forming his style. He was only seventeen when he entered. The big roll of miscel-

FIG. 92.—HAMILTON : PORTRAIT OF HON. RICHARD VAUX, PENNSYLVANIA ACADEMY.

laneous work, drawings, water-colors, landscape studies in the style of Calame and copies after the old masters, which he showed to gain admission, led Carolus to remark that he had much to unlearn, but his fellow-students (all much older than he) were amazed at their quantity and facility. This same ease of execution remained with him. As a student working from the model he would cover a whole canvas with color while others were fussing over a little patch. Such facility is apt to be dangerous. Hundreds of artists have stopped in their development because the ability to do a pleasing sketch easily has rendered them content with that and incapable of the hard work and self-criticism necessary to completeness. Sargent, however, had no such lethargy nor were his talents checked or diverted into a false channel, as might have happened had he entered another studio. Carolus-Duran was probably the best master that he could have had. Contemplating some of his later work, especially the portraits executed in America, we are apt to forget what a superb draftsman he was at the time he painted the " Femme au Gant " of the Luxembourg or the " Lady with the Dog " of the Museum of Lille ; but in addition to this and almost alone among the artists of Paris he taught painting to his pupils. The basis of instruction was not an infinitely elaborated charcoal drawing of the nude figure, but a head blocked in with paint, the great construction planes kept simple, their edges meeting in harsh, straight lines in the work of the beginners, but the paint laid on thickly, and all the attention concentrated on getting the just relations of mass, tone, and color. Not until this had been done were the pupils permitted to soften the edges and elaborate details.

The feeling for this underlying construction in form and tone Sargent gained thoroughly. It is the framework unseen but all pervasive on which his pictures are built, and differentiates them absolutely from the most skilful of his imitators. To this must be added his ease in the mechanical manipulation of paint which would be encouraged and developed by the teaching and example of Carolus. To spread great surfaces of pure clean color, to touch on them lights and shades and details with a flowing brush, but so surely and firmly that they lie bright and clear on the wet underpainting, to invent strange and apparently accidental turns of the brush that give effects with an accuracy beyond the reach of the most persevering labor, — all this is of his nature. The beholder stands in delighted bewilderment as before a juggler more mystifying than any that India or Japan has produced. To other painters such dexterity has come, if at all, after long labor ; but it was Sargent's from the first. His portrait of Carolus-Duran with which he made his début was hailed as a masterpiece of cleverness, and so it was ; but alongside of the "Girl with a Rose" that followed, it seemed labored and academic — as if he had been hampered by his master's presence. It is the only one of his works that looks as if it might have been done bit by bit and worked over; his other canvases have the air of absolute spontaneity. There is no under-painting, overpainting, or glazing, there is no heavy body color, the paint, made fluid with oil and turpentine, is brushed on exactly as it should be and left. A head is ordinarily finished in a single sit-ting, for the purity of the tone must not be impaired by alterations or reworking.

What desperate hard work, what struggles constantly renewed the artist has gone through that he might paint with ease, he alone knows. Traditions tell of heads painted and scraped out thirty and forty times, of portraits that required countless sittings, but in the end they had the lightness and swiftness of a sketch. One result of this method is the ability to grasp an instantaneous effect and render it in all its complexity. In " El Jaleo," one of his earliest pictures, as well as in other Spanish dances, or in the study of an Egyptian girl from the back with the body twisted into profile, what with most men would have been mere thumb-nail sketches became life-size pictures. But the power is more important when it is less obvious, when it catches the passing expression on a face or the naturalness of a gesture before it relapses into the rigor of a set pose. Take the " Girl with a Rose" just mentioned, the arm is at right angles to the body, — a position that could not be held for a moment with-out fatigue; but no suggestion of fatigue comes to the spectator, because he recognizes that the pose is but momentary, that it has just been taken, and that the hand will be drawn back at once. Almost all of his portraits show somewhere the same effect, — in the turn of the head, the nervous twisting of hands, or the flow of a scarf, — and it helps to give them their wonderful vitality.

Another result of the direct fluent painting is the purity and brilliancy of the color. Softness, a sort of indwelling glow, may be obtained by glazing and manipulation, but nothing else is as bright as pure color laid on a clean canvas and left unmolested. It was, as has been said, a time of examination and experimentation in colors, of elaborate investigation and discrimination of all varieties of lights and shadows, of tones and half-tones, and reflected lights.

It tended after all to subtlety rather than strength. Titian used throughout his life the same reds and blues to dress his virgins, just as Homer's ships are always black, his sea wine-colored, and his Greeks well-greaved; but the complexity of nature had replaced the simplicity of tradition. Flaubert, the Goncourts, Daudet, wrestled over the ultimate refinements of exactitude in the choice of words as the painters did in colors. Sargent was of his time and as little trammelled by tradition as Courbet, and his craftsmanship was even better though entirely different. There was no rich, solid impasto plastered on with the palette knife, but a surface of fluid paint, in spite of all its strength and richness, thin as in the canvases of Rubens, or more exactly Franz Hals. He belonged also in a different social class than Courbet, but he looked at the visible world with much of Courbet's directness, and he was not led into the excesses of men like Manet, whose originality was not exempt from pose. He was a portrait painter, too, and the problems of the open-air school did not affect him greatly, but from the prevailing realism he gained a freedom from prescribed or conventional methods. He had no fixed scheme to which all heads were more or less fitted, as had been the method of some of the greatest masters of the past. The shadows were not uniformly brown or even warm, and the half-tones had all the infinite variety of nature with a special clearness and brightness from the direct workmanship. The same influence extended to the backgrounds, which were neither the conventional dark shadows of Bonnat nor the carefully composed tables and columns of the eighteenth century, but the actual surroundings of the sitter, the walls and furniture and floor, with glimpses of other rooms through open doors, all in the sharp foreshortening in which they were seen, varying with each sitter and fitted to each as their clothes or their gestures.

But the triumph of realism was in the way in which the sitters themselves were comprehended. " Heraclitus saith well in one of his aenigmas, 'dry light is ever the best.'" Even Lord Bacon might admit that the maxim is not so generally applicable in art as in life, yet Sargent has accepted it with a completeness unknown since Holbein, and even Holbein scarcely saw his sitters in a light so little "infused and drenched in his own imagining."

The older master, for all his sincerity, was sympathetic; but before a group of portraits by the younger man we wonder whether he cared at all for the people he painted, either for their past or future, or for anything except the moment that they stood before him twiddling their watch-chains or spreading their fans. Of that moment, though, we have the absolute record, and a terrible one it is sometimes, for the artist, without illusions himself, is pitiless for those of his sitters. If a lady thinks to renew by artifice the freshness of her youth, she appears not with the roses and lilies of nature on her face, but with rouge and pearl powder manifest and unmistakable; if the statesman bends his brows and puffs up his chest, he is displayed not as a thunderbolt of debate, but as a pompous ass. An adoring family wails that instead of their young goddess they have been given a picture of a Gibson girl, and magnates of all sorts hear with bewilderment the inferences as to their personal characters which an enthusiastic public draws from their counterfeit presentments. One genial moralist has even had his faith in Providence strengthened because certain of the great of this world, who seemed beyond the reach of human vengeance, with no outside duress or intimidation, have gone to Sargent and paid considerable sums to have their likenesses given to the world.

And in these pictures, even the most terrible of them, there is not a grain of malice. The features are painted as dispassionately as the necktie or the boots. Nothing is caricatured or exaggerated, but the people are alive and demand our judgment as real people. Nor is that judgment usually hostile; on the contrary most of the portraits awake in us conflicting, but on the whole favorable, emotions, and there are many beautiful women and high-bred men whom it is a pleasure to have met. At times the charm is strangely intense and personal. When a year or so ago a young girl died just as she was on the point of entering society, there were hundreds who felt it as a private bereavement of their own, though they knew her only as the little wistful child in the portrait with the parrot. In fact, almost all of the portraits of children are tender, and the series of them from the Beit children in the hall with the great blue and white vases down to those of the present day is of wonderful and varied charm. One suspects a special tenderness toward them; but even in the

2 F

soft outlines of childhood there is yet the discrimination of personal character, the minute details that make the individual different
from all the rest of the world.

This display of character is the intellectual quality in Sargent's
work to which all of his technical attainments are subordinated.
When an artist has mastered the meaning of a face, he may try to
paint it dispassionately and exactly, but the inner meaning will be
more vivid to the ordinary man in the picture than in the flesh, and
no one, not even the greatest masters of the past, has read ordinary,
everyday character as minutely and completely as Sargent.   He is
not profound.   He does not touch on the eternal mysteries or try to
lay bare the soul.   He is incurious as to whether his sitters have
souls or what will be their future state; but as to this present commonplace world of business and pleasure he is full of the most minute
and valuable information.   He tells whether they are pompous or
cordial or shy, if they have or have not a sense of humor, whether
they are nervous or stolid, sensible or eccentric, kindly or malicious.
He diagnoses their health, shows their degree of education, displays
the style of their establishment, and suggests approximately their
annual expenditure.

On these and on a thousand other points he is rarely at fault,
and some of the deductions drawn from his portraits by utter
strangers are amazing in accuracy.   His portraits of public men are
historical documents as illuminative as the most elaborate memoirs,
and it is not too much to say that the political situation in Europe
would be clearer to us to-day if he had painted the Czar; but no
ruler by divine right has ever sat to him, wisely perhaps from the
point of view of the ruler; for it is doubtful if the divine right would
have been made as prominent as the human weaknesses, and yet
posterity will regret that it cannot know Queen Victoria or the
Emperor William with the same intimacy that it may Thomas
Brackett Reed, for instance, also once upon a time called Czar.

This penetrative analysis of character is not confined to those
whose characters are important or distinguished.   It is lavished
on all alike and even on inanimate things, the silks and velvets, the
furniture and bric-à-brac are all eloquent.   A gleam of gold in the
shadow has the dusty tone that proclaims that it is old gilding even

FIG. 93.— SARGENT : HENRY G. MARQUAND, METROPOLITAN MUSEUM.

though its form is indistinguishable. The porcelain in the Beit hall is evidently not in the same class with that behind the Misses Wertheimer. The personality of a room, of a place, is given absolutely and unexpectedly. Venice has been painted thousands and tens of thousands of times, — the canals, the Campanile, the Doges' Palace and St. Mark's, both inside and out, but there is a sketch by Sargent of a slatternly, red-headed girl with a black shawl over her head coming over the stones of a shabby little street that *is* Venice as none of the other representations are. The canals may be filled up, St. Mark's may crumble as the Campanile has done ; but as long as the race and the climate remain, so long will remain the clear, colorless morbidezza of the face, the limp, clinging skirts with all the stiffness taken out by the moist sea air, and the gentle lassitude of the loafers leaning against the wall draped in their dark cloaks. The curious thing is that while the picture is in grays and blacks, without a single bright touch, it is not only more true but infinitely more beautiful in color than the customary blaze of orange and red ; and while there is not a trace of old carving or Gothic architecture, yet it somehow gives the grace and mystery of Venice as Ruskin's painfully elaborated drawings do not. Sargent has painted but few canvases of this kind in proportion to the number of his portraits, and yet set apart by themselves they form an important group. They have the same qualities as the portraits, they might well be called Portraits of Places, but not official portraits nor of "show" places. They are intimate, personal, and it is only a passing mood that is noted, the sunlight on a sea beach, the spacious, shadowy depths of an Italian palace interior, the rosy glow of the pink shaded candles on the silver and linen of a dinner table, but each wonderfully seen and rendered.

Sargent's work has its limitations, but they are largely set by its qualities. If a transcript of life is to be made vivid, with all its changing effects struck instantly upon the canvas, there can be no brooding and musing and dreaming. The surface of the paint is smooth and flowing, the color is brilliant and pure, but neither have that absolute and subtle perfection that comes when an artist holds a canvas by him, looks at it long and often, searching it, adding a touch here and a glaze there with loving care until all fuses into unity.   The composition likewise has no such absolute perfection.   The figures are usually well placed and well grouped, they fit well in the frames; but after all the composition is taken as nature gave it, with some choice from different poses and some suiting of the dimensions of the canvas to them, but no weaving of light and shade, line and spot, into a complete decorative arrangement.   His portraits rarely have distinction in their patterning.   This amounts about to saying that Sargent is not Whistler.   It has already been hinted that he is not Rembrandt, and it may be added that he is not Raphael.   It is even possible to doubt whether he is Velasquez, though both he and Whistler have each been claimed as reincarnations of that master.   But he has no need to claim a reflection of another man's qualities, for he has his own and they suffice.

With a certain temperament it is quite permissible to dislike his work, as it is permissible to dislike the work of Rubens; but with all limitations and reserves made, he has talents manifest and unmistakable that give him securely his position as the first portrait painter since Reynolds and Gainsborough.

CHAPTER XXIII

RECENT LANDSCAPE PAINTING IN AMERICA

PRESENT DEVELOPMENT OF LANDSCAPE IN AMERICA. — FOLLOWERS OF CHURCH AND
KENSETT. — W. L. PALMER, E. M. TABER, H. BOLTON JONES, R. W. VAN BOSKERCK. —
FOLLOWERS OF INNESS AND THE BARBIZON PAINTERS. — LOUIS C. TIFFANY, GEORGE
INNESS, JR., CHARLES H. MILLER, ROBERT C. MINOR, CHARLES MELVILLE DEWEY. —
BLAKELOCK, BOGERT, RANGER. — DEARTH, F. BALLARD WILLIAMS, DESSAR, WILL S.
ROBINSON, CARLETON WIGGINS. — BUNCE, MURPHY, CRANE, BIRGE HARRISON, SNELL,
COFFIN. — PICKNELL, DONOHO, DAVIS. — ROBINSON, W. S. ALLEN, TWACHTMAN,
HASSAM, METCALF. — TRYON, OCHTMAN, APPLETON BROWN. — BEN FOSTER, W. L.
LATHROP. — NETTLETON, POTTHAST, WALTER CLARK. — SCHOFIELD, REDFIELD. —
MARINE PAINTERS. — EICHELBERGER, KOST, REHN, WOODBURY, CHAPMAN

FOR American painters residing mainly abroad remoteness in
space replaces remoteness in time and gives a perspective so that
it is possible to write of them with a certain dispassionate detach-
ment, which is aided by the fact that there are not so many of them,
their aims are more or less alike, and the honors for which all have
contended, and which most have received, in some measure grade
them into a sort of hierarchy. In America, while the number doing
work good enough technically to entitle it to serious consideration
is naturally much greater, formal honors like medals are contended
for so intermittently and awarded on such varied grounds that they
do not settle relative rank. Moreover, less stress is laid here than
in Europe on workmanship and more on sentiment, the indwelling
emotion which may be felt, but its quality or genuineness is hardly
measurable by any definite standard. There is a certain loose union
into groups resulting from similarities of training or temperament,
but quite as often as not the affiliations are impermanent and traceable with difficulty. Under such conditions criticism becomes
increasingly difficult, and to characterize properly any artist and show
how he varies from those doing similar work would require space and
reproductions of his paintings far beyond the possibilities of a book
like the present. The most that can be done is some general

439

characterization of the groups, with reference to individual painters only here and there by way of illustration.

Of the recent painters, including under that head those that have come forward since the founding of the Society of American Artists the only ones that hold at all to the traditions of the American past are the landscapists. It was the strongest and most characteristic branch of the old school, as it probably is of the new. It perfected itself as a school more gradually than figure painting, feeling and adapting the foreign influences earlier and more naturally. When the figure painters returned with all the novel and revolutionary methods of the Munich and Paris schools, men like Inness and Martin had already assimilated the inspiration of the best of the French masters of landscape, but they had assimilated it on a basis of native training and practice. Even the younger landscapists went abroad less unprepared and spent less time in the schools than the figure painters. In this way they got less out of touch with the taste of the country, and for a long time they were the only painters to enjoy even a modest popular vogue.

Already in the seventies the American landscape school was divided more or less between the men who painted detail and those who looked for broad effects. The point of view represented by Church had practically no followers, all the tendencies of the time were away from the panoramic arrangement of the wonders of nature; but many learned the methods of Church or Kensett or Colman, and developed them — men like Henry A. Ferguson, Joseph Lyman, or J. C. Nicoll whose work has much the characteristics of that of the older men. Walter L. Palmer was even a student under Church and shows stronger traces of his early discipleship than of his later one under Carolus-Duran. It is not that he delights in icebergs or volcanoes, or that he seeks out the strangeness of the tropics or the glories of Greece; but all the minute detail that his eye can see interests him, and he does not fail to reproduce it. He has painted most forms of landscape, including many views of Venice, but he has made the winter with its snows his especial province. It is not the snow of Europe damply evaporating into a leaden sky, but the New England article, crisp and dry in the keen cold and shining dazzling white against the blue horizon. All the

FIG. 94.—TABER: MT. MANSFIELD IN WINTER.

resources of the open-air school are resorted to in order to get the exact tone of the shadows and keep them keyed up to their natural brilliancy and yet have a higher, brighter note for the sunlit snow itself.   This brilliancy is given perhaps better than by any one else, and yet detail is pushed to the ultimate point of elaboration, every twig or track in the snow has the sharpness and completeness of nature.

This crystalline clearness of our winter air we share with Norway and Sweden, to judge by the works of their painters; but it is not common elsewhere in Europe, and we get no formulas for represent-

FIG. 95. — H. BOLTON JONES: SPRING, METROPOLITAN MUSEUM.

ing it.   In this way Palmer's work is original and equally original was that of E. M. Taber, who painted not only the immediate foreground but the distant Vermont mountains on the days when every rock and tree shows sharp and clear though miles away.   He analyzed the forms and the shifting tints of sapphire and amethyst with infinite delicacy and feeling and with a handling peculiarly his own, — smooth, solid, and minute.   It seemed as if, had not an untimely death intervened, he might have developed the art of Kensett into something finer, more responsive to our own climate and land than has yet been done.   Something of this same completeness of finish is also characteristic of H. Bolton Jones, although the seasons which appeal to him are the summer and especially the spring with its fresh bright greens and the delicate tints of the budding trees. The interest in all the minutiæ of nature which characterized the old Hudson River school is there, but the execution is surer and more artistic, and the coloring in its truthfulness and delicacy and in the absence of the brown studio tones shows the influence of the French open-air school.

Allied to the older work also, both by their completeness of finish and by their frank and unaffected enjoyment of prettiness, are the pictures of R. W. Van Boskerck with their tranquil streams, great trees, white cottages, and calm summer skies with rosy clouds. There is a direct connection, too, for Van Boskerck was a pupil of Wyant; but the pupil does not seek the delicate, rather melancholy sentiment of the master. The grass and flowers shine bright in the sunlight, cheerfulness is over all; but for all their prettiness the planes of the pictures hold together with absolute solidity.

In contrast to these men with their completeness, their clarity, their occasional hardness, are the followers of George Fuller or of Inness, who seek a richer harmony of color, a more decorative composition, and a unity of effect less broken by insistent details. Some of these were pupils of the older men. Louis C. Tiffany, for instance, was a pupil of Inness, but his work shows more traces of his other masters, — Samuel Colman and Leon Belly. There was, in fact, much of Colman's love of warm, pure color in his paintings in transparent wash or in gouache on rough straw board, of Italian or Mexican scenes that used to light up the early exhibitions of the Water Color Society, the firmness of outline and energy of drawing being probably the result of the French training. Like La Farge, however, and even more than La Farge, of late years Tiffany's love of beautiful color has diverted his energies from painting to glass and enamels and similar fields of decorative art, so that now his pictures and even cartoons for stained glass are infrequent, though in exchange the beauties of the " Favrile " glass are admired throughout the art-loving world.

While Tiffany numbered Inness among his instructors, he never followed his methods or style closely. George Inness, Jr., however, can at times paint in a way almost deceptively resembling his father's later work. There is the same soft, rich haze of color with the light glowing through it. And if the son has somewhat less of rigid underlying construction in his landscapes, in the figures and animals that he introduces (and which latter are important enough to give him a right to rank as an animal painter as well as a landscapist), there is a fuller, more complete draftsmanship. The group of horse and man dashing into the breakers in the " Surf Horse," in its vigor and firmness, seems traceable to his short stay in the Bonnat *atelier* or at least to the general influence of his studies abroad.

Not many men, though, were actually pupils of Inness, and his name is rather used to characterize a certain class of work somewhat resembling his. In some cases the resemblance came from direct admiration, but quite as often from following similar models, usually the " Barbizon " landscapes; and sometimes only from a similar liking for warm tone, richness of surface, and unity of composition that fitted the canvas into the frame and gave a decorative quality to the whole. One of the earliest of this group, Charles H. Miller, was born as far back as 1842, and his training was mostly German. He brought the browns of Munich into his landscapes, but not with the broad, sweeping brush work of Shirlaw. In spite of Munich, Vienna, Leipsic, Berlin, Dresden, and Paris, in all of which places he studied, he belongs with the older school, and also returned to the country earlier than most, and was an A.N.A. in 1873.

Robert C. Minor was older by two years than Miller, but he came under different influences. He studied under Diaz, as well as at Antwerp and elsewhere, and his pictures retained to the last something of Diaz' composition in his massing of light and shade. Charles Melville Dewey, on the contrary, was self-taught, yet his pictures have much in common with Minor's, — the same liking for the subdued light of morning and evening, the same tree masses dark against the sky, the depth and mistiness of the twilight foliage, and the glow of the twilight sky. It was the picture of sentiment so called. There were many more artists doing work of the same general type and often doing it extremely well, with truth and feeling, though in weak hands it had a tendency to degenerate into the formlessness common to weak sentimentality all over the world. It

represented one side of the Fontainebleau school, having especially
a strong infusion of Corot.   It was the softer, more emotional side, but
there was another.   The followers of Minor or Dewey might imitate
Diaz or Rousseau in the massing of lights and shades, but there was
no attempt to reproduce the full strength of their color, the solidity
of their brush work, and the rich, lacquer-like quality of their surfaces.

FIG. 96. — RANGER: MASON'S ISLAND CLASSIC.
[Photographed by Curtis Bell.]

This question of texture, of using pigment and varnish so that
they should be beautiful in themselves, counted for little with the
earlier landscape men.   Inness and some others achieved it as a sort
of by-product, without apparently giving much thought to it.   Ryder
and Fuller began to treat matter as quite as important as ideas, or
rather to have ideas that required glazings and varnishings to express.
Often the idea (an emotional not an intellectual idea) lay in transparent brown shadows, spots of color or interesting patterns rather than
in any accurate transcript of nature, and sometimes in Ryder's work,
and still more in that of a man like Blakelock, the component ele-

ments, the trees and rocks and streams, had been so adapted by the artist to his purpose as to resemble their prototypes in nature only suggestively, somewhat as a heraldic lion resembles a real one. Blake-lock is an extreme example, but there are canvases by Bogert and Ranger and the others where the concept of a tree seems to have been founded on the representation of trees in other pictures rather than on the green, leafy, growing reality, and clouds have had a dark-ness that completed the composition, but scarcely agreed with the ordinary laws of light.

Such unveracities, however, are not common, and are men-tioned simply to show that to the mind of the painters it was more important to have an effective picture than a literal tran-script of nature. This is almost the only tie between the two men whose names have been mentioned. Bogert has done a great amount of work, most varied, not only in subject (landscapes, marines, views of cities chosen from all over the world), but also in handling and in color scheme. Ranger holds more closely to the New England hill-sides and autumn woods, but with a steadily increasing development both of skill and feeling, so that his later canvases are not only a more beautiful pattern of golden or russet masses than the earlier, but also a more intimate and exact rendering of the spirit of the woods. Both at their best have done work which will stand in any company of their contemporaries, and the same may be said of Henry G. Dearth, of F. Ballard Williams, of Louis Paul Dessar, of Will S. Robinson, or of Carleton Wiggins. This lumping of names together in a class, though of necessity it must frequently be resorted to in this and the succeeding chapters, is unjust and unsatisfactory. There is a certain similarity in the men mentioned above. They all paint the decorative landscape, rather low in key, rich in color, and with the paint laid on solidly and with a pleasant, though varied, sur-face, but there is no further resemblance. The works of each are dis-tinct, unmistakable for those of any of the others. There is not even such similarity as there is between the canvases of Rousseau, Diaz, and Dupré. Each has his own personal view-point apart from the question of execution, and the twilights and moonlights of Dearth vary no more in sentiment from the idyllic note of Williams than they do from the gravity of Wiggins, the broad, sweeping lines of whose landscapes call up vague memories of men like Old Crome or some of their Dutch prototypes.

Allied to these by their sense of tone and tint, but more delicate, less robust, delighting in broad stretches of finely modulated color rather than in vigorous patterning, is another group equally dissimilar among themselves, but whose tendencies may be suggested by the names of W. Gedney Bunce, J. Francis Murphy, Bruce Crane, Birge Harrison, Henry B. Snell, and William A. Coffin.   Bunce

FIG. 97. — TWACHTMAN : SNOW SCENE.

would seem as a connecting link between the two; for while his "Venetian Sails" or "Fishing Boats," or whatever he calls the myriad repetitions of his favorite theme, may be founded on long and patient watching of the shifting tints of sky and water, and frequently reproduce them with delicacy and veracity, yet there are other times when facts are used simply as a basis for elaborating subtle and beautiful color schemes which nature would find difficulty in duplicating.   Like the preceding group, it is the picture that interests him, not the subject, the harmonies that he discovers himself and works out with thin, transparent washes of tinted varnish over the surface of the panel. It is this preponderance of the decorative element that allies Bunce to men like Ranger or Dearth, but in the simplicity of his composition (usually little more than two approximately equal bands of sea and sky interrupted by a group of boats), as also in his lack of heavy impasto, he resembles rather Murphy and Crane. But these latter men, however much they seek to make beautiful pictures, are not content to venture far beyond effects and tones for which nature herself gives them warrant. The hill-sides of Murphy may perhaps have a tinge of brown, pleasing rather than exact; but that is his single weakness, and in the ploughed fields of Crane, with their violet tones and in his stretches of farming land, whether parched by summer or covered with winter snow, the veracity is manifest. The same may be said of the snow scenes of Birge Harrison, softer in their morning or evening light than those of Palmer, less crisp and sparkling, and of the marines of Snell, misty and gentle, or of Coffin's Pennsylvania landscapes. In this last case the strong greens of summer, the cold gray of the rain, the raw brilliancy of the sunset clouds, are seen with a peculiar personal and uncompromising directness and simplicity which are true but hardly " tonal " like the others, and put them rather in a class by themselves.

This " tonal " quality which runs through so much American landscape work that it has become a sort of descriptive epithet of a school is not uncommon abroad. It came originally from the study of the Barbizon masters and similar works, and it has always been influenced by foreign examples; but in no other country has it affected any such proportion of the landscape work as in America. And nowhere else is the attempt so general to infuse personal feeling into the copying of nature. To any one who compares from this point of view exhibitions abroad with those in this country the contrast is striking. Even in France, whence the impulse so largely came, most men content themselves with a skilful transcript of the facts and let the beholder furnish his own emotions. To do this demands perhaps a surer, stronger workmanship than when sympathy may be expected to dim the critical sense; but it was probably not the lack of skill so much as of public appreciation which diverted the painters from the more literal rendering. Works like the " Route

2 G

de Concarneau" of William L. Picknell or "La Marcellerie" of Ruger Donoho are fully up to the best Salon standards, the latter especially being beautifully painted, but it is noticeable that they were both done in France.

Perhaps the strong, simple landscape work of Carlsen may find its place here as well as elsewhere. It has the quality of his still-life studies of game or fish; broad, unbroken masses of color strongly relieved against each other whether sunlit trees against a deep blue sky or a white swan against a dead wall, the contrast not being relied on alone for the effect, but the color being made as absolutely true as in less vigorous work. Other men, notably Charles H. Davis, have brought similar direct vision and workmanship back from the Paris *ateliers*, but they have usually developed more in accord with a popular taste that knows too little about sound workmanship to enjoy and buy it on its own account.

Another Parisian movement, however, the so-called impressionism, was imposed by the artists upon a decidedly recalcitrant community. It was opposed to the solid Salon work just described, and yet it had at least one quality in common with it, —the lack of sentimentality. As a rule, the painters cared for the actual things which they represented nothing at all. They were interested in the play of light and shade, but what the light and shade played on was a matter of indifference. Monet painted his haystack and his cathedrals dozens of times in pink or purple or gold, caring much for the shifting film of color, but not for the stack or church that it lay upon. Not thus did Daubigny or Millet work, but somewhat so worked most of the Americans that followed the new light.

This is not the place to analyze the principles of the school. Its chief innovations were the extremely high key in which the pictures were painted in order to reproduce the brilliancy of the open air, the careful study of tints of light and shadow, so that their opposition might be given as much as possible by contrast of color without strong darks, and a peculiar broken handling composed of touches of pure color which was to give at once the vibration and the brilliancy of sunlight. It took on some eccentric forms, and as a separate revolutionary movement it has largely died out; but almost all modern art shows something of its influence. It appealed particu-

FIG. 98. — HASSAM: LANDSCAPE.

larly to the Americans studying in Paris in the eighties, and among them are found some of its most brilliant practitioners. Theodore Robinson was a pupil and friend of Monet himself, and toward the end of his short life perfected a method of work sure, brilliant, and original, and about the same time William Sullivant Allen produced a series of studies of Fontainebleau and the neighborhood charming in their delicacy of color and a certain odd originality of composition.

These men did not remain in France, but returned to America and with them returned others like Willard L. Metcalf, John H. Twachtman, Childe Hassam, and Robert Reid. J. Alden Weir would also find a place here, if he had not already been mentioned among the founders of the Society of American Artists. While they all belong to the same school they paint no more like each other than the "tonalists." Twachtman was the most delicately sensitive of the group, unequal, varying in execution, sometimes elaborating, sometimes leaving his canvas partially bare, but always with a feeling for grace, for variations and contrasts of tint. The work, although differing entirely in key and color scheme, yet resembles Whistler's in its analysis of the subtle nuances of tone, imperceptible save to the most delicately trained eye. Hassam is robuster, surer, with a less varying *technique* and one that with its dry touches of pure, contrasting colors comes nearest to what is considered typical of the school; and in his work (landscapes, street scenes, and interiors with figures) he shows how well it adapts itself to all requirements. Its quality is shown when it is contrasted with Metcalf's handling, the subjects are often similar and painted in the same out-of-door key of color; but Metcalf lays on his paint smoothly, thinly, so that the characteristic vibration is lacking and is replaced by a stiller, quieter surface which takes the work out of the strict impressionist school.

This same smooth surface was also common to the work of Charles A. Platt before his desertion of painting for decoration and architecture, but in his case brilliancy, or at least interest, is given by handling the thin, fluid paint with something of the freedom of water-color. The subjects, too, the stretches of Vermont or New Hampshire hills, are treated with sympathy and understanding, and their native character, whether covered with winter snow or spotted with the blue shadows of the summer clouds, is truthfully reproduced. The coloring is true to out-of-door light and with its freedom from brown tones was considered rather an innovation when the pictures were painted; but such coloring has now become rather the rule than the exception. The critics would class it as even less impressionistic than Metcalf's, yet it shows the influence of Monet as well as of Bastien-Le Page.

This complete adaptation and assimilation of the new theories and methods, developed in Paris during the seventies, so that they might be applied to the rendering of the spirit of American scenery naturally and without trace of their foreign derivation, culminated in a group of men like Tryon, Ochtman, J. Appleton Brown, who stand somewhat in the place that Inness and Homer D. Martin occupied twenty years or so before. They are not as yet such commanding or such isolated figures, and it is not possible to tell what consecration time may bring. While they are spoken of as having received foreign influence, it is not so manifest as in the case of those classed among the impressionists. They followed only indirectly the *plein-air* school, whose inspiration was hardly so noble or so purely artistic as that of Rousseau, Daubigny, or Corot, but was mixed up with a desire to innovate, with scientific theories of light, and with the exigencies of exhibitions. It is with the earlier men that the artists under consideration are in sympathy. They studied and admired their works (Tryon was even a student of Daubigny), but they expressed themselves in manners modified by the later practice. They carried on the best inspiration of the earlier American school.

More than his direct followers and imitators, Tryon is the successor of Inness. Not that their work is alike. Even in his earlier paintings, which were apt to be brown and dark, Tryon shows no special resemblance to his predecessor; but they both paint American landscape with deep, personal feeling and with a *technique* complete, original, and modern. The temperament expressed is not the same. It is easy (when once we know the fact) to trace the mystic, spiritual side of Inness in all his work. The vision is seized and drawn into constructive lines and planes, firmly, sanely, but yet in neglected corners the picture has a tendency to

FIG. 99. — TRYON: EARLY MORNING, SEPTEMBER.

[Copyright, 1905, by N. E. Montross.]

remain mysterious and elusive. In Tryon's work, on the contrary, the poetry is built upon the solid fact. Rocks, groves, streams, and sky are knit together as firmly and logically as a proposition of Euclid; but on this reality he begins to work with mists and shifting lights and feathery spring foliage until it almost disappears under the shimmering web of poetry that he has wrapped about it, yet underneath still lie the stone walls and the gray ridges of New England rock ready to emerge in all their uncompromising strength the instant that the east wind sweeps up the enveloping veil. In spite of this greater solidity of foundation the spirit is more delicate, less robust, than with Inness. There are no mighty oaks, no whirling thunder clouds, no glowing color. The trees are slender, delicate, with something of the adolescent grace of the Early Renaissance sculptures, and they are not collected in solid masses, but stretch across the picture in a diaphanous line only kept from monotony by the delicate differentiation of detail, the individuality of the trunks, the spots of light breaking through, the varied line of their tops. The color is kept within one milky, luminous tone that softens and transmutes whatever more violent tints may lie beneath to something in harmony, though there is no monotony. It is not a messing together of warring colors into one soiled monotone but each is pure and distinct for all its delicacy.

The harmony is as great, though the contrasts are stronger, in the autumn scenes of Ochtman whose rolling hills and woodlands have an ampler composition and a graver, less lyric note, — a difference not inherent in the seasons, for both men are alike painters of the spring and autumn, but in their temperaments. Ochtman achieves most when he attempts most. His larger canvases differ not only by their size, but they are also more finely balanced in composition, more subtle and refined in color, more profound in feeling than the smaller ones, which are apt to be direct studies from nature, skilful and varied, but, from the very ease with which they reproduce the subject, lacking in the emotional quality which the artist puts into a picture by repeated labor. The smaller canvases of Tryon, on the contrary, have a sentiment as fine and as complete as the greater.

More broadly treated and more gayly, but with a gayety which

had always its air of distinction and breeding, were the spring and
summer landscapes of J. Appleton Brown, with their sunny clouds
in the soft blue sky, their green meadows, and the pink and
white of their blossoming fruit trees. They do not resemble Corot,
but there is a touch of his inspiration in them, and Brown was a
fervent admirer of the older master and caught something of the
charm of his misty skies; but his handling was smooth and broad,
and his pictures stand a little by themselves in their apparent ease
of execution and their light, opaque color, which suggests some
perfected kind of gouache.

Here, too, belong the series of moonlights by Ben Foster,
with the mysteries of their enveloping hazes and shadows, and
his autumn hillsides and rolling waves; and here should come in
the works of many other men, for the group represents the general
tendency of our art to copy American landscape according to
methods assimilated from foreign (mainly French) practice. Even
men like Murphy and Crane might be included. A distinction has
been attempted in their case on the ground that the obtaining of
a decorative quality in the canvas seems by them to be held more
important than the rendering of the spirit of nature, but the distinction is obscure and no fixed line can be drawn. The men cited
above as representative have been chosen rather more for the beauty
and diversity of sentiment shown in their works than for their
technical skill.

A considerable degree of skill is becoming fairly common, and
incompetent work is generally recognized as such. There is a
mass of pictures painted each year not only respectable from the
training and application of their authors, but worthy of serious
consideration for their beauty and artistic merit, often little if at
all inferior to the works mentioned. They represent all shades of
feeling, sentimental or literal. Each favorite artist has his imitators
and there is some seeking among our American hills and groves for
effects like those admired in the works of the masters of France; but
there is also much painting of our landscape with the sincerity of
the old native school, but with a greater skill by men like W. L.
Lathrop, for instance, who, in some of his work at least, does not
avoid the dry, clear light and the irregular, uncentralized heaping

FIG. 100.—OCHTMAN: AUTUMN SUNRISE, OWNED BY ANDREW CARNEGIE.

together of our hills. Greater possibilities in this direction seem hinted at by certain tentative essays that have never been pushed to their ultimate development — things like some of the early land-scapes of La Farge or the wintry mountains of Taber. Some day perhaps the predestined man may come and give us a new school as Constable or Rousseau did, some one who can adapt Whistler's color to a draftsmanship like Van Eyck's, or do something of the sort.

At present the tendency is rather toward strength both of con-ception and execution than subtlety. Walter Nettleton, Edward H. Potthast, Walter Clark, all alike see nature frankly and paint her with a sure, solid handling, rich and harmonious in color — some of Nettleton's snow scenes deserving a special mention. The same may be said of Charles Warren Eaton and Frank Russell Green, though their color is softer and sweeter and they prefer the evening light to the blaze of midday; while Elmer W. Schofield and Edward W. Redfield bring in a different, a more up-to-date element. They both lay on their pigment in broad, firm touches, and the picture has a tendency to lie on the surface of the canvas as a decorative pattern. The subjects of Schofield, the line of foreground trees through whose interwoven branches one sees the little towns and streams beyond, have the quality of a tapestry of delicate gray and buff spots, and though Redfield's contrasts of color are usually stronger, some of his stretches of river and field have much the same character. Both of these latter men are younger than most of the others mentioned, and they represent a later form of French train-ing, the ideals of the new Salon rather than the old, though not such ideals in their exaggerated or extreme form. The new dis-ciples of Manet, though prominent in Paris, have hardly appeared yet in this country.

Landscape painting has thus far been treated in its stricter sense as something different from marine painting; but the distinction has not as a rule been greatly respected by the artists, most of them occasionally painting marines. Some, however, have made of the sea, the movement of its waves, its mists and lights, a special province. Of the older men, both Winslow Homer and William T. Richards have been mentioned, and almost every phase of work within the wide limits which they represent has been attempted. One of the earliest and most promising men, Robert A. Eichelberger, died in 1890, the year that his "Surf and Fog" was exhibited. Although he had been by no means a painter of the sea, it was by far his best picture and seemed to promise a special development in that direction. Frederick W. Kost and F. K. M. Rehn are peculiarly marine painters, with the same solidity of *technique* and delicacy of tone as the best of their *confrères* of the land. Howard Russell Butler paints the long stretches of the Long Island beach and surf rather than inland views. Charles H. Woodbury gives the sweep of the blue ocean water, rising and falling with the swell of the open sea or eddying around the hidden rocks of the shore with something of the freshness and breadth of Homer if without his grandeur; while Carlton T. Chapman, in addition to reproducing the sea itself, has made a feature of recording the glories of the American navy upon it, and has recorded the long series of conflicts from the days of Paul Jones to the Spanish War with a curiously complete knowledge of the structure and also of the tactics of the privateers and three-deckers of the days of hemp and canvas, as well as of the steel-armored battleships of to-day.

CHAPTER XXIV

RECENT FIGURE PAINTING IN AMERICA

RECENT FIGURE PAINTING. — MANY OF THE BRANCHES OF EUROPEAN PAINTING UNAVAILABLE. — ITS IDEAL SIDE. — F. S. CHURCH. — THAYER. — THE GROUP OF BOSTON PAINTERS. — REID. — DEWING. — OTHER FIGURE PAINTERS. — COX. — LOEB. — THE ROMANTIC SCHOOL

THE figure painting of the present period has not as much unity as the landscape work. Among the landscapists every man stands in some sort of relation to others and, with a little insistence on analogies, the later work can be connected with the earlier in a fairly unbroken series. This is hardly possible with the figure painters. The well-defined break with the past as to technical training represented also a break in feeling, in the point of view; but this breaking with old tendencies gave the men no solidarity among themselves. It was a time when traditions were weakening, and innovation and original genius were demanded to infuse new life into the art. More even than the average the American art students were assured of their ability to meet that demand unless led astray by insidious academic influences, and each was vigorously defending his personality against every possible diminution.

In Europe this did not prevent them from painting work resembling sufficiently closely that of their fellow-students, but those that returned found innovation forced upon them. To paint the regular Salon pictures in America was difficult, to sell them well-nigh impossible. They were (and still are) brought back from Munich and Paris on the return of the young practitioner. From their size and often also from their skill they made a rather brave showing on exhibition walls throughout the country, but this same size unfitted them for private houses, and the amount of talent displayed rarely filled the wide expanse so amply, as to overcome that and other hindrances to domestication. They brought no money to the artist nor any reputation which made the sale of his other works easier. Even if he were willing to paint them for the sake of painting them, most of the materials were lacking in America. There were no Moors from Algeria, no Gypsies from Spain, no Breton or Dutch peasant girls in sabots and picturesque caps, nor even any workingmen in blouses, nor interesting, well-determined types of any kind in their old-established settings of cottage or shop. Most of the people whom the young artist saw looked and dressed pretty much alike, and the costumes and sur-roundings, though comfortable, did not strike him as worth record-ing. There was no official pomp, the wealthier social life was as private as any other, and it was expensive rather than beautiful. The old, simple industries that were comprehensible to the eye and which had the consecration of centuries of use were vanishing. The mowing machine had replaced the scythe and the sickle, and the great factory the hand-loom. The new machines were complex, unpicturesque, and even if successfully painted the result would have been incomprehensible. Their appearance was too novel and too changeable to become typical.

There were difficulties likewise in the nobler, imaginative themes of the "grand style." The painter's public was neither naïve enough to accept religious painting with simple devotion nor scep-tical enough to admire in it only the skill displayed. The classical mythology, vaguely understood even by the unlearned in Europe, was here unknown to the average spectator who was equally unac-quainted with history save some vague ideas about the Revolution and the Civil War. And the artist himself was not much wiser. Even if he wished to paint history or historic *genre*, all costumes and accessories were lacking, and yet he could not dispense with costumes and paint the nude. Trained as they were by the study of the undraped model, many of the returning artists naturally ex-hibited nude figures; but such subjects were not in accord with the national habits. Our prudishness in the old days was notorious. Vanderlyn's " Ariadne " when exhibited in New York in 1822 was looked on with disfavor, and of his reproduction of Correggio's " An-tiope," the owner (who had given an order for a copy from an old painting without specifying the subject) cried : " What can I do with it ? It is altogether indecent. I cannot hang it in my house, and

FIG. 101.—THAYER : A VIRGIN.

my family reprobate it." Mrs. Trollope's account of her visit to the collection of casts in the Pennsylvania Academy shows Philadelphia in even a worse state than New York, and in the middle of the century, Greenough, who had the fine orotund style of the epoch, declared of his "Chanting Cherubs": "Those infantine forms roused an outcry of censure which seemed to have exhausted the source from which it sprang, since all the harlot dancers who have found an El Dorado in these Atlantic cities have failed to reawaken it. I say seem to have exhausted it, for the same purblind squeamishness which gazed without alarm at the lascivious Fandango awoke with a roar at the colossal nakedness of Washington's manly breast," which recalls the tempest raised in Boston hardly more than a dozen years ago by Saint Gaudens's decorative figures over the entrance of the Library.

Against the paintings there was no such protest from outraged modesty. They were not bought, but they were admired and praised with few dissenting voices; but, nevertheless, the nude has become imperfectly acclimated among us. We are a northern nation and a decorous nation, unlearned in artistic traditions and unacquainted with the artistic view-point. Interest in a picture is apt to depend on the object represented and not on the manner of its representation, and before a painting of the nude the average beholder experiences something of the same embarrassment that he would feel before the reality. This is not so strange nor so derogatory to the national intelligence as it at first seems to artists and their friends. There were honest burghers in the Greece of Pericles who were horrified at an undraped Aphrodite, and equally excellent people of the Renaissance insisted that costumes should be painted over the figures in Michael Angelo's "Last Judgment." In those favored periods, as to-day, purely æsthetic delight in the human figure and comprehension of its beauty and expressiveness was limited to a comparatively small number of cultured people, but among them were some so powerful in the state as to be able to defend the artists and impose their taste upon the public. Even to-day the British Philistine and the French Bourgeois (the strength of the two nations) are hostile, and only the long list of acknowledged masterpieces and the authority of the cultured classes keep them from protest. In America, culture is democratic, the leisure class is small, its opinions carry little weight, and it is not very sure of its opinions. The very wealthy have much the same views on art as the rest of the people, and being founded on social habits and moral considerations, they are not likely to be changed by ampler artistic knowledge. The suggestion may seem grotesque, but it is possible that public toleration of the nude is more advanced by certain widely circulated advertisements of soaps and porous plasters than by all the efforts of culture. Whether these considerations are sound or not, the fact remains that in the annual exhibitions paintings of the nude are not numerous, are usually small in scale, and are treated decoratively rather than realistically. The carefully finished life-size study such as crowds the walls of the French and German salons is practically unknown.

With religious, mythological, historical, and nude painting unavailable or to be practised only under unfavorable circumstances it would seem as if there were little field left for imaginative art, and that the painters would be forced to realistic copying of the life about them. Such is the conclusion to which Fromentin comes after summing up the situation in Holland in the seventeenth century: " A nation of bourgeois, practical and consequently little given to dreams, very busy, not mystic in the least, anti-Latin in spirit, without traditions, of parsimonious habits." All the conditions except the last fit America even better than Holland, and yet the conclusion that the nation would "insist on having its own portrait," so excellently true in one case is false in the other — which shows how easy it is to prophesy after the event. The American people are practical and energetic not only from their environment, but also from their race; for however much it may have been diluted it was the English blood which gave its character to the nation, yet like the English, at heart they are enormously sentimental. They do not display their feelings (except their anger). Something of Puritan tradition, but more of personal pride, has convinced them that to be unable to conceal emotion is the part of a weakling or one lacking in breeding, but there are matters on which they feel profoundly. These are mostly abstract ideas of faith or loyalty for which they have as yet found no visible representation. They have no god-

FIG. 102. — TARBELL : A GIRL CROCHETING.

[Copyright, 1905, by N. E. Montross.   From a Montross Print.]

desses or saints, they have forgotten their legends, they do not read the poets, but something of what goddess, saint, or heroine represented to other races they find in the idealization of their womankind. They will have such idealization decorous; there is no room for the note of unrestrained passion, still less for sensuality. It is the grace of children, the tenderness of motherhood, the beauty and purity of young girls which they demand, but especially the last. The American girl is placed upon a pedestal and each offers worship according to his abilities, the artist among the rest. All of the papers from the yellowest of the daily press to the most digni- fied of the magazines are filled with representations of her. Gibson has created the best-known type, to which his name has been given, a creature rather overwhelming in her perfections, with no occupa- tion in life save to be adored by young athletes in tennis clothes or by disreputable foreign noblemen. Gibson, however, respects the child of his imagination; but some of his brother-illustrators for the weekly papers, though they undoubtedly stand ready personally to assault the temerarious man who should assert that the American girl is not modest and mannerly, have yet fallen into the way of representing her as if she were neither. This is certainly not from malice, but rather from the following of foreign types, the difficulty of being perennially funny which leads to the harping on purely conventional ideas, and also, perhaps, from a certain lack of breeding both in the artists and the great public to which they cater.

This side of the representation of the girl, moreover, is simply a homage to the eternal feminine and has little distinctively Ameri- can in it. Sketches of pretty girls are the staple product of popular illustrated papers all over the world. The painters naturally have tried for and attained a higher achievement. One of the earliest, F. S. Church, also did much work as an illustrator, and is interesting because he never studied abroad nor ever obtained a complete tech- nical training. He never even supplemented his deficiencies by careful study from nature, so that some of his birds and beasts — his sandpipers, for instance — are hardly more than schoolboy hiero- glyphics; and yet, in spite of a manifest amateurishness, there was a charm and freshness about his works that not only captured the public, but appealed to the men returning from the Continental studios, so that he was one of the earliest members of the Society of American Artists.   They are not profound, they are not subtle — these maidens skating with polar bears or lecturing to flamingoes or making Welsh rabbits for an admiring circle of miscellaneous beasts; yet, if they have the simplicity of a story told to children, they have also freshness and charm.   If the drawing is loose, it is also graceful; the light, bright tints keep, even in oil, the quality of washes of water-color, and there is real decorative feeling.

Church stands quite alone, however, in this simplicity of subject and workmanship; all of the other men have the learning of the foreign schools, which implies also more complexity of thought.   One of the most prominent of these, Abbott H. Thayer, has some analogy with Church in his admiration of triumphant maidenhood, but the feeling is profounder.   They do not make Welsh rabbits or go skating, those virgins of Thayer.   They are set up frankly for our adoration, and it goes to them at once without reserve, they are so strong and beautiful and pure.   It is a noble ideal, a sort of revivifying of the figures of Phidias with modern spirituality, and the execution corresponds with it.   The draftsmanship is large and ample, the color pure and strong and held in large, simple masses, the arrangement well balanced and decorative, and the handling also large, neglecting details, with a good weight of pigment and much use of the palette knife.   The execution shows some tendency to fall off in unimportant details, as if it were not done without an effort, but one must have a special curiosity for such matters to notice it. The general effect is of a peculiar unity and loftiness of inspiration. It is, as has been said, a noble ideal.   It could not have been produced on the Continent, and scarcely in England; but, though Thayer gives to it its highest expression, the conception is widespread in America.   At base it is the woman of Winslow Homer, less robust, more graceful, but with her soundness of body and mind.   Thayer spiritualizes her until she becomes almost as a sacred thing; others abating no whit of her charm and grace, still make her human, — a creature capable of playing tennis, pouring tea, or even sitting in a hammock; a creature that is real, and whom we have met.

Benson, Tarbell, Reid, and others so paint her, with an easier, surer skill, if with an inspiration less celestial.   These three men

FIG. 103.— BENSON : IN THE SPRUCE WOODS.

studied together in Paris, at the Academie Julien and also under
Dannat, but on their return Benson and Tarbell settled in Boston
or its vicinity instead of New York.   There were other students
from the Academie Julien, like Major and William W. Churchill;
later men like Philip L. Hale accepted their methods, and the
spirit of the old Hunt training and of Duveneck's class was enough
like theirs in the desire for breadth, simplicity, and strong direct
work to give to the whole body of painting produced in Boston
a distinct character of its own, which cannot be said of another
American city.   It is a little like the Glasgow school in Great Britain,
not only in its solidarity as against a great heterogeneous metropolis,
but also in the sort of work which it does.   It follows more the
artist's standpoint and seeks artist qualities in handling and light
and color, a certain breadth, a rougher texture, a quivering light.
The artists do not confine themselves to ideal pictures of young
women.   All have painted portraits more or less.   Vinton, who belongs in the group, is exclusively a portrait painter.   But most of the
men made their studies at the period which gave them a peculiar
interest in open-air tints and coloring.   They painted landscapes,
they painted figures in the open air and in darkened interiors, they
studied all forms of light with the resulting shadows and reflected
tones, and they succeeded in producing pictures of brilliant but
pleasing color.   Its frankness, its directness, suggests again Winslow Homer, with more of grace and of the training of the schools,
and with less of originality and elemental force.

Reid, who settled in New York, belongs clearly to the same
group and has the same inspiration, though his handling is less
sweeping, more broken, in a way that suggests the influence of
Manet, and his figures have a slender gracility that is personal
to him.

All of the men already mentioned in this chapter, and the larger
group of which they are representative, paint clearly, strongly, and
frankly; there is feeling, but there is no mystery.   There is nothing
like the "Winifred Dysart" of Fuller, and nothing that corresponds,
as that does, to the work of the sentimental, or "tonal" landscape
painters, nor have these latter among the younger figure painters
any exact counterparts.   The fact is rather strange, and to be

accounted for, perhaps, by the almost universal training in the Paris *ateliers* which the figure painters received to a far greater degree than the landscapists. Clarity was insisted on. In art as in letters, " what is not clear is not French," and though by a certain reaction some French artists have latterly attempted the mysterious, Americans have not yet imitated them.

But clearness does not exclude sentiment even the most delicate and subtle. If Ryder or Blakelock, for instance, have no corresponding figure painters, the spirit of work like Tryon's is closely matched by that of Dewing. It is not shapeless, it is not incoherent; the things that count, the faces and hands and certain bits of detail, are drawn with the extremest and minutest perfection. Yet it is not the completeness of the drawing that strikes one, but its quality. It is infinitely delicate and refined, the contour fading into the background or reappearing with the changing light, and the color matches it, soft, shimmering, evanescent. The canvases, unless decorative work, are usually small. There were one or two early productions, like the " Prelude " of 1883, that were of considerable size and filled with an infinity of delicate detail, flowers and marbles, but these were not repeated, the tendency being toward the elimination of detail. There are many portrait heads and graceful single figures seated or standing, and when a group is given, it is apt to be as a decorative spot or pattern against a wide expanse of soft green or gray background. They are wonderful, these little figures and heads in their distinction, and they thrill us with something of the strange poignant charm of Gainsborough's women.

No one else has quite equalled the " Lady in Yellow," the " Lady in White," " Comœdia," and the other subjects of Dewing's which the mind recalls, but others have worked in a similar spirit. Mrs. Dewing has given to flowers almost the personal charm of her husband's figures. Edward A. Bell has the soft, enveloping light and color, and there is something of it in the work of Henry Prellwitz and of Edith Mitchell Prellwitz. Bell particularly has done some groups of slender classical figures or of young girls in gauzy modern dresses of a delicate decorative effect. But this group is not large. The painters even of ideal figures do not usually wrap them in mist, though here, as with the landscapists, there is no sharp

FIG. 104.—REID : FLEUR DE LYS.

division to be made. H. Siddons Mowbray, Irving R. Wiles, Francis C. Jones, Charles C. Curran, George R. Barse, F. V. Du Mond, and many more have painted easel pictures wherein, under a more or less plausible title, lovely girls are grouped in suitable surroundings.

The object of them all is charm, the external charm of beautiful forms beautifully rendered. As with all works of real merit, these are personal, the style of each man perfectly distinguishable on sight, but difficultly by description. All are masters of their trade, delicate and sure draftsmen and colorists. Mowbray's rendering of form resembles Dewing's in its subtle refinement; Wiles has a certain breadth and sureness of brush work even in his smallest pictures; Jones has a tenderness for children and works in a brighter, higher key than the others; Curran has a wider range of subjects, and, if possible, a draftsmanship more sure, minute, and unwearied; Barse and Du Mond have each a decorative quality of their own, the one broad and simple, the other crowding a multiplicity of detail into harmonious masses.

All of these men have done other work besides the small, ideal, or poetic subjects which have been taken as a bond between them. Wiles has latterly turned to portraiture; Mowbray has also done some small portrait heads of great charm, but is now devoting himself to mural painting, as are several of the others, notably Barse. Nearly all have painted scenes of contemporary life, but they have done so seeking grace rather than character, painting the gowns in the same spirit as Greek robes. For it is noticeable that all these figure painters from F. S. Church down have been confined to two types of costume — a sort of a classic and a sort of a modern, sometimes accurate in detail and spirit, but usually loosely adapted and fitted out with draperies and studio odds and ends, and with one style running into the other as freely as in Reynolds's portraits. None of the painters has been interested in the character and cut of a costume as representing a specific period or nation, and this not from the difficulty of obtaining exact historical costumes in America (already much harped of), but because they sought abstract qualities of line and color and form, and were indifferent as to the dress in which they found them.

These qualities they also found in the nude and painted it at

times, although from the general feeling of their work, as well as for
other reasons already given, not realistically nor usually on a large
scale.   Almost the only man to paint the nude as it is understood
in Europe, except as part of decorations, was Kenyon Cox.   In the
years following his return from Europe he painted repeatedly
large life-size studies of the same general type as the Études
of the Salons, and painted them well and learnedly.   More than
almost any one else he represents the academic traditions as they
are understood abroad.   He knows the great work of the past; not
only has he seen and admired, but he has studied and analyzed
it with exceptional sympathy and clarity, as his writings show.
There was in his nudes, as in his compositions and his portraits,
a conscious striving for the qualities which may properly be called
academic, rhythm of line and mass, rendering of form in accord with
the old traditions, and sometimes the expression of a symbolic idea.
This may be said, too, of the works of Elliott Daingerfield, who has
also tried for some breath of the inspiration of sixteenth-century
Italy, and has attained at times to a glow and richness of color which
belongs to that age rather than this.

As far as the nudes of Cox were concerned, he received small
encouragement from the public, and he has been led, like so many
other men, more and more into mural decoration for which his
qualities peculiarly fit him, just as Mrs. Cox with somewhat similar
qualities (more graceful if less robust) has turned from ideal composition to paint very personal and charming portraits of children.

With entirely different methods from Cox or Daingerfield and in
a different spirit, too, Louis Loeb also paints classical scenes like
" The Temple of the Winds," with its luminous figures in sunlight and its fluttering draperies, but the landscape has each year
usurped a larger place until it has dominated the picture.   It has become a landscape with figures now where through Arcadian groves
nymphs and shepherds rove in the golden glow of evening.   It has,
more than most of its companions in the exhibitions, a European
completeness of execution, and strangely enough this very completeness detracts somewhat from its interest.   It is not Düsseldorfian, —
far from it, — but it lacks the personal note so strong in the other
works that approach it at all in quality.   Obvious, recognized

FIG. 105. — DEWING: THE SPINET, OWNED BY JOHN GELLATLY, ESQ.

[Copyright, 1904, by John Gellatly.]

beauties are accumulated with such perfect ease and sureness that the effect is a little over-sweet, a quality that is also felt in such charming ideal heads as the "Blossoming." This is not to blame the work of Loeb, but to explain that it, in its own way, is also academic. Perhaps, because having returned more recently from Paris than the other men, he still holds somewhat more foreign standards than they.

The distinction may be felt by comparing it with work which may vaguely be called romantic, the work of a group which would include J. Humphreys Johnston, Albert Herter, Bryson Burroughs, and Arthur B. Davies. These, if any, represent among us the romantic school, although it would be difficult to define just wherein the special characteristics of that school consist. It no longer, as in the days of Delacroix, takes its subjects from Walter Scott or Byron, nor does it delight in swan-necked heroines in ringlets; but the name, for want of a better, may stand for a revolt against the commonplaceness of life. The escape from its prosaic details is made not by spiritualizing them, by giving their inner essence freed from all unessential detail, nor yet by turning to the accepted beauties worked out by a long succession of artists and consecrated by academic tradition, but rather by trying to make a world of one's own where one may enter as into a walled garden suited to his mind and there enjoy his vision with all discordant sights shut out. Even here the difference is of degree rather than of kind. Most artists have some such realm more or less elaborated and removed from reality; it is only necessary to recall figure painters like Dewing or landscapists like Tryon, but the group under consideration, perhaps because they are for the most part younger men, seem to have moved farther into the realm of dreams. They are not alike in the completeness of their visions.

Herter, for instance, seems without definite point of view. He should perhaps have been classed with the non-resident Americans, not only because he has worked at least as much abroad as in this country, but even more because he still paints Salon pictures — pictures whose whole conception and execution is based on the requirements of great crowded galleries. To many they are his least successful works. Living from his boyhood in beautiful surroundings, producing notable work almost before he was in his teens, studying and travelling under the best auspices, the very multiplicity of his appreciations seems to have hindered his achievement. He has been inspired by Japanese kakemonos and by Greek vase paintings, he has drawn Renaissance ladies and Norse demigods, he has painted his figures nude, and he has wrapped them in all the splendors of Oriental or "Liberty" fabrics; but in it all there is felt no clear, personal note. The execution is often amazingly skilful, but it has been said of him that it was a pity that a man able to paint anything should not as yet have discovered anything particularly worth painting. This remark, called forth by the sight of one of his Salon pictures, might be excusable under the circumstances, but it goes too far. Herter has done much charming work, especially in water-color of which difficult medium he is a complete master. His drawing is sure and graceful, his color rich, and when he wishes surprisingly strong, and there is an unfailing decorative quality aided by his fertility of invention of costume and detail. In connection with her husband's work mention should also be made of that of Mrs. Herter, which resembles it in its beauty of color and its decorative quality, but is apt to be softer and more delicate, done in pastel rather than oil, and turning to portraiture rather than ideal subjects.

Johnston must also now be counted among the non-residents, having settled in Europe with no fixed date of return, but he shows clearly an influence which is not European. At the very beginning of his career he served as aid to John La Farge in his decorations in Trinity Church and elsewhere, and more than any other of the many assistants of that master he assimilated not only the methods but the essence of his work. It has not limited his personality. The "Portrait of the Artist's Mother," now in the Luxembourg, or the "Mystère de la Nuit," could have been painted by no one else, but the influence of La Farge's color theories is manifest, and equally manifest is the large sympathetic grasping of the underlying spirit of the subject. There is, too, about the work as a whole something of the unsatisfying quality of La Farge's earlier work, as if the artist were capable of ampler achievements, and for that reason the lover of American art cannot but wish that his production should be greater.

FIG. 106. — COX : HOPE AND MEMORY.

[Copyright, 1900, by Kenyon Cox; from a Copley Print. Copyright, 1900, by Curtis & Cameron, Publishers, Boston.]

The works of Burroughs, although they are mentioned here, are not always romantic, they are often academic or realistic, but whether they are decorative panels of colossal archers or country girls hanging out clothes, a mother and child, or the Norns, the same animating spirit runs through each and receives in each complete and artistic expression. The feeling is difficult to analyze apart from the form in which it is clothed; there are vague memories of the old myths, there is a feeling for the tenderness of motherhood, for the slender grace of half-grown childish form; but whatever the subject, it is rendered with a peculiar large simplicity of drafts-manship, a soft luminous coloring and particularly with unity in the masses, each color forming a spot by itself, carefully placed so as to combine into a harmonious composition within the limits of the frame.

These men and others like them belong in a way to the imaginative school but all at times drop away from it more or less completely. The romantic painter *par excellence* is Davies, and his work is as personal and as interesting as any done in the country to-day. Never once does he wander from his dream, his vision. His enchanted garden is not visited at rare intervals; it is not one of many resorts, it is his home, his retreat from which he never departs. It is a wonderful land of which he gives us glimpses, — of flowery meadows and bosky groves peopled by youth and childhood. It is a world that touches the real world only remotely, choosing from it bits with the odd, impulsive likes and dislikes of a child; blossoms and wide-eyed babies and blue distances, pinafores and the bits of nude rendered with exquisite tenderness. It all has a naïveness, a belief in its own imaginings, which recall early Florentine workers, the painters of allegories and decorators of *cassone*. These men probably had some formative influence on Davies, for one of the earliest remembered of his works was a study sent in to the competition for the decoration of the Criminal Courts Building in New York, a study where most of the virtues and vices were personified and woven into a composition that looked like a sketch from some forgotten fresco by Botticelli, while for the elucidation of the allegory the most emotional and least critical of critics, Pater, Ruskin, and the rest, were cited as authorities. The Italian influence, however, though it shows now and then in the drawing of a siren or satyr, is seldom noticeable in later work.

This consists mostly of small panels or canvases varying from a few inches to a couple of feet in length. Sometimes as in the " Two Step " the figures fill the canvas, sometimes they are but incidents of the landscape, sometimes the landscape or marine is without them. Considering that the artist is still a young man, the production has been very considerable, but in all the series, even in the little things, there has been no repetition. Certain habits of handling recur more or less, but the subjects, the coloring, the arrangement, are infinitely varied. The coloring especially, which with ideal painters is apt to crystallize into a formula, is constantly shifting in rich and varied combinations. Each work has its own sentiment too, of grace or tenderness, or perhaps only of curious patterning. It is not all equally good, purely imaginative work rarely is, and at times the spectator may regret that there seems to be a trend toward William Blake rather than Giorgione; but as a whole it is capable of giving keen delight to a mind in sympathy with it. It is regrettable that it is so little seen. It rarely appears at any of the annual exhibitions and must be sought in a dealer's gallery. That, like the work of Whistler, it should suffer from the neighborhood of canvases done in a different spirit is inevitable and yet such haphazard association is sometimes tonic and illuminative.

FIG. 107.—BURROUGHS : ARIADNE.

BRUSH : MOTHER AND CHILD.

CHAPTER XXV

RECENT FIGURE PAINTING IN AMERICA (*Continued*)

Brush. — Blum. — Horatio Walker. — Subjects from American Life less frequently chosen by Painters than by Illustrators. — Causes for this. —
Ulrich. — Ward. — Painters of Frontier Life. — Remington. — Hovenden. —
Painters of the Civil War. — Other Paintings. — The Most Recent Development. — Henri. — Glackens. — Water-Color

The previous chapter has been devoted to men who sought
beauty. Without exception they have sought it, where it was most
obviously to be found, in beautiful persons and things. They are
not oblivious to the inner beauty of the spirit, in some cases it dominates the work, but it is always gloriously lodged. The example
of the Flemish and Dutch painters and of Germans like Holbein,
who disregarded grace of form for the intimate and personal expression of character, is less attractive and more difficult to follow.
Against all those who see the noble character through graceful
forms and faces in the freshness of youth, there is hardly more than
one to be found who finds it beneath features neither classical nor
youthful, yet so human, so intense, and so sympathetic is the character revealed in the pictures of George De Forest Brush, that his
name is among the first mentioned when the standing of our art
is to be defended. He does not paint the mother radiant, strong,
and incredibly young, seated among a group of rollicking chubby
cherubs; she is, on the contrary, if not sad, at least grave, and holds
tenderly the very human child in her arms. Youthful freshness and
something of health and strength have been paid as the price of
maternity, but there is no sign that the price is regretted or even
considered. There is a strange penetrating peace that fills the
group, so manifest and so appealing that, in reproductions, the pictures have had almost the popularity of those exploiting the graces
of youth.

A charm so delicate as this is only obtainable by a craftsmanship equally delicate and perfect.   It is not alone for the sentiment
that the great art of Holbein, of the Van Eycks, or of Terburg
is recalled.   Their complete and calm mastery of their trade with
no trace of effort or of difficulties evaded is not for our day but
something of their quality Brush has.   His canvases seem to have
been done with their unhastening, absorbed labor.   They have unity
of sentiment and completeness of rendering.   The composition both
in line and spot is usually carefully poised and complete; the color,
as befits the sentiment, is in a subdued, grave harmony and the
drawing of great beauty — the details subordinated to the chief
masses, but seen in all their changes of form and texture with
a minute fidelity which never loses interest or degenerates into the
commonplace.

Besides these groups, taken usually from his own family, Brush
has with similar skill and feeling painted a number of portraits,
and it is worth while to recall also the earlier Indian subjects, like
the " King and the Sculptor," where he showed himself an excellent
pupil of his master, Gérôme, or the " Moose Hunt," on a larger
scale, and far more original in its realization of the chase of the
unwieldy beast by a canoeful of red men.   There is even a Salon
picture of his, a girl and a grizzly bear, both life size, which is incomprehensible except as an illustration of one of Bret Harte's
stories — and it illustrates the story very badly.   Such tentative
essays were made by many men when they left the studios, and
before they found their true path.   There is by Dewing a " Sor-
ceress," which might match the " Aztec King " of Brush, and
Thayer painted a notable series of summer meadows with white
and red cows in the heat-dried grass, which in spite of their merits
(the dry sultriness of the season has not been equal!y well given
since) are yet almost as much ignored by the general public, as the
bulldogs and other animals that he did, back in the early seventies
before he saw Paris.

Brush stands by himself.   Many paint mothers and children,
and do not make them pretty, but they lack either his sentiment
or his skill.   There is no one else who does the same kind of work.
Equally difficult to place in any general group are Horatio Walker

and Robert F. Blum, and these unclassified independents may serve to mark the division between the seekers of beauty and the seekers of truth. Both Walker and Blum are notable executants, their *technique* is brilliant and interesting in itself, and both occasionally have imitated with surprising skill the handling of other men ; but they have not imitated the same men, nor is there any other resemblance between them. Blum began as an enthusiastic admirer of Fortuny, whose influence shows through all his early work, in his pen drawings, his etchings, his pastels, his water-colors, and his oil paintings, for he tried all mediums for the pleasure of developing the peculiar qualities of each. Often, as with Fortuny, the subject was nothing but an excuse for a display of a skill that was in reality the subject. Every bit of drawing was crisp and dashing, every spot of color sparkled, the ink lines or the water-color washes were touched on with a cleverness that savored of legerdemain. With time his outlook widened. His Venice pictures have something of Rico and something of Whistler. He saw and studied the Dutch water-colorists ; a long stay in Japan made him acquainted with its art. But whichever of these varying inspirations he follows, his work itself is good and does not need the reputation of its prototype to sustain it. In fact, the things which seem most closely to approach some model when actually compared with it only show how different they are. Through them all is seen Blum's own temperament, brilliant, witty, with a touch of poetry and a touch of sentiment. In his later work he has worked out a *technique* of his own, and shows less and less disposition to imitate others until in his great decorations the only remaining trace of his early tendencies is the determination to make every portion interesting in itself, and interesting in the way that it is executed.

Walker never played the sedulous ape (to borrow Stevenson's phrase) to other men's work to any such extent as Blum. In being influenced by Millet and Troyon he but followed the general tendency of the time, nor has Millet's method of painting been copied by him so much as his feeling for largeness of composition and for enveloping atmosphere. Above all he has been influenced by Millet's sentiment toward the soil and its workers. This sentiment had an enormous vogue in America ; it was fostered by tales

of his poverty, by sales of his pictures at sensational prices, by
reproductions of his work in the magazines, and by much uncritical writing everywhere; but at base the admiration was sincere and
profound. The American public love and comprehend sentiment
in a work of art as they do not technical merits (many of them still
think Millet a poor draftsman); and, moreover, Millet's sentiment
needed no tinge of European culture or tradition for its comprehen-

FIG. 108. — BLUM: STREET SCENE IN TOKIO.
[Copyright, 1893, by Charles Scribner's Sons.]

sion and touched the great sympathetic, democratic heart which
had but recently freed the slave and hoped to make of its land a
refuge for all the oppressed.

In spite of this, however, Millet's influence on our painting is less
than that of the others of the Barbizon school. American painters
and students were among his earliest admirers, and several of them
while in France painted subjects somewhat resembling his; but
when they returned home they found it impossible to convey the
spirit of Millet in terms of the American farmer — he was too inde-

pendent, too sophisticated ; his machinery, his reapers and threshers, lacked the epic note; they were new like his clothes, his house, and all his surroundings. There was no long, intimate association of the man with the soil, each moulding the other until both were in harmony.

The result was that the artists either continued to paint French peasants or sought a newer inspiration. Walker alone found among the habitants of Canada a corner of the new world whose manners and customs were older and simpler by far than anything that Barbizon could offer. It is seventeenth- or eighteenth-century France, uncontaminated by later intellectual or mechanical developments. The families are rooted in the soil and as the year revolves they go through the old august labors of ploughing, sowing, and reaping, as simply and naturally as the birds build their nests or the salmon mount the rivers in the spring. When Walker paints this life, he gives like Millet its large, ample, classic simplicity. His works have the same Virgilian touch of sympathy with the field and the forest, but the human interest is not so dominant or profound. Millet's peasants are himself, their families are his family. They are obscure of thought and inarticulate of expression, but he has felt and thought for them and made himself their spokesman. There is no such intimate personal unity between Walker and his habitants. He likes and sympathizes with them, but after all they are only a part of the fauna of his pictures, like the sheep or the great oxen ; what he is painting is the spring ploughing or the winter wood-cutting.

If the sentiment of Walker, for all its similarity, is always distinct from that of Millet, his handling at times is absolutely that of Troyon. This is not a reproach. Troyon's *technique* was the most masterly and painterlike of any one of the group of French landscapists with which he is usually associated, but it differed from that of men like Diaz or Dupré mainly by its sureness and perfection. No one knows so well as he all the varieties of texture and surface: how to simplify too aggressive details, how to mass the light and dark, how to paint a sky of solidly modelled but luminous clouds, to blend the distance into it, to glaze rich, transparent shadows in the foreground and then to put over them sure touches of solid impasto that glow like spots of real sunlight on the trees, the grasses, and the red or white coats of the cattle. This perfection of workmanship of Troyon's in his smaller canvases (it is less interesting in his great Salon pictures) Walker has succeeded either directly or indirectly in acquiring perfectly. He can reproduce it when he will in a manner that need fear no comparison with his prototype. He does not always do so. As befits a man of a later generation, his coloring is more varied, more subtle, and usually with more of blue and less of brown in the shadows, and his handling is usually looser, more free but not less sure. This is especially true of his smaller pictures and his water-colors, which latter closely resemble Mauve; but in this case there is no necessity of referring the similarity to imitation, conscious or unconscious. It is the natural development of Troyon's *technique*, used with an increasing ease and adapted to a swifter, lighter medium. Besides, excellent artist as Mauve is, in the works where they most closely resemble each other, Walker is distinctly the better — more varied in subject, more subtle in color if not in tone, more sympathetic in drawing and not inferior in sentiment.

The charm of Blum's pictures lies in the execution rather than in the subjects, which are chosen from every land except America. The same cannot be said of Walker, who paints a land that geographically is American and very near to the United States, yet it may be questioned if he gives its peculiar, characteristic essence. That he paints it truthfully none can doubt, but there is a suspicion that he chooses in it the scenes and effects which approach nearest to those admired and painted by French masters. The same suspicion arises in the case of some of our best landscapists, and among the figure painters the disposition is curiously small to do as Fromentin says they should — paint the portrait of the American people. The quest for beauty dominates that for truth. There is hardly a painter who could be depended upon to refrain from pinning a bow of bright colored ribbon to a dress if it gave him a wished-for spot of color, no matter how much the addition might conflict with the immutable rules of the milliners of the day. Two or three centuries from now those curious to learn what manner of people lived at the beginning of the twentieth century can

FIG. 109. — HORATIO WALKER: OXEN DRINKING.

cull out from the art production of France, of Germany, or of England an infinity of pictures, many of high artistic merit, that will give to them the very age and body of the time. From America they will get hardly anything of the sort, at least in oil painting.

It is strange that it should be so, for we do not lack the ability to see ourselves with sincerity and sympathy; the illustrators are there to prove it. They are not to be discussed in this volume, so it must suffice to recall out of many names the wonderful rendering by Frost of our great democratic life on the farm, in the workshops, in the crowded quarters of our great cities, and in the raw little towns of the far West; and Smedley's pictures of the wealthier classes, with the pretty girls sitting in the parlors in wonderful toilets, and the well-groomed old gentlemen in their offices or clubs. These things are not only true, but they are typical and illuminative; but no painter has worked with the more deliberate choice of subject and the ampler treatment that he should command to mirror our life to us more perfectly or more profoundly. No one has painted the political or financial or social habits of to-day. It is not at once clear why this should be so. The same training that our artists received in the Paris *ateliers* has enabled the French painters to fill the Salons with transcripts from life of all degrees of merit. Stewart could paint his " Hunt Ball " and like subjects there, but they are not done here.

For this there may be suggested a number of contributing causes. One is the transitory and trivial character of the setting of our social life. This does not refer so much to the vagaries of dress, which is on the whole one of the most satisfactory artistic factors in our modern life, as to the mass of accessories with which our existence is cluttered up — furniture and bric-à-brac, wall-papers and carpets. Every detail is usually inartistic in itself and almost certainly incongruous in its surroundings, and all avow their unsatisfactory character by shifting and changing more swiftly than even the styles in dresses. All of this has at times been painted, but such a task was distasteful to the younger men. They had for the most part learned during their studies abroad to dislike the average American furnishings. They avoided them in their own surroundings as well as they could and did not much care to elaborate them

in their pictures.   When draftsmen like Smedley left illustrating
for work in oil it was to portraiture and landscape that they turned,
and Tarbell's "Crocheting," which suggests Vermeer in its tranquillity and the beauty and perfection of its lighting, does not
impress us at all as holding within itself an epitome of the home
life of its time as the works of the Dutch masters do.

Life in the country and in the open air is more inspiring than
that penned up in city rooms and it has been more painted, but even
there the tendency has been to make a thing of beauty rather than
to give the " true truth."   Not only the artists but their patrons preferred it so.   The American man finds enough of prose in the day's
work.   It does not sadden him ; on the contrary, he enjoys it and
puts all his energies into it, and when he turns from it he demands
that art shall do its duty in furnishing delight and that uncompli-
cated by too much subtlety.   He dislikes problem plays that finish
badly and realistic novels that simply give again the life he knows,
and he wants his pictures beautiful or at least pretty.   He doesn't
know anything about art, but he knows what he likes, as he proudly
proclaims, and no perfection of craftsmanship is going to make him
change his likes.

There was, besides, a practical reason perhaps more potent than
any of the others for this lack of realistic painting.   During the
eighties and nineties, French and German *genre* pictures had an
enormous popularity.   The dealers' galleries were filled with them,
and they were bought greedily by a public which would not consider
native work.   American oil paintings were almost unsalable, but for
illustration there was a steady demand with sure pay.   Most of the
figure painters worked at times for the publishers and those of them
who had the facility and other qualifications necessary to reproduce
the life about them in a way acceptable to the readers of the magazines were sure of incomes far higher than they could gain by more
ambitious work.

These are all excellent reasons why America should not have
to-day painters to interpret her daily life and yet one suspects also
that it is partly a matter of chance.   J. G. Brown, Winslow Homer,
Eastman Johnson, all painted certain sides of it, the last named having
even represented the interior of the New York house of the seventies,

and not unacceptably.   There are reasons why the younger generation should be less inclined to such subjects, but they are not prohibitive.   Apparently the predestined man might have occurred just
as Winslow Homer did.   Several have touched upon the province.
Ulrich, after he had painted his " Glass Blowers," a marvel of minute,
careful observation and rendering, did also a " Land of Promise," a
scene of arriving immigrants at Castle Garden which was quite as fine
technically and with a profounder meaning.   Douglas Volk, Edgar
M. Ward, August Franzen, and many others have all done among
other things scenes from our country life.   Another group has preserved the traditions of the now vanished frontier and the long
guardianship of it against the Indians by our little army.   E. Irving
Couse and De Cost Smith have told the story of the red man, his
life and habits ; Charles Schreyvogle, the fights and friendships of
the cavalrymen who held the settlements against his inroads ; but
the authoritative chronicler of the whole western land from Assini-
boine to Mexico and of all men and beasts dwelling therein is Frederic Remington.   He, at least, cannot be said to have sacrificed truth
to grace.   The raw, crude light, the burning sand, the pitiless blue
sky, surround the lank, sunburned men who ride the rough horses
and fight or drink or herd cattle as the case may be.   The record is
invaluable and the execution is direct and sure.   Perhaps it would
lose something of its force if it were completer, but even in his work
in oil Remington is an illustrator rather than a painter.   The subject is more to him than the purely artistic qualities displayed in its
representation, and the same may be said of some of the other men
just mentioned.

   There was one man, however, who was a painter and who
might have become the recorder of the simpler, wider side of
our common life had it not been for his untimely death.   It is
noticeable that Thomas Hovenden, like J. G. Brown, Guy, and
other painters of American life, was born abroad (in County Cork,
Ireland, 1840) and did not come to America until 1863.   He had
begun painting in Cork ; he worked here at the Academy of Design,
and in 1874 went to Paris, where he studied six years under Cabanel.
The apprenticeship was long and the school training very complete, but it was some time before he found the work fitted to him.

He painted Brittany scenes in France and after his return " Elaine," a composition of many figures, laborious and frigid. About the same time, however, he began a series of studies of negro life, " Chloe and Sam," " Dem was Good Ole Times," and the rest. They were followed by " In from the Meadows," " The Village Blacksmith," and similar subjects culminating with " Breaking Home Ties," a country boy leaving home to make his fortune. It is as good a picture of the kind as has been painted in the country — less artistic, perhaps, than Eastman Johnson's work, but still excellent in its craftsmanship and profound and sincere in its sentiment.

It is, of course, the story-telling picture, the anecdote is forced on the spectator as it is not by Johnson, still less by the old Dutch masters — but the story is told clearly and beautifully. The sentiment rings true. The Spartan repression of emotion between the mother and the great overgrown boy, the sisters, the stage driver with the bag, the flawless neatness and comfort of the room, are all typical. The same typical quality is in another, unfinished picture, representing the taking possession of their section of prairie land by a young farmer with his wife and child. It tried to show how the external problems of life were being worked out on the new soil. Through both pictures, and in fact through all Hovenden's work, there runs the simple, kindly character which showed in every action of the artist and which glorified his end, for he gave his life instantly and unhesitatingly to save a child from being killed by a railway train. It was a serious loss to our art. He was in the prime of life, his important works, the ones in which he had painted most skilfully and displayed the deepest feeling, had been produced in the preceding three or four years, and it seems but reasonable to suppose that had he been spared he would have developed still further.

One of Hovenden's pictures was historical — the " Last Moments of John Brown." The subject, the unsubdued old agitator stopping as he walked to the scaffold to kiss a negro child, must have appealed to the artist; but the picture was an order, and he did no other work of the kind. Few of the recent artists have tried to paint their country's history, such subjects, like the social life, being left mostly to the illustrators. Julian Scott, who had served himself in the army from 1861 to 1863 and afterward studied under Leutze, has done a

number of war scenes; but a more skilful artist is Gilbert Gaul, whose
series of pictures of the conflicts of the blue and the gray, "Charg-
ing the Battery," "Saving the Colors," and the rest bring back the
almost forgotten days and stir the blood like the sight of the lines of
veterans on Decoration Day.   They are excellently well painted and
moreover they are truthful,—the types of faces, the ragged uniforms,
the country fought over with its stone walls or fences, all the little
tricks of attitude and expression, are racy of the soil.   W. B. T.

FIG. 110. — HOVENDEN: BREAKING HOME TIES.

Trego, too, has shown the "Light Artillery," the wheels sunk to the
hubs in the mud, while the weary, straining horses and men force the
guns along a road like a morass in the pouring rain.

Others have occasionally chosen a subject from the same time,
but the American soldier has had no De Neuville or Detaille to
record his prowess, and with our earlier heroes the case is even worse.
Howard Pyle is the only man who seems to know thoroughly the
colonial and Revolutionary epoch, and he is above all an illustrator,
though he has done enough independent work to permit mention of

him among the painters and to merit a special note of thanks in that he has represented the founders of the Republic as they were, — sturdy, hard-headed folk, with strong characters and few graces, who wore the rather rigid costumes of the time with dignity and not like singers in comic opera or dancing masters. It is difficult not to go farther with Pyle and discuss his other work, his Knights of the Round Table, his mediæval poets and ladies, and his pirates (surely never before were pirates so satisfactorily bloody-minded offered for the delectation of youth); but though frequently completely and elaborately painted in oil, these subjects were yet intended for books or periodicals, and so must count as illustrations.

Outside all these various groups of landscape and figure painting, the description and classification of which has been attempted, and equally outside of portraiture and decorative painting which are to follow, there remains an enormous mass of work, perhaps equal to all the rest, too great to be treated individually and yet too varied for successful generalization, the painters themselves adding to the confusion by their changes of style and subject. There are transcripts from everyday life and its familiar detail, and contributions from the picturesqueness of distant lands, strange peoples and places, character heads of old men, mothers with children, girls reading or walking or sitting in hammocks, kneeling angels with gold halos, bits of old houses, a man with a sword or a lady with a rose, still-life and decorative panels, — all the things, in short, of which the average exhibition is made up and which in their totality represent what the man in the street understands by a picture. They are not, as a rule, of such high inspiration as to be classed as ideal work nor of such deep insight into character as to be typically realistic, but they are well done. Technical standards are understood now, and incompetence is rarely displayed in the larger annual shows. The work seen there is generally speaking good, one would say on the average quite as good, though in a different way, as is found in the Salons and Academy exhibitions of Europe.

Recalling the past, numbers of pictures like some of the children of Sergeant Kendall, the " Boy with an Arrow," by Volk, the beautiful ideal compositions of Henry O. Walker, or some of the early *genre* pictures of Eakins, " Mending the Net," or the " Chess Players," come to mind and seem imperatively to demand mention.   Most of these painters, however, are to be spoken of in other connections, but some record must be made of the animal painters represented by J. H. Dolph, William H. Howe, and Henry R. Poore.   They merit it, for even Dolph, though forced by the exigencies of the popular demand to produce an interminable series of puppies and kittens, was yet never led into slighting his work, while the cattle of Howe and the hunting dogs of Poore touch a higher plane.   They are pictures well drawn and well composed in excellent landscape settings, which in the case of Poore are becoming more and more important, so that his figures are often but an incident of his luminous autumn woods.

Last of all, mention should be made of the most recent development of artists who are now beginning to be called the younger men and to be matched against those who bore the title twenty-five years ago.   There is no such sharp line of demarcation as there was in the seventies.   American painting is now in touch with that of the rest of the world, and changes are made gradually here as elsewhere, but from this very intimacy with foreign art currents it was inevitable that there should be developments of groups corresponding to the " New Salons " and " Secessions " of the Old World.   Academic traditions and official influences have no such power here as there, consequently there has been no such organized opposition, nor has the work been pushed by opposition into the extravagances sometimes seen in Paris or Munich; but the artistic principles of the new school have their followers.   These principles consist, for the most part, in a revolt against what is commonplace and tedious, no matter how much labor or learning is displayed.   The execution and conception must seem facile and spontaneous, and above all the work must be personal and striking; given these qualities, a painful accuracy can well be spared.   As for the works of the elders, even if they had at one time merit, their repetition during a generation has enabled their message to be assimilated and they are now but the most wearisome of platitudes.

There is nothing particularly novel about these principles; rising generations have proclaimed them often enough before, and they are as sound as general principles can well be, in spite of the fact that the "School of Athens" successfully avoids most of them and still remains a meritorious work. Their interest lies in their application, which in the present case has something of the tradition of Manet and something of the sentiment of Whistler, both tempered by individual originality. Form must be rendered by mass and not by line; there must be no tinting of a carefully prepared underlying drawing but a broad, painterlike laying on of pigment with masterly and striking brush work and if possible some peculiarity of handling which shall serve as the artist's sign manual.

Robert Henri is perhaps the most characteristic of this younger group, for although he is, strictly speaking, a portrait painter, his best works are not from the casual sitter of commerce, but from carefully chosen models, and are hardly more portraits than the "Virgins" of Thayer. These latter, however, are classic and simple. The girls in "white" or "black" of Henri are modern, complex, and rather mysterious, as they stand slender and graceful, with their faces showing light against the dark background. The workmanship, as principles of the group demand, is broad and sure, insistently masterly, with great richness of surface and harmony of tone in the simple schemes of black and white and flesh-color.

An even stronger contrast of light and dark, and a handling even more aggressive, is seen in some of the canvases of Jonas Lie, which are dashed in with the *furia* of a sketch and retain much of a sketch's vigor, and at times something of its inaccuracy. The drawing of Jerome Myers, on the contrary, is rather careful and there are no forcible contrasts of dark and light. His street scenes in the poorer quarters belong in the group more from the mellow tone in which they are enveloped, the simplification of uninteresting detail and their sentiment, than from any strangeness of composition or of brush work. This is to be found in the pictures of Maurice B. Prendergast, who translates the groups of children and nurses playing in the parks or on the beaches into a curiously decorative mosaic of pink, blue, and green spots, which give in their color and texture something of the joyousness suited to the occasion.

But the best picture of childhood as it disports itself *en masse*

FIG. 111.—HENRI: YOUNG WOMAN IN BLACK.

in the open air is William J. Glackens's "May Party," where a
crowd of pupils from the public schools play, roll about, or scuffle
on the grass under the trees of the park.   Glackens is best known
as an illustrator.   He has made a few careful and elaborate compositions, but many more drawings in a style somewhere between
Charles Keene and Forain, slightly indicated, with little light and
shade or background, but with much character and expression in
the little figures.   All of this expressiveness is given in the "May
Party," which is realized with truth and humor, and moreover
painted brilliantly and broadly, the composition holding together
well in tone and color.   Glackens has already painted some figures
and portraits, but nothing in quite the same vein as the "May
Party," and should he continue in it he might take the vacant
place of recorder of the popular life.

Thus far the painters referred to have all worked in oil.   When
any were skilled in other mediums besides that, mention has usually
been made of the fact.   It is not possible or particularly desirable
to speak at length of those who have worked solely in such other
mediums which practically are limited to pastel and water-color, for
painting with turpentine, benzine, and petroleum essences or varnishes
does not vary materially from that in oil, and not many have been
curious to go beyond the ordinary materials obtainable at the color
shops.   Experiments in true fresco, in tempera, or in wax or egg
medium have been so rare and inconclusive as to be unimportant.
Pastel has been employed by many men but irregularly, no one has
limited himself to it alone, and few have cared to develop its full
resources.   Of water-color there has been, on the contrary, an enormous production.   All over the country, water-color societies have
been formed and exhibitions held, its apparent facility commending
it to all classes of amateurs.   The medium has been used in every
possible way and naturally much feeble and mediocre work has been
produced.   Even the better exhibitions are apt to show a preponderance of work which is merely pretty, but the best is very good.
Very little of it, however, is done by painters who confine themselves
to the medium, using it alone.

Mrs. Sarah C. Sears has painted a number of ideal heads in water-
color, recalling in their refinements and dignity the work of Thayer;

and Frank Hopkinson Smith has produced in the same medium his series of views of Venice, of Holland, of England — but especially of Venice.   They are widely known and admired, these glimpses of little canals hemmed in by old palaces or vine-covered walls, these bits from the Piazza or the Riva degli Schiavoni or stretches of water ending in the great dome of the Salute, and the admiration is deserved.   They are not emotional, they are not subtle, they are not "tonal," but they are very charming with their delicately colored skies, their luminous air, their soft, sunlit marbles and clear, cool shadows.   The execution is exhilarating, it is so sure, with such an economy of resource and so manifest an enthusiasm.

These two and a very few besides have been in reality water-color painters, but the others who have done notable work have either been masters in other mediums, like La Farge, Horatio Walker, Winslow Homer, and Blum, or else they have been illustrators.   It is hard to draw a line between the two camps and to decide that Albert Sterner and Arthur I. Keller, for instance, are not painters; and logic has still greater violence done it when the title is denied to Maxfield Parrish because his very complete and beautiful paintings in oil are made to be reproduced in the magazines.   Jessie Wilcox Smith, Violet Oakley, and Elizabeth Shippen Green are naturally grouped together in the minds of all those acquainted with their works, and yet the fact that one of them happens to have done an important piece of decoration separates her from the others.   The divisions are difficult, and yet these names and others like them must be regretfully omitted, for if they were placed among the painters the historian of American Illustration would have but an ungrateful task.

FIG. 112.—ALEXANDER: A PORTRAIT.

[From a Copley Print.   Copyright by Curtis & Cameron, Publishers, Boston.]

CHAPTER XXVI

THE MODERN PORTRAIT PAINTERS

IN the earlier days of American art, the most important branch of painting was portraiture. It is almost the only branch in which examples of colonial and Revolutionary work remain, and even in the succeeding period it maintained its supremacy. Not only was it more practised, but the work done was better than in other branches until well after the middle of the last century. Since then there has been a change. Portraiture has become less important as compared with other forms of figure painting and especially with landscape, and besides it may be said that, in spite of some notable exceptions, it has developed less brilliantly.

The main cause for this diminished importance is not far to seek. In his *Annals of the National Academy of Design*, Cummings gives a copy of the letter of invitation sent him in 1839 by a pupil of Daguerre just arrived in New York, in which he was invited to a first view of a collection of proofs by Daguerre and others, "perhaps the most interesting objects which have ever been exposed to the curiosity of a man of taste." Cummings justly objects to calling the new art a "marvellous process of drawing," and (writing in 1861) compares disadvantageously the works shown with the "beautiful specimens done by Brady, Gurney, and Fredericks"; but he seems to have had no impression that the invention was even then changing the whole course of American art.

Up to that time there had been one customary and authorized entrance on the painter's career. The Youth of Genius, with or without instruction, as the case might be, succeeded in painting a head that showed some likeness to the sitter and then started out to furnish portraits at whatever price he could get. In every little town or village there were people that wanted likenesses of themselves or their families, and they contented themselves with poor ones if they could get no better. The spread of intelligence, the increase of wealth, the greater facilities for intercommunication, had made standards of taste more sophisticated, but that was not what prevented the impecunious painter of the seventies and eighties from going through the country in the old way doing heads for ten or twenty dollars. It is interesting to imagine what the situation would be to-day had not photography intervened. We are eighty millions of people not, as elsewhere, for the most part peasants or necessitous laborers, but rather a bourgeoisie with money to spend. Allowing but one portrait painter to each thousand, there would be eighty thousand of the craft, and with miniaturists and workers in pastel, crayon, and other draftsmen the number would probably be several times as great. Never yet has painting anywhere been practised on such a scale, and it is fair to suppose not only that the best of the artists would have formed a school of portraitists of the highest merit, but that the skill so acquired would have spread to other branches of art. The vision of what might have occurred is entrancing; the reality was different. The daguerreotype, the tin-type, the carte-de-visite or the crayon-finished enlargement replaced the work of the humble, unskilled craftsmen, from whom the better painters developed.

Another influence was also active which attacked the field unaffected by photography so that not only did those of small or moderate means desert the American painter, but the wealthy also ceased more and more to patronize him. Some of the older men like Huntington or Eastman Johnson still kept their clients, but the younger portrait painters of the eighties suffered as all painters suffered at the time. Foreign work was having its greatest vogue. The purchasers of foreign pictures began to have themselves painted abroad by foreign artists; but soon the dealers who had imported the pictures imported also the painters, so that it was no longer necessary to cross the ocean to have portraits done in a style in harmony

FIG. 113.—EAKINS: THE CELLO PLAYER, PENNSYLVANIA ACADEMY.

with the new houses and new furniture and by artists with all imaginable medals and decorations.

The men who came thus under the sheltering wing of the great dealers were almost, without exception, men of ability. Some of them ranked among the best of contemporary portrait painters. The work they did here was at times worthy of their reputations and at times not. The circumstances under which they labored were too frankly mercenary to be inspiring. No French artist could pretend even to himself that he journeyed to America to improve his art, or that he cared for any honors that were to be won here. They had no high opinion of the taste of their patrons, and when they did their best it was for the most part to satisfy their own consciences. Those artists whose work was admired for its artistic quality by their fellow-craftsmen and by the severer critics had less success here, or at least repeated their visits less frequently, than what may be called the society portrait painters whose regularly recurring visits are still so much a part of painting in America as to demand some notice.

The reputation of these latter artists was quite as widespread as that of the others, their medals and decorations were possibly more numerous, but they wore them with a difference. Their admirers came from a different class. They had been patronized by those highest in rank or most abounding in wealth or most prominent socially. They were not unskilful; on the contrary, they knew their trade, and more. They worked surely and swiftly, the drawing was clever, the color was bright, the silks and satins shimmered, the texture of the furs and laces was wonderful, and the faces of the sitters were beautiful but yet recognizable, with lips that smiled and liquid eyes that sparkled. In America there have been few dissenting voices in the chorus of admiration, and those mostly from artists and their friends who may justly be suspected of bias and whose opinions, rarely put forward so as to have any wide circulation, may be considered as negligible.

In Paris (the painters under consideration are mostly Parisians) the dissenting group is larger and more important. In it, too, there are a number of artists and art critics and art collectors, but the opinion of artists about their art carries a certain weight in France. For these dissenting artists are also prominent. They may not have any more medals to their credit, but the French medals are apt to be a trifle larger, likewise the red rosettes, and occasionally the wearers of them are members of the Institute, which is very distinguished.   In the same way the critics, in addition to the *Figaro* or the *Temps*, write for the *Gazette des Beaux Arts* or the *Revue des Deux Mondes*, which is also distinguished, and one or two are members of the Academy, which is most distinguished of all.   For some reason the portraits just described have the power to set on edge the teeth and rasp the nerves of this group.   Mostly they are silent or coldly civil, but at times they break out into savageries of speech which pass all decorum.   The work maddens them.   They declare that it is meretricious in the most offensive sense of the word, that there is no feeling for noble form or color, no true rendering of character, no beauty of craftsmanship, but instead a slippery, superficial execution made up of a lot of tricks, an insistence on every trivial and vulgar detail, and an utter failure to see the things worth seeing.

And in so saying the critics are right.   They should not lose their tempers, but those who struggle for the higher qualities in their art are naturally exasperated at work which shows no consciousness of the existence of such qualities, and it does not diminish the exasperation to see this trivial work gaining enormous pecuniary rewards.   They are even apt to ignore the possession in a high degree by the objects of their scorn of other qualities not indeed of the first rank, but still laudable although appealing to a popular and uncultured taste, and they take no account whatever of such immensely important practical factors as promptness in finishing the work, skill in fitting the picture to its surroundings, and the social qualities of the artists.

The foreign invasion, however, although it has seemed to bear heavily on the native artists, is not likely to prove in the long run an injurious influence in portraiture any more than in other branches of art.   It is doubtful even whether it has diverted many commissions from the native-born.   Those who patronized the visiting artists wanted Parisian portraits just as others wanted pictures by Toulmouche or Baugniet, and if they could not get them they went without instead of taking an American substitute.   As in the case of the *genre* painters, the preference was not inexcusable.   Some of

FIG. 114.— MISS BEAUX: CHILDREN OF R. W. GILDER, ESQ

the foreign portraitists were artists of great merit, and (though there has since been an independent influx of all degrees of capacity and incapacity) all those brought over by the dealers knew their trade thoroughly.   The patron who engaged their services was reasonably sure to receive promptly after a limited number of sittings a picture such as he expected, with approximately the same qualities as the sample which had been shown him and which had influenced him to give his order.

With the Americans it was different.   The general characteristics of the older and the younger men have been described, and the qualities of the latter were such that a score of years ago the con- scientious person who was asked for advice about the choice of a portrait painter might indeed recommend home talent, but he was yet obliged to make certain reservations lest he should later be called to account.   One man would do work not surpassed anywhere, but there would probably be interminable sittings which might continue for a year or even two; another would be sure to do a brilliant piece of painting, but the resemblance might or might not be satisfactory; still another might introduce some eccentricity of details or of posture which would offend the owner or his family; and the other men whose work was dependable were growing old and their recent productions were not equal to their earlier and also often not up to the newer standards.

Portraiture was, in fact, in a much worse condition than land- scape or ideal figure painting.   The rigid discipline in drawing from the model which most of the new men had undergone in the Parisian schools, and which was such an admirable foundation in the other branches, would seem to be peculiarly fitted to form the portrait painter, but, reasoning from results, it is doubtful if it was so.   At all events, when we consider how few men comparatively were trained outside of the *ateliers* of the École des Beaux Arts and kindred schools like Julien's or Colarossi's, and yet how many of our good portrait painters are among these outsiders, the con- viction is strong that the severer training was not the best.

The students of Couture rather antedate the period under consideration, though some of them like George Butler were still doing admirable work; but from the *atelier* of Carolus-Duran, who almost alone in Paris based his instruction on painting rather than drawing, came, besides Sargent, J. Carroll Beckwith, Irving R. Wiles, Frank Fowler, and William M. J. Rice. W. M. Chase was of Munich and J. W. Alexander, Frederic P. Vinton, J. R. De Camp, Julian Story, all were among the pupils of Duveneck and felt (like Dannat, also) the Munich influence. Wilton Lockwood formed his style under La Farge before going to Paris, Benjamin C. Porter was practically self-taught, and the same may be said of Cecilia Beaux.

It would be difficult to place against this an equal list of American painters distinctively portraitists who were formed by the stricter training of the École des Beaux Arts and similar academies. Even when these achieved success it is felt that they did it by force of temperament, and that their training often hampered them. In the first place, they were taught no method of painting. All formulas and recipes, preparing of grounds, setting of palettes, underpaintings, overpaintings, and glazings, everything that came under the head of *la cuisine* was neglected. A minutely accurate drawing was covered with color beginning at the head and ending at the feet, each spot being finished as completely as possible before another was begun. This was not supplemented by copying the old masters or by much other study except some anatomy and perspective. The student produced a series, partly of life-size heads, but mostly of small, full-length figures, from weary, ungainly, nude models, admirable in construction and in truthful rendering of the uninspiring originals. There was rarely beauty of form or color, of workmanship or inspiration; but the discipline and the knowledge thus gained were invaluable when the student turned to express himself in new channels. Then it remained as a foundation on which he built his new workmanship and his new ideas. But portraiture was so like the school work that it was difficult to avoid its defects.

The very restriction in portrait painting to so simple a subject demands that every resource of composition and handling and texture should be employed to add interest, otherwise it remains a school study and hopelessly uninteresting. Furthermore, the circumstances under which the artist works demand that he should do so as freely and easily as possible. Carolus-Duran and Duveneck, like West and later Couture, taught each a method by which the canvas was

FIG. 115.—LOCKWOOD: PORTRAIT OF JOHN LA FARGE.

promptly covered with color and then brought forward as a whole by regular, well-defined steps, and which gave their students as soon as possible familiarity with the brush, the instrument they were to use rather than the charcoal point or the crayon. They worked freely and easily, even if sometimes inaccurately. The students of Gérôme or Lefebvre, on the contrary, had too deep a conscience for drawing as the probity of art to slight it even for an instant. As has been seen, it served them far better than the Munich facility in other branches of art, but in portraiture before their sitters it seems to have paralyzed them. They felt more deeply than the others all the delicacies of modelling, but they had no facile methods of rendering them; a fleeting expression was not to be hastily caught, but rather the bored look of the sitter; even the clothes could not be slighted or be hastily done, but required the same deliberate thoroughness.

The consequence was much tedium for the sitters and much wofully prosaic work. Even when the work was admirable, as in the case of Alfred Q. Collins or Thomas Eakins, the lack of painter-like training told terribly. Collins, at his best, has the insight into character, the simplicity and the completeness of the old Dutch masters that he admired. He saw with splendid unity and thoroughness, but he had learned no facile method for putting down what he saw and had to invent one for himself,—laborious, variable, wearying the artist by the constant effort and consuming much time before completion was attained. In the same way, Eakins with a like grasp of the personality of his subjects, and an even greater enjoyment of the picturesqueness of their attitudes and apparel, yet fails of the popular appreciation that he merits because of his neglect of the beauties and graces of painting, — not the beauties and graces of his subjects. No one would wish his sitters more modishly clad or more self-conscious. Their interest lies in their personality, and that is excellently given. The drawing is the most searching and delicate, the figures are well constructed and stand with notable firmness on their feet, and every line of face and raiment has character. The artist seems to say, " Here is the man, what more do you want? " but the paint is apt to be laid on inelegantly. There are vast expanses of background that are thin or dry or muddy or cold. The eye longs for beauty of surface, richness of impasto, or transparent depths of shadow, and the lack is the more felt because the artist has shown that when he will he is quite competent to give them, but they do not come naturally. Compare his work with that of Beckwith and see how much more effective was the training given by Carolus-Duran, for Beckwith has kept the quality of his master's handling better than almost any other of his pupils. It does not change his own personality, it does not make him a copyist, but it enables him to say what he has to say easily and rather sumptuously, with heavy impasto, rich shadows, and broad, strong handling. In like manner, Vinton and De Camp by adding sureness and solidity to the Munich brush work have arrived at a result not far different in workmanship.

Another representative of the Munich training besides the two pioneers of the school, Duveneck and Chase, already spoken of, is John W. Alexander; but his art developed in a peculiar and personal way much influenced by the art movements of Paris, but standing as much by itself there as in Munich or New York. It is interesting as introducing certain new elements into art, and especially as adapting itself to certain peculiarly modern conditions. It has fitted itself both for the moderately sized rooms of a private house and for the enormous exhibitions, where thousands of canvases contend for the attention of the public.

In the works of the old masters each has its general effect apart from its elaboration. Their greatest merit may lie in that general effect, but the elaboration is rarely omitted, not even by men like Hals or Velasquez, whom we think of as working most broadly. They did it with splendid ease and sureness; but a figured velvet doublet that counts only as a solid black mass will yet, when closely examined, show all of its elaborate pattern accurately rendered. But to-day the question naturally arises, Why take the trouble for a public which never does closely examine? One reason is that, although not understood, the elaboration of pattern or modelling yet gives texture, and without it the mass would look flat and empty. This drawback Alexander avoids by using a coarse absorbent canvas and painting with a turpentine or petroleum medium, so that the rough, unglazed surface helps to avoid monotony and heightens the interest

FIG. 116. — PORTER: PORTRAIT OF A BOY.

of every variation of brush work. Having thus simplified his work, he turns all his effort to the originality and completeness of the first general effect. The art in the suppression of the unessential resembles poster art. Nothing is included that does not actually interest. This is the merit of an unfinished sketch, but the peculiar quality of Alexander's work is that though much is omitted (even the hands are apt to be only summarily indicated), yet the effect is of complete· ness. The mind desires no more for the comprehension of the subject, and the shadowy tones which fill the vacant spaces both please and satisfy the eye. This stopping as soon as the interest stops is characteristic of some schools of Japanese art, and the coloring frequently has the same underlying principle as the Japanese colored woodcuts. Each picture represents a destinct color scheme of yellow and buff and black or of rose and gray and green, carefully balanced within itself and kept very simple and comprehensible. The darks also are at times spotted in a way that suggest the Japanese *notan*, and the lines have a long decorative caligraphic sweep like those of Yeishi or Utamaro. All this makes a decorative canvas, a canvas that, apart from its meaning as a picture, increases the beauty of a wall on which it is hung whether the wall be of the new Salon in Paris or of a parlor in America. And with this decorative quality the canvas remains a portrait. The interest is drawn to the personality of the sitter, and the characterization, though not elaborate, is direct and truthful.

It is noticeable that Alexander, whose art many consider as characteristically French, never studied in Paris, although he lived there a number of years as a practising artist; while Lockwood, who has had years of training in the French schools, shows a subtle harmony of coloring, an enveloping atmosphere, and a perception of character intimate and profound, which he is not likely to have gained there, but which may be traced closely to the influence of La Farge. In other cases, too, it would be difficult to divine the place and character of the schooling from the works of the artist. Just as at an earlier date Charles Loring Elliott, who never went abroad, seems to show more than most of his contemporaries the qualities that might be supposed to be the result of foreign study, so two other artists who picked up their training as they could and

2 M

mostly in America, have each in a different way much in their work that would indicate not only a longer foreign schooling, but also more favorable opportunities for the assimilation of foreign feeling and tradition.

Benjamin C. Porter has distinctly an echo of the French eighteenth century, the poses, the arrangement of the costumes and accessories, the decorative quality, and a sort of air of the figures as if on parade, all recall the painters of the court of Louis XV. His canvases have even the warm, mellow tone which age, rather than the painters, has given to their prototypes that hang in the Louvre or at Versailles, but here he stops. The sitters that he paints do not figure in memoirs like those of the Comte de Gramont. They are American ladies, dignified, well bred, opulent, and (in spite of their airs and graces) as clearly and candidly moral as the sitters of Huntington.

The art of Miss Beaux is the antithesis of this. It is modern in every way; the people sit in their ordinary dresses in their familiar surroundings and in their easiest, least conventional poses. It is not Latour or Tocqué that is suggested, but Sargent. Yet here again it is only adaptation of what is congenial and that as much from the general practice of the freer, more skilful painters in Paris as from the peculiarities of any one man. Comparison is often made between the two, but not with much profit. Miss Beaux' handling is broad and strong, the color flowing free and pure from the brush with many of those felicities that seem most accidental when they are the highest art; but neither in her work nor in that of any other artist is there the amazing jugglery of Sargent which has something aggressive in its force and sureness, nor has she his impersonal, vivid insight into character. She is in sympathy with her sitters, and they are likable and charming and enlist the affections of the spectator as those of Sargent rarely do after they get beyond the age of eight or ten.

Besides these who have been mentioned, for the most part because they are representative of different groups or tendencies, there are many more men and women who paint good portraits; indeed, a list was made of some thirty or forty names all seeming to call for special mention. Each of these has individuality and so would require in justice a rather careful analysis, but space forbids anything more than

FIG. 117. — WILES: MRS. AND MISS WILES.

certain general considerations. One is that during this period there have arisen in America no portrait painters of the old type nor any that as yet approach their predecessors in proficiency or productiveness. No one "taxes himself to six sitters a day" or counts his works by the hundreds or even thousands. Apart from the lack of patronage and a possibly unsuitable training, a portrait demanded much less mental effort from the artist fifty years ago. Then each man arranged his picture according to certain definite rules; he set his palette in a fixed way; he posed his models in the same light; he put in the same background. He had, as it were, a typical portrait which he painted, varying the drawing and in a less degree the color to suit the sitter, but seldom going far from the type except on great occasions. This the Paris student of the seventies or eighties could not do, not only from lack of training in the schools, but from certain influences outside of them.

The realm of art was being widened, knowledge was being increased. Effects of outdoor light rarely attempted by the old masters were being discovered and analyzed. The "Portrait of his Grandfather," by Bastien-Le Page aroused the emulation of hundreds. In vain the old professors warned that "genius would really be too cheap if you could get it by painting in the yard"; many youths thought to obtain it at that very moderate price. They painted portraits out of doors, studying with enthusiasm all the delicate and novel variations of tone, they refused to accept the old conventions for studio shadows, but insisted on dissecting them anew; they even succeeded in seeing in their studios the violet shadows of sunlight. By all this not only was labor greatly increased, but the chief interest for the artist was diverted from the character of the sitter to the analysis of novel tones which, however much it might divert the advanced group of critics who were eager for some new thing, did not please the plain man who desired a portrait, for not only was resemblance to the sitter frequently considered a negligible detail, but the gray monotone of the *plein-air* school was apt to make the pictures show to disadvantage in an ordinary room, and the sad sincerity with which every detail was finished from nature diverted attention from the head and often resulted in ungainly compositions.

The divergency of view between the artist and his client was thus sharper in portrait painting than in the other branches, one desiring to produce a picture and caring nothing for the likeness, the other wishing a likeness and naught else. It consequently took longer than in landscape or figure painting before a compromise could be arranged. It has been made at length, and even the comrades of Bastien paint portraits that are appreciated and enjoyed both by the painter and the sitter. The later generation has a less difficult task. The open-air school has run its course. Its main principles have been absorbed into the great body of art practice, and its eccentricities have ceased to interest aspiring students. Some of the errors of the earlier training have been avoided, painting is better taught, and the merit of technical methods is more considered. The visiting painters have shown the necessity of skilled work without fumbling or hesitation, and the public is beginning to consider more dispassionately the relative merits of native and foreign work.

The last five or ten years have shown a great advance in the quality of the mass of American portrait painting. There is no one practising in the country who holds such a position as Stuart did in the old days or as, for instance, is held in London by Sargent, who in spite of his occasional visits must be considered an expatriate, but the place stands open for such a man to-day as it did not twenty years ago. If Sargent had come to America then, with his returning fellow-students, it would have been impossible for him with all his talent and with all his industry to have attained anything like his present position. It seems as if a young man of equal endowment returning now and working steadily here might not only develop his art to its highest expression, but might also find that with advancing years he had gained a reputation and an authority in matters of art in accord with his abilities. It is the recognition by the public which fails at present rather than the talents of the artists, and in that, too, there have been recently signs of a change for the better.

With the other branches of portraiture, the last dozen years or so has also seen a notable revival of the art of the miniaturist so important in the early days of the Republic. It is an artistic

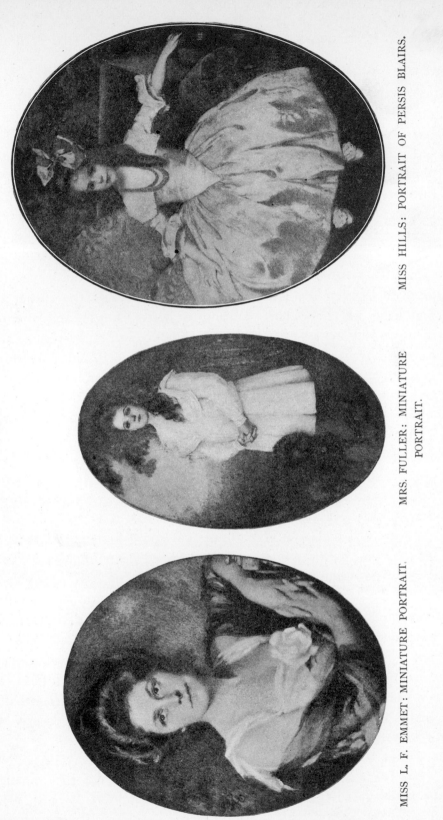

FIG. 118.

MISS L. F. EMMET: MINIATURE PORTRAIT.

MRS. FULLER: MINIATURE PORTRAIT.

MISS HILLS: PORTRAIT OF PERSIS BLAIRS.

revival, too, something better than a timid stippling of photographic likenesses. The artists put into their work the same qualities of handling, of composition, and of character that are demanded of workers on a larger scale. The best is very good, so good, indeed, that it has withstood the competition of foreign artists far better than the life-size work. There is an organized "Society of Miniature Painters," and the number of skilled practitioners is so great that it must suffice to present illustrations of some of the best work without entering into the merits and characteristics of the individual artists.

CHAPTER XXVII

RECENT MURAL DECORATIONS

WHILE portrait painting which was the chief occupation of our earlier artists has lost something of its primary importance, mural painting which was practically unknown to them has had of late a great and gratifying development so that it may fairly be claimed at present as the most interesting and the most promising branch of our art. In saying that it was unknown to our earlier painters, exception should, of course, be made of West, who under the king's patronage adorned the walls of chapels, churches, and halls with many square rods of painted canvas; but apart from the fact that West's work was indifferently decorative, all of it, done for specific places, remained in England. The great canvases like the "Christ Healing the Sick" and the "Death on a Pale Horse" were painted for no particular place and usually, like similar works by his pupils, were intended for itinerant exhibition.

The first opportunity for mural decoration in America was connected with the Rotunda of the Capitol at Washington, and we have seen what jealousies and intrigues were stirred up by the award of the commissions for the eight panels. Even here, however, there is no mural painting properly speaking. The eight panels remain eight pictures in heavy frames, with no attempt to fit them to the architecture or to unite them in a decorative whole. It could hardly be otherwise, for not only were there no traditions of mural work in America, but both in England and France, from which we

BLASHFIELD : DECORATION FOR BALTIMORE COURT HOUSE.

received our inspiration, the art was at its lowest ebb, being either little practised or with its fundamental requirements misunderstood. This explains why the real decoration of the Capitol was done not by native artists but by Constantino Brumidi, a political refugee who came to this country from Italy in 1855, and who was employed for many years at a fixed salary of ten dollars a day (with occasional extra allowances) to paint mythological allegories in the dome and along the friezes.

Brumidi was a decorative painter. Not only did he know the technical side of the craft, how to draw and paint large figures in distemper on the curved plaster surfaces, but he was the inheritor of the great Italian traditions which started with Raphael and Correggio, and were harmonized and codified by the later eclectic schools. He knew all the gods and goddesses of classical antiquity, their attributes and accessories, their floating, formless draperies, the way in which they should be grouped together, the scale on which they should be drawn to fit a given space, the architectural details necessary to bind the whole together, and when to paint in color and when to give variety by working in monotint. While thus certainly a decorative painter, Brumidi was with equal certainty a very bad one. Even in Italy the school to which he belonged was worn out and every particle of life and inspiration had departed from it. Its practitioners put together the old materials according to the old formulas with no feeling but with some skill. Brumidi and his compatriots who were associated with him, Capellano, Causici, Castigini, and the rest, lacked even this skill, being according to the Italian standard but indifferent workmen, and yet it is difficult to see what better could have been done at the time. The Art Commission appointed by Buchanan in 1859, which consisted of H. K. Brown, sculptor, and James R. Lambdin and Kensett, painters, criticised the work of the Italians and recommended the employment of native talent. But native artists would probably have done still worse if they had been able to work at all, which is doubtful.

The "frescoing" of the Italian journeyman painter was the only style of mural decoration recognized in the country at this time, and furnished what Goddesses of Liberty, figures of Justice, sporting cupids, or flowery garlands were needed for public buildings or for

private parlors.   One native school of decorators there was.   The old
painters of signs, coaches, and transparencies long persisted, and the
crowning triumphs of their skill, the Fifth Avenue stages of the
sixties and seventies, may still occasionally be seen serving as hotel
omnibuses in remote rural towns, their interiors adorned with ideal
landscapes and their exteriors gorgeous with golden scrolls enclosing
the " Battle of the Monitor and the Merrimac " or " Dexter lowering
the World's Trotting Record."   But the school rarely attempted
mural work and died out or was submerged by foreign competition
soon after their most glorious effort.

When during these years Congress voted money for a work of
art it was usually for a picture — a portrait of Washington or a landscape by Bierstadt.   But there is one exception, the commission
given to Leutze to decorate one of the staircases with the " Course
of Empire," and the result is interesting.   Leutze was both capable
and conscientious.   He was himself a part of the German art
movement of the time, which under the leadership of the older
Munich school had turned to covering the walls of palaces, churches,
and museums, both within and without, with allegorical and historical compositions.   He made a special trip to Germany to learn
the *technique* and another to the Rocky Mountains to be sure of
the scenery.   His decoration is a serious piece of work, carefully
drawn and carefully composed, although not in the least decoratively.   It is practically an enlarged Düsseldorf easel picture with
all the thoroughness of execution and commonplaceness of inspiration characteristic of the school, and yet it compares very well as
work with Kaulbach's enormous compositions in the stairway hall
of the Berlin Museum.   It would be more effective if its surroundings were better fitted to it; but, in spite of the decorative border
which the artist added at his own expense, it remains a patch of
color surrounded by whitewashed walls.   The texture of the surface
is particularly pleasing and as it has stood now for some forty years
without appreciable change, the technical methods employed would
seem worthy of study by some of our present decorators.

The " Course of Empire " had no successors and stands quite
alone in this country as an example of German decorative work.
Like other painting, decoration from this time on developed under

influences that had their origin mostly in France. The leadership in the movement belongs clearly to John La Farge. There is a decorative quality obvious in his easel pictures and in his illustrations, but in addition to this he had early made tentative essays in decoration on a larger scale. The "Saint Paul Preaching" was originally intended for the church of the Paulist Fathers; he had begun a "Crucifixion" of which only the side panels were completed, there had been work done in private houses, so that he was not entirely inexperienced when he received from Richardson, in 1776, the commission for the decoration of Trinity Church, Boston. The painting of such an interior so as to make of it an artistic whole was an undertaking of a sort absolutely unknown hitherto in the country. The artist has related the material difficulties under which the work was done, the unfinished state of the building, the haste imposed by limitations of time, the lack of trained workmen, the unreliability of the ordinary pigments furnished by the trade. He has also told the spirit that animated him. "I have always been impressed by one great quality never failing in the works of the past that we care for. It may be bungling like some of the Romanesque, for instance, or it may be extremely refined, like the Greek; but it is never like our usual modern work, which suggests machinery, that is to say, the absence of personality. I knew that our work at Trinity would have to be faulty, but this much I was able to accomplish, that almost every bit of it would be living, would be impossible to duplicate."

In order to do this he not only taught to the more intelligent of the ordinary workmen higher ideals, but he called to his assistance a number of the younger artists, unskilled in such work but able to understand his view-point, — Francis Lathrop, F. D. Millet, Saint Gaudens, George W. Maynard, S. L. Smith, Edwin G. Champney, George Rose, nearly all of whom afterwards did important independent work of their own. When the scaffolding was taken down and the stained glass windows were put in place, America possessed for the first time a complete and beautiful piece of interior decoration. The figure work, the borders and arabesques, the flat tints of the walls, all united into a harmony enlivened and diversified, but with no jarring note. Not only was it beautiful, "a construction in colors " (to use the artist's own phrase) with that distinction which only resolute avoidance of the commonplace in each minutest detail can give, but it was also emotional, stirring the feelings in the deep, vague way given only to fine color and fine music.

The work in Trinity Church was for La Farge the beginning of a season of decorative activity. Among the first commissions were the paintings in the chancel of St. Thomas Church in New York (recently utterly destroyed by fire together with the reredos by Saint Gaudens) and the paintings in the Church of the Incarnation, and there was also the color decoration of the interior of churches, — the Brick Church and the Paulist Church in New York and others in Newport and Portland, Maine, besides the work in private houses, as the ceiling with its inlaid panels done for Cornelius Vanderbilt or the two beautiful lunettes painted for Whitelaw Reid. The same year with these last he painted on the chancel wall of the Church of the Ascension in New York "The Ascension of Christ," his largest figure composition, and up to that time his most important work. There is no such unity of impression as at Trinity; the picture does not as there fuse into an indivisible unity with the rest of the church, but there is no jarring dissonance, and its separateness gives to the composition a deserved prominence. It is a noble work, and it would be difficult to find in recent times one that possesses more fully those qualities that we admire in the greatest masters of the past. With the "Ascension" there came a pause in La Farge's activity as a decorative painter, and when he recommenced the conditions had somewhat changed. Before describing those conditions, mention must be made of the decorations of William M. Hunt, who (for all their differences of temperament) did work more in harmony in style and feeling with La Farge than any of the later men.

It was within two years of the time that La Farge was asked by Richardson to decorate Trinity Church that Hunt received from Leopold Eidlitz, who had been jointly employed with Richardson to complete the State House at Albany, the commission for the Assembly Chamber of that building. In spite of its crowning his earlier ambitions, Hunt hesitated to undertake the unaccustomed task, but urged by admiring friends he finally accepted. As in the case of Trinity Church, there were material and technical difficulties, besides the artistic ones. The time was, as in the former case, absurdly short. There was also the question of the methods to be employed, there were the drawings and studies to be made and the scaffoldings to be erected, so that while the whole planning, preparation, and execution of the work took some six months the actual painting of the two lunettes, each forty-five by fifteen feet, was done in two months, just as the work at Trinity was undertaken and carried through in four.

It is likely that the limited time aided rather than hindered Hunt, for he was of the ardent, enthusiastic temper that rises to its fullest height in difficulties. He chose two subjects, " The Flight of Night " and " The Discoverer," which under various titles had long occupied his mind and on which he had already worked in various forms, and he painted them in his usual way, broadly, directly, careless of minute detail, and also of the construction of the picture which was an unfamiliar task for him. It seemed in places as if he had taken separate studies that pleased him and forced them together arbitrarily. As a whole, however, the pictures were very successful. They fitted admirably in their places, the figures were good in scale, the compositions were original and effective both in line and spot, and the color, always Hunt's strong point, was particularly fine. The plunging horses in the " Flight of Night " were relieved against contrasting clouds, and the backs of the sea nymphs glowed around the bark of the " Discoverer "; but they did not and could not harmonize with the rest of the room. The Assembly Chamber had an enormous vaulted roof of a yellowish sandstone, across which there had been cut bands of flat, stencil-like ornament, the bands being painted alternately vermilion and ultramarine, which, with the color of the stone and the other fittings, gave a tone to the room against which the paintings seemed to protest.

This, however, did not affect their merit. It was a time of art enthusiasm, and when they were displayed they were greatly admired. A bill was passed appropriating $100,000 for further decorations, and Hunt was filled with enthusiastic ideas for them when the governor vetoed the bill. Hunt's death followed soon after, and within a few years the vaulted roof, which had been boasted of as the greatest of its kind in the world, showed signs of weak-ness, and had to be taken down and replaced by a flat, wooden ceiling, which started from below the bottom of Hunt's pictures. Above it in the dark still remains all that is left of the "Discoverer" and the "Flight of Night," for they were painted directly on the stone and could not be removed.

Hunt's work at Albany was done in 1878, at the time when the returning "younger men" were beginning to make their presence most actively and aggressively felt in other fields of painting; but although it was a time of notable development in interior decoration, furniture, and all forms of applied art in which they had their share, the newcomers had to wait over a dozen years before they had a chance to show what they were capable of in figure decorations. As the Centennial Exhibition of 1876 had turned the popular attention to the beauties of industrial art, so the Columbian Exhibition of 1893 gave an opportunity for a display of mural painting. The manage-ment, wise in that as in other departments, chose the best available men, regardless of local or personal considerations. F. D. Millet was made director with C. Y. Turner as assistant, and under their influence Weir, Blashfield, Shirlaw, Reid, Reinhart, Beckwith, Sim-mons, Cox, Melchers, McEwen, and Lawrence Earle were chosen to decorate the Manufactures and Liberal Arts Building. The remu-neration was small, but the men seized eagerly the chance to attempt a branch of art new to almost all of them. The conditions were such that the painting had to be done on the grounds. The sayings and doings of the group of enthusiastic artists were written up and illus-trated in all the papers and magazines throughout the land, and when their work was finally disclosed, it was received with a chorus of praise. Looked at dispassionately across the intervening lapse of time it seems, while some of it was better and some worse, to have been as a whole rather bad. The men were inexperienced but the spaces were peculiarly difficult to decorate; and no skill could have solved the problem satisfactorily. In the dazzling whiteness of the huge colonnade that stretched for thousands and thousands of feet about the building, the eight little domes (they were in reality twenty odd feet across) could only be discovered with difficulty and studied with discomfort.

FIG. 119.—SARGENT : DOGMA OF THE REDEMPTION, PUBLIC LIBRARY, BOSTON.

Apart from this, however, the four colossal figures, which each artist placed within his dome, rarely came together in a decorative harmony of line and color. Blashfield's were probably the best, and he alone among the painters of domes possessed previous experience in decorative work. Experience told also in Maynard's Pompeian decoration of the Agricultural Building, which without having the novelty of that of some of his *confrères* was probably the most effective of any on the grounds. For the work was not confined to any one building. William de Leftwich Dodge had a huge composition in the dome of the Administration Building, Millet had a ceiling in the New York Building, and the work of Miss Cassatt and Mrs. MacMonnies, of Miss Lydia Field Emmet, Mrs. Sewell, Mrs. L. F. Fuller, and Mrs. Sherwood in the Woman's Building, while the difficulties of execution may not have been so great, certainly averaged as good as that of the men.

All of this mass of decoration mercifully vanished with that "White City" which contained it, but it had served its purpose. It had aroused the interest of the public and had done something toward training the artists. It was followed by some private orders, but the next great public commission went to men none of whom was represented at Chicago. Boston had just finished a very beautiful building for its Public Library, and private liberality offered a very considerable sum for its adornment. It was not a case for giving opportunities to untried men. The first commission went to Puvis de Chavannes, not only the first of European mural painters, but standing quite alone, with no rival of even approximately equal merit. In the other commissions, however, courage as well as discretion was shown, for they went to Abbey, Sargent, and Whistler, artists of the highest reputation, to be sure, but with little or no experience in decoration.

The work of Puvis was done under rather unfavorable circumstances. For the first time he prepared decorations for a building that he had not seen. The panels were small, the main decoration placed behind a row of arches, and the walls were of a highly polished yellow marble, but in spite of these hindrances the work is worthy of his great reputation. It is not American painting, but it is noted here because the stairway hall that contains it is perhaps the second example of complete, harmonious, and noble interior decoration in the country, as Trinity Church on the other side of Copley Square had been the first, — the clear, classic tranquillity of the one contrasting finely with the deeper, more emotional quality of the other.

It was not to be expected that a portrait painter, entirely unversed in decorative work, who had never represented anything not actually seen, and who was so bound to reality that he would not even alter the jarring tint of a necktie "out of his head," but required an actual change of the offending piece of apparel — it was not to be expected that such a man should at all equal the work of the most renowned decorative painter of the time; but all who were interested in art were enormously curious to see what Sargent with his amazing skill would make of his task. The statement that the work was to illustrate in some way the theological side of the library made conjecture no clearer, and when finally the decoration for the north end of the gallery was completed and shown in the Royal Academy, the British critics knew not what to make of it. It was too important to be ignored, and they described its size and shape, they explained at length the names and characters of the different figures; but of its artistic qualities, whether it was good or bad, hardly one ventured to express an opinion. Their reticence was natural, for the work was of a character to confound all pre-conceived notions of what it was likely to be. The brilliant painter of incisively personal portraits had produced a great imaginative composition filled with ideal figures, not the old classical gods and allegories, but strange, mysterious beings from obscure mythologies, typifying cruelty, hatred, and lust, and all the formless horrors and superstitions of the early ages; and amid these inextricably inter-woven and incomprehensible terrors, a subject race crushed beneath the yoke of the Egyptian and Assyrian cried to a great, unknown God, whose mighty hand stayed the arms of the oppressors, while beneath, a frieze of very human prophets denounced, mourned, or looked for the coming of a brighter day.

The intellectual element, the "invention," to use the old term, was as great as it was unexpected; the artistic quality was almost an equal surprise, for it was likewise of the greatest originality, and of a sort not displayed previously in the painter's work. The crimson, dull greenish black, and gold made a harmony of color strange but beautiful, the raising of much of the gilded ornament gave variety of surface, while the strongly colored figure of Moses in high relief bound the upper composition to the frieze, whose whites and grays united with the light wall beneath.

There was a long interval between the completion of this work and its successor. During the time the public had learned to appreciate the merits of the first decoration, and they confidently expected the same qualities in the second, only more brilliant, more strange, more dazzling. When it was finally in place it was found to be none of these things. The colors were mostly a dull, greenish blue and a brickish red, and for composition and arrangement the artist had frankly gone back to Byzantine models. After the first shock of surprise, however, the conviction began to gain ground that here was a work finer even than the first, a work so perfect technically that it might serve as a canon almost to decorative painters. All of the problems of the art, proportion, scale, symmetry without monotony, are solved with absolute and delicate sureness. The dull, dead color keeps the wall perfectly flat, the modelled and gilded ornaments vary the surface, the borders, the figures, the raised relief of the Crucifixion hold together within the limiting space with a perfection of balanced relation to each other; while the lower limb of the crucifix, breaking through the intervening moulding, joins the upper half to the lower in a perfect unity. Furthermore this method of treatment is felt to be not accidental but intentional, typifying the compression of freer, vaguer, and more human faith within the rigid bonds of dogma.

There remains to be decorated a long panel of wall. The subject chosen is said to be the Sermon on the Mount, the most difficult of all if, as may be conjectured, the intention is to contrast the simple tenderness of the Gospels with the savagery of the Old Testament and the aridity of the later theologians. The unexpected has already happened twice though, and we may confidently hope the artist will conclude his work with equal success. If in that case a suitable decoration should be added to bind the separate parts together, Boston could boast of still a third interior not easily surpassed in beauty and interest elsewhere.

The work of Abbey in Boston is hardly less remarkable technically than Sargent's. When he received the commission he was already painting pictures and had even done a small decoration in a New York hotel; but his handling was still inclined to be minute, and his values a trifle uncertain, as in the decoration mentioned. Suddenly, without any transitional work of which the public knew, he displayed the paintings for the Delivery Room of the library, canvas after canvas, crowded with more than life-size figures painted in the broadest, freest manner. There was something of Sargent in it and doubtless Abbey learned much from his friend, but there was more of his own, for Sargent's portrait *technique* could not be transferred to imaginative work. The easy, flowing brush work was a pleasure to see, and besides the new skill of the painter, all the old skill of the illustrator was there. The grouping of the figures, the faces, the costumes — all the little accessories were interesting and beautiful. The labor and ingenuity employed in creating the surroundings and paraphernalia of a mythic age were incalculable — the beholder entered into and dwelt in the strange land of legend as if it were reality.

When the canvases were finally in place, however, the effect was felt to be not so entirely and completely satisfying as that of the other work in the library. The Delivery Room was dark, with dark ceiling and woodwork, the pictures placed in a frieze about the room were separated only by flat mouldings a few inches wide, so that the light edge of one came next to the dark edge of another with disquieting effect, which was increased by the fact that the pictures were not painted flat on the surface of the canvas like a tapestry, but had atmosphere and depths of transparent shadow as pictures should, but as decorations, as a rule, should not. The color, too, in the faint light showed strangely blackish and dead in spite of crimson and azure and gold, in marked contrast to the prophets of Sargent on the floor above, who fairly glowed in their black and white against the gray background. These criticisms, it must be remembered, are made in comparison with the other work in the Boston Library. It is only in such company that we recall that no man masters all the resources of his art at once. There is recent work of Abbey's, like his " Trial of Queen Catherine," that

FIG. 120.—H. O. WALKER: LYRIC POETRY, LIBRARY OF CONGRESS, WASHINGTON.

[Copyright, 1896, by H. O. Walker; from a Copley Print. Copyright, 1899, by Curtis & Cameron, Publishers, Boston.]

though not painted as a decoration is more decorative than his Boston series.

The fourth commission for the Library, which was given to Whistler for a panel in the Reading Room, was not completed, if indeed it was ever seriously undertaken. At the time that it was offered the artist had no longer the enthusiasm and possibly not the physical force for a work requiring long-continued application. It is regrettable, for there is little work by Whistler of the first importance on public exhibition anywhere in the country, and doubly regrettable if the execution of the commission would have involved the supervision of the decoration of the rest of the room, for Whistler was a born decorator of peculiarly delicate and personal taste. The famous " Peacock Room," however, which is his best-known achievement in this branch of art, is not characteristic of his usual work, which was, on the contrary, of an extreme simplicity with a minimum of ornament, depending for its effect on refinements of tint, accent, and proportion.

While the Boston decorations were being completed, a great enthusiasm for mural painting had sprung up throughout the whole country. The amount of serious artistic work which has been accomplished in the last ten years is amazing. Few among the artists themselves would be able to give a complete list even of the more important commissions. Much of this work has gone into private houses and clubs, where it is not readily accessible to the public; much into hotels and banks and theatres, and much into public buildings properly so called. The cost of modern construction has become so great, interior fittings have become so elaborate, that the price of mural paintings is but a slight item in the grand total, and their employment is at times an economy as compared with the colored marbles, the inlaid wood, or the gilded bronze that would be expected in their place.

One of the earliest of the commissions was for the decoration in the Criminal Court building in New York, offered to the city by the Municipal Art Society and awarded to Simmons after an interesting public competition. About the same time, Blum began his two great compositions for the Mendelssohn Glee Club, and Cox, Thayer, Vedder, and La Farge were asked to decorate the new Walker Art building of Bowdoin College, Maine.   But the building which brought together again the great body of artists in friendly competition, somewhat as at Chicago, was the new Library of Congress at Washington.   Here, though, the conditions were not so impossible as at the great fair, skill had become greater and the work was to be permanent.   Most of the men who had served their apprenticeship at Chicago reappeared, but many more were added to them, — H. O. Walker, Benson, Alexander, Reid, Vedder, Charles Sprague Pearce, Barse, William B. Van Ingen, a score or more in all, and to each was given a room, a gallery, or a ceiling wherein to display his ability in accordance with the general comprehensive plan.   The Library, largely owing to its decoration, was a great popular and artistic success.   It was epoch-making in a way, for it was the first government building to be erected in the country where the architect had planned a complete artistic adornment as an integral part of the structure.   From it the public first learned what it had a right to expect in costly public works, and also that competent professional management not only produced better results than incompetent, but that it was cheaper — for the building was finished within the estimates contrary to all political precedent.

The decoration of the Library was a success — even the most captious critics admitted that — but it was not without defects.   If in the great reading room all of the details, from Blashfield's dome above down to the pavement below, united in perfect harmony, the same could not be said of the entrance hall, beautiful and effective though it was.   The tone of the marbles was cold and raw, the decorations were spotty and on the ceilings of the galleries insufficiently connected by intervening arabesques.   In the lesser rooms and corridors also the pictures often were in no close relation with their surroundings. They were, however, almost invariably good in themselves, there was very little inferior work, and there were some notable successes. Benson and Alexander made their first appearance as mural painters, as did also Walker, whose decorations were charming both in execution and sentiment, breathing the very spirit of the lyric poetry that they illustrated.   Simmons's work marked a great advance on anything that he had previously done, and Vedder's lunettes, which in spite of their great beauty of line and composition had seemed dull and almost muddy in color when shown by themselves, took their place as part of the architecture of the building more perfectly perhaps than any others.

The Library of Congress exercised an enormous educational influence, though it took a few years for it to become effective. The interval was filled by constantly increasing private orders. When the Waldorf-Astoria Hotel was enlarged, the architect for the decoration of the great ballroom secured the services of Blashfield and of Low (who had already done under most difficult conditions a charming ceiling in the ladies' parlor of the older building), while to Simmons was given a gallery which he filled with figures of the months and seasons, freer, surer, and more delightful even than his work in Washington. The Hotel Manhattan ordered an important decoration by Turner; Blashfield, Vedder, Mowbray, Simmons, Low, R. V. V. Sewell, were repeatedly called upon for the adornment of private houses; while banks and insurance companies gave commissions for lunette or ceiling decorations. Soon public commissions from the states and cities were added to these. Boston, while preserving the venerated dome and Beacon Street front of her ancient State House, enlarged the body of the building to many times its original size, and Simmons, Walker, and Reid were given orders for mural paintings in the Rotunda and Hall. The architect of the new Appellate Courts building in New York, under the promptings of the newly formed Society of Mural Painters, made the interior of his building a glowing mass of color and gold. Baltimore had a Court-house with peculiarly successful decorations by Blashfield and Turner, and Harrisburg, St. Paul, Des Moines, all had new State Houses that are even now receiving their crowning ornament at the hands of the painters. It is impossible to give the list of such orders, great or small, which have continued down to the present time.

It would be a mistake to suppose that this movement was confined to painting; it represents, on the contrary, a simultaneous advance in all the allied branches of the fine arts. In the Court of Honor of the Chicago Exposition, the soul of the great untravelled American public was stirred at the sight of a beauty undreamed of before, and in the Congressional Library it saw something of that

beauty made permanent and fitted for daily use. Those who beheld
had no theories of art, nor did they care much for professional standards; but they knew what they liked, and when increasing wealth
and population made new public buildings necessary, they took the
advice of the men whose works they had admired. These men had
that general agreement of opinion that comes from thorough training
along the same lines, and so professional authority was in a way
established. It was the architects that usually directed the choice
of sculptors and painters for the decorative work, and they did it as
a rule with excellent discretion.

While the recent increase of knowledge and ability in the three
arts has thus been along similar lines, it may be fairly claimed that
mural painting is, more than the rest, of native development. The
great exodus of architects to Paris to learn their trade was later than
that of the painters, and the traces of their training in the École des
Beaux Arts are still much in evidence; many of the decorative sculptors were both born and trained abroad, and much of the work is
not clearly distinguishable from that done in Europe; but with the
painters, while the principles of their art were learned in France,
the whole adapting of it to decorative purposes was done to fit local
conditions. The quantity of good work in proportion to our wealth
and territory is still small as compared with foreign countries, but
its quality is cause for satisfaction.

It is unmannerly to boast, and yet in justice it should be pointed
out that there is no living mural painter in Europe with the high
inspiration of John La Farge. Justice also demands the admission
that there is no other in America; but there is a group of men such
as Blashfield, Simmons, Vedder, Cox, and four or five others, whose
work is on a level with the best of the Old World. Like the easel
painters, they produce their effect by simpler means and with less
accumulated knowledge than the Europeans, but the effect does not
suffer from that. The decoration of the Library of Congress has
been admitted to be unsatisfactory, but it stands comparison with
that of the Hôtel de Ville in Paris. The latter is much the more
important building, and there was much more work put into it.
The body of French painters who were called in to adorn its halls
and salons was much larger than the corresponding body here,

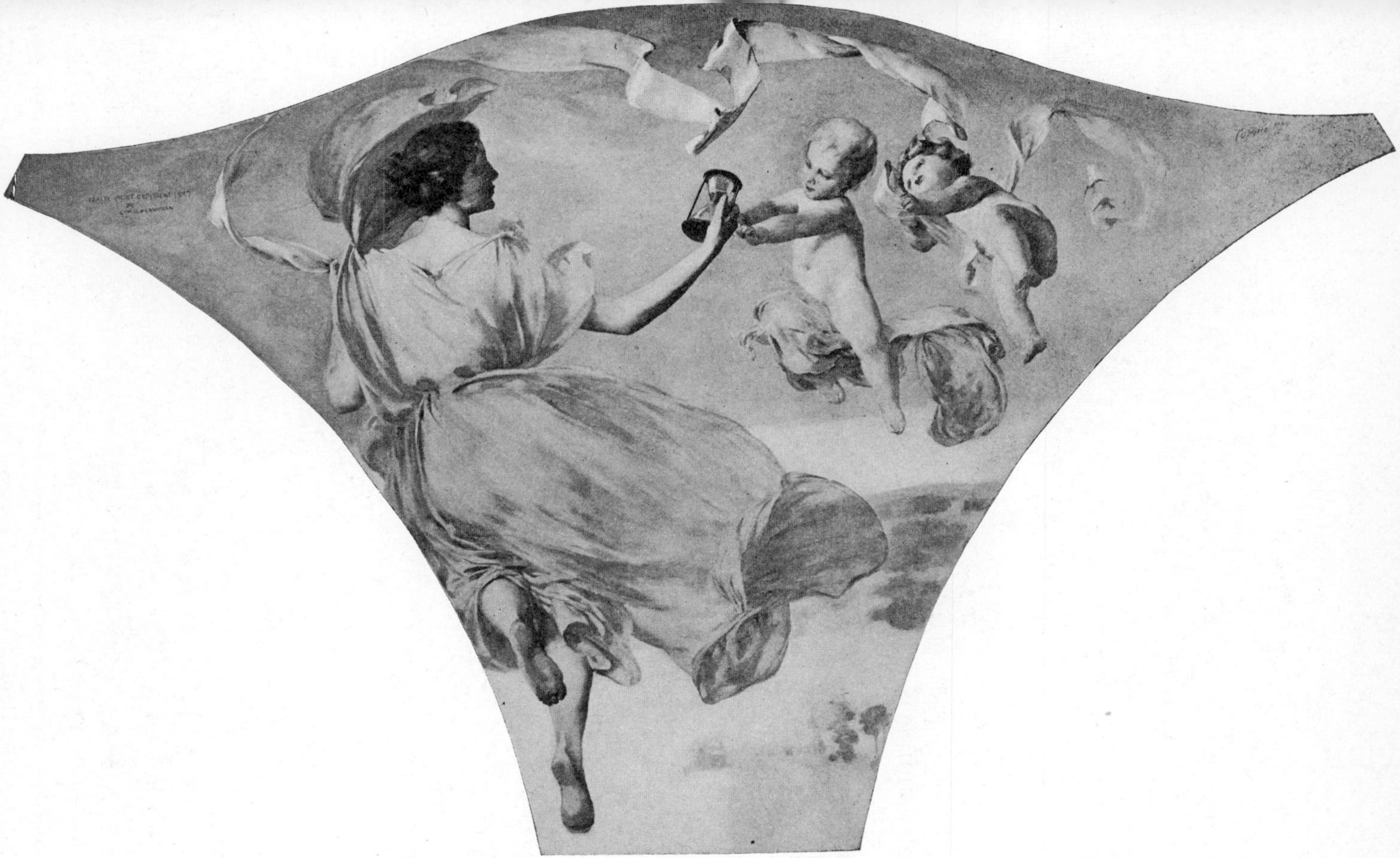

FIG. 121.—SIMMONS: JANUARY, WALDORF-ASTORIA HOTEL, NEW YORK.

[Copyright, 1899, by Edward E. Simmons; from a Copley Print. Copyright, 1899, by
Curtis & Cameron, Publishers, Boston.]

their skill was greater, their styles more original and varied, their knowledge of the resources of their art more complete. And yet the result, in proportion to the effort, was no better. Unity and dignity failed as often, and some of the canvases were offensively bad in their unfitness for their places, which was not the case in Washington. In the Congressional Library, moreover, American decoration was still in a formative state. In later works, like the St. Paul State House, it has approached far nearer completeness. There the whole building within and without forms a harmonious whole, with its hallways glowing with colored marbles, its Court Room decorated by La Farge, and its Assembly Chamber with decorations by Garnsey and two great allegorical compositions by Blashfield. These last, with their pure, sweet color, their delicate drawing, their multiplicity of detail, united with perfect clearness of general composition, their fulfilment of all the special requirements of mural painting, — scale, flatness, carrying power, — must satisfy the most exacting critic of *technique*.

What is lacking in American decorative painting generally is not skill. Any insufficiency in that is readily detected and sure to be supplied; what is lacking is a wider inspiration and a deeper emotion. Few men except La Farge have attempted to decorate a church. Lathrop did some painting in St. Bartholomew's, and many have designed stained glass windows, Reid especially having had a commission for all the windows and interior coloring of a small memorial church, but there has been almost no religious figure painting. This is mainly because the Roman Catholic churches are either poor or prefer to spend their money in other ways, while such decoration is not in accord with the customs of the other denominations; but there is also a feeling that though the artists might produce beautiful decoration, they are unlikely to enter into the deeper spirit of the place.

The younger artists no longer have the "deep insight into spiritual things" that Page or Inness possessed. They are of their time, with its cheerful optimism, its absorption in material affairs, and its desire to know and to enjoy. From this it comes that their work is also lacking in austerity, where austerity would be more suitable than richness or grace. The judgment of the humbler critics from the East Side that the Appellate Courts "looked like a music hall" expressed admiration, but not exactly of the type that Appellate Courts should produce. The spirit of our recent decorations has suited better the costly private houses, the banqueting halls, the ballrooms, the libraries, and the like than the graver judicial or legislative rooms where the minds of the occupants, it is supposed, are absorbed in serious thought upon the problems before them and averse to too insistent external beauties. Simmons's decoration in the Criminal Court building has a touch of this gravity, and there is something of it in the works of Vedder and Cox, but in general the artists seem to think with Filippo Lippi that "if you get simple beauty and naught else, you get about the best thing God invented." This richness, when it is a merit as well as when it is a defect, is not entirely due to the painters, but rather to the architects, who bring together all manner of precious marbles, gilding, mosaics, and stained glass, so that the canvases have to be keyed up to a similar degree of sumptuousness.

A chapter on American mural painting should not close without acknowledging side by side with the achievements of the figure painters the services of men like Maitland Armstrong, Frederic Crowninshield, and Elmer E. Garnsey, who, fully competent to do figure work themselves, and on occasion turning to it, have yet devoted the best of their talent to the more modest but not less important or difficult work of harmonizing the coloring, planning the arrangement, and designing the borders, arabesques, and all the infinite subsidiary detail. The present advance of artistic decoration is largely owing to their intelligence and good counsel.

FIG. 122. — HAWTHORNE: THE FISH, THE BOTTLE, AND THE BOY.

FIG. 123.— MILLER: THE OVAL MIRROR.

CHAPTER XXVIII

THE TURN OF THE CENTURY

ELEMENTS IN THE DEVELOPMENT OF PUBLIC TASTE. — ARCHITECTURAL INFLUENCE. — NEW ORGANIZATIONS. — THE ARMORY SHOW. — INDIVIDUALISM TO THE FORE

THIS book, first published in 1905, opens with a frank admission of the European origin of American painting and in succeeding chapters the persistence of European influences is freely recognized. But Isham had not traversed his subject over a period of more than a hundred years without sympathetically feeling the development of native traits and he was especially aware of their pressure at the turn of the century. He was chary, it is true, of drawing more than tentative conclusions as to the condition of the art in his own day, the subject of his closing pages. "The final standing of the different men is not yet established," he said, "the real tendency of the different artistic movements cannot yet be clearly foreseen." Yet on certain fundamental points he could see definitely enough. In the whole body of our painting he found sanity and wholesomeness. We were notably free from the baleful influence of the "Salon picture." It was characteristic of our art, too, to be cheerful and optimistic. Our annual exhibitions told of "the joy and beauty of life with hardly a discordant note," and the matter was summed up in the following passage :

"It is observable that the aim of the great majority of our painters is for purely artistic qualities rather than for intellectual or anecdotic ones, for beauty of line or form or composition or tone or color. . . . The present condition of painting in this country is thus, on the whole, sound and satisfying."

In other words the principles laid down by the forefathers have steadfastly endured. In taking over the British tradition Stuart and the rest took over a mode which passed with the social epoch with which it was allied, but as time went on the ideal of sound workmanship underlying that tradition was retained. It is one of the curious paradoxes of art that Benjamin West, while himself a mediocre painter, nevertheless inculcated in his American disciples the notions of technical efficiency which are indispensable to good painting. From his time down they got into the American blood and all through the evolution described in the foregoing pages, through earlier and later portraiture, through the mutations of genre and landscape painting, from the era of convention to that of individuality, the story is one of preoccupation with technique. Workmanship has improved along something like national lines. The prevailing aim has been that which Isham defined as one "for purely artistic qualities."

In a sequel to his reflections, embracing the activities of some twenty-odd years, it is, however, necessary to take account, at the outset, of elements outside as well as inside the studios. We must reckon with the atmosphere in which American painting has passed through its latest phases. The historian writing in 1905 must have had, necessarily, his doubts about public taste, and, consequently, the support given to artistic endeavor. It was not to be supposed, then, that "in America any more than elsewhere, the average man will ever become a discriminating art critic." But Isham had some prophetic insight and confidently remarked: "It seems probable, however, that we are on the eve of a great increase of artistic appreciation among the people." His surmise has been ratified. The movement to foster that appreciation is one of the leading phenomena of the last twenty-five years and it has had its effects.

It received powerful impetus from the renaissance in architecture begun by such masters as Richard M. Hunt, H. H. Richardson and Charles F. McKim and carried on by a host of their successors. In the nature of things there are no statistics available to buttress this contention, but it is nevertheless obviously permissible to assume a beneficent impact upon the American mind of the dignity and beauty embodied in countless public and private buildings all over the country. Slowly but decisively this enrichment of the background of our national life has contributed to the erection of better standards of taste, has stimulated artistic appreciation in all directions. Contemporaneously other educational forces have been reinvigorated and multiplied. Museums increase in number, their material resources are expanded with amazing rapidity, and these institutions are centres of more and more constructive administration. In enlarging the knowledge and sympathies of the

FIG. 124. — SEYFFERT: ROSE AND SILVER.

community they enlarge the artist's public and give him that much more encouragement.

The synchronous development of the art schools is one more salient outgrowth having a peculiar relation to our subject. Where the beginner was once virtually driven to seek instruction in France, Munich or Antwerp he may now find, on every hand, quite as adequate training at home. The new régime began some years ago, when men like Frank Duveneck, in Cincinnati, and William M. Chase, in New York, dispensed the ideas they had worked out abroad. But the American genius for organization has vastly extended the scope of the movement which they did so much to energize. The young painter is no longer required to depend upon Paris. His needs are abundantly supplied by the schools in New York, Boston, Chicago, Philadelphia and numerous other cities. Europe remains a stamping ground for the man of talent but as often as not he goes there not to learn his craft but to exercise it. As a school it is, for us, to-day, chiefly a "finishing school," as McKim saw it when he founded the American Academy in Rome. The fellowships there are for picked men, who have already learned their trade at home well enough to compete on serious terms for the prize of three years in Italy. Having mastered the rudiments they go to Rome to fertilize their minds, to see what the contemplation of grandeur and beauty will do to their imaginations. This is characteristic of a growing number of young American painters. Many of them, no doubt, enter as students the ateliers of Paris, but more of them go abroad on independent adventure bent. It is significant that those American painters who, in their maturity, reside more or less continuously in Europe, send home works which retain an individual accent. The point is stressed because in the pursuit of that accent lies the key to what the American painter has accomplished since the twentieth century was ushered in.

Resistance to crystallization may occasionally lead men to unfortunate, even grotesque lengths, but it is a truism that in itself it makes for progress, liberating personality and making breathing space for new ideas. Nothing is more characteristic of American painting than its recurrent disposition to change its moorings. As far back as 1877, as Isham has related, the Society of American Artists unfolded its own banner, flaunting it bravely until 1906, when the members went back in a body to the Academy of Design. Even while the Society was proudly functioning some of the best men in its ranks formed themselves into a detached group. Frank W. Benson, Joseph R. De Camp, T. W. Dewing, Childe Hassam, Willard L. Metcalf, Robert Reid, Edward Simmons, Edmund C. Tarbell, J. H. Twachtman and J. Alden Weir came forward in 1898 with their first exhibition as the "Ten American Painters." They thus went on for years until they, too, lapsed, as an organization, from the scene. They foreshadowed further ventures of a kindred liberalism. Perhaps the most important of these was the founding of the New Society of Artists in 1918 and the holding of its first exhibition in the following year. Childe Hassam was the first president and on his retirement after a year's service Gari Melchers was elected to the office. The personnel was much larger than that of the Ten, there being about fifty members, including such painters as George Bellows, George Luks, Maurice Sterne, Van Deering Perrine and Rockwell Kent, and, among the sculptors, Andrew O'Connor, James Earle Fraser and Paul Manship. There was a difference, too, in what might be designated as "the corporate aim." The varying individualities of the Ten were united by a predilection for exquisiteness in painting; they served, in the main, an ideal of beauty essentially gracious. The New Society, much larger in scale and consequently much more varied in scope, has bound together more diversified types and has included, along with graciousness, the conception of beauty which is content with the process of keeping a disinterested eye on the object. Its principal object has been to group together what it considered the best of every school or tendency.

The inference that the New Society was started in opposition to the National Academy has been denied and on ample authority the denial is repeated here. But the dominant tone of the exhibitions has clearly been one antipathetic to that conservatism which goes so often with academic discipline, and, indeed, the whole testimony of the newer movements now under discussion has been on the side of individualism. This is what makes them typical, representative, symptomatic of the latter-day drift of American painting. For twenty-five years reaction against academic, or, for that matter, any rule, has been in the air. The tendency which Isham hesitated to define, because its goal was not apparent when he wrote, by and by declared itself in one aspect at least, that disclosing a rebellion against authority, and, peculiarly, in har-

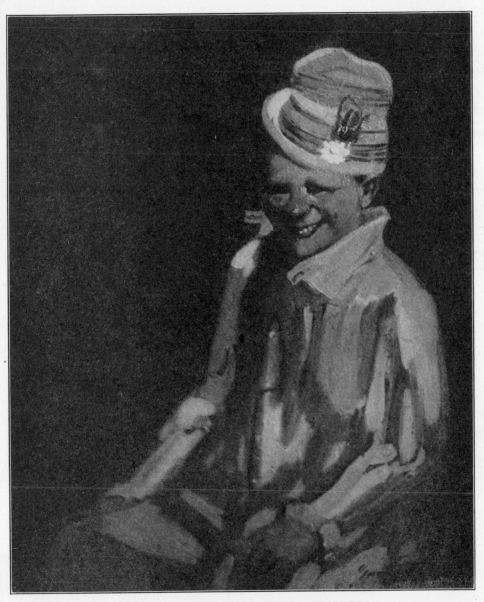

FIG. 125. — LUKS: NEW YEAR'S SHOOTER.

mony with the revival of experimentation all over the world. Group movements as well as personal initiative count in a situation of this kind. Hence the references to exhibitions in these pages and the citation now of one or two more which have served to illustrate a growing mood.

The Society of Independent Artists has had something of this illustrative character. It was incorporated in 1917, under the presidency of William J. Glackens. It was formed for the purpose of "holding exhibitions in which all artists may participate independently of the decision of juries." One section of its preliminary announcement should be quoted at greater length:

"There are no requirements for admission to the Society save the acceptance of its principles and the payment of the initiation fee of one dollar and the annual dues of five dollars. All exhibitors are thus members and all have a vote for the directors and on the decisions made by the Society at its annual meetings."

The character of the successive annual exhibitions held since 1917 has not been precisely thrilling. But that point is, in a sense, irrelevant. What justifies allusion to the Society of Independent Artists is its organized contribution to the sentiment of "self expression" which has especially marked the activities of the last two decades. The outcropping of this sentiment has often been associated with the dislocation of old tradition ascribed to the World War, but as a matter of fact the period of unrest antedates that cataclysm. The Post-Impressionism which brought Cezanne, Gauguin and Van Gogh to the fore was in being long before the war. Futurism and Cubism, in fact the whole apparatus of Modernism, arose in pre-war days. Glimpses of it were repeatedly afforded at "291," the gallery in Fifth Avenue where Alfred Stieglitz, the photographer, pioneered for its types, and it was as far back as 1913 that a memorable demonstration in favor of the newer hypotheses was made in New York. That affair was fathered by the Association of American Painters and Sculptors and the aim of this body was explained in a statement by the president, Arthur B. Davies, from which these extracts are taken:

"This is not an institution but an association. It is composed of persons of varying tastes and predilections, who are agreed on one thing, that the time has arrived for giving the public here the opportunity to see for themselves the results of new influences at work in other countries in an art way. In getting together the works of the European Moderns, the Society has embarked on no propaganda. It proposes to enter on no controversy with any institution. Its sole object is to put the paintings, sculptures and so on, on exhibition so that the intelligent may judge for themselves by themselves."

The exhibition forthwith opened in the Armory of the 69th Regiment that February was a notable gesture of openmindedness and rendered a valuable service. It was welcomed as a fine and stirring episode, marked by a tone of healthy independence. The sensationally eccentric nature of some of the exhibits gave to this "Armory Show," as it came to be called, a dubious notoriety, but in truth it was not freakish violence that was the determining factor in the character of the ensemble. The Association of American Painters and Sculptors was true to its manifesto. It began with Ingres and Delacroix, went on to Courbet, neglected the Barbizon group but came out strong for the Impressionists, and made a point of including such American exemplars of their influence as Alden Weir, John H. Twachtman and Childe Hassam. Places were found for paintings or drawings by Puvis de Chavannes, the American Albert P. Ryder, Odilon Redon, Matthew Maris, Whistler, Augustus John, George Bellows and others in a multi-colored array. Every here and there, piercing through the equable tone of this chorus, there could be heard the shrill notes of the Modernist — a Matisse, a Marcel Duchamp, a Desnoyer de Segonzac or a Kandinsky. To counterbalance the antique dignity of a Bourdelle in the department of sculpture there would be the curious exaggeration of an Archipenko. It was a banquet of "fine confused feeding." If it gave the American public an opportunity to judge the newer movements for itself, it as undoubtedly did much to stimulate the young American painter in his already fixed resolution to "gang his ain gait." The question of the intrinsic value of this or that work at the Armory is a question apart. What gave the exhibition its significance was just its demarcation of a line between the older generation, entrenched upon established ground, and the younger generation, discontented, inquisitive, and resolved to strike out for itself. There was no melodramatic levelling of traditional walls. The older generation carried on undisturbed. But it had received a challenge, the specific affirmation of a greater restlessness than any of which Isham had dreamed.

FIG. 126.— BELLOWS: EDITH CAVELL.

CHAPTER XXIX

THE SERVICE OF THE VETERANS

Last Glimpses of Whistler, La Farge and Their Generation. — The Fathers of the Cult for Brushwork. — Arthur B. Davies and Romantic Idealism. — The Factor of Mystery

THE melting of one generation into another, in the development of a school, usually involves the substitution of a new set of dominating ideas for an old one, a general re-orientation. But the transition is never made at a step, its phenomena "overlap," and then, too, there are events which detach attention from matters of influence, of tendency, and concentrate it upon purely personal issues. This is the case in regard to American painting at the stage now being considered. The leading men with whom Isham's later chapters were concerned were nothing if not distinctive individualities. They paid tribute to a common denominator of taste but each paid it in his own way. Whistler, for example, achieved his renown without ever taking on — or wanting to take on — the status of a *chef d'école*. As an etcher, to be sure, he blazed a trail which many have followed, but as a painter he remains isolated, a master of pure originality and incommunicable inspiration. The commentator on some of his earlier canvases may recall Courbet, or in the presence of some of his portraits may "drag in Velasquez." Before the "Nocturnes" which reveal his essential genius it is possible to think only of the Whistlerianism of Whistler, a vision of beauty such as no man preceding him ever had and no man since has renewed. The circumstance is typical of nearly the whole group reared in American art in the second half of the nineteenth century and giving the school in that period its special distinction.

Most of the men to whom reference is made were still living when Isham wrote, but have died since, and retrospective memorial exhibitions have afforded the opportunity to study them in a perspective which he admittedly lacked. In so far as such testimonials render a verdict they fill out the record which he could not carry to the end. Whistler, whose career he could trace in full, has been thus honored in Boston and New

York.   So has Sargent.   At the Metropolitan Museum there has been a long series of these historical affairs, summing up the life work of George Fuller, Thomas Eakins, Albert P. Ryder, Winslow Homer, Alden Weir, William M. Chase.   A later type, George Bellows, has had his place in the series, but the type now before us is he who helps to round out an epoch.   The men in question are the veterans upholding a long regnant tradition, destined, if the figure may be changed, to illuminate as with the rays of a sunset the explorations of their juniors.   They were, as has been intimated, significant of what is most precious in any school, unconventional genius.   Winslow Homer had it.   No one was ever more racily American than he, more intensely personal in a direct, almost artless dramatization of the sea.   He let the truth speak for itself, without any adventitious glamour, yet gave it an unmistakably free and new accent.   George Fuller spiritualized the truth.   Ryder based upon it moving interpretations of poetic, romantic and Biblical themes.   La Farge invested it with a profound beauty of color and with the distinction of style. If these artists are touched upon in this chapter it is not because Isham neglected them, but to emphasize the service rendered by the veterans down into very recent times.   A remark of Isham's on La Farge — "he seems to have rarely done anything where the result was not intended to be in itself beautiful or interesting," — applies to a great deal of the activity in which the older men shared.   Their generation is for nothing more gratefully to be remembered than for its point of view, its habit of "seeing beautifully."   This triumphed, in Fuller and Ryder, over technical limitations.   With Abbott Thayer, who knew all about technique, the urge toward beauty swept almost disdainfully above technical admonitions.

Thayer had been trained at the École des Beaux-Arts, under Gerome. He could draw like an angel when he was in the mood.   An appropriately scientific spirit was in him, as was shown by his discovery of the principle of protective coloration.   He needed the niceties of draughtsmanship in the working out of his hypothesis and whether with brush or pencil he could use them as he wanted them.   But, for his creative imagination, the beauty of his "Caritas," or "Winged Figure," or "Diana," was the main thing.   This duality of Thayer's was one of the most interesting things about him.   He was a born naturalist.   "Thayer's law," the subject of his great book published in 1909, "Concealing Coloration in

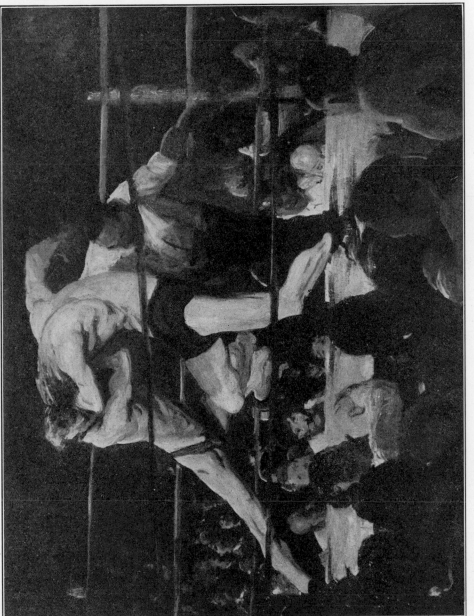

FIG. 127. — BELLOWS: STAG AT SHARKEY'S. THE HINMAN B. HURLBUT COLLECTION. CLEVELAND MUSEUM OF ART.

FIG. 128.— DU BOIS: ART LOVERS.

the Animal Kingdom," and the basis of that art of camouflage which was so potent in the World War, was the outcome of woodland studies which he had carried on all his life. Yet when he turned to pictorial invention the preoccupations of the scientist fell away like a garment and he was as much the creative designer as La Farge or Ryder or Vedder, the deeply sensitive interpreter of motherhood and childhood, the protagonist of a noble and wonderfully tender idealism. Beauty, it must be repeated, was predominantly his mistress, the beauty which in one form or another was the artistic aim of his epoch. It was a gracious epoch if it was anything. There is no mistaking the amenity uniting its diverse types. They painted charming pictures, a now comparatively unfashionable process. One or two of the veterans have gone on steadily painting such works — Thomas W. Dewing, with his visions of feminine loveliness in exquisite costume against simple backgrounds; George De Forest Brush, with his portraits and pictures marked by a Florentine sentiment and polished workmanship. In their workmanship, indeed, the older men have followed a consistently high standard and some of the strongest figures among them have brought it very much into the foreground, richly playing into the hands of the younger generation.

Duveneck and Chase, as has already been intimated, were of prime importance in this matter. Both were *virtuosi* of the brush and both excelled as teachers. The former in Cincinnati, his friend in New York, were the inspiring masters of countless students and they did more than develop amongst their pupils a turn for brushwork — they kept broadly in the air the idea to which the Society of American Artists owed so much, the idea that a picture, to be good, must be well painted. It would be difficult to exaggerate the value to our art of the precept and example given by the two men. They were the spiritual fathers of any number of capable craftsmen. Sargent exercised a more impersonal influence. He had pupils, now and then, but his gospel was disseminated chiefly through his works. Isham's hearty estimate of him was written when the painter's career had still many years to run but in respect to both merits and limitations it applies to the closing as well as the middle phase of Sargent's art. He continued as he began, the technician *in excelsis*, in his astounding manual efficiency a brilliant type of the American genius. His rank as a great portrait painter and a mighty man of his hands remains unshaken. Many attempts have been made to bend his

bow. His influence upon numerous portrait painters has been obvious.
But he died unrivalled in his *métier*. Others might beat him in the mural
decoration toward which he had a mistaken leaning. No one could
beat his best portraits and no one could beat his mastery and *élan* in
the painting of a realistic picture, in oils or in water colors.

The trail of Sargent leads inevitably into the domain of that more
objective mode of painting which is characteristic of recent groups. On
what a different note from that of a La Farge or a Thayer are his impressions pitched! Yet the old delicacy of feeling contrived to have its way
and though so many of its elder practitioners have passed from the scene,
the play of imagination goes on here and there. In 1905 Isham cited
Arthur B. Davies as "the romantic painter *par excellence*" and regarded his
work as being "as personal and as interesting as any done in the country
today." The career whose fuller unfolding the historian was not permitted
to register has abundantly confirmed this judgement and gives to Davies
a significance warranting further details on his art and its growth.

Davies was born at Utica in 1862 and received his earliest training
from his father's friend, Dwight Williams. That artist found him
already a budding draughtsman. He sought to make him a better one
but stimulated him also to form a finer habit of vision, a process in which
he was surprisingly soon successful. From his earliest works down
Davies has shown that half his art has been a matter of seeing and
feeling. Always he appears to have been an artist with an inner sense
of the beauty of the visible world. For a time it looked as if he were
to have no artistic development at all. Our pioneer landscapists,
Inness and Homer Martin, made a deep impression upon him in the early
seventies, when he was still only a lad, and deepened his taste, but a few
years after that he was still so far from following in their footsteps that
he had entered business in Chicago. The setback, if it is so to be regarded, was only nominal. It was as a draughtsman that he joined an
engineering expedition to Mexico in 1880 and when that venture was
concluded he was busy again as a student, first at the Art Institute in
Chicago and later at the Art Students' League in New York. In New
York he was occupied also as a magazine illustrator. He made his
début with a picture in a public exhibition in 1888. It was in the late
eighties that he made his first voyage abroad and in Italy surrendered
to the enchantment of Giorgione.

DAVIES : CHILDREN DANCING.

FIG. 129.—SLOAN: THE DUST STORM.

He could draw at this time with power and delicacy, his studies from the nude having an almost academic rectitude. But even then he had made his choice, to superimpose upon knowledge, upon searched-out structure, the romantic fabric which Isham so definitely signalized. The allusion just made to Giorgione connotes no specific Italianizing of his art. He was akin to the Venetian, as he was to the Florentine Piero di Cosimo, through a spontaneous and entirely natural *flair* for grace and charm. He came back to paint native scenes and figures, often mothers and their children, but they seized upon the imagination as denizens of a world which he had himself invented. When in the process of time he turned to mythological themes it was with the same originality. His Hylas goes through his amazing adventure with modern sails showing upon the horizon. Davies can mingle the motives of Pagan Greece and Puritan New England, his imagination somehow working the fusion and making it convincing. He comes of that sparse line of artists in whom a certain sublimely romantic make-believe takes on a beguiling reality. It is generally a little naïve and Davies has often seemed naïve. But this rare strain in old and modern art always really knows what it is about, which is to bring the beauty of remoteness nearer. Davies is representative of his time in that he is an experimentalist. His presidency of the organization responsible for the Armory Show has been noted in the preceding chapter. He was so far in sympathy with the Modernism there exploited that he turned Cubist for the decoration of a room and embellished it with a scheme of dancers in the new mode. He has worked in all the media and has tackled all kinds of subjects. He is a lithographer as well as a painter. On late travels in France he has made some remarkable water colors of the buildings in the château district, water colors in which landscape beauty counts as well as the picturesqueness of architecture. As recently as 1926 he was putting in place in International House, on Riverside Drive, in New York, a set of mural decorations, and at last accounts he was turning to the production of tapestry. He has manifested extraordinary versatility. Yet his place in American art is due to certain fixed, central elements, to his refined imagination, to his passion for romantic beauty, to his gift for enhancing the appeal of a theme not by deliberately poetizing it but by divining the poetry latent in it. He is the capturer of things which eyes less subtle would miss.

It is a golden gift, so seldom asserting itself in any school, anywhere, that every trace of it is doubly to be prized. American painting owes much to the men who have kept alight the tapers of imagination and fancy. Isham named some of them, La Farge, Vedder, Ryder, and Davies in his earlier manifestations. Davies, as we have seen, has carried the fire well on into the present day and it burns in the work of divers others. Eugene Savage is one of these torch bearers, a former fellow of the American Academy in Rome. He belongs more in the sphere of the mural painters but he has done many easel pictures striking an imaginative note, original in color, splendidly drawn and distinguished in style. Kenneth Hayes Miller is another of the band, grave in ideas and strong in workmanship. Gerald Leake is a third, working a vein kindred to that of Davies as regards themes and working it with some technical accomplishment. Through artists of such tendencies as these there goes on functioning the old instinct for the saturation of subject in reverie, in poetic emotion, in the feeling that springs not so much from the observation of life as from dreaming upon it. They touch the skirts of mystery. That was more characteristic of the older generation than it is of its successor.

FIG. 130.—BLUM: THE DANCE—FRAGMENT OF MURAL DECORATION.

CHAPTER XXX

PICTURE MAKING OLD AND NEW

Our period has been one of change, yet, as has been indicated, more than one previously established habit has had its later exemplars and there is a remark of Isham's, concerning the American student returning from Europe in the seventies, which perfectly fits the man of a subsequent movement. "He was rarely able to paint a clever genre picture, nor as a rule did he desire to do so. His ambition as well as his real feeling directed him to more purely artistic qualities, to refinement of drawing, beautiful color, skilful handling." The figure men amongst the Ten American Painters perfectly illustrated these observations. Tarbell's "Girl Crocheting," reproduced on an earlier page of this book, might be chosen as embodying the dominant mood, that of the figure portrayed with complete rejection of any dramatic purpose and enveloped in the charm of technical mastery, purely, with the note of personality tincturing that quality. The individual technician achieved his individually beautiful impression. With Weir an indefinably subtle refinement had its way. Tarbell had serenity and Benson vivacity. Reid and De Camp were the emphatically "decorative" members of the group. With all these varied contributors the group, as a group, stood for anything but the "mystery" to which attention has been called in the work of a man like Davies. On the contrary, keeping its eye on the object, it painted the figure as so much still life. That is one of the points of view that have been steadily maintained and made more general. Differences of temperament have promoted differences both of feeling and of style, but fundamentally the pictorial hypothesis that excludes sentiment or any "literary" implication has been a stable factor amongst innumerable American painters. Their appeal has been, too, very persuasive on just those grounds of technique and decorative taste.

Occasionally the work of the day is touched by a deeper emotionality.

Charles W. Hawthorne is a representative of the movement as it is tempered by reflection. A pupil of Chase's, he has exercised great skill in drawing and brushwork and to these elements he has added powerful color. On the less ponderable side of his work he has oscillated between striking virility and exceptional tenderness. He has painted pictures having a spiritualized maternity for their theme, in portraits bearing impersonal titles he has painted young women and girls from something like an idealistic angle, graceful, flower-like images — and then he has turned to the vigorous celebration of rude Gloucester fishing types. He is a finished, free craftsman with sympathy and an imaginative impulse directing his brush. The late Max Bohm disclosed a warm personal quality. He painted fishermen and their boats, women and children against natural backgrounds, and though his subjects were of the open air his gamut of color, resting on a low key, had the charm of invention rather than that of observation. He drew and painted with a large, bold gesture, his specific contribution. He, too, was essentially "decorative" but he raised the motive to a level of great dignity.

The foregoing painters, and others, point to a characteristic development — the exercise of technical ability touched by a delicate feeling. In pictures or in portraits which, like Hawthorne's, are half pictures, a pleasing figure is heightened in effect by grace of tone or workmanship. Karl Anderson, Edmund Greacen, Lilian Westcott Hale, R. Sloan Bredin, are among the leading types who give to adroitly painted things this faintly complex interest. The adroitness is widespread, with or without the intangible accent. Some of this abundant cleverness suggests sharply enough the influence of Paris. That is recalled by the pretty women of Frederick C. Frieseke and Richard E. Miller, drawn with all the necessary ease and accuracy, in the garden or at the dressing table, doing nothing in particular but having a certain surface engagingness of which their respective painters make the most. The light touch is constantly apparent in the paintings of such artists as Hilda Belcher, Leon Kronberg, and, to tell the truth, in those of a fairly large company of talented performers. It has a sedater gait, as though steadied by more or less academic discipline, in the work of Maurice Fromkes, Malcolm Parcell, Arthur Spear and others. A good deal of this work,

FIG. 131.—SAVAGE: BLESSED ARE THE POOR IN SPIRIT.

FIG. 132.—WINTER: CEILING—GREAT HALL IN CUNARD BUILDING.

grave or gay, has the defect of its quality. It denotes a livelier interest in the detached *morceau* than in the art of design, a reliance upon execution rather than upon invention.

The subject picture, as such, remains as it were in abeyance, save, chiefly, where more or less ambitious treatment of the nude lifts the still-life motive a bit above its wonted plane. The nude is ably handled by Leopold Seyffert, W. Sargeant Kendall, William Paxton, Philip Hale, Lilian Genthe and others. Seyffert recalls the temper — and polished facility — of the Salon. Philip Hale and Sargeant Kendall make a more imaginative approach to the subject. In their productions, typical of a considerable mass, the standard of workmanship is high and remains, on the whole, the principal thing to admire. They imply the atmosphere of the studio rather than that discovered through contact with life in the everyday world. Exceptions arise, to revert to the draped figure. John Costigan paints pastorals, pictures of sheep and their shepherdesses, carrying the theme out of doors definitely enough. The Taos painters, a group identifying themselves with the southwest country, have assiduously cultivated an Americanism having a more primitive picturesqueness than that of the great cities. The field supplied by the Indian has been actively explored by E. L. Blumenschein, Walter Ufer, Victor Higgins and numerous companions. In substance the group has brought into American painting romantic motives studied against a notably vivid background. Technically the Taos men have tended to a certain hardness and they have maintained, too, in spite of obvious relations with nature, a modicum of that studio atmosphere to which reference has been made.

It is a delicate distinction, this one between the studio and the external world, but it asserts itself clearly enough. It is in the studio that masterpieces are made — but they spring from communion with life and do not suggest, as so much modern work does suggest, the thing "posed." Consultation with life, conscious or unconscious, has been at the bottom of some of the most conspicuous phases of the subject here to be traced. When Isham signalized Robert Henri as, then, a member of the "younger group," he found his paintings "hardly more portraits than the 'Virgins' of Thayer." The girls in white or black of this painter were characterized as, among other things, "rather mysterious." As time has gone on Henri has succeeded, and has led a school, through nothing so much as

his glittering actuality.   He is of the tribe of Manet, leaving imaginative
picture making to other hands and contenting himself with the deft
registration of the thing seen.   His brush is supple and sure.   Travelling
much, he has portrayed any number of racial physiognomies.   The
ebullience of life is in them.   It is the object of some of his most representative contemporaries.

George Luks is one of them, a stalwart protagonist of the new philosophy which, if not flatly committed to art as prose, is still pretty
confident that it is not poetry.   It is based not so much on "seeing
beautifully" as on the virtue of seeing truthfully, a principle having at
least this to recommend it, that it may easily lead the man who practises
it to such beauty as resides in fine workmanship.   In the art of George
Luks it is the beauty of simple human things that is sought, the beauty
of things dispassionately regarded and set down with an exultant directness and strength.   It is not probable that he has depicted the tall
tenements of the East Side in New York City, the barrows at their base
and the tide of humanity flowing all through the scene, without some
response to its drab drama; but it is not philanthropic sentiment that
guides him.   He has no cause to champion.   He does not paint the poor
because they are poor.   He simply finds them so much honest, forth-
right, paintable material.   The slice of life available in the open streets
is, to him, thrillingly alive and that is enough.   He has attuned himself,
at rare intervals, to a delicate key.   "The Little Milliner," a notable
portrait-picture of his, is a most sensitively painted, charming thing.
At the other extreme, in "The Old Duchess," as he has ironically called
some battered derelict of the slums, he has been, in his aloof way, tragic.
But as a rule he is matter-of-fact, recording the character and movement of metropolitan life with a candid, brutally powerful simplicity.
Energetic and sweeping in style, he defines a contour with the force of a
blow, a technician with an inspiriting bravado about him.

George Bellows had much of this tempestuous virility, a man of great
gifts and solid achievement.   Born in Ohio in 1882, he died in 1925, one
of the dynamic figures of his generation.   The mass of work he left
behind him, paintings, drawings and lithographs, made inevitable the
memorial exhibition which was held at the Metropolitan Museum shortly
after his death.   He got his training from more than one instructor —
Kenneth Hayes Miller and Robert Henri among them — and he came to

HE WHO TOILS HERE
HATH SET HIS MARK

FIG. 133.—COVEY: TAPPING A CUPOLA.

put into practise in some of his pictures the recondite ideas of design developed by Jay Hambidge. He was a thoughtful picture maker, especially in his later years, when he painted his "Edith Cavell," a solemn nocturnal prison scene, and even produced, two years before his death, a "Crucifixion." Among his many lithographs, which not only exhibit mastery of a medium but include some of the finest passages of his draughtsmanship, there are designs both thoughtful and imaginative. It is tolerably certain that if he had lived he would have become a redoubtable composer. He could paint landscape, too, in some moods, having extraordinary depth and suggestiveness, landscapes like "A Wet Night" in which the very spirit of a moment and a place is expressed. But in the length and breadth of his art what distinguished Bellows was the energy and gusto with which he delineated familiar truth.

He was a natural realist, clear-eyed, racy, sincere, with a technique perfectly adapted to his frank impressions. He soon matured, expressing himself in direct fashion. His independent faculty swiftly declared itself during his pupilage under Henri and was almost immediately directed into channels of his own choosing. He painted much about New York, at one moment the upper shore line, with the Palisades looming beyond the river, at another some wagon-load of snow, halted in an obscure street. He would drift into the Park and paint the *frou frou* of feminity in his "Day in June," or beneath the shadow of the bridge he would extract beauty from the antics of the "wharf rats," noting lithe forms, odd movement and the amusing play of light and shadow, using a touch as eloquent as it was rapid. He was built like an athlete and had the tastes of one. He went to polo games, to the circus, to prize fights, and wherever he went he got the materials for pictures having the instantaneity of snap shots but nothing else of the camera. In a word, he painted life, the pulsing, multifarious life of his own day and generation, his own city and countryside. Though he would withdraw now and then into a seemingly "dated" world, to paint a portrait insistent upon some old-fashioned detail of dress or furniture, his work was rarely immobile. His impressions have animation, they have a bite partly due to the smashing celerity of his workmanship and partly due to his kindling human sympathy. Allusion has been made more than once in these pages to the vogue of experimentation in recent American painting. Bellows was an indefatigable experimentalist. His "Crucifixion" showed him to be hardly more than that and in a notable contrast that he painted in 1924, the "Two Women," he invited the same dubious verdict. He was an artist of uneven judgement. Perhaps it is truer to say that he was one of intermittent inspiration. When the dæmon visited him unqualifiedly in his valiantly adventurous career, always trying for some new goal, he could reach a splendid plane. The "Edith Cavell" proves that.

The realization of the scene, the poignant truth with which the painter puts before us the terrible walls, the soldiery, the noble figure of the victim and the dramatic light bringing one episode into relief and throwing the next into obscurity, afford arresting evidence of the power with which imagination can master unseen facts. Bellows rose to something near to greatness in this picture. It is interesting to observe that in painting it he escaped the limitations which usually dogged him as a colorist, and in quality of surface also improved upon his wonted habit.

Luks and Bellows have not by any means stood alone in the fearless interpretation of the raw incident in life. In fact they are indicative of the broad tendency which has been noted as breaking away from that of the older régime. The latter-day outlook upon life has been one incurious, objective, and more often cold than emotional. Here and there temperament has overflowed into a piquant enhancement of the subject. The little vignettes of urban life painted by Guy Pene Du Bois are edged by mordant wit. John Sloan has approved himself a sardonic satirist in his etchings. But in his paintings it has been his power rather than his humor that has brought him to the front. The pictures of what must presumably be called his middle period, pictures of streets, ferries, humble interiors and the like, have been noticeable for their able drawing, their handsome tone, and, above all, their bald truth.

A deep sincerity unites all these men and many more who have found the independence so sought after in our day. It vivifies the austere portraits and pictures of Eugene Speicher, the pondered workmanship of Leon Kroll, the works of men otherwise as unlike as the blithe Gifford Beal and the crisply exact Sidney Dickinson. Along with the sound craftsmanship that prevails it specifically denotes the main line that figure painting is following. It is no new thing in American art, but now it takes its start from a newer point of view and is allied with a measure of change. The purpose allied to this sincerity is not exactly, as in the

FIG. 134. — METCALF: LATE AFTERNOON, WINTER.

old days, to charm. That very word, it would seem, is a trifle out of date, and one can imagine the newer artist of to-day positively shying at ideas of grace, loveliness and the like. The truth is enough and in some cases it is a little dull. But from under some hands it emerges with unquestionable dignity and interest. Maurice Sterne, for example, has developed a high order of pictorial statement with small regard for "charm." He is a fine draughtsman and in the little Italian hill-town of Anticoli has given himself to meditations which have told perceptibly in the simple gravity of his compositions. Mention is made of his gravity. It is a trait found in numerous types, in Samuel Halpert, Henry L. McFee, and Andrew Dasburg. They are somewhat heavy-handed, as though the prosaic nature of their feeling affected their workmanship. It is a familiar note among the younger men. In their independence they have been indisposed to pursue either charm or the elasticity which springs from technical ease and authority.

CHAPTER XXXI

FURTHER STEPS IN MURAL PAINTING

THE RELEASE FROM CONVENTION. — ROBERT BLUM. — EDWIN A. ABBEY. — NATIONAL LIFE AND
THE SYMBOLIC MOTIVE. — EUGENE SAVAGE. — FORMAL ORNAMENTATION

How recent a growth American mural decoration has been is clearly
shown in an earlier chapter of this book. John La Farge practically
invented the subject with us in 1876, when Richardson turned over to
him the walls and windows of Trinity Church, in Boston. When Isham
wrote, mural painting could fairly be described, he thought, as "the
most interesting and most promising branch of our art," for it felt its
way with singular precocity. He testified to the value of the great venture at the Chicago Exposition in 1893, paused upon such later developments as those in the Boston Public Library and the Congressional
Library at Washington, and, alluding to divers public buildings like those
at Harrisburg and St. Paul, observed that they "are even now receiving
their crowning ornament at the hands of the painters." That was in
1905 and in the subsequent period Isham's optimism has been substantially ratified.

The architectural expansion which has been cited as a stimulus to the
betterment of public taste has in nothing more decisively made its influence manifest than in the widespread demand for collaboration amongst
architects, painters and sculptors. Isham noted the extension of this
activity from monumental structures into private houses. The whole
subject has been widened in scope. The decorative painter may be
called upon either to adorn an heroic wall or to design an overmantel.
He may be detached from full color and restricted to *grisaille*. He may
be employed like Robert W. Chanler in the production of screens, or he
may deviate, like Jules Guerin and Barry Faulkner, into the making of
huge, delightful maps. The mural painter has revived far more than the
designer of easel pictures the old practise of "doing a job of work" as it is
needed. There has been a change in him, as in his brethren. Isham
considered that the younger artists at work when he was writing no longer

FIG. 135.— PERRINE: IN THE PATH OF LIGHT.

had "deep insight into spiritual things." In its place the mural decorations of our time, broadly surveyed, have a closer contact with American life, thereby displaying the common impulse. It is a practical, material age and the painted pageants on our walls are primarily studies in form and color, of the ponderable element fitting a composition to its space. After that the symbolism employed, while often reverting to classical ideas, tends strongly to meet the modern mind half way and to ease the strain of traditional convention. The old, rather rigidly symmetrical pattern in which plow-shares, hour-glasses, cog-wheels and such-like accessories played a weighty part, is more often tempered nowadays by the free individualism to which reference has so often been made in these pages. All the time the mural painter has been entering more and more into the spirit of our period, pulling his share in the boat, no longer the tentative, even amateurish experimenter that he was when the National Society of Mural Painters was founded in 1895, but a sophisticated craftsman, executing with confidence the commissions which flow out of an advancing prosperity.

Again it is necessary to glance at the continuance of careers still progressing when Isham closed his narrative. La Farge was busy, especially in the west, up to the time of his death, painting monumental decorations which still left his vast canvas of "The Ascension" his greatest masterpiece but well maintaining the standard set therein. Kenyon Cox was similarly active down to the end and E. H. Blashfield has never laid down the brush. After his work in the Boston Public Library Sargent undertook an elaborate set of ceiling panels in the Art Museum of the same city and was occupied upon the completion of it in the last year of his life. These notes are pertinent as emphasizing the long sway of the older men who did so much for this, the youngest of all the branches of painting in American art. They were indispensable to its maturity as well as to its beginnings. And there will always remain something astonishing and admirable about the manner in which they turned from the easel to the wall, establishing here a virtually unprecedented idiom. Certain exemplars of the step demand further attention.

Robert Blum, born in Cincinnati in 1857 and lost to American art while in his prime, in 1903, was one of the natural technicians in our school, the inevitable comrade of a virtuoso like Chase. He had a deft turn of the wrist, a butterfly touch, which gave to his emulation of Fortuny and

Martin Rico an air of original ability.   When he painted his two panels
for the Mendelssohn Glee Club, long withdrawn from view on the
demolition of that organization's building, the emprise seemed flatly
impossible.   A light-handed improvisatore was set to the task of making
a great frieze for an architectural scheme.   To increase the problematical
nature of the episode he had to produce the work in a comparatively
small studio, stretching his canvas from roller to roller and painting it
with only a limited area visible at one time.   Yet on being put in place
these panels had unity and proved exactly adjusted to conditions, the pro-
cessions of merry dancers and minstrels beautifully embellishing the hall.

Blum's transformation from a painter of easel impressions into one
of mural decoration was accomplished at a leap.   Edwin A. Abbey,
born at Philadelphia in 1852, passed gradually from one phase of art to
another.   He began as an illustrator, using the pen, and achieved a fame
in that rôle, especially through his drawings for Shakespeare, that in
ordinary cases would leave a man satisfied.   He went on, instead, to
win distinction as a painter and after producing a large number of
admirable pictures still further developed his art.   He did not strike
twelve in his first decorations.   The traits of the illustrator survive in
the Grail panels that he did for the Boston Public Library.   Though he
took unimaginable pains with them, even going to Bayreuth in order
that a hearing of "Parsifal" might help him to recreate the atmosphere
of his theme, he made them picturesque without making them inalienable
parts of the wall.   Then, characteristically, he forged ahead and conquered a new field.   For the State Capitol of Harrisburg he painted a
portentous series of lunettes and panels, grandiose in scale but intimate
rather than grandiose in the interpretation of Pennsylvanian history
and industry.   When he commemorated "The Spirit of Vulcan" he
caused the god to hover over the scene but below he reproduced the
aspect of a modern steel mill and portrayed the workers in it from careful
studies of form and movement.   The old reconstructor of the world of
Herrick had come to grips with his own American cosmos and though
the decorations were painted in London they are in harmony with the
flair for life itself, here, in the America of to-day, which is the mark of
modern American art.   The symbolist in him was also a realist.

The immutable laws of mural decoration, laws of balance and order,
of a kind of inner organic symmetry answering to that of architecture,

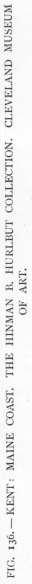

FIG. 136. — KENT: MAINE COAST. THE HINMAN B. HURLBUT COLLECTION. CLEVELAND MUSEUM OF ART.

react even upon that wayward factor called temperament, and recent developments in the art do not share altogether in the impressionism discernible in other forms. A monumental wall cannot be painted as the *morceau* is painted. The solidarity of mural decoration with other branches of painting is of the spirit, discreetly governed. The decorative mind has been liberated from preoccupation with exclusively academic modes but it still pays tribute to the unity which is the core of good design. This may be emphasized by reference to painters who have moved boldly upon the solution of modern problems through the unfolding of modern motives. Abbey's excursion into the mines and mills of his native state is a case in point. So is the work of John W. Alexander on the staircase walls of Carnegie Institute at Pittsburgh, the home of steel. Another effective exploiter of the same vein is Arthur Covey, whose decorations for a manufactory in the west drew their inspiration from the business going on in the establishment itself. "He Who Toils Here Hath Set His Mark," runs the legend inscribed upon one of them and the picture shows the brawny workmen at their accustomed stint, handling their hammers, managing their grim machines and the glowing metal passing through them. The decorator chants the epic of labor and "prettifies" nothing about it. At the same time he marshals the actors in his scene and delineates the background in such wise as to make the work an integral part of the wall. It is above all in their technique, in the acceptance of the peculiar conditions of their craft, that the mural painters have kept progress going. Constructive ideas underlie the productions of the most varying personalities.

The variety is obvious. It is true that, as Isham said, "deep insight into spiritual things" is, generally speaking, absent; but it is not quite without its spokesmen. There is spiritual force, supported by vibrating color, in the religious designs of Augustus Vincent Tack. Davies fuses realistic passages with others of pure idealism in his panels for International House. A notable leader among the younger men, Eugene Savage, who was born in Indiana in 1883, has produced for the Elks National Memorial at Chicago a series of large panels dedicated altogether to an idealistic symbolism. The elevated characteristics of his easel pictures, mentioned on a previous page, are carried into his decorative work and so manipulated as to ally themselves with monumental architecture. His Roman experience fostered in him a predilection for simple dignity in composition and for largeness in style. He has great linear authority. La Farge would have been interested in these paintings, related as they are to the classical tradition, though he would probably have admonished the artist on their occasional lapse from clarity into obscurity in the illustration of the Beatitudes as part and parcel of a memorial to those who shared in the World War. They stand high, nevertheless, as examples of intellectual painting and disciplined technique. In Italy Savage devoted himself to the Primitives and, among later masters, copied Raphael. He is representative of a feeling for Italian precedent which again and again crops out in the short history of American mural decoration.

Kenyon Cox was a reverent disciple of Veronese and he had a distinct influence. H. Siddons Mowbray owed as much to Pintoricchio when he abandoned the fantasies that he used to paint on the easel and gave himself to mural decoration in the library of J. Pierpont Morgan and in that of the University Club in New York. He revived with uncanny authority the formalized habit of the Renaissance, its lovely blues, its raised ornamentation in gold, its conventional design and its exquisite detail. His achievement and that of divers others gave a higher status to what Isham called the "more modest but not less important or difficult work" of the mural painter, the work which makes less of the figure than it does of arabesques, of the abstract and floral pattern. Isham mentioned the men in this nominally subordinate category active at the time, Maitland Armstrong, Frederic Crowninshield, both since dead, and Elmer Garnsey, who is still living. A fuller record must embrace the decorations by Mowbray cited above, similar designs by the late James Wall Finn, and, to-day, the work of Ezra Winter, who besides his figure work in various places has done some memorable ceilings in the great Cunard Building in New York. Miss Hildreth Meiere very recently has made an honorable place for herself in the corps of decorators dealing with formal motives. In any contemporary exhibition of decorative painting it is immediately plain that the cult for sheer ornamentation has taken on a greater importance than it once enjoyed; it has to-day a prouder relation to the more pictorial side of decorative art.

The latter phase of the subject renews here appreciation of the individuality which has been repeatedly designated as the prime agent in late developments. James Monroe Hewlett symbolizes the genius of

FIG. 137.— DAVIS: TRANQUILLITY.

Greek, Roman and Mediæval architecture in three huge decorations for a Masonic Temple. Bancel La Farge goes back to the church for his themes. Arthur Crisp is content to be playful. The late Howard Cushing was delicately and elegantly ingenious. Fred Dana Marsh, like Arthur Covey, has dared to paint a handler of steel at his job. Jules Guerin, whatever his subject, whether he be placing figures on the walls of the Lincoln Memorial or defining big maps on those of a railway station, makes mural decoration a restrained affair, one of a thin veil of color. The company of mural decorators is very large, much larger than Isham had occasion to observe, and its character is true to the canon fixed for it at the outset, workmanlike, architectural. But it is freer now than it was then. The invigorating contact of the American painter with contemporary life tells in this province as in others, that and the tendency to self-expression.

CHAPTER XXXII

OUT OF DOORS AND IN THE STUDIO

UNITY OF THE LANDSCAPE SCHOOL. — IMPRESSIONISM. — JOHN H. TWACHTMAN. — VAN DEERING PERRINE. — ROCKWELL KENT. — CHARLES H. DAVIS. — THE PORTRAIT PAINTERS. — MODERNISM

THE landscape painters have received extended treatment in this volume and their claim to consideration is always being renewed. In the nature of things, speaking as they do for our natural background, they make a strongly characteristic appeal. In the terminology of criticism they command beyond all peradventure the designation of a national school. Isham traced the evolution of that school from its inception, followed the Hudson River men along their path, and paused upon the major achievements marked in the works of Inness, Wyant and Homer Martin. The record was carried further, touching upon the traits of many of their juniors, but twenty-five years ago the full tale as regarded certain of these still remained to be told.

John H. Twachtman was in the upshot to prove a remarkable contributor to American art, a fact hardly foreshadowed by his earlier performances. Born in Cincinnati in 1853, he came to be one of Duveneck's young men, submitting to his influence at home and afterwards in Munich. He painted then under the canonical north light and though he broke away from the low tonality which Duveneck inculcated in his Rembrandtesque way he was very deliberate about it. When Twachtman proceeded to France he adhered to the cool grey illumination of a Parisian studio. A skilful craftsman, he produced acceptable but in no wise startling pictures. Nor was he immediately impressive as he became aware of the impressionistic ideas which Monet was putting into circulation. He was a man of original character and had to beat out a method for himself. When he had done this he emerged an artist of distinction.

He, too, has had his memorial exhibition, one filling a large room in the San Francisco Exposition of 1916, where the similar tribute paid to

FIG. 138.—UFER: MANUEL LA JEUNESSE.

Duveneck brought out in sharp contrast Twachtman's divergence from the direction of his apprenticeship. The old reliance upon an interior atmosphere had been altogether rejected. He had plunged into the open air and whether under the blaze of summer sunshine or the moist skies of winter had sought out the last tremulous nuances of atmospheric beauty. In his prime he was all for the most elusive delicacy, for the fugitive diaphanous effect, and without dreaming of a poetic purpose (Twachtman was one of the least "literary" of painters) he gave to his work a charm so exquisite that it seemed poetic. Charm exhales from his landscapes and from his almost ghostly impressions of flowers, the charm that is attributable to creative originality — and it rests upon the firm foundations of truth and design.

Twachtman was one of a group whose work, interesting in itself, is doubly so as demonstrating the growth of independence in American painting. Speaking of Weir's susceptibility to the influence of Manet and Monet, Isham parenthetically adds that he was moved "rather by the spirit of the time of which they were manifestations." The distinction was more deeply enforced by the pictures painted long after those words were set down. As Weir found himself he became only nominally a disciple of Monet. The silvery vibrations of his leafage and its fine texture denoted a wholly personal impressionism. It was so with Twachtman, in his infinitely delicate modulations of tone. It has been so with Childe Hassam, whose sparkling light and resonant color have revealed a singularly strong and confident temperament. Willard Metcalf also had this freshness of attack. His personal characteristic was a renunciation of the extreme breadth so often associated with impressionism. He availed himself to the full of the modern hypothesis of diffused luminosity, but he never let go the meticulous definition of form commended to him by his first master, the academic George L. Brown. The facts in Metcalf's pictures are beautifully drawn. What all these men did in their independent emulation of Monet, was to acclimatize here a principle, purely, and not a manner. Their Americanism counts pre-eminently in the establishment of their rank. The racy originality of impressionism in this country is by itself a piquant episode in the history of the subject. It could not, perhaps, have been otherwise, the whole landscape school is so thoroughly "of the soil."

There is some difficulty in distinguishing between the objective and subjective strains in our landscape painting. The disposition to paint a disinterested portrait of a place is undoubtedly in the ascendant, so that almost any collection of pictures in this field brings home first of all the tang of the American countryside. But this very type of record is often so sensitive that it amounts to much more than mere accurate statement. In some cases the heightening of the fact is explicable on the score of intentional or temperamental leanings toward romanticism. The visionary compositions of Elliot Daingerfield offer one instance. Others are supplied in the tapestry-like landscapes, with figures, of Frederick Ballard Williams, the exotic sumptuous pictures of George Elmer Browne, and the sylvan improvisations of Van Deering Perrine. Perrine is one of the most curiously interesting figures in recent American painting. When his talent first revealed itself, his pictures, done along the Palisades on the Hudson, were in so low a tone as sometimes to seem positively inky. They were original and fresh but left a desire for more light. When that came within the artist's scope it revolutionized his conception of nature and made his harmonies sing. He painted woodland glades, blown by the wind and flecked with flying leaves. Dancing children fluttered across the scene and playing over their little figures went a blaze of half-white, half-golden luminosity. The key of his earlier work was sombre. His new mood has been declaratory of a happy spirit. He has done some enchanting things, intensely individualized.

It was with the power and glamour of individuality that Rockwell Kent rose above the horizon, making his début with rocky coast scenes full of character, giving even the bleak face of a tall cliff something akin to a dramatic interest. He went on painting them with a notable feeling for mass and for line, using a simple but very appealing arrangement of color, and in general conveying the new, original conception of truth that lifts an artist well above the ruck. There has been no mistaking the distinctive nature of work like Perrine's and Kent's. It has flavor. It has, too, conspicuously, the note of the world of land and sea that lies beneath the American sky. Isham touched upon the "tonal" quality running through a great deal of American landscape painting that he had to describe, the low key that had developed, perhaps, from looking at pictures of nature rather than at nature itself. That habit has receded.

FIG. 139. — SPEICHER: MLLE. JEANNE BALZAC. THE HINMAN B. HURLBUT
COLLECTION. CLEVELAND MUSEUM OF ART.

It has not gone wholly down the wind but it no longer prevails as it once did.   There has kept pace with the diffusion of technical ability a great sharpening of the power of observation.   If a distinguishing merit of the school is to be named it is that of seeing things as they are, generally sympathetically, sometimes emotionally, and always faithfully   It is a realistic school, indebted alike to the broad naturalism which the Barbizon painters cultivated, to the taste for detail which the Hudson River men exaggerated, to the prismatic vision of the impressionists, and, most of all, to a certain matter-of-factness in the American blood.   It is a clearly recognizable portrait of nature that the representative painter of landscape gives us, intimate, often subtle, but rarely sentimental.

When Isham wrote of Charles H. Davis he underlined the fact that that artist had brought back direct vision and workmanship from a Parisian training.   In his maturity Davis recalls no French precedent whatever.   He paints a New England pasture with its fence of stones or rails, a meadow or a hilltop, trees standing beneath fleecy clouds, in such a way that the character of an American scene breathes from it as unmistakably as from a page of Thoreau.   He has a fluent technique and a faculty of design.   He is a true interpreter and one of the leaders of a surprisingly large host of landscape painters.

It is in the solidarity and abundance of their seemingly artless veracity that those painters have lifted their work to the plane of a national asset. Their realism has, also, an extraordinary range, revealing in this category the individuality to which it has been necessary again and again to recur. Contrast the desert scenes that Francis McComas paints in the west with the fishing streams that Frank W. Benson paints in the east.   The differences are not greater in the matter of subject than in that of style. Go from the keenly defined effects of Daniel Garber to the broad masses of W. L. Lathrop, or to the opalescent canvases of Ernest Lawson, or to the robust "natural magic" of John F. Carlson, Hobart Nichols, John Folinsbee, Edward Bruce, and so on through an always lengthening list. The spectacle is so rich, so varied, so convincing, that it leaves axiomatic the progressive movement of the school since this book first appeared.

For the same certitude in respect to portraiture it is necessary to look to fewer individuals.   There is no school of American portraiture as there is a school of American landscape art.   The portrait painters who have excelled have succeeded by virtue of very differently marked charac-

teristics.   The failure of anything like a common denominator to declare
itself in this field has been, on the other hand, satisfying enough.   It
implies the elimination of some of the dryness of academic formula.
The frank realism of the picture makers has been carried over into portraiture, a fact signally illustrated by the excursions of such men as
Luks and Bellows.   In their portraits a kind of ruthless bluntness has
superseded the suave convention which we fostered in an earlier generation.   Though sometimes momentarily disconcerting it is, among other
things, a relief after the more fashionable superficiality and "prettiness"
still much in evidence.   The serenity and the careful composition of the
historic schools is discouraged a good deal not by the habit of the studios
alone.   The high nervous tension of American life has irresistibly shaken
the poise of many an artist.   The business man of to-day, his wife and his
daughters, would hardly be pleased, or seem quite themselves, if they
were imaged forth in the style that satisfied their forefathers, sitting to
Stuart, Neagle, Sully or Inman.   The demand, which is met by a ready
supply, is for a brisk, direct and brightly decorative type of portrait.
Side by side goes occasional acceptance for work less flashing but
weightier.

Even the unhurried artist has his chance.   A pervasive calm marks
the grave portraits painted by Eugene Speicher.   Tenderness lurks
beneath those by Charles W. Hawthorne.   And there are many who
deal in penetrating characterization, in sympathetic vitalizing touches,
exercising, too, the crispest, deftest workmanship.   The group suffers,
as Isham found his contemporaries suffering, from the incursions of the
foreigners, many of whom are decidedly unworthy competitors.   Time
alone can redress the balance in this matter, but meanwhile the native
productions are aiding toward correction of present conditions.   There
is plenty of workmanlike, persuasive portrait portraiture.   Women
have made a fine record in the art.   Cecilia Beaux has had notable
colleagues in Helen Turner, Ellen Emmet Rand, Cecil Clark Davis and
Lilian Westcott Hale.   The men, besides those already mentioned,
include Charles Hopkinson, Albert Sterner, John C. Johansen, L. S.
Ipsen, Leopold Seyffert and others.   They are not as numerous as the
landscape painters or the figure men, though it must be remembered that
the craft, as a craft, has representatives among men active in other
fields.   Bellows painted both pictures and portraits.   Tarbell does the

FIG. 140. — HOPKINSON: NIKOLA PASHICH

same. So does Hawthorne. In their dual activity and in that of many others, it may be added, lies an indication of the groundswell of American painting, its eager, zestful participation in the movement of the time. Frank W. Benson, once almost exclusively a figure painter, is now chiefly known for his large and beautiful studies of still life. He turns from these frequently enough to depict the life of sportsmen, duck-shooters and the like, occupied in the midst of wild nature. He illustrates the temper of the whole school, energetic and adventurous.

How far will modernism carry those members of the school who are engaged upon that latest experiment of all? Isham was unsuspecting of the developments to be dated in this country, roughly, from the Armory Show. The period of unrest goes further back, as has been shown, but the purely modernistic hypothesis is very new, so new that it cannot be said to have entered at all into the body of American art. Any allusion to it here must constitute a post-script to the present volume rather than a continuation of Isham's narrative. It has been the subject of much discussion but this is scarcely relevant, the burden of proof resting upon the painters themselves rather than upon the assertions made about them. It is talent, not propaganda, that must determine the matter. Such talent as has come to the surface has seemed to justify itself apart from whatever recondite purpose may nominally have animated it. Charles Demuth may be taken as fairly illustrative. He paints, in a rather rigidly linear manner, a couple of chimneys leaning toward one another and calls the picture "Aucassin and Nicolete." The *jeu d'esprit* is no doubt harmless, but it is not particularly interesting. Then he draws a still-life motive, a cluster of fruit or what not, and takes the beholder captive with his pattern and the brilliance of his color. What modernism, as such, has done for him is not clearly perceptible. Georgia O'Keefe's floral forms wake the same dubiety. They are lovely in color and they are well drawn, but their æsthetic intention is elusive. John Marin, the water colorist, in whose works there sometimes appear fine passages of color, permits himself a looseness and obscurity in form that are merely baffling. Charles Sheeler, making amusing play with the sails of yachts and using polished line in the delineation of his objects, nevertheless inspires wonder as to the validity of his manner. Stefan Hirsch can draw and both in landscape and portraiture reveals talent, but when he reduces the skyscrapers of New York, rising above the river, to a cubical pattern, he briefly beguiles without quite establishing his impression as conclusively artistic.

The broad effect of these and many other modernists is one of a revulsion from academic convention, unaccompanied by more than a vague search after some new apparatus in the field of technique and design. Very often, too, amongst the rank and file, there is the suggestion of inchoate thought, imperfect observation of natural objects, and a kind of crude negation of ordinary ideas of sound workmanship. These ineffectual experimenters point simply to an order of ill-equipped "self-expression." Leaders and followers alike, those who pay more or less tribute to the unwritten laws of a craft and those who pay no tribute at all, remain merely puzzling. They have been functioning a very short time and their ultimate destination remains to be seen. Meanwhile the fact already noted is beyond question, that the bulk of American painting is untouched by modernism.

FIG. 141.—HIRSCH: NEW YORK. THE PHILLIPS MEMORIAL GALLERY, WASHINGTON.

BIBLIOGRAPHY

Compiled by Henry Meier, Prints Division, New York Public Library.

BIBLIOGRAPHY

CHASE, F. H. A Bibliography of American Art and Artists before 1835. (In: Dunlap's . . . The Arts of Design . . . v. 3, pp. 346-377)

DISTRICT OF COLUMBIA PUBLIC LIBRARY. Contemporary American Painters, Reference Lists Nos. 13-19. Washington, D. C., 1914-1926.
  Extensive periodical references.

GENERAL FEDERATION OF WOMEN'S CLUBS, Art Division. Study Outlines and Bibliography of American Art. Bridgewater, Mass., 1922.

INTERNATIONAL INDEX TO PERIODICALS. New York, 1907 to date.
  Indexes: American Magazine of Art, Arts, Arts and Decoration, and Memoirs and Proceedings of the American Academy of Arts and Sciences.

READERS' GUIDE TO PERIODICAL LITERATURE. New York, 1900 to date.
  Indexes: Art and Archæology, Arts and Decoration, and The International Studio.

SHAW, C. B. American Painters. Greenboro, N. C., 1927.

GENERAL BIOGRAPHY

APPLETON'S CYCLOPÆDIA OF AMERICAN BIOGRAPHY. New enlarged Edition. New York, 1887-1926. 10 v.

BENEZIT, E. Dictionnaire critique et documentaire des Peintres, Sculpteurs, Dessinateurs et Graveurs de tous les Temps et de tous les Pays. Paris, 1911-1923. 3 v.

BRYAN'S DICTIONARY OF PAINTERS AND ENGRAVERS. New Edition, New York, 1903-1905. 5 v.

CHAMPLIN AND PERKINS. Cyclopædia of Painters and Paintings. New York, 1886-1887; reprinted 1927. 4 v.

CLEMENT, C. E. Women in the Fine Arts. Boston, 1904.

CLEMENT AND HUTTON. Artists of the Nineteenth Century. Fully revised, Boston, 1907.

DEUTSCH-AMERIKANISCHES CONVERSATIONS-LEXICON. Edited by A. J. Schem. New York, 1869-1874. 11 v.
  Contains biographical sketches of American and German-American artists.

DICTIONARY OF NATIONAL BIOGRAPHY, with Supplements. Edited by Stephen and Lee. London, 1885-1913. 74 v.

FIELDING, M. Dictionary of American Painters, Sculptors, and Engravers. Philadelphia, 1926.

FRIENDS OF AMERICAN ART. Yearbook. Chicago, 1911-1915. 5 v.
  With bibliography, particularly periodical references, prepared by the Ryerson Library.

LIST OF PAINTERS, ETC., WORKING IN THIS COUNTRY BEFORE 1835. (In: Dunlap's . . . The Arts of Design . . . v. 3, pp. 281–343)

MICHIGAN STATE LIBRARY. Biographical Sketches of American Artists. 5th Ed. Lansing, 1924.

 With bibliography and periodical references.

NATIONAL CYCLOPEDIA OF AMERICAN BIOGRAPHY. Edited by distinguished Biographers. New York, 1893–1926. 19 v. Current v. A. 1924.

THIEME, U. AND F. BECKER. Allgemeines Lexikon der bildenden Kuenstler von der Antike bis zur Gegenwart. Leipzig, 1907–1927. 20 v. (Aa-Knilling). In Progress.

 The international standard dictionary of artists with copious references.

WHO IS WHO IN ART? (In: American Art Annual, 1925)

GENERAL HISTORY

AMERICAN ART ANNUAL. Washington, D. C., 1898 to date.

AMERICAN ART REVIEW. Boston, 1880–1881.

AMERICAN ART UNION. New York. Bulletin, 1848–1851; Transactions, 1839–1849.

AMERICAN ARTISTS AND THEIR WORKS by leading American Art Writers. Boston, 1895.

BALCH, E. S. Art in America before the Revolution. Philadelphia, 1908.

BENJAMIN, S. G. W. Our American Artists. Boston, 1886.

 Contents: W. H. Beard, A. F. Bellows, G. L. Brown, W. M. Chase, S. Colman, J. J. Enneking, R. S. Gifford, S. R. Gifford, D. Neal, W. Shirlaw, W. Thompson, T. W. Wood.

BRYANT, L. American Pictures and Their Painters. New York, 1925.

CAFFIN, C. H. Story of American Painting. New York, 1907.

CORTISSOZ, R. American Artists. New York, 1923.

CRONAU, R. Drei Jahrhunderte deutschen Lebens in Amerika. 2nd Ed. Berlin, 1924.

 German-American painters, pp. 549–574.

CUMMINGS, T. S. Historical Annals of the National Academy of Design. Philadelphia, 1865.

DUNLAP, W. A History of the Rise and Progress of the Arts of Design in the United States. New Edition by F. W. Bayley and C. E. Goodspeed. Boston, 1918. 3 v.

EHRICH, H. L. and W. L. One hundred early American Paintings. New York, 1918.

ELY, C. B. Modern Tendency in American Painting. New York, 1925.

FAUST, A. B. The German Element in the United States. Boston, 1909. 2 v. Bierstadt, Leutze, Marr; v. 2, pp. 293–306.

HENDERSON, H. W. The Pennsylvania Academy of the Fine Arts. Boston, 1911.

HOWE, W. E. A History of the Metropolitan Museum of Art with a Chapter on the early Institutions of Art in New York. New York, 1913.

KELBY, W. Notes on American Artists, 1754–1820, copied from Advertisements appearing in the Newspapers of the Day. New York, 1922.

LESTER, C. E. The Artists of America. New York, 1846.
> Contents: W. Allston, J. DeVeaux, H. Inman, R. Peale, G. Stuart, J. Trumbull, B. West.

LOW, W. H. A Painter's Progress. New York, 1910.

McSPADDEN, J. W. Famous Painters of America. New York, 1923.

MATHER, JR., F. J. The American Spirit in Art. (The Pageant of America, v. 12) New Haven, 1927.

MORGAN, J. H. Early American Painters. New York, 1921.

RÉAU, L. L'Art Français aux États-Unis. Paris, 1926.
> Treats of French artists in the United States, and of American artists in France.

SHELDON, G. W. American Painters. New York, 1879.

—— Recent Ideals of American Art. New York, 1888.

SHERMAN, F. F. American Painters of Yesterday and Today. New York, 1919.
> Contents: A. B. Davies, W. Eaton, G. Fuller, J. F. Murphy, D. W. Tryon, H. Watrous, B. West.

TUCKERMAN, H. T. Book of the Artists. New York, 1867.

VAN DYKE, J. C. American Painting and Its Tradition as represented by Inness, Wyant, Martin, Homer, La Farge, Whistler, Chase, Alexander, Sargent. New York, 1919.

STATE AND LOCAL HISTORY

CONNECTICUT. *French, H. W.* Art and Artists in Connecticut. Boston, 1879.

INDIANA. *Burnet, M. Q.* Art and Artists of Indiana. New York, 1921.

LOUISIANA. *Cline, I. M.* Arts and Artists in New Orleans during the last Century. New Orleans, 1922.
> *Cline, I. M.* Contemporary Art and Artists in New Orleans. New Orleans, 1924.

MASSACHUSETTS. *Belknap, H. W.* Artists and Craftsmen of Essex County, Massachusetts. Salem, 1927.

NEW ENGLAND. *Robinson, F. T.* Living New England Artists. Boston, 1888.

PENNSYLVANIA. *Sartain, J.* Reminiscences of a very old Man, 1808–1897. New York, 1900.
> Early Philadelphia artists.

RHODE ISLAND. *Arnold, J. N.* . . . Art and Artists in Rhode Island. Pawtucket, R. I., 1905.

SPECIAL SUBJECTS

FIGURE AND LANDSCAPE PAINTING. Book of American Figure Painters. Philadelphia, 1886.
> *Sherman, F. F.* Landscape and Figure Painters of America. New York, 1917.

MINIATURE PAINTING. *Bolton, T.* Early American Portrait Painters in Miniature. New York, 1921.
> *Foster, J. J.* A Dictionary of Painters of Miniature, 1525–1850. New York, 1926.
> *Foster, J. J.* Miniature Painters, British and Foreign, with some Account of those who practised in America in the Eighteenth Century. London, 1903, 2 v.

Wehle, H. B. and T. Bolton. American Miniatures, 1720–1850. Garden City, N. Y., 1927.

Wharton, A. H. Heirlooms in Miniatures . . . with Reproduction of the best Examples of colonial, revolutionary, and modern Miniature Painters. 1898.

MURAL PAINTING. *Allen, E. B.* Early American Wall Paintings, 1710–1850. New Haven, 1926.

Blashfield, E. H. Mural Painting in America. New York, 1913.

King, P. American Mural Painting. Boston, 1902.

Mural Paintings in the Public Buildings in the United States. (In: American Art Annual, 1922, v. 19, pp. 407–438)

PORTRAIT PAINTING. *Baker, W. S.* The engraved Portraits of Washington with Notices of the Originals and brief biographical Sketches of their Painters. Philadelphia, 1880.

Bayley, F. W. Little known early American Portrait Painters. Boston, 1915– 1917. 3 v.

Bolton, T. Early American Portrait Draughtsmen in Crayons. New York, 1923.

Hart, C. H. Catalogue of the engraved Portraits of Washington.
The Grolier Club, New York, 1904.
Portraits engraved after Peale, Trumbull, Stuart and others; supersedes Baker.

Johnston, E. B. Original Portraits of Washington. Boston, 1882.
With biographical sketches of their painters.

Munn, C. A. Three types of Washington portraits, John Trumbull, Chas. Wilson Peale, Gilbert Stuart. Philadelphia, 1908.

STILL-LIFE PAINTING. *Bye, A. E.* Pots and Pans. Princeton, 1921.

WATER-COLOR PAINTING. *Gallatin, A. E.* American Water-colourists. New York, 1922.

INDIVIDUAL PAINTERS

ABBEY, E. A. *Lucas, E. V.* Edwin Austin Abbey, the Record of his Life and Work. New York, 1921, 2 v.

ABDY, R. M. Old California, being ten Reproductions of original Water-colors by Rowena Meeks Abdy with a Foreword by G. Piazzoni, and an Introduction and descriptive Text by H. B. Abdy. San Francisco, 1924.

ALEXANDER, J. W. *Agar, J. G.* Address at a Testimonial to John W. Alexander. New York, 1916.

John White Alexander Memorial Exhibition. Carnegie Institute. Pittsburgh, 1916.

ALLSTON, W. *Flagg, J. B.* Life and Letters of Washington Allston. New York, 1892.

Peabody, E. P. Last Evening with Allston. Boston, 1886.

Sweetser, M. F. Life of Allston. Cambridge, 1879.

ATKINS, A. *Porter, B.* Arthur Atkins, Extracts from the Letters with Notes on Painting and Landscape. San Francisco, 1908.

BELLOWS, G. George Bellows Memorial Exhibition. Metropolitan Museum of Art. New York, 1925.

BINGHAM, G. C. *Rusk, F. H.* George Caleb Bingham. Jefferson City, Mo., 1917.

BLACKBURN, J. *Park, L.* Joseph Blackburn, a colonial Portrait Painter, with a descriptive List of his Work. Worcester, Mass., 1923.

BLAKELOCK, R. A. *Daingerfield, E.* Ralph Albert Blakelock. New York, 1914.
   Young's Art Galleries. Blakelock, his Art and his Family. Chicago, 1916.

CASSATT, M. *Segard, A.* Un Peintre des Enfants et des Mères. Paris, 1913.

CHASE, W. *Roof, K. M.* The Life and Art of William Merritt Chase. New York, 1917.
   Newhouse Galleries, Inc. William Merritt Chase, Paintings. New York, 1927.

CHURCH, F. E. Paintings by Frederic E. Church. Special Exhibition of the Metropolitan Museum of Art. New York, 1900.

COLE, T. *Bolton, S. K.* Lives of poor Boys who became famous. New York, 1913.
   Greene, G. W. Biographical Studies. New York, 1860.
   Noble, L. L. Life and Works of Thomas Cole. New York, 1853.

COPLEY, J. S. *Amory, M. B.* Domestic and Artistic Life of John Singleton Copley. Boston, 1882.
   Bayley, F. W. The Life and Works of John Singleton Copley, founded on the Work of A. Th. Perkins. Boston, 1915.
   Letters and Papers of John Singleton Copley and Henry Pelham, 1739–1876. Massachusetts Historical Society Collections, v. 71. Boston, 1914.
   Perkins, A. T. Life of Copley. Boston, 1873.

CUCUEL, E. *Ostini, Fritz von.* Der Maler Edward Cucuel. Amalthea Verlag. Leipzig, 1925.

DAVIES, A. B. *Phillips, D. and Others.* Arthur B. Davies; Essays on the Man and his Art. New York, 1924.

DEMMLER, F. A. *Price, L.* Immortal Youth, a Memoir of Fred. A. Demmler. Boston, 1919.

DEMUTH, C. *Gallatin, A. E.* Charles Demuth. New York, 1927.

DEVEAUX, J. *Gibbes, R. W.* A Memoir of James DeVeaux. Columbia, S. C., 1846.

DURAND, A. B. *Durand, J.* The Life and Times of Asher B. Durand. New York, 1894.

DUVENECK, F. *Heermann, N.* Frank Duveneck. Boston, 1918.

FUCHS, E. With Pencil, Brush and Chisel, the Life of an Artist. New York, 1925.

FULLER, G. *Millet, J. B.* George Fuller, his Life and Works. Boston, 1886.
   Tack, A. V. Centennial Exhibition of the Works of George Fuller. Metropolitan Museum of Art, New York, 1923.

FULTON, R. *Colden, C. D.* Life of Robert Fulton, New York, 1817.
   Dickinson, H. W. Robert Fulton, Engineer and Artist. London, 1913.
   Sutcliffe, A. C. Robert Fulton and the Clermont. New York, 1909.

GIFFORD, S. R. Memorial Meeting of the Century. New York, 1880.
   Weir, J. F. Sanford R. Gifford. Metropolitan Museum of Art. New York, 1881.

GLACKENS, W. *Watson, F.* William Glackens. New York, 1923.

HARDING, C. H. *White, M. E.* A Sketch of Chester Harding, Artist, drawn by his own Hand. Boston, 1890.

HASSAM, C.   *Pousette-Dart, N.*   Childe Hassam.   New York, 1922.

HEALY, G. P. A.   *Bigot, M.*   Life of George P. A. Healy.   Chicago, 1913.
   Healy, G. P. A.   Reminiscences of a Portrait Painter.   Chicago, 1894.

HENRI, R.   *Yarrow, W. and L. Bouche.*   Robert Henri, his Life and Works.   New
   York, 1921.

HOMER, W.   *Downes, W. H.*   The Life and Works of Winslow Homer.   Boston, 1911.
   Cox, K.   Winslow Homer.   New York, 1914.
   Pousette-Dart, N.   Winslow Homer.   New York, 1923.

HUNT, W. M.   *Angell, H. C.*   Records of William Morris Hunt.   Boston, 1881.
   Bartol, C. A.   Principles and Portraits.   Boston, 1880.
   Knowlton, H. M.   Art-Life of William Morris Hunt.   Boston, 1898.
   Shannon, M. A. S.   Boston Days of William Morris Hunt.   Boston, 1923.

INNESS, G.   *American Art Association.*   Oil Paintings and Water-Colors by George
   Inness, the Collection of the Artist's Daughter.   New York, 1927.
   Daingerfield, E.   Fifty Paintings by George Inness.   New York, 1913.
   Daingerfield, E.   George Inness, the Man and his Art.   New York, 1911.
   Inness, Jr., G.   Life Art and Letters of George Inness.   New York, 1917.
   Trumble, A.   George Inness, a Memorial of the Student, the Artist, and the
   Man.   New York, 1895.

JONES, R. E.   Drawings from the Theatre by Robert Edmund Jones.   New York,
   1925.
   Macgowan, K.   The Theatre of Tomorrow.   New York, 1921.

KENNSETT, J. F.   Proceedings at a Meeting of the Century Association in Memory
   of John F. Kennsett.   New York, 1872.

LA FARGE, J.   *Cortissoz, R.*   John La Farge, a Memoir and a Study.   Boston, 1911.
   Waern, C.   John La Farge, Artist and Writer.   London, 1896.

LE MOYNE.   *Stevens, Henry.*   Thomas Hariot . . . with Notices of his Associates
   . . . London, 1900.
   Contains much information about Le Moyne.

LESLIE, C. R.   Autobiographical Recollections.   Boston, 1860.

LEUTZE, E.   *Blanckarts, M.*   Duesseldorfer Kuenstler.   Stuttgart, 1877.
   Mueller, W.   Duesseldorfer Kuenstler.   Leipzig, 1854.
   Schaarschmidt, F.   Zur Geschichte der Duesseldorfer Kunst insbesondere im
   XIX.   Jahrhundert.   Duesseldorf, 1902.

LOW, W. H.   A Chronicle of Friendships, 1873–1900.   New York, 1908.

MACKNIGHT, D.   *Fitzgerald, D.*   Dodge Macknight.   Brookline, Mass., 1916.

MARTIN, H. D.   *Carroll, D. H.*   Fifty-eight Paintings by Homer D. Martin.   New
   York, 1913.
   Mather, Jr., F. J.   Homer Martin, New York, 1912.

MILLET, F. D.   *American Federation of Arts.*   Francis Davis Millet Memorial
   Meeting.   Washington, D. C., 1912.

MORAN, E.   *Sutro, T.*   . . . Thirteen historical Marine Paintings by Edward
   Moran, New York, 1905.

MORSE, S. F. B.   *Morse, E. L.*   Letters and Journals of Samuel F. B. Morse.
   Boston, 1914.   2 v.
   Prime, S. I.   Life of Samuel F. B. Morse.   New York, 1875.

MOSLER, H. COLLMANN.   *S. M. Jews in Art.*   Cincinnati, 1909.

MUNN, G. F. M. *Munn, M. C. and M. R. Cabot.* The Art of George Frederick Munn. New York, 1916.

MURPHY, J. F. *Hudnut, A. M.* An Appreciation of Mr. Murphy and his Work. (In : Paintings and Drawings by J. F. Murphy) American Art Association. New York, 1926.

NEAGLE, J. *Pennsylvania Academy of the Fine Arts.* Catalogue of an Exhibition of Portraits by John Neagle. Philadelphia, 1925.

OERTEL, J. A. *Oertel, J. F.* A Vision realized, a Life Story of Rev. J. A. Oertel, D.D., Artist, Priest, Missionary. Milwaukee, 1917.

PEALE, C. W. ; J. ; and R. *Pennsylvania Academy of the Fine Arts.* Exhibition of Portraits by Chas. Wilson Peale, and James Peale, and Rembrandt Peale. Philadelphia, 1923.

PYLE, H. *Abbott, C. D.* Howard Pyle, a Chronicle. New York, 1925.
   Morse, W. S. and G. Brincklé. Howard Pyle, a Record of his Illustrations and Writings. Washington, Del., 1921.

REMICK, C. *Cunningham, H. W.* Christian Remick, an early Boston Artist. Boston, 1904.

RICHARDS, W. T. *Morris, H. S.* William T. Richards. Philadelphia, 1912.

RIMMER, W. *Bartlett, T. H.* The Art Life of William Rimmer. Boston, 1882.

RYDER, A. P. *Sherman, F. F.* Albert Pinkham Ryder. New York, 1920.

SARGENT, J. S. *Charteris, E.* John Sargent. New York, 1927.
   Downes, W. H. John S. Sargent, his Life and Work. Boston, 1925.
   Manson, J. B. and Mrs. Meynell. The Work of John Sargent. New York, 1927.
   Metropolitan Museum of Art. Memorial Exhibition of John Singer Sargent. New York, 1926.
   Museum of Fine Arts. . . . Memorial Exhibition of the Works of the late John Singer Sargent. Boston, 1925.
   Pousette-Dart, N. John Singer Sargent. New York, 1924.
   Wood, T. M. Sargent. New York, 1909.

SCHREYVOGEL, C. My Bunkie and Others. New York, 1909.

SELLSTEDT, L. G. From Forecastle to Academy . . . an Autobiography. Buffalo, 1904.

SIMMONS, E. From Seven to Seventy, Memoirs of a Painter and a Yankee. New York, 1922.

SLOAN, J. *Gallatin, A. E.* John Sloan. New York, 1925.

STUART, G. *Fielding, M.* Gilbert Stuart's Portraits of George Washington. Philadelphia, 1923.
   Fielding, M. Paintings by Gilbert Stuart not mentioned in Mason's Life of Stuart. (In : Pennsylvania Magazine of History and Biography, Philadelphia, 1914, v. 38, pp. 311–334)
   Mason, G. Life and Works of Gilbert Stuart. New York, 1879.
   Park, L. Gilbert Stuart, an illustrated descriptive List of his Works compiled by Lawrence Park, with an account of his Life by John Hill Morgan and an Appreciation by Royal Cortissoz. New York, 1926. 4 v.

SULLY, T. *Biddle, E. and M. Fielding.* The Life and Works of Thomas Sully. Philadelphia, 1921.
   Hart, C. A Register of Portraits painted by Thomas Sully. Philadelphia, 1908.

SULLY, T. *Pennsylvania Academy of the Fine Arts.* . . . Memorial Exhibition of Portraits by Thomas Sully. Philadelphia, 1922.

TANNER, H. O. *Brawley, B.* The Negro in Literature and Art. New York, 1921.

THAYER, A. H. *Carnegie Institute.* Exhibition of Paintings by Abbott H. Thayer. Pittsburgh, 1919.

 Cortissoz, R. Introduction to Abbott H. Thayer, Memorial Exhibition, Metropolitan Museum of Art. New York, 1922.

 Pousette-Dart, N. Abbott H. Thayer. New York, 1923.

TIFFANY, L. C. The Art Work of Louis C. Tiffany. Garden City, N. Y., 1914.

TRUMBULL, J. Autobiography, Reminiscences and Letters of John Trumbull from 1756–1841. New York, 1841.

 Morgan, J. H. Paintings by John Trumbull at Yale University of historical Scenes and Personages prominent in the American Revolution. New Haven, 1926.

 Weir, J. F. John Trumbull, a brief Sketch of his Life to which is added a Catalogue of his Work. New York, 1901.

TRYON, D. W. *Caffin, C.* The Art of Dwight W. Tryon. New York, 1909.

VEDDER, E. The Digressions of V. Boston, 1910.

 Reminiscences of an American Painter. (In: World's Work, New York, 1910, v. 19, pp. 12459–12470, 12559–12570, 12684–12694, 12815–12824)

WEIR, J. A. *Phillips, D. and Others.* Julian Alden Weir, an Appreciation of his Life and Works. New York, 1922.

WEST, B. *Farington, J.* The Farington Diary, 1793–1811. Edited by J. Greig. New York, 1923, 6 v.

 Galt, J. Life, Studies, and Work of Benjamin West. London, 1820.

 Galt, J. The Progress of Genius, or authentic Memoirs of the early Life of Benjamin West. Boston, 1832.

 Hart, C. H. Benjamin West's Family. Philadelphia, 1908.

 Jackson, H. E. Benjamin West. Philadelphia, 1900.

WHISTLER, J. A. M. *Seitz, Don C.* Writings by and about James Abbott McNeill Whistler, a Bibliography. Edinburgh, 1910.

 Bacher, O. With Whistler in Venice. New York, 1908.

 Duret, T. Whistler. Translated by Frank Rutter. Philadelphia, 1917. New French Edition, Paris, 1914.

 Freer Gallery of Art. Gallery Book of the Whistler Collection. Washington, D. C., 1926.

 Menpes, M. Whistler as I knew Him. New York, 1904.

 Pennell, E. R. and J. The Life of James McNeill Whistler. New and revised 6th Edition. Philadelphia, 1920.

 Pennell, E. R. and J. The Whistler Journal. Philadelphia, 1921.

 Pousette-Dart, N. James McNeill Whistler. New York, 1924.

WILGUS, J. W. *Sellstedt, L. G.* Life and Works of William John Wilgus. Buffalo, 1912.

WILLARD, A. M. *Devereux, H. K.* "The Spirit of '76"; some Recollections of the Artist and the Painting. Cleveland, O., 1926.

WIMAR, C. *Hodges, W. R.* Carl Wimar. Galveston, Texas, 1908.

WITH, J. (JOHN WHITE). *Binyon, L.* Catalogue of the Drawings by British Artists . . . in the British Museum. v. 4, p. 326–337. London, 1907.

WYANT, A. Clark, E. Alexander Wyant. New York, 1916.

INDEX OF PAINTERS' NAMES

(See Supplementary Index also)

INDEX TO SUPPLEMENTARY CHAPTERS

(Pages 561–592)

By Royal Cortissoz

WITHDRAWAL